DICTIONARY

Tohono O'odham/Pima to English

English to Tohono O'odham/Pima

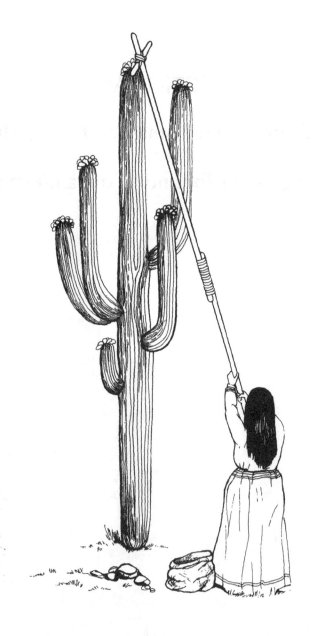

Papago woman harvesting saguaro cactus fruit

DICTIONARY

Tohono O'odham/Pima to English
English to Tohono O'odham/Pima

Dean Saxton
Lucille Saxton
Susie Enos

SECOND EDITION / REVISED AND EXPANDED
Edited by R. L. Cherry

THE UNIVERSITY OF ARIZONA PRESS
Tucson

Since the publication of the second edition in 1983, the Papago Indian Tribe has officially changed its name to *Tohono O'odham* (Desert People). This change became effective with the adoption of the new constitution in January 1986 by members of the Tohono O'odham Nation.

The University of Arizona Press
© 1983 The Arizona Board of Regents
All rights reserved

Library of Congress Cataloging-in-Publication Data
Saxton, Dean.
[Dictionary, Papago/Pima–English, O'othham–Mil-gahn, English–Papago/Pima, Mil-gahn–O'othham]
Dictionary: Tohono O'odham/Pima to English, English to Tohono O'odham/Pima / Dean Saxton, Lucille Saxton, Susie Enos. – 2nd ed., rev. and expanded / edited by R. L. Cherry.
p. cm.
Originally published: Dictionary, Papago/Pima–English, O'othham–Mil-gahn, English–Papago/Pima, Mil-gahn–O'othham. 2nd ed., rev. and expanded. 1983.
Includes bibliographical references (p.).
ISBN 0-8165-1942-0 (pbk.)
1. Tohono O'odham dialect—Dictionaries—English. 2. Pima language—Dictionaries—English. 3. English language—Dictionaries—Tohono O'odham. 4. English language—Dictionaries—Pima. I. Saxton, Lucille. II. Enos, Susie. III. Cherry, R. L. IV. Title.
PM2123.Z5   1998   98-41620
497'.45–ddc21

Manufactured in the United States of America on acid-free, archival-quality paper.

This Second Edition of
The English—O'odham Dictionary
is dedicated to
Juan Dolores
who began the work of
producing a dictionary
and a written literature
of his O'odham language

Contents

Foreword

This vocabulary is of great importance for the contribution it makes to the Papago-Pima speaking peoples of the southwestern United States and northern Sonora and to the many persons—including teachers, doctors, missionaries, officials—who have voiced a strong desire for scientifically sound, practical material which can be used in acquiring an understanding of the Papago-Pima language.

Papago and Pima constitute one of the most important American Indian languages of the Southwest. Since the appearance of the first edition of this dictionary, a number of valuable works on the language have appeared—including the Saxtons' *Legends and Lore of the Papago and Pima Indians*, the rich textual material contained in Bahr et al. *Piman Shamanism and Staying Sickness*, Ofelia Zepeda's *A Papago Grammar* (all by University of Arizona Press), and Madeleine Mathiot's *A Dictionary of Papago Usage* (Indiana University, 1974, 1978). In general, scientifically sound information on Papago and Pima is becoming more abundant. An especially important development in Piman linguistics is the involvement of a number of excellent native-speaking language scholars, such as Albert Alvarez and Ofelia Zepeda, who are not only continuing the rich tradition begun by the late Juan Dolores but are also building a solid foundation for future Piman linguistic scholarship through their writing and teaching.

It is most appropriate that this revised version of the dictionary should now appear, as a part of the growing body of Papago-Pima linguistic literature. This volume constitutes the most practical single-volume compendium of Papago-Pima lexical and phonological data. Its scientific validity, accuracy, and practical usefulness make it valuable for linguists and laymen alike.

The Piman languages, of which Papago-Pima is the northernmost, are of considerable interest for the fact that they constitute a close-knit, well-defined subfamily within Uto-Aztecan. As such, they provide an especially good laboratory for the study of linguistic change. Despite the close relationships that the languages show to one another, the linguistic boundaries are surprisingly clear. The recent separate, though similar, developments in the phonology and syntax of the Piman languages promise interesting and theoretically significant insights into the ways in which successive generations reinterpret grammatical systems—that is, insights into the notion 'possible grammatical change.' It is precisely the kind of material contained in this volume that is needed to further this work.

I join the group of linguists and educators who can be truly grateful to Dean and Lucille Saxton and Susie Enos for this latest contribution to linguistics and pedagogy.

KENNETH L. HALE
Professor of Linguistics
Massachusetts Institute of Technology

Acknowledgments

The authors would like to express appreciation to the University of Arizona Press and to its director emeritus, Marshall Townsend, for guidance in the preparation of this edition, and to R. L. Cherry, who prepared the English—Papago/Pima Dictionary and accomplished the editorial and lexicographical work on the book.

Sincere appreciation is also due to the Papago and Pima speakers who shared their rich knowledge of the language and culture to make possible a growing bilingual dictionary. Chief among these were: Irene Adams, Albert Alvarez, Sam Angelo, Edith Antone, Juan Antone, Jose Bailey, Samuel Cachora, Juan Dolores, Ramon Chavez, Andrew Enos, Enos Francisco, Sr., Joe Garcia, Lena Garcia, Ramon Garcia, Mahila Harvey, Eleanor Hendricks, Josemaria Hendricks, Jose Ignacio, Raymond Johnson, Ventura Jose, Roe Lewis, Antonio Lopez, Chica Manuel, Cipriano Manuel, Francis Manuel, Jose Manuel, Loleta Manuel, Molly Manuel, Cruz Marks, Juan Mattias, Lorenzo Pablo, John Pedro, Joe Thomas, Juan Thomas, Lupe Thompson, Thomas Segundo, Frank Stein, Henry Throssel, and some whose help is remembered although their names are forgotten.

Sincere appreciation is also due to Kenneth Hale for his encouragement and sharing of ideas. Appreciation is also due to Adrienne Lehrer for opportunity to progress in the work in lexicology classes at the University of Arizona.

The authors and editor are indebted to the University of Arizona Foundation and its director Richard Imwalle for providing funds for much of the preproduction editorial preparation. They are also grateful to the University of Arizona Press both for effecting publication of this second edition and for the very generous amount of time given for preproduction editorial work.

The editor also wishes to thank Peter Kasenenko for a lot of typing, and Alex Ochoa for a lot of checking. He is especially indebted to Tim Hilliard, who worked for several months on the dictionary doing typing and the large majority of the checking and acjing as lexicographical assistant to the editor. The general appearance of the dictionary material is due in large part to his tireless efforts.

D.S.
R.C.

The Alphabet

The alphabet used for Papago-Pima in this dictionary was formed by testing speakers of the major dialects from 1953 to 1973 for preferences and ease of reading. This alphabet differs slightly from that of the first edition, which was published before the tests were completed, but is the same as that used in *Legends and Lore of the Papago and Pima Indians,* the *Papago-Pima New Testament,* and various smaller books.

Native speakers have usually written the sounds of Papago-Pima like the sounds of Spanish and English. Spanish has had the primary influence on writing preference because of hundreds of Spanish words adopted into Papago-Pima during three centuries of Spanish and Mexican rule. The sounds written like Spanish are given below, with an example Spanish source word and Papago-Pima adopted word for each sound.

	a	b	ch	g	i
Spanish	Padre	bola	Chino	granado	pico
Papago-Pima	Pahl	bohl	Chihno	gal-nayo	pihgo
English	Father	ball	Chinese	pomegranate	pickax

l	m	n	n (=ng)	o	p	s
lámpara	mula	novillo	chango	oro	peras	santo
lahmba	muhla	nowiyu	chahngo	ohla	pihlas	sahnto
lamp	mule	steer	monkey	gold	pear	saint

t	u	y
tanque	tubo	yugo
tahngih	tuhwo	yehwo
tank	tube	ox yoke

Where Spanish and English differ in writing a similar sound, the Papago and Pima speakers tested preferred the English spelling because of the last century of contact with English and because of extensive literacy in English among the Indians. The English basis for spelling preferences is shown in the example same-word pairs below.

	a	b	ch	d	e	g
Papago-Pima	tachchua	bohl	chuchul	tadai	jeg	gawos
English	want	ball	chicken	roadrunner	open	gun

	h	**i**	**j**	**k**	**l**	**m**
Papago-Pima	huhch	chi-lihhi	ugijith	keihin	liat	mashath
English	hooves	police	jostling	kicking	lariat	moon

n	**n (=ng)**	**n (=ñ)**	**o**	**p**	**s**	**sh**	**t**
s-nakosig	wahngo	huniga	hothai	pihba	sihl	shuhshk	tahtami
noisy	bank	bunion	stone	pipe	saddle	shoe	teeth

th (voiced)	**u**	**w**	**y**
ihtha'a	kuintakud	winthani	yehwo
this	ruler	window	yoke

The glottal stop ('), as in ho'i 'thorn', is a stop in the throat, as between the parts of Oh oh! in English. Since it pronounced automatically before all initial vowels in Papago-Pima—as it is in English—the speakers tested preferred not to write the glottal stop in initial position.

The speakers tested preferred to indicate duration of vowels with h, as in pahl 'minister' and wehs 'all,' which are patterned after English words like ah, eh, oh, ohhh, etc.

Being a product of field tests to determine native speakers' preferences and ease of reading, this is a practical alphabet, not a technical one. For a key to technical alphabets in use see the phonological description in Appendix One. For a convenient guide to pronunciation, see the *Pronunciation Guide* at the end of the book.

Guide to the Dictionary

The dictionary material in this book is in two parts. The first part is *Papago/Pima—English,* and the second part is *English—Papago/Pima.*
The *Papago/Pima—English* section has complete information on all Papago and Pima word forms, part-of-speech labels that apply to Papago and Pima, and complete information on English definitions. Also, where they exist, this section gives subentries, variant forms, restrictive labels, illustrative examples, taxonomy, cross references, usage notes, and etymology. All of these are explained below with examples from the dictionary. Pronunciation of Papago and Pima words is not given in this section but can be found in the *Pronunciation Guide* at the very end of the book. All of the information that follows in this guide applies only to the first section.

The *English—Papago/Pima* section is basically a cross-reference dictionary in which only essential information is given. This section has its own information guide, which can be found immediately preceding this second section.

For the purpose of saving space, several abbreviations and symbols are used. For those used in the *Papago/Pima—English* section, see the section entitled *Abbreviations and Symbols* that follows this guide. The *English—Papago/Pima* section has its own *Abbreviations and Symbols* list.

Grammatical terms are used in this guide only for the purpose of explaining the layout of entries. Illustrative examples of how the perfectivity, reflexivity, the various forms of transitivity, etc., of Papago/Pima verbs translate into English can be found in the *Abbreviations and Symbols* list following, but no other grammatical information on English or Papago/Pima is in this book.

Main Entries

Main entries are words printed in **boldface type** that extend into the margin. They are in alphabetical order letter by letter. A main entry can be a single word (such as **chekopig** and **edapk**), a phrase (such as **Chehthagi Mashath** and **Akimel O'othham**), a prefix (such as **chu___** and **e-**), a suffix (such as **___kon** and **___dag**), or a combining element (such as **ku___** and **alo**). Prefixes, suffixes, combining elements, and individual parts of speech are discussed below.

Subentries

A subentry is a main entry that has a suffix or a combining element attached to it, producing a new word with a new meaning. Suffixes and combining forms can also produce different parts of speech from the main entry. All subentries are in alphabetical order letter by letter.

> **gagka** *N* a clearing; ~**t** *Vt* clear (land); ~**t|a** *N* brush (for burning).

The first subentry is **gagkat** (**gagka** + **t**), and the second subentry is **gagkata** (**gagka** + **t** + **a**).

A subentry can also be a main entry that combines with another word or words.

> **mo'o** *N* the head; ~ **ko'okthag** *N* a headache.

The subentry here is **mo'o ko'okthag.**

Spelling

Some words have variant spellings. Variant forms follow a slash.

> **lasan/lason** *N* a ration.
> **hahawa/haha/-aha** *Adv* afterward, then.

Lason is a variant spelling of **lasan,** and **haha** and **-aha** are variant spellings of **hahawa.**

Variant forms are also indicated by information in parentheses.

> [2]__**dag** (__**d** before __*kam*)/__**lig** *suffix added to gerunds to form abstract nouns* . . .

Some words are spelled the same but have different meanings and different etymology. These are listed separately with small numbers in front of them.

> [1]**chehchk** *Vt* name.
> [2]**chehchk** *Vcmpl* dream.

Singular, Plural, and Distributive Forms

Some words have different spellings for the singular, plural, and distributive forms. These are presented in main entries in different ways. Plural and distributive forms are extensions of the singular, just as, in

English, *dogs* and *men* are extensions of *dog* and *man*. These extensions usually follow a set pattern, and when they do, they are presented in the dictionary in an abbreviated form. These are explained in the following examples. When a plural or distributive form is irregular, however, it is spelled out in full.

If a main entry has only one form, this form is used for singular, plural, and distributive.

> **gagka** *N* a clearing...
> **nuhkuth** *Vt* tend, take care of...

If a noun main entry has two forms separated by a semicolon, the first form is singular and the second is plural.

> **shonigiwul;** *sho N* a ball used in a racing game.

This plural is an abbreviated form and can be reconstructed by putting this *sho* after the first vowel of the main entry: **sho/sho/nigiwul.** The full form is therefore **shoshonigiwul.**

This is also true for suffixes and combining forms.

> **hik___;** *hi CE* cut:...
> [2]**___chk;** **___kumia***k* *suffix added to transitive verbs to intensify the action...*

The full plural of **hik___** is **hihik___** (**hi/hi/k___**). The italicized *k* in **___ch***k* and **___kumia***k* is discussed under *Verbs* below.

Subentries can also carry singular and plural forms.

> **hiwchu;** *hi N* the groin; the side of the body; ~**-wegi;** ~**-wepegi** *N* the black-widow spider (lit. a creature with a red groin).

Hiwchu, the singular form of the main entry, is used with **-wegi,** the singular form of the subentry, producing **hiwchu-wegi. Hihiwchu, (hi/hi/wchu)** is the plural form of the main entry, and this is used with **-wepegi,** the plural form of the subentry, producing **hihiwchu-wepegi.**

Some suffixes that have more than one form are accompanied by (*).

> **huni___** *CE* corn:... ~**med*** *V* go grocery shopping...

The (*) means to look under the main entry **___med** for other forms of this suffix. The singular form of the main entry (**huni___**) is used with the singular forms of the subentry, and the plural form (**huhuni___**) is used with plural forms of the subentry.

A few plural forms are also abbreviated in another way.

Hi-lihpih; *hi —li* *Adj,N* Filipino ...

Here, *hi* is inserted after the first vowel in the part of the main entry before the hyphen, and *li* is inserted after the first vowel in the part of the main entry after the hyphen. The plural here is **Hihi-lilipih (Hi/hi-li/li/pi)**—not **Hihi-lili***h***pih.** Whenever material is inserted after the first vowel (in either part of the word in a situation like this), that vowel loses any length that it originally had. The "h" (which signifies length in this spelling system) is therefore lost in the second part of this word when *li* is inserted.

When a main entry has two forms separated by a semicolon with "*(dist)*" following the second form, the first form is used for both singular and plural, and the second is used for distributive.

> **hajuni;** *ha* (*dist*) *N* a relative, a relation ...
> **gegos___;** *g* (*dist*) *CE* eat: ...
> **shakal;** *'ash* (*dist*) *Adv* side by side; ...
> **shawad;** *'ash* (*dist*) *Adj* thick (in diameter); ...

The full distributive forms here are **hahajuni, geggos, sha'ashkal,** and **sha'ashwad.**

If a main entry is a verb, adjective, adverb, or preposition, and has two forms separated by a semicolon, the first form is used for both singular and plural, and the second is distributive.

> **kegchuth;** *he* *Vt* beautify; repair ...
> **shopol;** *'osh* *Adj* short (in measure) ...
> **thahm;** *'atha* *Prep* over or above ...
> **ga'ajed; ga'agajed** *Adv* from there.

The full forms here for the distributives are **kehegchuth (ke/he/gchuth), sho'oshpol (sho/'osh/pol),** and **tha'atham (tha/'atha/m).** The distributive form **ga'agajed** is spelled out because it is irregular.

If a main entry has three forms all separated by semicolons, the first form is singular, the second is plural, and the third is distributive.

> **mahgina;** *m; mma* *N* a car ...
> **¹wo'o; wohp; wo'owop** *Vs* (of things that can move ...) to be lying flat ...

The plural form of **mahgina** is **mamgina,** and the distributive form is **mammagina**—not **mamhgina** and **mammahgina.** Whenever material is inserted after the first vowel, that vowel loses any length that it originally had. The "h" (which signifies length) is lost here.

Pronouns can also be distributive but do not have special forms for this. When a pronoun is to show distributiveness it is used with the distributive form (**hehe'ejel**) of the emphatic adjective **hejel**.

Alternate Forms

Alternate forms are different forms of the same lexical item that are used in different ways in a sentence. These forms are separated by a comma.

ehp, ep *Adv* again; also; more...

Number can also be shown in alternate forms, as with

²**eda, ed; 'e** *Prep* in; among; during...

Eda and **ed** are both singular and plural, and **e'eda** is distributive.

Alternate forms must not be confused with variant forms. In the following example, **heg** is an alternate form of the two variant forms **hegai** and **hega'i**.

hegai/hega'i, heg *Pron* that; that one...

Variant forms are explained under *Spelling* above. Other forms are explained under the individual parts of speech following.

Part-of-Speech Labels

Part-of-speech labels are abbreviated in italicized type and follow main-entry and subentry material.

kommo'ol *N* a millipede.
wothalt *V* vote; ~a *N* an election.

Some words can be two different parts of speech with the same meaning.

al; 'a *Adj,Adv* little...
kohmagi; ko *s-Adj,s-Vs* (be) gray...

S-kohmagi as an adjective means "gray," and as a verb means "be gray."

Some words can be two different parts of speech with different meanings.

> **mahth** *N* one (*used in counting*); *Prep* except...

For main entries that are prefixes or suffixes, these words are spelled out in full.

> **e-** *prefix added to nouns and prepositions to indicate a second or third person subject*...
> **__kud** *suffix added to gerunds to form nouns*...

Some words are special elements that do not function as a part of speech. Their purpose is explained, and examples of usage follow.

> **²chum/chem** *indicates that something is unexpected, or is expected, attempted or accomplished in vain*...: **Bat-o chum juh**= He is expected (or supposed) to do it (but won't)...

Definitions

Definitions are in regular type and follow the part-of-speech label.

> **bihinod;** *hb Vt* wrap.

A comma is used to connect words of similar or near similar meaning.

> **ushabi;** '*u N* resin, sap, or pitch.

A semicolon is used to separate words of dissimilar meaning.

> **uskonakud** *N* a scoop; a fork.

Sometimes numbers are used in involved definitions or where other material is included.

> **²__g** *suffix added to transitive verbs to form nouns:* **1.** a product for or of (an activity): **cheposig**=a brand mark...; **2.** any one of the five senses: TAHTKAG.

Some elements do not have any lexical meaning but have a special purpose. These are followed by examples of usage or cross-referenced words that show usage.

> **²__chk; __kumiak** *suffix added to transitive verbs to intensify the action:* HIKUCHK, HIKKUMIAK.

Some verbs have obligatory subjects. These, or examples of restricted subjects, are shown in parentheses.

> **thoahim** *V* (of thunder) to rumble...
> ¹**kehk;...** *Vs* (of a person or animal) to be standing...
> ²**toni; tohoni** *s-Adj,s-Vs*...; ~**h** *Vp* (of weather, food, etc.) to get hot...

Some verbs have obligatory objects. These, or examples of restricted objects, are shown in parentheses.

> **mohto, momtto;** *m* *Vt* ...bear (responsibility or guilt)...
> **kahiobin;** *k, kk* *Vt* cross (as a road; or one thing with another, as the legs)...

Some words have both an obligatory subject and obligatory object.

> **ih'e, i'i__; ih'i** *Vt* drink; (of a plant) to absorb (moisture); (of a machine) to use (gasoline, oil, etc.)...

Similarly, other restrictive information is in parentheses.

> **gahsh/gahj** *Adv* over there (facing toward).
> **luhya;** *lu* *Adj* gray (of a horse)...
> **ahith__;** '*a* (*dist*) *CE* a year or a cycle of a year: ... ~**kam** *N* someone or something of a (specified) age: **hemako** ~=a yearling.

Ambiguity of word order in phrases is made clear by the insertion of extra information.

> **hia** *N* a sand dune; ~**sh|ch** *Vts* have (someone or something) buried.

The words "someone or something" are inserted to show that the verb is not in the present perfect tense (which would be "have buried") but that a person or thing is the object of the verb "have," as in the sentence *We have grandfather buried in the new cemetery.*

Some words are used only literally and some only figuratively. Some words can be both. This restrictive information is in parentheses.

> ¹**ka'al** *N* the gall bladder; ~ **shuhthagi** *N* gall (lit. only).
> **gewkath** *Vt* ...strengthen the hand of (fig. only).
> ²**esh...** *Vt* sow (usu. lit.).
> **hothaichuth** *Vt* petrify (lit. and fig.); stupefy.

Some lexical items in Papago are descriptive expressions which translate into English as simple names for things or persons. Literal translations are given in parentheses.

> **huni__** *CE* corn:... ~**med*** *V* go grocery shopping (lit. go to get corn).
> **jiawul;** *ji* *N* a devil or demon; ~ **wuhi** *N* a television (lit. the devil's eye).

Prefixes

Prefixes attach to the beginning of a word and have various purposes.

> **s-** *prefix added to verbs of ability and existence to indicate the intensive:* **S-melithag o**= He's good at running.

Suffixes

A suffix is a meaningful grammatical unit that is attached at the end of certain words, producing a new word with a new meaning. The new word formed is often a different part of speech from the original word.

> **ali; a'al** *N* a child; ~**chuth** *Vt* treat like a child;... ~**th|t** *Vt* beget; become the father of.

A suffix can also be added to another suffix or suffixes. These suffixes are separated by horizontal lines "**|**".

> **nawoj;...** *N* a friend; ~**m|a** *s-Vs* be friendly; ~**m|a|kam** *N*** a friendly person...

Some subentries have suffixes whose meanings are usually predictable. These are called run-on words and are listed in alphabetical order with other subentries. Run-on words are not defined because their meaning can be determined by adding the meaning of the suffix to the meaning of the main entry.

> **hogi;** *ho* *N*** leather, hide; ~**dath** *Vtp* saddle; put leather on; ~**dath|ch** *Vts;* **huawi** ~, **sihki** ~ *N* buckskin; ~**mag** *Vs.*

The run-ons in this entry are **hogidathch** and **hogimag.**

Combining Elements

A combining element is a form of a word that carries lexical meaning, but, unlike a regular word, it cannot stand alone. It either has a suffix attached to it, as with

> **nehn__** *CE* sight: ~**t** *V* gain sight; ~**thag** *N* sight, the ability to see;...

or will attach to another part of speech, as with

> **em-** *CE* you (pl.,obj.); your (pl.): **em-eniga**=your possession...

or is used unattached with another word or words, as with

> **alo** *CE* limited: **chum** ~ *Adv* almost, not quite; **sha i** ~, **sha al i** ~ *Adv* in a while.

Number can also be shown in combining elements.

> **ki'i__**; **kih~** *CE* an action of the teeth: ~**hin*** *Vt* bite off...

Ki'i__ is singular and **kihki'i__** is plural.

Combining elements will have either one or more subentries, as with

> **am__**; **'a** *CE* friendly: ~**kam** *s-N*** a friendly person; ~**thag** *s-Vs* be friendly

or will have examples to show usage, as with

> **__d, d** *CE* *added to combining elements to indicate a time in the distant past* used to, had, was: **Kunid** (or **Nid**) **am chikpan**=And I used to work there...

Nouns

Countable nouns are distinguished from noncountable nouns by the use of an article *a, an,* or *the.*

> **gaso; g** *N* a fox; ~ **mad** *N* a kit or young fox.
> **sisiki** *N* the sparrow hawk (*Falco sparverius*).
> **a-saithi** *N* gasoline; **chuk** ~ *N* oil.

For many words that are frequently used as both a countable and a noncountable noun, an article appears in parenthesis.

> **sil-wihsa** *N* (a) beer.

All articles that appear with nouns in the dictionary, however, must be added when the words are used in sentences since the article is not included in the definition of the noun.

Ambiguities are made clear by the use of supporting material.

> **lai; *hla*** N   a king or ruler.
> **oh'og** N   a tear from the eye.
> **ha'a; ha~** N   a jar (container).

The words "ruler," "tear," and "jar" would otherwise be ambiguous.

Words that are used only in plural are defined in plural and are accompanied by a "*(pl)*" marker.

> **gogs; go~** N   a dog; **~i|g** *s-N* *(pl)*   many dogs...

Nouns that are normally plural in English are defined in plural.

> **chapa-lihya** N   leg chaps.

Sometimes nouns can be used interchangeably in singular or plural. Parentheses are used to show this.

> **edawek; 'e** *(dist)* N   intestine(s), gut(s)...

Verbs

Main-entry verbs and verb-forming subentries give the basic forms from which all other verb forms are derived predictably. In main entries, forms for aspect and mood are separated by commas within any number category. Verbs labeled *Vs* have forms for imperfective aspect only. Verbs labeled *Vp* have forms for perfective and repetitive aspects. (Imperfective aspect is usually called the "continuous" or "progressive" form of a verb in English, that is, verbs that end in -ing. Perfective aspect is usually called the "regular" form, that is, verbs that do not end in -ing.) All other Papago-Pima verbs have neutral, customary (also called habitual), perfective, repetitive, and perfective imperative forms. Since any form that is the same as the main-entry form is not given, forms must be recognized by their derivational pattern.

If the customary form of a verb is distinct, it is derived from the neutral form by repeating the initial sound(s), and lengthening the first vowel if short, as in *gehgew* 'strikes' from *gew* 'to strike.' The succeeding forms are derived from the customary form, which may be distinct from the neutral form.

If the perfective form is distinct, it is derived by deleting certain sounds, as in *gehg* 'strike,' from *gehgew* 'strikes.' When practical, the sound(s) deleted for the perfective form are given in italics, as in "geh*gew*."

If the repetitive form is distinct, it is derived by repeating the initial consonant after the first vowel, and deleting vowel length, as in *geggew* 'strike repeatedly,' from *gehgew* 'strikes' (the *h* following a vowel represents vowel length in this spelling system). When practical, only the repeated sound is given, here the *g*, which is in italics to indicate that it is so inserted.

If the perfective imperative form is distinct and formed solely by adding the suffix *i* to the customary form, only the suffix *i* is given, as in *gehgewi* 'strike (imperative),' from *gehgew* 'strikes.'

Thus the entry

     gew, gehgew, *g,* ~**i** *Vt* strike...

represents the following forms with their aspectual and modal meanings: *gew* (neutral), *gehgew* (customary), *gehg* (perfective), *geggew* (repetitive), *gehgewi* (perfective imperative).

While the verb forms can be recognized by the pattern of derivation given above, any distinct form that is not readily predictable is given in full, as in

     him, hih, hihhim, hihm; *hi* *V* move along...

Here, *him* is customary as well as neutral, since the next form shows deletion of *m* for perfective. (Any verb with the same neutral and customary form does not change for perfective if it is immediately before its own conjunction *k*; thus the neutral form may be imperfective or perfective in contrast to the perfective form, as in *Am o him* = He's going there; *Am at him k-bei* = He went there and got it; *Am at hih* = He went there.) In the above entry, *hi* is inserted after the first vowel in each singular form, except the repetitive, to make the corresponding plural form. The repetitive plural is identical to the repetitive singular unless otherwise indicated. The forms and functions indicated by this entry are: *him* (neutral, sing.), *him* (customary, sing.), *hih* (perfective, sing.), *hihhim* (repetitive, sing.), *hihm* (perfective imperative, sing.), *hihim* (neutral, pl.), *hiḩim* (customary, pl.), *hihih* (perfective, pl.), *hihhim* (repetitive, pl.), *hihim* (perfective imperative, pl.).

Some Papago verbs translate into English as phrases.

     kohmch *Vts* have in the arms.
     kubswua *V* puff out smoke.
     maskogi*th; m* ...*Vr* reveal one's powers or intentions...

Adjectives

Adjectives can be a single word or a phrase.

> **mukima** *s-Adj* deathlike; expecting to die;...

Participles that are often used as adjectives in English are defined as adjectives.

> **kopoth;** *'ok Adj* swollen;...

Many stative verbs are contained in adjectives.

> **kubjuwi;** *ku s-Adj,s-Vs* (be) brown or gray;...

Here, when **kubjuwi** is used as an adjective, it means "brown or gray"; when used as a verb it means "be brown or gray."

Adverbs

Many adverbs translate as a part of a verb. Often these adverbs carry mild force with no special meaning. The adverb, which does not have to be used, is in parentheses.

> **ba'iha***m***; bahbhia***m Vt* store (away), stow (away);...

Here, the verb can mean "store," "store away," "stow," or "stow away."

Similarly, other such adverbs can be left out or used.

> **shuhthath; shuhshuth** *Vt* fill (up).
> **shaj___;** *sha CE* scrape; chip; ~**kon*** *Vt* scrape; chip (off).

Most adverbs that accompany verbs cannot be omitted because the meaning would be changed.

> **shoni___** *CE* an action of the hand...; ~**ch***k*; ~**ak** *Vt* chop down;...

Adverbs can be a single word or a phrase.

> **epai** *Adv* also; again.
> **edapk** *Adv* at this very time.
> **gahnai/gahna'i, gahn** *Adv* far over there to the side or in a position facing sideways.

Pronouns

Pronouns are not separated in the dictionary into class, as personal, relative, demonstrative, etc. All restrictive material is in parentheses.

> **ha'i** ...*Pron* some; any (used only in neg.); others.
> **hegam** *Pron* those; they or them (at a distance).

Prepositions

Some prepositions translate as phrases.

> **edawi; 'e** *Prep* in the middle of; ...

Some prepositions translate as part of verbs.

> ¹**gew** *N* ice; (a) snow; ~**shp*** *Vt* snow on.
> **nahj**ith; **ntha; n** *Vb* make a fire for (someone).

Interjections

Explanatory material is often given for interjections, together with a common English equivalent or an example of usage.

> **hah** *Intj* an expression used to **1.** get attention: Hey!; **2.** show surprise:
> Oh!

Taxonomic Classification

Taxonomy of many generally unfamiliar plants and animals is in *italicized* type following the common name.

> **nehpod; ne** *N* the lesser nighthawk (*Chordeiles acutipennis*).

Taxonomy is not given for common plants and animals.

> **okstakud** *N* a mushroom; a toadstool.

Cross References

A cross reference sends the reader to another word for full information on the word in question. The cross-referenced word is in SMALL CAPITAL LETTERS.

> **o'ohia** See O'OD.

Cross-referenced words are also used for showing examples of usage.

> __bim, __bij *suffix added to adverbs to form transitive verbs* go
> around, pass by: NE'IBIM, TA'IBIM.

Information at both **ne'ibim** and **ta'ibim** shows how this suffix is used.

Etymology

Where etymology is given, it appears in brackets at the very end of the
entry. Words in etymology that do not have a language marker are
Papago and Pima words.

> **komba-nihya** *N* a business company. [<Sp *compañia*]
> ²**komal; *k*** *N* a griddle. [<AmSp *comal*]
> **puhl** *N* a swimming pool. [<Eng *pool*]
> **hobinol; *ho*** *Vs* be wrapped. [<hobinod and i]

Usage Notes

Usage notes appear in two forms. Some are used with or in place of a
part-of-speech label.

> **pen** *indicates an attempt of the speaker to remember something* ...
> **ku__, k** *CE* (may be deleted if it does not end a word) ...

When there is a usage note further on in an entry, it is preceded by the
symbol "▶".

> ²__t, t *CE added to pronoun combining elements to indicate contempo-*
> *rary time, any time from the recent past through future:* **Kut** (or **T**)
> **am hih**=And he went there; ... ▶ __t is omitted before __*s*, and in
> incompleted action unless it is conditional or future: **Pi ani maheh**
> **mas-o juh**=I don't know if he's going to go there ...

Abbreviations and Symbols

Adj/ective
Adv/verb
AmSp   American Spanish
App./endix
CE   combining element (combining forms and special words that combine with other words)
colloq./uial
Conj/unction
Correl.Conj correlative conjunction (Example: He is *not only* intelligent *but also* quite rich.)
dist/ributive (denoting groups composed of individuals acting individually)
Eng/lish
fig./urative
habAdj   a *hab*-class adjective
habN   a *hab*-class noun
habs-Vr   a reflexive verb that prefixes both *hab* and *s*. See *Vr*.
habs-Vt   a transitive verb that prefixes both *hab* and *s*. See *Vt*.
habV   a *hab*-class verb (also *habVt, habVr, habVinf*, etc., for which see *Vt, Vr, Vinf*, etc.)
has   the indefinite form of *hab*
infm   informal
interrog./ative
Intj   interjection
joc./ular
Legends   *Legends and Lore of the Papago and Pima Indians* (University of Arizona Press, Tucson, 1973)
lit./erally
MexSP   Mexican Spanish
N/oun
N*   a noun that can also be used like an adjective
neg./ative
pl/ural
PNT   *Papago New Testament* (World Home Bible League, Chicago, 1976)
pos./itive
Prep/osition
Pron/oun
rel./ative
rep./etitive

s-Adj   an *s*-class adjective
s-Adv   an *s*-class adverb
sing./ular
s-N   an *s*-class noun
Sp/anish
spec./ifically
s-V   an *s*-class verb (also *s-Vs, s-Vt*, etc., for which see *Vs, Vt*, etc.)
usu./ally
V   an intransitive verb, a verb that does not take a direct object.
               (Example: He *runs* very fast.)
Vb   a verb with a benefactive object, that is, for someone's benefit.
               (Example: He *got firewood for* his neighbor—''got firewood for''
               is the verb and ''neighbor'' is the benefactive object.)
Vbcmpl   a verb that takes both a complement clause and a benefactive
               object. See *Vb* and *Vcmpl*. (Example: I *said* for John's benefit that
               I was leaving—''that I was leaving'' is the clause and ''John'' is
               the benefactive object.)
Vbinf   a verb that takes both an infinitive and a benefactive object. See
               Vb and *Vinf*. (Example: I *wanted* to wash clothes for Frank, that
               is, for Frank's benefit.)
Vcmpl   a verb that takes a clause for a direct object. (Examples: I *under-
               stand* that Mary is leaving soon—''that Mary is leaving soon'' is
               the direct-object clause. He *announced* where he was going—
               ''where he is going'' is the direct-object clause.)
Vdt   a ditransitive verb that takes two objects. These can be either two
               direct objects (Example: I *bet* him [direct object] five dollars
               [direct object]), or a direct object and an indirect object (Exam-
               ples: I *gave* Susan [indirect object] the pencil [direct object], or I
               gave the pencil [direct object] to Susan [indirect object]).
Vdtb   a verb that takes a direct object, an indirect object, and a benefac-
               tive object. See *Vb* and *Vdt*. (Example: I *gave* John [indirect
               object] the package [direct object] for his mother [benefactive], or
               I *gave* the package to John for his mother.)
Vdts   a stative verb that takes two objects. See *Vs* and *Vdt*. (Example:
               He *had* the broom *lying against* the wall—''had lying against'' is
               the verb, and ''broom'' and ''wall'' are the two objects.)
Vinf   a verb that takes an infinitive as the object. (Example: Mary
               wanted to leave early—''to leave'' is the infinitive object.)
Vp   a perfective verb, which is a verb that expresses completion of an
               action. (Example: He *moved* to Chicago last week.) This verb can
               also be in future tense. (Example: He *will move* next week.) A
               verb that is not perfective is imperfective, that is, it expresses
               ongoing or continuous action, as in The boy *is running* down the
               street.
Vr   a reflexive verb in Papago, although the reflexivity may not be
               expressed, or even felt, in English. (Examples: She *put on an
               apron*, The man *winked* at the waitress—''put on an apron'' and
               ''winked'' are the reflexive verbs.)

Vrcmpl   a reflexive verb that takes a clause as the object. See *Vr* and *Vcmpl*. (Example: He *decided* that he would go down town.)

Vrinf   a reflexive verb that takes an infinitive for an object. See *Vr* and *Vinf*. (Examples: The family *got ready* to leave, The little boy *can* swim very well, She *tried* to hit the ball. See **nakog** for these verbs.)

Vrs   a stative verb that is reflexive. See *Vr* and *Vs*. (Example: He *was ready* for the test.)

Vs   a stative verb, a verb that shows relationship or state of being but no action, like "be" and "have." (Examples: Building the house *was lots of work*, The children *were noisy*, Chili *has a* spicy *taste*—"was lots of work," "were noisy," and "has a taste" are the stative verbs.) Note that a noun or an adjective is part of the verb.

Vscmpl   a stative verb that takes a clause. See *Vs* and *Vcmpl*. (Example: It *was shown* that the man was wrong—"was shown" is the stative verb, and "that the man was wrong" is the clause. Note that "was shown" in English is a passive verb, and the clause is its subject.)

Vt   a transitive verb, a verb that takes a direct object. (Examples: The woman *searched through* her pocketbook for some change, The clerk *wrapped* the package—"searched through" and "wrapped" are the verbs, and "pocketbook" and "package" are the objects.)

Vtb   a transitive verb that has a benefactive object. See *Vt* and *Vb*. (Example: The little girl *colored* a picture [direct object] *for* her teacher [benefactive object]—"color for" is the verb.)

Vtbs   a stative verb that is transitive and has a benefactive object. See *Vt*, *Vb*, and *Vs*. (Example: He *had* a big dinner [direct object] *prepared for* his friends [benefactive object])—"have prepared for" is the verb.)

Vtcmpl   a verb that takes both a noun and a clause as objects. See *Vt* and *Vcmpl*. (Examples: He *reminded* me [direct object] that he had to go [direct object]. I *told* him [indirect object] that I was leaving [direct object].)

Vtinf   a verb that takes both a noun and an infinitive as objects. See *Vt* and *Vinf*. (Examples: My father *reminded* me to do my homework—"me" and "to do" are the two objects. They *let* the prisoner go after three weeks—"prisoner" and "go" are the two objects. We *told* him to leave—"him" and "to leave" are the objects. Note that in English "me," "prisoner," and "him" are often considered as subjects of their respective infinitives.)

Vtp   a perfective verb that is transitive. See *Vt* and *Vp*. (Example: He *hid* (or *will hide*) the money in his desk drawer.)

Vtr   a reflexive verb that is transitive. See *Vr* and *Vt*. (Example: He *took up* [i.e., studied] engineering in college.)

Vts   a stative verb that is transitive. See *Vt* and *Vs*. (Examples: The hiker *had* a knapsack *on his back*, The little girl *had* her doll *clothed*—"had on his back" and "had clothed" are the verbs.)

/   when used with English phrases, it means "or," as in *his/her pencil, in that /those way(s);* when used with Papago material it means that the word following the slash is a variant form of the first, as in **hi wa/hi-a**—"**hi-a**" is a variant of "**hi wa.**"

| separates suffixes, as in **hiw|kon|a**—"**hiw**" is the head word, and "**kon**" and "**a**" are two different suffixes.

~   a swung dash, which replaces the main entry, or head word. It is used with suffixes to form subentries. (Example: **huhud** *Vt* lubricate...; ~**a** *N* lubrication...—"~**a**"=**huhuda.**) It is also used with other words to form subentries. (Example: **watopi** *N* a fish.,.; **wamad** ~ *N* an eel—"**wamad** ~"=**wamad watopi.**)

—   used with suffixes and combining elements to show that the element is always attached to other material, either in front of it (as with __math and __bad), or behind it (as with ge'el__ and shah__), or in the middle (as with wa__absh).

†   signifies words used only by the Pima, as **ablis**†.

‡   signifies words used only by the Papago, as **gihko**‡.

*   when used with a noun part-of-speech label, it means that the entry can also be used as an adjective, as **hogi** *N** leather. When used with a main entry or subentry it means to look under that form (as a main entry) for other forms of this element.

Papago/Pima— English Dictionary

A

a *Intj* an expression of surprise: oh!

a__ ('a after a vowel), __a__ *CE* indicates that the clause is not a command: ANI, APT. ▶a__ is deleted before *ku*__, as in *kuni, kupt*.

¹__a *suffix added to adverbs to form s-class stative verbs* be (of a specified characteristic): S-A'ALIMA.

²__a (__h after *i*; __i after vowels, *g, k,* or *n*) *suffix added to transitive verbs to form abstract nouns* a (specified) activity, or an instance or product of it: KIHTA, CHEHCHKI, CHEHGI.

³__a See __TA.

__a__ (__i__ after *ch, j, l,* or *s*) *a transitional sound between consonants where there is no vowel following:* S-A'ALIM.

a'ag; a'ag (*dist*) *N* a horn (of an animal); ~a|m *N** any horned creature; ~chuth *Vt* put horns on; disguise.

a'ag__; a''ag__ *CE* secret: ~chuth *Vt;* ~i *s-Adj* secret; ~i|m *s-Adv* secretly; ~i|m|a *s-Vs;* ~ko *s-Adv*.

a'aga *Vt* point to. [<ahg]

a'ahe, a'ahesh *Vt* reach (a point in a cycle of events); *Vr* (of time) to reach (a certain point). [<²aha]

a'ai See AIGO.

a'al See ALI.

a'al__; a'al__ *CE* child: ~i|m *s-Adv* childishly; ~m|a *s-Vs;* ~m|a|kam *s-N* a crybaby.

a'amichuth *Vt* solve. [<amichuth]

a'an; a''an (*dist*) *N* a wing; a feather; ~a|m *N** any winged or feathered creature; ~chuth/~dath *Vt* put feathers or wings on; fletch, feather; ~chuth|a *N;* ~chuth|a|s *Vs;* ~dag *Vs;* ~t *Vp* grow feathers; ~ta|him *V*.

A'an-wonamim *N* a plains tribesman (lit. someone with a feathered hat).

a'aphun See A'APPEM.

a'appem/a'aphun *Vt* test, put to the test; try out; ~a *N* a test; a trial; the act of testing.

a'as__ *CE* laughter; humor: ~chuth *Vt;* ~chuth|a *N* fun; humor; laughter; ta ~ki|m *s-Adv* humorously; ta ~ki|m|a *s-Vs*.

a'ath *Vt* divine (the cause of sickness); ~a *N* divination; ~a|med* *V;* ~a ne'oki *N* a speech made to empower the medicine man for this act.

¹ab *Prep* at; on; on the basis of; about; (be recognized, known, or understood) by.

²ab See ABAI.

abai/aba'i, ab/b *Adv* there close by facing this way; (in a relationship) directed toward; *indicates an abstract relationship:* ab has elith=*respect;* ab wui kehk=*oppose, stand against*.

abam, ~k, ~muk *s-Vt* give good fortune to; ~thag *N* fortune; luck.

abchuth; 'a *Vdt* accuse (of); give credit for; ~a *N* accusation; ~a|s *Vs;* ~ch *Vdts* have under accusation of; ~tham *N** an accuser. [<¹ab]

abkam; 'a *N* a relative.

ablis† *N* an apple. [<Eng *apple*]

adawi; 'a *N* the buffalo gourd and plant (*Cucurbita digitata*).

ag__; 'a *CE* a horn: ~chk|wua; ~ch|shulig* *Vt* gore; ~wuan *Vr* avenge oneself; ~wu|i *N* avenging; ~wu|i|mk *s-Vr* want to avenge; ~wu|i|thag *N* vengeance.

agshp; 'a/kuawith† *Adv* (slanting) downward; ~a|dag *N* a slant; *s-Vs* be slanting downward; ~t *Vt*.

¹aha *Conj* or. ▶Conjoins an alternative question: ... aha napt pi am hu wo hih?= ... *or aren't you going to go?*

²aha, a'ahe, ah'i *Vtp* overtake; reach (a place or condition); continue until (a specified time); infect; *Vr* (of time) to arrive.

-aha, -ahawa See HAHAWA.

ah'ach N a head louse; lice; s-Vs have head lice.

ah'at N the desert lily (*Hesperocallis undulata*).

ah'ath, a''ath ‡ Vt send; dispatch; Vdt, Vtcmpl promise; ~a N a messenger, an emissary; a missionary; a prophet; the act of sending; ~a|s Vs; ~jel*ith* Vdt; ~tham N a sender; a dispatcher.

ahchim Pron (*emphatic*) we; us.

ahdho; '*a* N the peafowl (*Pavo cristatus*).

ahg, ahgi, a'aga Vt say; sing; discuss, talk about; call or name; Vr be said; talk about oneself; identify oneself or one's position; Vcmpl say; habVtcmpl tell; habVt, habVcmpl mean; habVinf,Vrcmpl plan; decide; think; ~am*k*/~im*k* s-Vt, s-Vcmpl want to say; ~a|s Vs; ~ch, ~k habVinf intend; habV have a reason or purpose. ▶Used with *ha'ichu* replacing *hab* to express that one intends nothing or something unspecified, and with *haschu* or *shahchu* to question what one intends: **Bant ahgk am hih mant-o nei g ni-nawoj**=*I went there (intending) to see my brother;* **Pi ant ha'ichu ahgk am hih**=*I went there with no reason;* **Shahchu ap ahgch am thaha?**=*Why are you sitting there?;* **chu** ~amk/imk s-Vs be gossipy; **chu** ~imkam s-N a gossiper; ~tham; '*a* N a speaker; a messenger.

ahga; '*a* N a message; an utterance; a discussion; a saying; a story; a tale; news; habN a meaning; an intention: **K hab d ahga mat-o hih**=*That means he'll go* (lit. *The meaning is that he'll go*); **K has d ahga?**=*What does it mean?;* ~chug/~chug Vt bear (as a message); Vcmpl; ~dag hasN criticism; gossip; ~him Vt go along saying.

ahgal*ith*, '*a* Vtb claim for (someone).

ahg*ith*, '*a* Vdt,Vtcmpl tell; ~am*k* s-Vdt; ~ch Vts; **ha'ichu** ~a N instruction; the act of instructing; **ha'ichu** ~a|dag N discipline; instruction; a story; a legend; a maxim; tradition; **ho'ok** ~a N a legend used for instruction.

ahgli; '*a* N an acre. [<Sp *acre*]

ahgowi N the crown-of-thorns or corona-de-Cristo plant (*Koeberlinia Spinosa*).

ahham See AHPIM.

ahhi CE flee; ~med* V flee; ~med|tham; ~o|kam N a refugee; a fugitive; a runaway.

ah'i See ²AHA.

ahi (ai before voiceless consonants); '*a* (*dist*) CE extend (to a point); complete (a cycle): ~chug Vt keep up with; ~him Vt catch up with; gain on; ~jith Vdt extend to; ~jith|a N an extension; ~jith|a|s Vs; ~jith|ch Vdts; ~m Adj enough, sufficient; that much; Adv enough, sufficiently; ~s Vts extend to (a specified place): **Pi o am hu ais g wohg hegai kihhim**=*The road doesn't extend to that village.* ahim *suffix added* **1.** *to non-stative verbs to indicate an action in progress in the past* was: NEITHAHIM; **2.** (after ²_k) *to stative verbs to show a past condition* was: S-OAMKAHIM.

ahith; '*a* (*dist*) CE a year or a cycle of a year: ~ag N a year or (specified) period of years. ▶The ag *may be omitted before prepositions which begin with a vowel;* ~ag|ga N one's age in years; ~kam N someone or something of a (specified) age: **hemako** ~=*a yearling;* **gohk** ~=*a two year old;* ~kam-tohlo-a'ag N a pickaxe (lit. the horns of a yearling bull).

ahlpa; '*a* N a harp. [<Sp *arpa*]

ahmo; '*a* N a boss; an employer. [<Sp *amo*]

ahn N the desert broom plant (*Baccharis sarathoides*).

ahnih/ahni'i Pron (*emphatic*) I; me.

ahni'i See AHNIH.

ahpih/ahpi'i Pron (*emphatic*) you (*sing.*).

ahpim/ahham Pron (*emphatic*) you (*pl*).

ahshos; '*a* N garlic; a garlic clove. [<Sp *ajos<ajo*]

ahth, ai, a'atha Vt hang (something) around the neck; ~ch Vts.

ahtha; '*a* N a palate or gum in the mouth.

¹ai Intj an expression of grief or sympathy: Alas! How sad!, etc.

²ai See AHTH.

aichug *Vt* keep up with.
aigo; 'a/a'ai *Prep* across, on the other side of; on each side of; *Adv* in return; *(pl)* back and forth, to and fro; ~**jed** *Prep* from across; on the other side from; from each side of; on each side from.
aihim *Vt* catch up to or with.
aj; 'a *Adj* narrow; slender; thin; ~**chu** *N;* ~**i|j** *Vs* be narrow; be slender or thin; ~**i|j|k|a** *Vp;* ~**i|j|k|a|him** *V;* ~**i|j|k|a|th*/**~**i|j|k|a|j***ith Vt;* ~**i|j|k|th|a** *N;* ~**i|j|k|th|a|kud** *N;* ~**i|j|k|th|a|s** *Vs;* ~**ma** *Adv* in a narrow fashion; ~**tha** *Vp;* ~**tha|him** *V;* ~**-wainomi** *N* a telephone, a phone; a metal wire; ~**-wainom|math** *Vt* telephone, phone; ~**-wohg** *N* a footpath.
aki; 'a *N* a ravine, arroyo, or wash; ~**mel** *N* a river; ~**thag** *N* the arroyo of or in.
Akimel O'othham *N* a Pima Indian (lit. a river person).
al; 'a *Adj, Adv* (*a diminutive*) little; *Adj* little old: **al Huan**=*little old Juan;* **al oks**=*a little old woman;* ~**chu** *N* a small or young person or thing; ~ **chum** *N* only/just a little; a bit of; ~ **ha'as** *Adj* only/just so big; ~ **i wehs** *N* the last bit, all there is.
alhin; 'a *N* a threshing floor. [<Sp *era*]
al-huanthi *N* an elephant. [<Sp *elefante*]
ali; a'al *N* a child; a baby; ~**chuth** *Vt* treat like a child; *Vr* act like a child; reach second childhood; ~**ga** *N* one's child; ~**thag** (~**th** before suffixes) *N* an offspring of a male; ~**th|bad** *N;* ~**th|kam** *N;* ~**th|t** *Vt* beget; become the father of.
alijk *N* the beginning of one's life.
alo *CE* limited: **sha i** ~, **sha al i** ~ *Adv* in a while.
a-lohs/shohs *N* rice. [<Sp *arroz*]
alshani; 'a *s-Adj, s-Vs* (be) sorrel (the color). [<Sp *alazán*]
Al-Shonk *N* Arizona (lit. place of a little spring).
¹am *Prep* at.
²am See AMAI.
am___; 'a *CE* friendly: ~**kam** *s-N** a friendly person; ~**thag** *s-Vs.*
amai/ama'i, am, m *Adv* there facing away; there.
am hu *a modal of possibility* may,

might: **T-o am hu chikp**=*He might work.*
am hu'i *Adv* about, referring to an estimated amount.
amichuth; 'a *s-Vt, s-Vcmpl* understand; learn; recognize; (*rep.*) estimate; *s-Vrs* be apt or skilled at; be knowledgeable; ~**a** *N;* ~**a|chuth** *Vdt;* ~**a|dag** *N* cleverness; understanding; wisdom; recognition; **chu** ~ *s-Vs* be understanding; be clever; **chu** ~**a|m** *s-Adv* understandingly; cleverly; **chu** ~**tham** *s-N*;* **ta** ~**a|m** *s-Adv* understandably; intelligibly; **ta** ~**a|m|a** *s-Vs;* **ta** ~**a|m|a|kam** *N** someone or something that is understandable.
¹amjed *Adv* then, subsequently.
²amjed; 'a (*dist*) (___**jed** after adverbs of place and prepositions) *Prep* from; about; concerning; ~**kam** *N* a person or thing from a (specified) place or ancestor; **mehk** ~ *Adv* from far; **thahm** ~ *Adv* from above.
___amk See ___IMK.
amog, 'a, ~**i** *Vt, Vcmpl* announce; preach; proclaim; orate; ~**ith** *Vdt, Vtcmpl;* ~**tham** *N* an announcer; a preacher; a proclaimer; an orator.
¹an *Prep* along; on the margin of.
²an See ANAI.
ana, ade *Intj* an expression of pain: ouch!
anagith, 'a *Vr* (of winged creatures) to flap the wings.
anai/ana'i, an/n *Adv* there close by facing across.
anghil; 'a *N* an angel. [<Sp *ángel*]
a-nihl; 'a—ni (*dist*) *N* blueing; ~**magi** *s-Vs* be blue; ~**magi|m** *s-Adv* blueishly; ~**math** *Vt.* [<Sp *anil*]
anilo; 'a *N* a ring. [<Sp *anillo*]
¹ap See ²___P.
²ap; 'a *s-Adj* good, normal; right, correct; *s-Adv* well, thoroughly; properly; appropriately; capably; right, correctly; ~**chu** *s-N;* ~**chuth/**~**'e|chuth** *Vt* prepare; arrange; approve; adjust; repair; improve; ~**chuth|a** *N* preparation; arrangement; approval; adjustment; repair; improvement; the act of preparing, etc.; ~**chuth|a|chuth** *Vtb* prepare, etc., for (someone); ~**chuth|a|chuth|a|mk** *Vtb* want to

prepare, etc., for (someone); ~**chuth|a|chuth|ch** *Vtbs* have (something) prepared, etc., for (someone); ~**chuth|a|mk** *Vt;* ~**chuth|a|s** *Vs;* ~**chuth|ch** *Vts;* ~**'e** *s-Vs* be good; be normal; be right, correct, or all right; *s-Vts* be good or opportune for (someone); ~**'e|kam** *s-N* the right; the righteous; the good; ~**'e|ma** *s-Vs* look, appear, seem good; look, appear, seem normal; ~**'e|t** *Vp* become good, right, normal, or correct; ~**'e|ta|him** *V* (begin, continue) to be all right; ~**'e|ta|ma** *s-Vs* look, appear, or seem improved; ~**'e|thag** *N* well-being; opportunity; a sphere (of influence); a license or permit; the right or liberty (to do); rights; **pi-**~**'e|kam** *N* evil.

apapa; 'a *N* one's father (in a clan of the Coyote moiety); ~**gam** *N*. See App. 3.

apkih; 'a *N* one's father (in a clan of the Coyote moiety); ~**gam** *N*. See App. 3.

apko; 'a *s-Adj* right (side); ~**chu** *s-N;* ~**g** *s-Vs* be well-formed; be in usable condition; be accessible; ~**jed** *s-Adv;* ~**ma** *N* a test; ~**t** *V* become opportune; ~**thag** *N* good condition; well-formedness.

a-pohla__ See APOLA__.

apola__/a-pohla__; 'a *CE* lining: ~**dag** *N* (a) lining; *Vs;* ~**dath** *Vt;* ~**dath|ch** *Vts*.

a-saithi *N* gasoline; **chuk** ~ *N* oil. [<Sp *aceite* oil]

ash *Vt* laugh at.

asim, __k, __muk; a'~ *s-Vt* want to laugh at; ~**chuth** *s-Vt*.

asugal/a-suhga; 'a (*dist*) *N* sugar; **chu'i** ~ *N* powdered sugar; ~**math** *Vt* sugar; ~ **mumkutham** *N* a diabetic. [<Sp *azúcar* sugar]

a-suhga See ASUGAL.

at; 'a *N* the anus; the buttocks; the bottom of a basket or jar; ~**chuth** *Vt* begin (a basket, story, song, etc.); ~**gith** *Vr* shake one's hips (as in a dance); ~ **hoabdag** *N,Vs* (be) the end of a story; ~**po** *N;* ~**sh|ch** *Vrs;* ~**shp*** *Vr;* ~**wua*** *V*.

ataio__; 'a *CE* breech: ~**dag** *N,Vs* (have on) a breech strap; ~**dath** *Vt;* ~**dath|ch** *Vts*.

atapud; 'a *N* a buttock.

at'ol; 'a (*dist*) *N* gruel; gravy; **kaij** ~ *N* saguaro seed gravy.

atosha; 'a *N* a diaper; a loincloth; ~**dag** *Vs;* ~**dath** *Vt;* ~**dath|ch** *Vts*.

atshnig; 'a *N* the trench between the buttocks.

a'ud; a''ud *N* any agave plant; specifically, the century plant and the lechuguilla.

auppa; a'uppa (*dist*) *N* the cottonwood tree (*Populus deltoides*); **mohmli** ~ *N* the poplar tree (*Populus*).

B

b See ABAI.

ba'a, bah, bab'e, bah'i *Vt* swallow.

ba'a__; bahb__ *CE* one's maternal grandfather or great-uncle: ~**bad** *N;* ~**mad** *N* the relationship of a man's daughter's child to the man and his relatives in his generation; a grandchild, grandnephew, or grandniece; ~**mad-ohg;** ~**mad-ha-ohg,** ~**mad-ha-o'og** *N* the relationship of a man's son-in-law to the man and his peers; the reciprocal relationship; ~**md|a|m** *N*;* *Nr* (*pl*). See App. 4.

ba'ag; hba *N* an eagle; ~ **mad** *N* an eaglet.

ba'ali See BAHB.

ba'ama *s-Adv* abundantly, plentifully.

ba'amad-o'ogam; **bahbmad-ha-o'ogam** *Nr* (*pl*) those mutually related as son-in-law and father-in-law. See App. 4.

babath; b (*dist*) *N* a frog; a toad.

babath ihwagi *N* the heliotrope plant (*Heliotropium curassavicum*) (lit. frog greens).

bab'e See BA'A.

babhe See BAHA.

babih See BAHB.

__bad (__**bd** before a vowel) *suffix* added to nouns to refer to a person no longer living or to a thing which no longer has its original use the late; something abandoned or non-functional: HOABAD. [<pad]

baga; b *s-Vs* be angry or mad; ~**chuth** *Vt* anger; ~**m** *s-Adv* angrily; ~**s** *s-Adj* boiling with rage; ill-tempered; pessimistic; ~**t** *Vp;* ~**t|a** *N;* ~**t|a|him** *V;* ~**t|a|lig** *N* anger; aggravation; ~**t|a|m** *N* one easily angered; **ta** ~**m** *s-Adv*

maddeningly; **ta ~m|a** *s-Vs;*
ta ~m|a|kam *s-N** something
irritating.
bagwul; ba *s-N* one easily angered.
bah See BA'A.
bah__ See HEBAI.
baha, bai, babhe, bah'i *Vp* reach a
ripe or cooked state.
bahb/bahbi or **ba'ali** *(infm);*
~a'a/~ab *N* one's maternal
grandfather; one's great-uncle on this
side; **~am** *N;* **~keli;** **~kekel** *N*
one's great-uncle on this side;
~keli|m; **~kekeli|m** *N;* **~oks;**
~o'oki *N.* See App. 4.
bahbagi *s-Adj,s-Vs* (be) slow; (be)
silent; (be) low-pitched; *Vt* defer to,
give place to; *s-Adv (with
intransitive verbs)* slow, slowly; at a
low pitch or volume; **~m** *s-Adv
(with transitive verbs)* slow, slowly;
at a low pitch or volume.
bahban ha-ihswigi *N* the strawberry
cactus *(Mammillaria microcarpa)*
(lit. Coyote hedgehog).
bahbas; b *(dist)* *N* a potato. [<Sp
papas<papa]
bahbgih *Vr* slow up, slow down; have
patience; **~m** *s-Adv* slow, slowly;
patiently.
bahbhai See ¹BAHI, ²BAHI.
bahbhaij *N* tail feathers.
¹bahi; bahbhai *s-Vs* be ripe; be
cooked; **~jith** *Vt* ripen; cook;
~thag *N* (a) fruit; *V* (of plants) to
have fruit; **~thaj** *N* fruit of the
saguaro cactus (unless otherwise
specified).
²bahi (bai__ before voiceless sounds);
bahbai *N* a tail; the tail end; **~gith**
Vr wag or switch the tail; **~kam**
N anything with a tail or long
handle; a frying pan.
bah'i See BA'A, BAHA.
bahmuth; hb *Vt* appeal to, plead to;
employ; invite; **~a** *N* someone
appealed to; an appeal; **~tham** *N*
an appealer.
bahni__ *CE* crawl: **~med*** *V* crawl;
creep; **~med|t** *V* learn to crawl;
~med|tham; **~o|kam** *N* one who
crawls, a crawler.
bahp-chehpo'ogam *N* a praying
mantis (lit. the one that a person
asks, "Where do you have your
grain-mashing hole?" so named
because its posture resembles that of
someone mashing grain).
bahsho; b *N* the chest; the breast; the

front of; *Prep* in front of; **~dag** *N*
an apron; **~dath** *Vr;* **~oh'o** *N*
the sternum.
bahtkhim; b *s-V* wilt.
bahwui *N* the coral bean or chilicote
plant *(Erythrina flabeliformis).*
bai See ²BAHI.
bai__; ba *CE* ripe; cooked: **~him** *V;*
~kam *N** ripe or cooked food.
ba'i__; bab'ai__ *CE* swallow:
~chuth *Vt.*
ba'ich; bab'aich *Prep* beyond; past;
ahead of; in front of; *Adj* the next
(specified unit of time): **ba'ich
tash**=*the next day;* **~ i** *Adv* more,
-er; further; more (. . .) than, -er
(. . .) than; **~ i s-hohho'ith** *Vt*
prefer; *Vcmpl* (would) prefer, had
rather, would rather; **~kam** *N*
someone ahead of or more important
(than); **wehs ha-~ i** *Adv* most.
ba'ichu; bab'aichu *N* the front of the
neck.
ba'i-chukulim *N* the black-throated
desert sparrow *(Zonotrichia
querula).*
ba'iham; bahbhiam *Vt* store (away),
stow (away); **~a** *N* a supply; the act
of storing or stowing; **~a|kud** *N* a
container for storage; **~s** *Vs.*
baik__ *CE* tail: **~ko** *Adv;* **~kon***
Vt.
ba'itk; bab'aitk *N* the throat; *s-Vs*
be clear-voiced.
baiuk; b *Vts* have around the neck;
~a *N* a leash; a necklace; **~t** *Vt*
string (as beads) for a necklace.
ba'iwichkhim *Vt* go beyond or
around, overtake, pass; surpass;
exceed; outlast.
ba'iwichkim *Adv* further; more.
balwuani; ba *s-Vs* be scarred; **~gith**
Vt scar.
bamuistk; b *s-Vs* be unflinching; be
even-tempered; **~thag** *N* an even
temper.
ban; hba *N* a coyote; one who flatters
or curries favor, a flatterer; **~kaj**
Adv in a coyote-like manner; **~ma**
s-Vs be greedy or gluttonous;
~ma|dag *s-N* greed; gluttony;
~ma|kam *s-N** a greedy or
gluttonous person or animal, a
glutton; **~math** *Vt* cheat, trick (lit.
apply the wiles of a coyote to); **~uw**
s-Vs have bad breath, have halitosis
(lit. smell like a coyote).
ban-bawi *N* the wild tepary bean
(Phaseolus acutifolius).

ban-chepla *N* the fish-hook cactus (*Mammillaria microcarpa*).

ban-chinishani *N* the daisy plant (*Compositae*).

ban-ihugga *N* the unicorn plant (*Probiscidea*).

ban-mawpai *N* the Thornber's cactus (*Mammillaria thornberi*).

ban-tokiga *N* the desert cotton plant (*Asclepias*).

ban-wihbam *N* the milkweed plant (*Asclepias*).

ban-wiwga *N* the coyote tobacco plant.

ban-wuhiosha *N* a mattock (lit. a coyote face).

bashpo *N* chest hair.

bawi; *ba* (*dist*) *N* the tepary bean; **o'am** ~ *N* an orange tepary bean; **tohta** ~ *N* a white tepary bean.

＿bd See **＿BAD.**

be＿; u'u＿ *CE* grasp: ~**ka'i** *Vt* take somewhere; ~**kch** *Vts*.

bebethk *V* make a rumbling noise; ~**i** *N* thunder; rumbling.

bebhe See **BEHE.**

behe, bei, bebhe, beh'i (*sing.*, *mass*); **u'u, ui, u''u, uh'i** (*coll.*, *dist*) *Vt* accept, acquire, get; take; assume control of; take over (as a business); **an** ~ *Vtp* arrest or apprehend; **i** ~ *Vt* pick up; move; ~**tham** *N* one who gets something; **uhg i** ~ *Vt* lift.

behi; u'i *N* booty; gain; a captive; the act of acquiring.

behi＿ (**bei＿** before voiceless sounds); **u'i＿** *CE* acquire, get: **chu** ~**mk** *s-Vs* be greedy; be thievish, be light-fingered; ~**chug** *Vt* carry; **chu** ~**m|kam** *s-N;* **hab hi** ~**th|ma*** *s-Vts* seem to acquire; ~**him** *Vt;* ~**hog** *Vt;* ~**jith** *Vtb;* *Vrs* be gotten; be captured; ~**kam** *N;* ~**kud** *N* a handle or knob; ~**med*** *Vt;* ~**mk** *s-Vt;* **ta** ~**ma** *s-Vs* be obtainable; be desirable to acquire; **ta** ~**ma|kam** *s-N* that which is a pleasure to acquire; ~**thag** *s-Vs*.

beh'i See **BEHE.**

bei See **BEHE.**

bia, bi, bbi, ~**'i** *Vt* dish out (food) into a serving dish; ~**kch** *Vts*.

bibijjim *N* a design; wavy lines.

bibith＿ *CE* harness: ~**sh|ch** *Vts;* ~**shp*** *Vtp* harness; ~**shp|a|dag** *N* a harness; ~**shp|i** *Vs;* ~**shp|i|'ok*** *Vt* unharness; ~**shp|i|'ok|a|s** *Vs*.

bibolmath *Vt* make a design with wavy lines on (someone).

bichpod *N* the pyrrhuloxia bird.

bih *N* food in a dish or container; ~**chug** *Vt*.

bih＿; *bi* *CE* wrap or surround: ~**sh|ch** *Vts;* *Vrs;* ~**sh|ch|i|m** *Adv* in a surrounded condition; ~**shp*** ❱ *Vt* wrap; tie (up).

bihad; *bi* *Vt* mob; surround.

bihag *Vt* surround; wrap (around); ~**ch** *Vts;* ~**s** *Vs*.

bihakud; *hbi* *N* a spool.

bihbhiag *N* the morning glory plant (*Ipomoea*).

bihim; *hb* *V* get constipated; ~**s** *Vs;* ~**thag** *N* constipation.

bihinod; *hb* *Vt* wrap; ~**ch** *Vts*.

bihiwig *Vt* wrap around.

bihiwin; *b;* *hb* *Vdt* wrap around; ~**i|s** *Vts*.

bihkud; *bi;* *bbi* *N* a serving bowl or pan.

bihs; *bi* *Vs* be dished out.

¹biht *N* feces, dung.

²biht, bihbt *V* defecate; ~**a** *N* defecation; ~**a|med*** *V;* ~**amk** *s-V;* ~**kud** *N* a toilet.

bihtagi; *b* *s-Adj,s-Vs* (be) dirty; ~**chu** *s-N;* ~**ga** *N* one's dirty clothes; ~**h** *Vp;* ~**h|him** *V;* ~**jith** *Vt;* ~**m** *Adv* dirtily.

bihth, *bi* *Vdt* serve (food) to; ~**ch** *Vtbs*.

bihugig *N* (a) famine; hunger.

bihugim, ~**k,** ~**muk; bihugk,** ~**k,** ~**ko'o** *Vp* become hungry, famished, or starved; ~**chuth** *Vt;* ~**kam;** ~**koi** *N*＊ a hungry person or animal; **si** ~ *Vp;* **ta** ~**ma** *s-Vs* (of a place) to be without food; ~**thag** *N* hunger.

＿bij See **＿BIM.**

bijim; *bi* *Vt* pass by, go or proceed past; ~**ith** *Vt* surround; compete with; run a relay race with; ~**s** *Vts* be lying along a course past (something).

＿bim, **＿bij** *suffix added to adverbs to form transitive verbs* go around, pass by: NE'IBIM, TA'IBIM. [<bijim]

binashwua; *bi* *Vr* play spin the top.

bischk; *bi* *V* sneeze; ~**chuth** *Vt;* ~**kud** *N* something that causes one to sneeze.

bit＿ *CE* feces: ~**uw** *s-V* smell of feces; ~**wua*** *V* defecate.

bith *N* adobe; clay; mud; plaster; ~**a|med*** *V;* ~**ha'a;** ~**haha'a** *N* earthenware; ~**hun** *Vt* contaminate; plaster; paint; ~**hun|a** *N;* ~**hun|a|kud** *N* a trowel;

~hun|a|s *Vs;* ~pig *Vt* remove
mud from; ~sh|ch *Vts* have
(something) plastered, sealed, or
pasted; ~shp* *Vt* plaster; ~shp|i
Vs; ~ shp|i|'ok* *Vt;* ~shp|i|'ok|a|s
Vs; ~shp|i|'ok|ch *Vts.*
bitikoi See BITITOI.
bititoi/bitikoi; *bi N* the stink bug
(*Pentatomidae*).
bitoi *N* oak, various species of
Quercus.
bohl; *bo N* a ball (for games); *Vr*
play ball (lit. only). [<Sp *bola*]

C

ch See KCH.
¹__ch (ch), ch__ (__t__ before __*t*)
CE *attached to combining elements*
a__ or ku__ we; (one of) us: **Kuch**
(or **Ch**) **am chikpan**=*And we're*
working there; **Kutt** (or **Tt**) **pi hebai**
chikp=*And we didn't work*
anywhere.
²__ch See __KCH.
-ch- See -K-.
chahbo; *cha N* a short-legged person.
[<Sp *chapo* a short, stout person]
chahgih; *cha N* a bank check. [<Sp
cheque]
chahngo; *cha; hcha N* a monkey;
~-**bahi;** ~-**bahbhai** *N* a pipe
wrench with a chain (lit. a monkey's
tail); ~-**mo'o;** ~-**mohmi** *N* a
coconut (lit. a monkey's head). [<Sp
chango monkey]
chahnsa *N* a chance; an opportunity.
[<Eng *chance* or AmSp *chansa*]
cha-lihgo *N* a vest. [<Sp *chaleco*]
cha-lihhi See CHI-LIHHI.
chapa-liia *N* leg chaps. [<Sp
chaparreras]
chea *N* hail, ice pellets; ~**shp** *Vt.*
cheadagi; *ch N* the Gila monster
lizard (*Heloderma suspectum*).
cheawuagi; *ch N* a germ; ~**g** *s-Vs*
be infectious; *N* infection; ~**th**
Vt infect.
chechga *Vt* inspect; examine;
investigate; ~**i** *N* inspection;
examination; investigation. [<chehg]
chechojim *s-Adv* generously; bravely;
~**a** *s-Vs* be generous; be manly;
~**a|dag** *N* generosity; manliness;
~**akam** *N** a generous or manly
person.

Chechpa'awi *N* the Pleides
constellation (lit. immoral women).
chedeni; *che Vt* thump (on), hit.
chedhaiwagi *Adj, Vs* (be) light blue or
light green; ~**chu** *N.*
chedhum† *N* a blanket.
chedk; *che s-Vs* be rough (not
smooth); ~**a** *V;* ~**a|lig** *N* a rash
on the body; ~**am** *s-Adv* roughly,
coarsely; i ~**a|th** *Vt* roughen.
chedkotham *N* the verbena plant
(*Verbena gooddingii*).
che'ew, ~**i; chehchewa** *Vt* glean;
pick up (bits of anything); ~**i|med;**
~**i|op** *Vt.*
che'ewhuith *Vt* cover with a blanket;
~**a** *N;* ~**a|dag** *N* any bed
covering, as a blanket, quilt, or
comforter; ~**ch** *Vts.*
cheggia; *che* (*dist*) *Vt* conflict with;
oppose; battle, fight; fight (an
opponent) in a boxing match, box;
wrestle; **chu** ~**dag** *s-Vs* be warlike;
chu ~**d|kam** *N** a warrior; a
fighter; **chu** ~**mk** *s-Vs* be full of
fight; ~**dag** *N* conflict; opposition;
battle; fight; boxing; wrestling; a
boxing or wrestling match; ~**d|kam**
*N** an able fighter; ~**him** *Vt;*
~**kud** *N* any instrument of battle,
as a sword, gun, cannon, missile,
etc.; a battleground or battlefield; a
boxing or wrestling ring; ~**kud**
wahlko *N* a battleship; any warship;
~**tham** *N* a fighter; a boxer or
wrestler.
chegima *s-Vt* notice; **pi** ~ *Vt* ignore.
chegito, chechegitod *V,Vcmpl* think;
~**him** *V;* ~**i** *N* a thought;
~**i|chuth** *Vtinf,Vtcmpl* remind;
Vdt; ~**i|lith** *Vdt* remind of;
~**i|thag** *N* an attitude; an opinion;
composure; frame of mind; *s-N*
memory; ~**kam** *N* a thinker; *Adj*
thinking.
chehani; *ch Vt,Vcmpl* command,
order; *Vt* hire; boss; **ab si** ~
Vt,Vcmpl demand; ~**g** *N* a law; a
command.
¹**chehchk** *Vt* name; name (someone)
(a specified name).
²**chehchk** *Vcmpl* dream; ~**i** *N* a
dream; ~**thag** *N* one's dream;
~**tham** *N**.
chehegam *N* a woodpecker; a tattletale.
¹**chehg,** ~**i, chechga** *Vtinf* find;
discover; *Vt,Vcmpl* find; discover;
learn; hear; *Vinf* learn; ~**i** *N* (a)
discovery; ~**i|med*** *Vt* go to visit;
~**s** *Vs.*

²**chehg**, ~**i, chehcheg,** *ch habVt* call by name.

chehgig; *ch N* name; reputation; *habVts* be named.

chehgimelhim; chehgiopahim *V* go to visit.

chehgimelimk; chehgiopamk *s-Vt* want to go visit.

chehgith; *ch Vdt* show; reveal; display to; exhibit to; *Vtb* find; *Vtcmpl* show; ~**a** *N;* ~**adag** *N* a showing; a revelation; a display (concrete); an exhibit; ~**a|him** *Vdt; Vtcmpl;* ~**a|kud** *N* an exhibition; ~**a|mk** *s-Vdt,s-Vtcmpl;* ~**a|s** *Vs,Vcmpl;* ~**ch** *Vdts.*

chehia; chechcha *N* a young female; a girl; **si s-ap** ~ *N* a virgin.

¹**chehk** '*eche Adv* high.

²**chehk,** ~**i, chechka** (*sing.*); **to'a, toa, to'aw, toa'i** (*pl mass*); **chehchka** (*dist*) *Vt* place, put, lay; store; **ab** ~ *Vt* patch; ~**him** *Vt.*

chehkith; to'ith *Vtb* place, put, lay; store; lay away (as a purchase) for (someone); set (something) aside for (someone) in a bet; offer (as a sacrifice).

chehkul/chehkol; *ch N* a squirrel.

chehm *Vr* gather into a group.

¹**chehmi** *N* the senita cactus (*Lophocereus schottii*).

²**chehmi;** *m;* **hche** *N* a heel (of the foot).

chehmo'o; *ch Vt* permeate; cover; reach the limits of and stop.

cheho; chehcho *N* a cave.

chehpa'awi; *ch N* an immoral woman; ~**dag** *Vs* (of a woman) to be promiscuous; ~**m** *Adv* promiscuously.

chehpithakud; *ch N* a stone for mashing food; a pestle.

chehpo'o; *ch;* **hch** *N* a mortar hole in a rock for grinding.

chehpsh *N* a flea.

chehthagi; *he s-Adj,s-Vs* (be) green; (be) blue; ~**chu** *s-N;* ~**m** *s-Adj* greenish; bluish; ~**-u'uwhig** *N* a bluebird; a parrot.

Chehthagi Mashath *N* February†; March‡ (lit. green month).

che'i___; *che CE* say: ~**s** *habVscmpl* be said; ~**sith** *Vt* mimic; repeat the sound of; *Vdt* repeat after; ~**thag** *N* (a) noise, (a) sound; pronunciation.

¹**chek___;** *ch CE* a pointed object: ~**ith** *Vt* vaccinate; ~**shan*** *Vt* draw a line on; make a border or boundary for (a place); set a course for (someone); ~**shan|i/~shn|a** *N* a line; a border, a boundary; a district.

²**chek___;** **to'ak___** *CE* put, place; store: ~**ch** *Vts;* ~**ch|i|m** *N* an appointee; *Adj* appointed; ~**i** *N* a stored item; ~**kud** *N* a container; a storage place; a closet; ~**shsh|a|s** *s-Vs.*

¹**cheka, chechkad** *Vt* put on (a shoe); ~**ith** *Vtb.*

²**cheka;** *hch* (*dist*) *Vp* reach a point in time or space.

chekai___, *ch CE* hearing: ~**chuth** *Vt;* **pi** ~**thag** *Vs* be deaf; be disobedient; *N* deafness; ~**thag** *N* the sense of hearing; *s-Vs* to have the sense of hearing; be cooperative; ~**th|kam** *N.*

chekith *Vtb* set (a time or course) for (someone); *Vr* pace oneself.

chekopig *Vt* undermine.

chekosh; *ch Vt* wrap around the ankle; ~**d|a** *N* an ankle rattle.

chekwo; *ch N* an ankle.

chel___; *che CE* a rough object: ~**kon*** *Vt* scratch off; ~**shan*** *Vt* rub; play (a stringed instrument); ~**win** *Vt* rub; file; polish; play (a stringed instrument); ~**win|a** *N;* ~**win|a|kud** *N* a file; a rasp.

chem See CHUM.

chemag *N* limestone.

chemait; *che N* a tortilla; *V* make a tortilla; ~**a** *N* tortilla making; ~**a|kud** *N* a tortilla griddle.

chemamagi; *che N* the horned toad.

chemhon *Vdt* scrape off or rub off; ~**a** *N;* ~**a|kud** *N* a scraper; a door mat; ~**a|s** *Vs.*

cheodagi; *ch s-Vs* be rough; be crusted.

cheoj; *ch N* a male; a man; ~**chuth** *Vt* medically, psychologically, or magically to change into a male or to male characteristics; ~**i|m** *s-Adv;* ~**pa** *N* a male homosexual; ~**pa|dag** *N* homosexuality; **si** ~ *N* a brave man, a manly male; ~**thag** *N* manliness; bravery; manhood.

cheolim‡ *N* the buckhorn cholla cactus or its edible bud (*Opuntia acanthacarpus*).

cheomi *V* contract venereal disease; ~**dag** *N* venereal disease.

cheopi; *ch N* a church; **ge'e** ~ *N* a large church; a temple; a cathedral.

che'ow*ith* Vt offend; excite; torment.
chepa; *ch* N a hole in bedrock for mashing mesquite beans.
cheped; '*ech* Adj even, level; flat-bottomed; ~chu N; i ~k|a|th* Vt; ~k Vs; ~k|a Vp; ~k|a|him V.
chepelim; *hch* s-Adv shallowly.
chepelk; *hch* Adj,Vs (be) shallow in concavity; ~chu N.
chepin Vt chip.
chepodk Vs be convex.
chepos___; *ch* CE brand: ~i|g N the brand on an animal; ~*ith* Vt brand; mark (for identification); ~ith|a N; ~ith|a|kud N a branding iron.
chepwin; *ch* V,Vt peck; tap; ~a N; ~ag s-Vs be chipped or rough; ~a|him V go along tapping or at a trot.
cheshaj, *chsh*; *ch* V climb; Vt ride; raise; elevate; ~chug V go climbing; Vt ride along on; gahi ~ Vt traverse or cross over (as in a boat or plane); ~him V; i ~chuth Vt raise, elevate; ~i|g N a ride; a climb; s-Vs be good at riding (as a horse or bicycle) or climbing; thahm i ~ Vt rise above (lit. and fig.); conquer.
cheshoni; *ch* N the bighorn sheep (*Ovis canadensis*); the moose (*Alces americana*); ~ mad N a bighorn lamb; a moose calf.
che-tondag/chetondag; chech-totondag/chechnodag N an upright support beam in a building.
chetto; *ch* N a fireplace stone; a stand for cooking.
che'ul; *ch* (dist) N the Goodding willow tree (*Salix gooddingii*).
chew; '*eche* Adj long; tall; ~a|j Vs; ~-chini|kam N a catbird (lit. a long-mouthed one); ~chu N; ~-kuswo|kam; k N a camel (lit. a long-necked one); ~ shuhshk N a boot (the shoe); ~th|a Vp elongate; ~th|a|him V; ~th|a|jith Vt lengthen; ~th|a|jith|a|s Vs.
chewagi; *che* (dist) N a cloud; ~g s-Vs.
chewaimed, chewaimmed; *che* Vt drag.
chewed V dwell temporarily; sojourn.
chewelhim; *hche* V (of ground plants) to grow long or spread out.
chiantho See TIANNA.
chichwi; *ch* (dist) V,Vt play (with); compete (with); trifle (with); ~dag N an activity; ~kud N a toy; a

recreation area; ~mk s-V; ~thag N competition; a game or contest; playful activity, play; anything trivial, a trifle; Vs be competitive; ~tham N a player; a competitor; a contestant.
chihgathih/chihgitha N chewing gum. [<Sp *chicle*]
chihil; *ch*; *hchch* N scissors. [<Sp *tijeras*]
Chihno; *ch* Adj Chinese; of or relating to the Chinese people or their language; N a Chinese person or the language.
Chihno ha-jewedga N China.
chihno-oag† N butter (lit. a Chinaman's brain).
chihpia; chichppiad (dist) Vp move with one's belongings; ~thag N travel; a pilgrimage; ~tham N* a traveler; a pilgrim, a sojourner.
chihwia; *ch* V settle, establish residence; ~pa Vr settle in a place permanently.
¹chikpan/chipkan N work; a job; business.
²chikp*an*/chipk*an*, *ch* (dist) V,Vt work (on); ~a N; ~a|chuth Vt put to work; employ; ~a|g s-Vs (of work) to be abundant; ~a|kud N a tool, an implement for working; ~a|med* V; ha'asa ~ V resign; ~*ith* Vb; Vtb; ~tham N* a worker.
chi-lihhi‡/cha-lihhi†; *ch*—li N a sheriff; a police officer, a policeman; s-wadag-jujkam ~ N a border patrolman. [<AmSp *charife*<Eng *sheriff*]
chimi-niia; *ch*—ni N a chimney of a house. [<Sp *chimenea*]
chimkko*n*; *chi* Vt nick; mar.
chi-mohn; *ch*— mo N a tongue on a wagon; a hitch; a whippletree. [<Sp *timón* the beam of a plow]
chini; *hchi* N a mouth (in any sense); aki ~; a'aki ~ N specifically, the mouth of an arroyo; ~dath Vt form a lip on; ~gith Vr move the lips; speak; ~sh|ch Vrs be close-mouthed (lit. and fig.); ~shp* Vr; ~wua* V hit one's mouth.
chiniwo; *chi* (dist) N a moustache; whiskers; s-Vs; ~t V.
chinniak; *chi*; *hchi* (dist) V yawn.
chintath; *chi* Vt press the lips to; kiss.
chipkan See ¹CHIKPAN, ²CHIKPAN.
chipshun, chipshush; *chi* Vt scrape (something, as icing, from a pan) and lick (it) from the fingers.

chiwi-chuhch

chiwi-chuhch *N* the killdeer bird
(*Oxyechus vociferus*); the sandpiper
bird (*Scolopacidae*).
¹__**chk** (__**ch** before __*shulig*),
__**chek**, __**chchek**, __**chki** *suffix
added to combining elements to form
transitive verbs* lean against or press
on (with the specified body part):
HONCHK.
²__**chk**; __**kumiak** *suffix added to
transitive verbs to intensify the
action*: HIKUCHK, HIKKUMIAK.
chogo-lahthi *N* cocoa. [<Sp
chocolate chocolate<Nahuatl
chocolatl]
cho-lihsa *N* Spanish chorizo. [<Sp
chorizo]
chu *prefix added to transitive verbs to
form s-class stative verbs indicating
a characteristic of the subject* be
__ing: **s-chu amichuth**=*be
understanding*.
__**chu**, __**chu'u** *suffix added to
adjectives to form nouns* a person or
thing (with a specified characteristic):
S-CHUKCHU. [<ha'ichu]
chu'a, chua, ch, chua'i *Vt* grind.
chu'a__; chucha__ *CE* a sharp
object: ~**kkad** *s-N* a bayonet;
~**kkan*** *Vt* puncture; ~**kkan|a** *N*
a puncture wound; ~**kkan|a|s** *Vs;*
~**mun** *Vt* tamp; poke; prod; incite;
~**mun|a** *N*.
chu'adk See CHU'ALK.
chu'adkim; chu *V* gallop; strut; hop.
chuaggia; ch *N* a net; a web.
chua'i See CHU'A.
chu'al; chu *s-Adv* straight up; erectly;
~**thaha;** ~ **thadha** *Vs* be
squatting.
chu'alk/chu'adk *Vs* be slender and
tall or long-legged; ~**a** *Vp;* ~**a|him**
V; ~**a|ith** *Vr* stand on tiptoe;
~ **him** *V* walk tall or tiptoe.
chuama; ch *Vt* roast in ashes; ~**i** *N*
a roast (meat).
chuawi *N* a ground squirrel.
chu'awogi; chu *Vs* be standing in
a group.
chuchkath *Adv* nightly.
chuchuis *N* the organ-pipe cactus
(*Lemaireocereus thurberi*).
chuchul; hch (*dist*) *N* a live chicken;
~ **chuhkug** *N* uncooked chicken;
~ **ha-hihiwthag** *N* chicken pox;
~ **hithod** *N* cooked chicken;
~**i'ispul/kuksho-wuhplim** *N* the
columbine plant (*Aquilegia*); the
larkspur plant (*Delphinium*) (lit. a

chicken spur); ~ **mad** *N* a baby
chicken.
__**chug‡/__chug†** *suffix added to
gerunds to form transitive verbs*
1. take up or continue (an activity):
AHGACHUG; **2.** carry (in a specified
manner): GI'ACHUG.
chuhch See ¹KEHK.
chuhcha See KEHSH.
chuhchim See KEHKAM.
chuhchpul *N** a square figure; ~**im**
s-Adv in a square shape, square;
~**k** *s-Vs*.
chuhchud; hch *N* a nephew or niece
by a younger brother or a male cousin
of younger ancestry; ~**am** *N* one
who has such a nephew or niece; *Nr*
(*pl*) those related as such a nephew
or niece and an uncle or aunt; ~**-je'e;**
~**-ha-je'e** *N* one's sister-in-law or
relative who is mother of this nephew
or niece; the reciprocal relationship;
~**-jehjim;** ~**-ha-jehjim** *Nr*. See
App. 4.
chuhd__ *CE* embers of wood;
charcoal: ~**agi** *N* embers; charcoal;
~**t** *V* make embers of wood, etc.
chuhhuni *s-Adj, s-Vs* (be) gray.
chuhi__ *CE* grind; mash: ~**wia** *N*
ground or mashed food; ~**win** *Vt*
grind (food).
¹**chuhk, chuhchku** *V* stop burning or
giving out light; ~**him** *V*.
²**chuhk, chuhchku** *Vt* carry on one's
back; ~**ch** *Vts* have on one's back.
chuhkug/chuhhug *N* the body; flesh;
meat; beef; the meat of any animal;
~ **gaki** *s-N* jerky; dried meat;
~ **shoniwia** *N* ground meat;
hamburger.
chuhl; chuhchpul *N* a corner; a hip
joint.
chuhsh, chui; hch *Vt* extinguish
(a flame or light).
chuhth *Vr* do a squaw dance.
chuhthk *N* a rise or hump in the
ground; *Vs* be humped; be high (as
a long-legged horse).
chuhthp; 'uchu *Adj, N* (a) six; (a)
sixth; one of the sticks used in the
game called ginis; ~**o** *Adv* six times.
chuhug *N* night; *Adv* last night;
~**a|m** *s-Vs* be dark; *s-N* darkness.
chuhugia *N* spinach; pigweed,
careless (*Amaranthus palmeri*).
chuhugith, chuchkith *s-Vr* faint,
pass out; go blank.
chuhwi *N* a jack rabbit; **chuk** ~ *N* a
black-tailed jack rabbit; ~**-tadpo** *N*

owl clover (*Orthocarpus purpurascens*, Figwort family) (lit. the foot hair of a jack rabbit); **toha** ~ *N* a white-tailed jack rabbit; **~-wuipo** *N* the fairy-duster plant (*Calliandra eriophylla*) (lit. a jack-rabbit's eyelash).

Chuhwi-Ko'atham *N* a lower Pima tribesman (lit. a jack-rabbit eater).

chuhwua; *chu* *V* (of a female) to reach puberty; ~'**am** *N** a pubescent female.

chuhwuathag *N* black resin from the mesquite tree.

chui See CHUHSH.

chu'i; *chu* (*dist*) *N* flour; ground food; pollen; *Adj* powdered; **~g** *s-Vs;* **~med*** *Vt* go to get (specified groceries); ~ **wua|tham** *N* a pollen sprinkler in the harvest ceremony. See App. 3.

chui___; *chu* *CE* wink: **~shp*** *Vr* wink.

chu'ichig; *chu* *N* character; fate; a plan; responsibility; credit; blame; guilt; **~ahg** *Vr* confess; **~ch***uth* *Vdt* blame for, accuse of; **pi ap** ~ *N* sin.

chu'ich*k* *Vdt* ask (a question) of; **~i** *N* a question; **~tham** *N** a questioner.

chu'ig; *hchu* *habVts* be like or similar to (someone or something, indicated by gesture or a clause); be (in a specified place).

chu'i*j* *habV* engage in a (specified) activity; **~kam** *habN* a doer; **pihk** ~ *V* make a mistake.

chu'iko; *chu* *Adv* in a secluded place.

chuishpa; *chu* *N* (a) lunch (usually packed and carried; **~med*** *V* go grocery shopping.

chuishpi*th;* *chu* *Vt* make a lunch for (someone).

chu'i*th* *Vdt* grind for (someone); **~a|s** *Vs.*

chu'ithag; *hchu* *N* a part or piece.

chuk; *ch* *s-Adj, s-Vs* (be) black; **~chu** *s-N* a dark or black person or thing; **i** ~ *s-V* become dusk or evening; **~ma** *s-Adj* dark; **~u** *Vp;* **~uj***ith* *Vt* blacken; darken; dim.

chuk mudagkam *N* six weeks grama grass (*Bouteloua barbata*).

chukmug *N* a gnat.

chukud; *hch* *N* an owl; **~-shosha; ~-ha-shosha** *N* a date (fruit) (lit. owl nasal discharge).

chukugshuad; *ch* *N* a cricket.

chukul-ba'ichuk *N* a horned lark.

chul__ *CE* the hip: **~sh|ch** *Vts* have (clothes) tucked or rolled up as when wading; **~shp** *Vt* tuck or roll up clothes as for wading.

__chulith *suffix added to transitive stative verbs to form causative passive verbs* cause (to be done): MAHCHCHULITH, IAGCHULITH.

[1]**chum/chem;** '*uchu/*'*eche* *Adj* small; insufficient; **~a|j** *Vs;* **~chu** *N;* **~th|a** *Vp;* **~th|a|him** *V;* **~th|a|j***ith* *Vt* make small, reduce; **~th|a|jith|a** *N;* **~th|a|jith|a|kud** *N;* **~th|a|jith|a|s** *Vs.*

[2]**chum/chem** *indicates that something is unexpected, or is expected, attempted or accomplished in vain, or that the subject acts like something is true:* T-kih o chum s-toha=*Our house is supposed to be white (but became discolored or never got painted);* T-kih o chum s-tohakahim=*Our house was white (but isn't now);* Bat-o chum juh=*He is expected (or supposed) to do it (but won't), He would have done it (but...), He'll try to do it (but will fail), He'll do it in vain (because its purpose will fail);* Am at chum nei=*He saw it unexpectedly;* ~ **alo** *Adv* almost, not quite; ~ **as** *Conj* even though, although, though; ~ **as hems** *Conj* even if; ~ **hekith** *Adv* always; ~ **hems** *Adv used in expressions of emphasis, surprise, or concession* even; **wabsh** ~ *Adj* any.

[1]**__chuth** (*replaces* [1]__*t and* [2]__*t*) *suffix added* **1.** *to non-stative intransitive verbs to form causative verbs* cause (to do): HIMCHUTH; **2.** *to stative verbs, adjectives, nouns, and prepositions to form causative verbs* cause (to be): AP'ECHUTH, O'OTHHAMCHUTH, HEMACHUTH.

[2]**__chuth** See **__**JELITH.

chuthwua; *hchu* *V* land on all feet.

__chu'u See **__**CHU.

chuwithani; *chu* *N* a pulse; *Vs* have a pulse.

chuwithk; '*uchu* *N* a mound; *Vs* be hunch-backed.

D

[1]**d** See **__**D.

[2]**d (d__)** See WUD.

__d, d *CE added to combining*

*elements to indicate a time in the
distant past* used to, had, was: **Kunid**
(or **Nid**) **am chikpan**=*And I used to
work there;* **Kud** (or **D**) **pi am hu
chikpan**=*And he hadn't been
working there.*

¹__**dag** *suffix added to nouns* **1.** *to
form stative verbs* have on (as
clothes, a harness, etc.): HOGIDAG; be
(buttoned, fastened, fenced, etc.):
KOLHAIDAG; **2.** *to form nouns:*
KOLHAIDAG.

²__**dag** (__**d** *before* __ *kam*)/__**lig**
*suffix added to gerunds to form
abstract nouns* -dom, -ship, -ing,
-ment: CHEGGIADAG.

³__**dag** See ²__THAG.

__**dath** *suffix added to nouns to form
transitive verbs* **1.** put on or attach
(as clothes, a saddle, a button):
ENIGADATH; **2.** fasten (as a button).

doh__ See HEDAI.

E

e *precedes verbs to indicate a second
or third person is acted upon by
someone or something unspecified*
oneself, himself, etc.; (usually with
hejel or *hehe'ejel*), one another
(usually with *a 'ai*): **Namt e
shonihi?**=*Did you get hit?* or *Did
you hit yourselves?* or *Did you hit one
another?;* **E at shonihi**=*He got hit* or
He hit himself or *They hit each other;*
Hehe'ejel at e shonihi=*They hit
themselves;* **A'ai at e shonihi**=*They
hit each other.*

e- *prefix added to nouns and
prepositions to indicate a second or
third person subject (of a sentence)
as possessor or object* **1.** his, her,
etc., own: **Am o u 'a g e-mad**=*She's
carrying her (own) child;* **2.** for
himself, herself, etc.: **Chikpan o
hehe'ejel e-we'ewejed**=*They work
for themselves;* **3.** one another's: **A'ai
at ha koktha g e-shoshoiga**=*They
killed one another's animals;* **4.** for
one another: **Chikpan o a'ai
e-wehhejed**=*They work for one
another;* **5.** one another's relatives:
Dam e-wepnagam=*You are cousins*
(i.e., *of one another*); **Do
e-mahmdam**=*They are mother and
child;* **6.** each in relation to the next:

Do e-o'og=*They are fathers each of
the next (in geneological succession);*
**Wehs o an e-thahm hab chu'ig g
shahmt**=*Each brick is on the next;*
**Wehs ihtha'a at am e-thahm hab e
juh**=*These events happened one
after another.*

ebkio*th* *Vt* scare, frighten; ~**a** *N* a
threat.

¹**eda** *Conj* but; yet; however;
~...**hekaj** *Correl. Conj*
since...then/therefore.

²**eda, ed;** *'e Prep* in; among; during;
at (a specified time); ~ **hugkam;** ~
hu Adj half; **s-**~/**si** ~ *Prep* in the
middle or center of; ~ **wa'ug** *N* the
spine (of a plant); ~**weso** *s-Adv* in
the middle.

³**eda** *Adv* then, at that time.

⁴**eda;** *'e N* the insides or interior (as of
a stem or seed); ~**pig** *Vt.*

eda__; *'e CE* shame: **ta** ~**m** *s-Adv*
shamefully; embarrassingly;
disgracefully; **ta** ~**m|a** *s-Vs* be
shameful, etc.; **ta** ~**m|a|kam** *s-N**
something shameful, etc.; someone
causing or deserving shame, etc.;
~**thag** *N* shame; disgrace; scandal;
embarrassment; ~**wua** *s-Vt* shame;
disgrace; scandalize; embarrass.

edagi*th*; *'e Vt* possess, have, own;
find; acquire, gain possession of, get;
Vr acknowledge one's identity;
~**a|chu***th* *Vt;* **chu**~ *s-Vs* be
acquisitive; ~**th|a|m** *N* a possessor,
an owner.

edapk *Adv* at this very time.

edastk; *'e s-Vs* be unruffled.

edawek; *'e (dist) N* intestine(s),
gut(s); inside(s).

edawi; *'e Prep* in the middle of; ~**ko**
Adv halfway.

edhaithag; *'e N* a blood vessel.

edho/~**i;** *'e N* the rhatany plant
(*Kremerin parvafolia*).

edmu*n* *Vt* crush (grain).

edpa; *'e N* a woven door (as of grass).

edtham; *'e N** one who is shy.

edwi*n* *Vt* pulverize (grain).

e'edobad *V* bleed from a natural body
opening.

e'es *N* a plant; a crop (of plants).

e'eshshelig *Vs* be tattooed on the
chin.

ehb; e'eb; e''eb *V* stop crying;
~**chu***th* *Vt.*

ehbith, ehbeni*th*, *'e s-Vt* fear, be
afraid of; become frightened by; ~**a**
N; ~**a|chu***th* *Vdt;* ~**a|dag** *N* fear;

~am *Adj* dangerous; chu ~ *s-Vs;*
chu ~a|m *s-Adv* fearfully; chu
~a|m|a *s-Vs* be fearful-natured;
chu ~tham *N** a fearful being; a
coward; ta ~a|m *s-Adv*
frighteningly; dangerously; ta
~a|m|a *s-Vs;* ta ~a|m|a|kam
s-N* something frightening.
eh'ed *N* blood.
ehk; 'e *V* get in the shade; ~a *Vp*
become shaded; become evening;
~a|him *V;* ~a|jith *Vt* shade;
~a|kud *N* an umbrella; a shade;
~ch *Vts;* ~chuth *Vt;* ~t *V;*
~t|a *N;* ~t|a|him *V;* ~thag *N*
shade; a shadow.
ehkeg/ehheg; *h'e N* shade; *s-Vs* be
shady or shaded; cast a shadow;
~chu *s-N** a black person; a dark
person or thing; ~ko *s-Adv;*
~wua* *Vtp* shade; ~wua|s *Vs.*
ehp, ep *Adv* again; also; more;
furthermore, moreover, in addition;
pi ~ *Adv* no longer.
ehs___, 'e *CE* stealth: chu ~k *s-Vs*
be a thief; chu ~kam *s-N** a thief;
~i|g *N* thievery, theft; stolen
goods, booty; ~ith *Vdt* steal from;
~ith|a|chuth *Vtb* steal for
(someone); ~i|th|amk *Vdt;* ta
~i|m|a *s-Vs;* ~to* *Vtp* hide;
~to|i *N;* ~to|i|s *Vs;* ~to|ith
Vtb; ~to|kch *Vts; Vrs.*
ei See ESH.
eie *Intj* an expression of fear.
el___; 'e *CE* skin or hide: chini ~thag
N a lip of a person or animal;
~i|thag *N* the skin of a person or
animal; the bark of a tree; ~kon *Vt*
skin, dehide; ~kon|a *N* the process
of skinning; a skin; a pelt; ~kon|a|s
Vs; ~kon|ith *Vtb;* ~pig *Vt* peel;
remove the peel, bark, or paint from;
~pig|a *N;* ~pig|a|s *Vs;* ~pig|ch
Vts.
elith, 'e *habVinf* plan; *habVt* form or
have an opinion about; think of (what
entity, location, time, or manner is
involved); *habVcmpl* assume; think;
expect; decide; conclude; wish;
hasVt fear; be in awe of; ~a *habN*
the act of planning or thinking; awe;
concern; a decision; ab ~ *hasVt*
respect; honor; worship; ~a|dag
habN a plan; thought; care; ~a|s
habAdj, habVs (be) planned or
assumed; ~ch *Adv; Vts;* padhog ~
s-V think evilly; *s-Vt* suspect, think
evilly about; padhog ~a *N;* padhog

~a|dag *N* evil thinking; suspicion;
obsenity; pornography; pi ~ *Vr* be
unashamed; have a clear conscience;
pihk ~ *Vr* concern oneself (about);
have deep love (for); *Vt* have
concern for; love deeply; pihk ~a
N; pihk ~a|dag *N* concern; love;
si ~ *s-Vr,Vr* be ashamed; be shy or
bashful; si ~a|dag *N* disgrace;
bashfulness; wehog ~/wohog ~
s-Vt respect; obey; wehog ~a *N;*
wehog ~a|dag *N* respect;
obedience.
em- *CE* you (*pl, object*); your (*pl*):
em-eniga=*your possession.*
eniga; 'e *N* (a) possession; clothes;
Vts possess, own; *s-Vts* have an
abundance of; ~chuth *Vdt;* ~dath
Vt clothe, dress; ~dath|ch *Vts;*
~d|pi'ok *Vt* undress;
e-wehngam ~ *N* a suit of clothes;
~kam *N* an owner; ~t *Vt* make
one's possession, become the
owner of.
ep See EHP.
epai *Adv* also.
es___ *CE* planting: ~i|med* *Vt;*
~thag *s-Vrs* be plantable (in a
specified place).
¹esh; 'e *N* the chin; ~po *N* a beard.
²esh, ei, e'esha, ehs *Vt* plant, sow
(usu. lit.); ~a *N* a living plant; an
act or an instance of planting;
farming; ~abig *N* the planting
season.

F

fa-mihlia See HUA-MIHLIA.

G

¹g/heg *article* the; a, an (with *hema*):
Hema ani neith g kawiyu=*I see a
horse; Adj* some, any (with *ha'i*):
Ha'i ani neith g kakawiyu=*I see
some horses.*
²g *an imperative indicator:* Ab g i
hihm=*Come here.*
¹___g *suffix added to nouns to form
stative verbs* be (a specified thing at
a specified place): Nam ia
o'othhamag?=*Are you people
here?;* Am o kuig=*There's a tree
there.*

²—g *suffix added to transitive verbs to form nouns* **1.** a product for or of (an activity): **cheposig**=*a brand mark;* **bihugig**=*hunger or famine;* **gegosig**=*a meal;* **heosig**=*a blossom;* **2.** any one of the five senses: TAHTKAG.

³—g See —GA.

—ga (—g *after certain loan words from Spanish;* —ka *after plant parts) suffix added to nouns and combining elements referring to that which is considered acquired, in contrast to that which is considered normally possessed, such as body parts, abilities, emotions, relatives, and man-made things:* KAICHKA. ►That which normally belongs to something may be acquired by someone: **hihijgaj g Huan** (or **Huan hihijga**)=*John's tripe* (but **hihij g haiwani**, or **haiwani hihih**=*cattle intestine*).

ga'a, gai, gag'e, gah'i *Vt* roast; broil.
ga'aba'i; ga'a/ga *Adv* over there; up there facing toward.
ga'ajed; ga'agajed *Adv* from there.
gadai/gada'i, gad/gd *Adv* over there out of range.
gagda *Vt* sell; betray; accuse; press charges against; judicate; translate; ~**kud** *N* a store; a shop; ~**tham** *N* a betrayer.
gag'e See GA'A.
gagih See KAHK.
gagka *N* a clearing; ~**t** *Vt* clear (land); ~**t|a** *N* brush (for burning).
gagli *N* any consumer item for sale.
gah*g* *Vt* look for; ~**him, gagahim** *Vt;* ~**hi|me*d*** *Vt;* ~**i** *N;* ~**i*th*** *Vtb.*
gahi, ~j; gahghai *Prep* across; back and forth across; on the other side of; on each side of; through: **si s-gahghai**=*completely across.*
gah'i See GA'A.
gahij See GAHI.
gahiobin; g *Vt* cross; criss-cross.
gahiobs; g *Vts* be lying across (something).
gahi wuhshanim *Prep* through; by means of.
gahj See GAHSH.
gahmai/gahma'i, gahm *Adv* far over there.
gahnai/gahna'i, gahn *Adv* far over there to the side or in a position facing sideways.

gahsh/gahj *Adv* over there (facing toward).
gaht; g *N* a bow (weapon); a gun.
gai See GA'A.
ga'i *N* roasted meat.
gai'iwesa *N* roasted and crushed boiled corn.
gaki; g *s-Vs* be dry; be skinny, be bony; ~**jith** *Vt* dry; ~**thag** *N* something dried; dryness.
Gakithag Mashath *N* September (lit. dry grass month).
gakimchul *N* the insect called the walking-stick.
gakodk; 'ag *s-Adj, s-Vs* (be) crooked or bent; (be) curved; ~**a** *Vp;* ~**chu** *s-N;* ~**him** *V;* ~**jith** *Vt.*
gaksim, gaksh; ga *V* become dry.
gal-nahyo *N* a pomegranate tree; the fruit of this tree. [<Sp *granado*]
galwash *N* a chickpea. [<Sp *garbanzo*]
gam/gm See GAMAI.
—**gam** *suffix added to nouns to form other nouns* a member of (a specified relationship group): MAHMGAM.
¹**gamai/gama'i, gam/gm** *Adv* over there; over there facing away.
²**gamai** *Conj introduces a number past ten or a multiple of ten* plus: **gokko west-mahm gamai gohk**=*twenty-two;* ~**ehp** *Adv* furthermore, moreover, in addition.
gan/gn See GANAI.
ganai/gana'i, gan/gn *Adv* over there facing in a transverse direction.
ganiwua; ga *Vt* dig up and remove (as earth).
gantan, gantad; ga *Vt* scatter; ~**ahim** *Vt;* ~**i** *s-Vs.*
gaso; g *N* a fox; ~ **mad** *N* a kit or young fox.
gaso-lihn *N* gasoline. [<Sp *gasolina*]
gaswua; ga *Vt* brush or comb.
ga-tohthi; g—to *N* a marble. [<Sp *catota*]
gatwua, gatwup; g *Vp* shoot off a bow or gun; ~**tham** *N* one who shoots, a shooter; a marksman.
gatwui*th*; g *Vt* shoot.
gawos; g *N* a gun; a rifle; **ge'e** ~ *N* a cannon. [<Sp *arcabuz* harquebus]
gawul; 'ag *Adj* different; separate; *Adv* differently; separately; ~**k** *Vs* be different; be separate; ~**k|a** *Vp;* ~**k|a|th*** *Vt* separate; differentiate; choose; ~**ko** *Adv;* ~ **mahs** *Adj,Vts*

be (look, appear, seem) different (from).

ge *Adj* all; big; own; positive; strange; unique; ~ **Jiawul** *N* the Devil (lit. the unique demon); ~ **kuhkunaj** *N* a male homosexual; ~ **tash** *Adv* all day.

ge'e; ~**ged** *Adj* great; large, big; elder; chief; *Adv* greatly; ~**chu** *N** the older or larger one; ~**j;** ~**aj** *Vs* be great, large, etc.; ~**ma** *s-Adv* greatly.

ge'eho *Adv* for a long time.

ge'ehog *s-Vs* be mature; ~**a|m** *s-Adv* maturely; ~**a|t** *V* become mature.

ge'ejig; *ge'e* *N* a leader; an officer; the head (of a family).

ge'el *N* maturity.

ge'el__; *ge'e* *CE* large: ~**him** *V;* ~**i|g** *N* growth; ~**ith** *Vt* raise (offspring).

Ge'e S-hehpijig Mashath *N* December (lit. great cold month).

ge'e shuhthagi *N* an ocean; a sea; a lake.

ge'etha; ge'ege *Vp* get big; grow; ~**him** *V;* ~**jith** *Vt* enlarge.

gegkio; *ge* *N* a shoulder (of the body).

gegok See KEHK.

gegokath *s-Vs* be standing firm; be steadfast.

gegoki__ See KEKI__.

gegos__; *g* (*dist*) *CE* eat: ~**ig** *N* a meal; a feeding; ~**ith** *Vr* eat; *Vt* feed, nourish; ~**ith|a** *N* nourishment; the act or an instance of feeding; ~**ith|a|mk** *s-Vr,s-Vt.*

gehgewa *N* wage; winnings.

gehgewi/gehgthag *N* a prize; spoils.

gehgewkam *N* a winner.

gehsh, gei, gegshshap, gegshshe, gehs; shulig, shuhullig *V* fall (lit. and fig.); bow; descend; **ab wui** ~ *Vt* befall, happen to; occur to; **ab wui i** ~ *Vt* appeal a case to; **gahi** ~ *Vt* cross (a space or body of water); **heki** ~ *Vt* spend; **wawich** ~ *V* fall from a height.

gehsig *N* a fall (lit. and fig.); **heb hu** ~ *N* a loss.

gehsim, gegsim; shulighim *V* go stumbling along; barely manage.

gehsith *Vr* become tired or intoxicated; pass out, faint.

gei See GEHSH.

gepi *N* (a) watermelon.

¹gew *N* ice; (a) snow; ~**shp*** *Vt* snow on.

²gew, gehgew, g, ~**i** *Vt* beat, strike; ring (as a bell); play (a stringed or percussive instrument); defeat; *Vdt* earn (wages) from.

__**gew** *suffix added to combining elements to form intransitive verbs* tremble; twitch; wave; undulate: WUHIGEW.

gewho; *ge* *N* a wildcat, a bobcat.

gewi__; *ge* *CE* strike, hit: ~**chk*** *Vt* strike, hit; ~**chk|wua;** ~**ch|shulig*** *Vt;* ~**kon*** *Vt* strike with a glancing blow; ~**kud** *N* a whip (as for driving animals); ~**shp*** *Vtp* lie against; ~**shun*** *Vt* crush with a blow.

gewito; gewitto; *ge* *Vt* defeat, finish victorious; ~**i** *N;* ~**i|dag** *N* (a) victory.

gewittan *Vt* whip, spank.

gewk; gewpk *s-Adj; s-Vs* (be) strong; ~**a** *Vp;* **ab-absh i** ~ *s-Adj,s-Vs* (be) stiff; ~**a|him** *V;* ~**a|jith** *Vt* strengthen; starch; stiffen; ~**am** *s-Adv* strongly; vigorously; ~**ath*** *Vt* strengthen; give hope to; strengthen the hand of (fig. only); ~**a|th|ch** *Vrs* be striving (toward), have one's hope set (on); ~**chu** *s-N;* ~**em|hun** *Vt* encourage; ~**em|hun|a** *N;* ~**em|hun|a|dag** *N* encouragement; **pi** ~ *Adj,Vs* (be) weak; *N* weakness; **pi-~am** *Adv* weakly; ~**thag** *N* strength, power; a spirit or spiritual power (see App. 3); ~**thag|kam** *N** a person or thing having great strength or influence; ~**th|a|kud** *N* starch.

gewkog, gewpkog; *ge* *V* tire; ~**him** *V;* ~**ig** *N* fatigue; **ta** ~**im** *Adv* tiredly; **ta** ~**im|a** *s-Vs.*

gewkthag; gewpkthag *N* strength; power; influence; authority; a spirit being; *s-Vs;* **ha'ichu thoakam** ~ *N* dangerous spiritual power associated with an animal (see App. 3); **pi-** ~ *N* weakness.

gi'a, gia, gig'ia, gia'i *Vt* grasp; link; fasten; ~**chug** *Vt* carry in one's grasp; ~**dag** *N* a handle; a string for fastening (as for a hat or shoe); ~**dath** *Vt;* ~**d|kam** *N* something with a handle (as a bucket or drawer).

gigi'ik; gi'igi'igik *Adj, N* (an) eight; (an) eighth.

gigiwuk *V* tremble; shiver; ~**chuth** *Vt;* ~**tham** *N* someone or something that trembles; gelatin.

gihg; *gi* *s-Vs* be fat; ~**chu** *s-N** a fat person or animal; ~**i** *N* body fat.

gihki; *g* *N* a plow or digger.

gihko‡/~a†; *g* *N* a crown (for the head); **wamad-** ~ *N* the strangleweed plant (*Cuscutaceae*) (lit. snake-crown).

gihkota *N* the globe mallow plant (*Spaeralcea laxa*).

gihnisi; *gi* *N* fifteen U.S. cents. [<Sp *quince* fifteen]

gihsupi *N* the black phoebe bird.

gihug *s-Vs* be in danger; be worried; be careful.

gi'i, gih, *g* *V* become fat; ~**chuth** *Vt* fatten; ~**him** *V;* ~**ho** *Vp* lose weight; diet; ~**ho|thag** *N* leanness; ~**pig** *Vt* remove bits of fat from (an animal).

Gi'ihodag Mashath‡ *N* January (lit. loss of flesh month).

gi'ik; gi'igik *Adj,N* (a) four; (a) fourth; one of the sticks used in the game called GINIS.

Gi'ik-tash *N* Thursday (lit. the fourth day).

gi'is *Vs* be connected (to); be grafted (on to).

gikuj; gikkuj *V* whistle; ~**i|g** *N* a whistle (the device); ~**ith** *Vt* whistle at; whistle for.

gimai; *gi* *N* a braggart; a proud person; ~**hun** *Vr* show off; brag; ~**m** *s-Adv* boastfully; ~**m|a** *s-Vs* be boastful; be haughty; ~**m|a|dag** *N* boasting; boastfulness; pride.

ginis *N* a wild game animal; a gambling game in which four flat, marked sticks (*ginis, sihngo, chuhthp, gi'ik*) are tossed to determine score; ~**kud** *N* any of the four sticks used in this game.

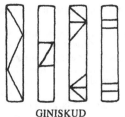

GINISKUD

gishaliwua*; '*ig* *V* become weak from hunger.

[1]**gishshum; gi'igshum** *N* a woven handle for a water jug.

[2]**gishshum** *Vt* bind (up) (lit. only).

gisoki *N* the purple-fruited prickly pear cactus (*Opuntia*); the fruit of this cactus.

gital; *g* *N* a guitar. [<Sp *guitarra*]

_gith (**_ith** after *k*) *suffix added*
1. *to body-part nouns to form non-stative transitive and reflexive verbs* move (a specified body part) to and fro: MO'OGITH; **2.** *to verbs to form transitive and reflexive verbs* cause to: JEHNIGITH, MUHKITH.

githag *N* mescat acacia (*Acacia constricta*).

githahim *Vt* go scouting (an enemy).

githahimed; githahiop* *Vt* go in order to scout (an enemy).

githahimel; *gi* *N* a scouting expedition.

githaihimdam; githaihokam *N** a scout; a raider.

githaihun; *gi* *Vt* seek (an enemy).

githwal; *gi* *N* any of various types of swallow (family *Hirundinidae*).

giumud† *Vt* strike (a match).

giushani, giushud‡ *Vt* strike (a match).

giwho/giho; *gi* *N* a basket for carrying things on the back, a burden basket.

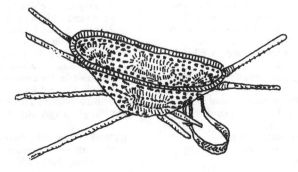

GIWHO

giwud; *gi*; **giwpud** *N* a belt; a band (as a headband); a strap; ~**dath** *Vt;* ~**dath|ch** *Vr;* ~**k** *Vs* be constricted; be narrowed.
giwul; *g* *s-Adv* carelessly; dangerously.
giwulk; *g*; **'ig** *Vs* be constricted; be narrowed; ~**thag** *N* the waistline.
gm See GAMAI.
gogs; *go* *N* a dog; ~**i|g** *s-N* (*pl*) many dogs; ~**i|m** *s-Adv* in a crude manner, crudely; ~ **mad** *N* a puppy; ~ **o'othham** *N* a monkey.
gohhim; *go* *V* limp.
gohih/gohui *N* the mulberry tree (*Morus microphylla*); ~ **bahithag** *N* a mulberry.
gohimeli *N* a ceremonial dance.
gohk; go'ogok *Adj,N* (a) two; second; ~**kam** *N** one who is second.
gohki *N* a footprint, a track.
Gohk-tash *N* Tuesday (lit. the second day).
gohui See GOHIH.
goikhim; *go* *V* limp.
gokko *Adv* twice.
gol__; *go* *CE* a raking motion: ~**shan*** *Vt* scratch out (a hole); ~**win** *Vt* rake; hoe.
golwis; *go* *N* a non-conformist; a fool; *Vs* be non-conformist; be a fool.
go'ol; go'ogol *Adj* other; ~**ko** *Adv* elsewhere; ~**ko|jed** *Adv*.

H

__h See ²__T.
¹ha *Intj* an expression used to ask for a repetition of something spoken: What?
²ha (-a after*pi*) *Adv* at all, in any way: **Pi ach ha gewkthag**=*We have no strength at all.*
³ha *Pron* them; someone; some (of a mass).
ha- *CE* their; someone's: **ha-kih**=*their house.*
ha'a; ha~ *N* a jar (container).
ha'a__ (*definite*), **he'e__** (*indefinite*); **haha'a__** (*dist, definite*), **hehe'e__** (*dist, indefinite*) *N* a quantity; ~**kia** *Adj* a number of a general category: **Ha'akia ani kakawiyuga**=*I have a number of horses;* **He'ekia ap i kakawiyuga?**=*How many horses do*

you have?; **Ha'akia**=*This many;* ~**kia|chu** *N* a person or thing with a number identifying its size, sequential order, etc.: **He'ekiachu apt i ha bei?**=*What numbered one did you get?*; ~**kia|jj** *Adj* a number of a particular specimen of a category: **He'ekiajj apt i ha ui hegam haiwani?**=*How many of those horses did you get?*; ~**kkio** *Adv* a number of times: **He'ekkio apt i ha ui g haiwani?**=*How many times did you get cattle?*; **Ha'akkio**=*This many* [<kia *and* ko]; ~**k|pa** *Adv* a number of places: **He'ekpa apt i kihkit?**=*How many places did you build houses?*; **Ha'akpa mani tachchua**=*As many as I wanted* [<kia *and* pa]; ~**s** *Adj* **1.** an amount of a general category of material: **He'es apt i ha bei g o'od?**=*How much sand did you get?*; **2.** a degree of a specified size: **He'es o i chewaj g ali?**=*How tall is the child?*; **Ha'as o chewaj mo g wo'ikud he'es i s-tadani**=*He's as tall as the bed is wide;* ~**s|chu** *N* a person or thing of a certain mass or size: **He'eschu apt i bei g huk?**=*What size lumber did you get?*; ~**s|i|g** *Vs* be a certain size: **Ha'asig o g gogs**=*The dog is this big;* ~**s|i|jj** *N* an amount of a particular specimen of material: **He'esijj apt i ha bei hegai o'od**=*How much of that sand did you get?*; ~**s|ko** *Adv* a distance; how far: **He'esko apt i hih?**=*How far did you go?*
¹ha'ab/ha'ag *Adv* in this or that direction; ~**jed** *Adv* from this or that direction.
²ha'ab *Adv* in a certain manner.
ha'ag See ¹HA'AB.
ha'ahama; haha'ama *s-Vs* be mean or tough; be bold†.
ha'akith *Adv* last year; **d hu hema** ~ *Adv* the third year previous; **hema** ~ *Adv* year before last.
ha'apaga *N* the flesh behind the upper teeth, the alveolar ridge.
ha'apapig *Vt* remove the alveolar flesh from (a horse).
ha'asa; ha *Vt* quit, cease, stop; ~**ni;** ~**nio,** ~**yogo** *V* imperative only Stop.
ha'athka; ha *Vp* become startled and gasp; ~**j** *V* open the mouth wide in surprise or wonder, gape.

¹**hab, b**— (*definite*), **has** (*indefinite, negative*), **shah**— (*indefinite, interrogative*) *CE occurs with or in place of the complement clause of certain verbs* (that); something; anything; what; that: **Huan o hab kaij** (or **Bo kaij g Huan) matsh gm hu wo hih**=*John says (that) he's going to go;* **Pi o hab kaij**=*He didn't say that;* **Pi o has kaij**=*He didn't say anything;* **Shah'o** (or **K has) kaij?**=(*And) what did he say?*

²**hab** *Adv* for the reason previously given: **K hab pi chikpan**=*For that reason* (or *That's why) he isn't working.*

³**hab** (*definite*), **has** (*indefinite*) *CE combines with adverbs of place to form adverbs* in a direction: **gan hab**=*there to the side;* **in has**=*some place to the side.*

hab—**; ha** *CE* flat: ~**ad|k** *Vs* be sitting flat; ~**al|i|m** *s-Adv* in a flat manner, flatly; ~**al|k|a** *Vp;* ~**al|k|a|him** *V;* ~**shun*** *Vt* deflate (lit. only).

hab-a'ap See HAB-A EHP.

hab-a ehp, hab-a'ap *Adv* also; in the same manner.

habba *Intj* an expression used to drive away animals: Shoo! Get away! etc.; ~**gith** *Vt* shoo (away).

hab hi *Adv* seemingly; supposedly.

had— *CE* cling: ~**am** *s-Adj, s-Vs* (be) sticky; ~**sh** *Vts;* ~**shadkam** *N* the teddybear cholla cactus (*Opuntia bigelovii*) (lit. something that clings); ~**shp** *Vt* glue; paste; ~**shp|a|kud** *N;* ~**shp|i** *Vs.*

hadam-tatk *N* globe mallow (*Sphaeralcea*) (lit. sticky root).

hadwuag; ha *V* belch.

hagito; ha *Vp* burn up; melt away.

hah *Intj* an expression used to **1.** get attention: Hey!; **2.** show surprise: oh!

haha See HAHAWA.

haha'atadkam *s-N* a good potter.

hahaha *Intj* an expression used to imitate laughter.

hahaisha *N* (*pl*) chips of food (as squash) for storage.

hahaisig *N* (*pl*) broken pieces (as bread, glass, etc.).

hahaw *N* a lung.

hahawa/haha/-aha *Adv* afterward, then; now; subsequently.

hahawk *V* pant.

hahbiw; ha *Vt* copulate with.

ha hekaj, wa hekaj *Adv* immediately.

hahg, ~**i, hahage** *V* melt; thaw.

hahgith, ha *Vt* melt; thaw.

hahhag *N* a leaf (of a plant).

hahk, ~**i, hahake** *Vt* roast (grain) with coals (in a basket); ~**i** *N* roasted grain; pinoli.

hahkkit See HAKIT.

hahkwod *N* mistletoe (*Phorodendron californicum*).

hahl *N* (a) squash; (a) pumpkin; ~**math** *Vt* break (as an engagement).

hahsa; ha; hha *N* an axe; **al** ~ *N* a hatchet. [<Sp *hacha*]

hahshani *N* the saguaro cactus (*Cereus gigantea* or *Carnegiae gigantea*).

Hahshani Bahithag (or **Bak) Mashath** *N* June (lit. saguaro ripening month).

hahsig *Vt* make fun of, ridicule.

hahth *N* the Papago lily (*Dichelostemma pulchellum*); ~**kos** *N* the Mariposa lily (*Calochortus kennedyi*).

hahwulith; ha *Vt* tie a knot in; *Vr* (*pl*) get tangled.

hahwul'ok; ha *Vt* untie.

ha'i *Adj* some; any (used only in negative); other; *Pron* some; any (used only in negative); others.

ha'ichu; ha (*definite*); **haschu** (*indefinite, interrog.*); **shahchu** (*interrog.*) *N* something; *Adj* of some kind; *Pron* something; someone of importance; the deity; ~**chuth** *Vt* honor, esteem; **has** ~ *s-N* something important; **has** ~**dag** *s-N* importance; **pi** ~**chuth** *Vt* belittle; **si** ~ *N* something important; ~**thag** *N* a part; a piece.

ha'ichug *Vs* exist, be in a (specified) place; **pi** ~ *Vs* be non-existent; be absent.

hain; ha *Vt* crack; burst; break in pieces; ~**amk** *s-Vt* want to crack, etc.; ~**i** *Vs* be cracked, etc.; ~**ig** *N.*

—**hain,** —**haish** *suffix added to body-part nouns to form transitive verbs* hit with (a specified body part): MO'OHAIN, TONHAIN.

haishan; ha *Vt* break off (a piece, as of bread).

haiwani; ha (*dist*) *N* cattle; a cow; ~ **mad** *N* a calf.

hajuni; ha (*dist*) *N* a relative, a

relation; ~m *N;* Nr (*pl*); ~m*k*
s-Vt; ~**thag/**~**talig** *N* a kin
relationship. See App. 4.

hakimad; *ha* *N* a nephew or niece by
an older brother or a male cousin of
older ancestry; ~**kam** *N; Nr* (*pl*).
See App. 4.

hakima-je'e; hahakimad-ha-je'e *N*
one's sister-in-law or cousin by
marriage who is mother of this above
nephew or niece; the reciprocal
relationship; ~**m;** ~**im** *N; Nr* (*pl*).
See App. 4.

hakit; *ha* /**hahkkit** *N* an uncle junior
to one's father; ~**kam** *N;* ~**-oks;**
~**-o'oki** *N* an aunt by marriage to
such an uncle; ~**-oksim;** ~**-o'okim**
N. See App. 4.

hakko/~**'o;** *ha* *N* a loop for carrying
burdens on the head, a looped
cushion; ~**dag** *Adj, Vs;* ~**dath** *Vt*
put a loop in (a lariat); put a cushion
on (the head); ~**dath|ch** *Vts;* ~**i|s**
Vs.

halibwua† *V* gallop; skip along.

hambthog *s-Vs* be esoteric; ~**im**
s-Adv in an incanting manner,
incantingly; ~**ith** *Vtr* incant.

ha-mohn *N* bacon; ham. [<Sp *jamón*
ham]

hanam *N* the cholla cactus
(*Cactaceae*); the edible buds of this
cactus.

Hapo-nihs *Adj* Japanese; of or
relating to the Japanese people or
their language; *N* a Japanese person
or the language. [<Sp *japones*]

hapot; *h; hp* *N* an arrow.

¹**has** *s-Adj* important; *Adv* (*in a
negative sense*) any way; *Pron* (*in
negative*) anything.

²**has** See ¹HAB, ³HAB.

haschu See HA'ICHU.

hash See WABSH.

hashaba See WABSHABA.

hashda; *ha* *N* a loose-woven basket.

hasig *s-Adj,s-Vs* (be) difficult; *s-Adv*
difficultly.

hasko; ha~ (*interrog.*), **shahko**
(*interrog.*) *Adv* somewhere; in a
given direction; ~**jed** *Adv.*

haths*ith; ha* *Vt* sprinkle.

ha'u; *ha* *N* a dipper (utensil).

hauk *s-Adj,s-Vs* (be) lightweight,
light; (be) easy; ~**a** *Vp;* ~**a|him**
V; ~**a|jith** *Vt.*

haupal; *h* *N* the red-tailed hawk
(*Buteo jamaicensis*); ~**-kosh** *N*

sticks gathered for kindling (lit. a
hawk's nest).

hau'u See HEU'U.

hawani; *ha* *N* the common raven
(*Corvus corax*); ~**-tahtad** *N* filaree
(*Erodium cicutarium*) (lit. crow feet).

hawol; hawpol (*dist*) *N* a lima bean.

hawpalithag *N* a group of buds on a
plant.

¹**hebai/heba'i, heb** *Adv* where; am
hu ~ *Adv* somewhere; **pi** ~ *Adv*
not anywhere; nowhere.

²**hebai/heba'i (bah__)** *Adv* where;
~**jed** *Adv* from somewhere; from
where?

**hedai/heda'i (doh__); hedam/hedai
(doh__)** *Pron* who; whom; whose;
which, which one; (no) one; (not)
anyone: **Doht hih?**=*Who went?;*
Kut hedai hih?=*And who went?;*
Dohpt nei?=*Who(m) did you see?;*
Dohpt mah?=*To whom did you give
it?;* **Dohp wecho chikpan?**=*Under
whom do you work?;* **Ha ant nei
hegam mat hedam hihih**=*I saw
those who went;* **pi hedai**=*no one;*
Adj. whose; (no) one's; (not)
anyone's: **Dohpt gogsga
melchkwua?**=*Whose dog did you
hit?;* **Pi ant hedai ha-gogsga
melchkwua**=*I didn't hit anyone's
dog.*

he'e__ See HA'A__.

he'edkath, he'edkai; *he* *Vr* smile,
grin; ~**ch** *Vrs.*

he'ek; *he* *s-Adj,s-Vs* (be) sour; ~**a**
Vp; ~**a|him** *V;* ~**a|jith** *Vt;* ~**chu**
*s-N** something sour.

he'eni; ~**o** *Vt* imperative *only* take;
accept.

¹**heg** See HEGAI.

²**heg** See G.

hegai/hega'i, heg *Pron* that; that one;
the one that; **si** ~ *N* the very thing
or person: **Do si hega'i**=*That's the
very one.*

hegam *Pron* those; they or them (at a
distance).

heh *Intj* an expression indicating
hesitation: uh.

hehekaj *N* a wing feather.

hehem, *h* *V* laugh; ~**imk** *s-V;* ~**kam**
*s-N** a laugher; **ta** ~**a** *s-Vs* be
funny; ~**thag** *s-Vs* be of a laughing
nature; *N* laughter.

hehewini *s-Adj* chapped; ~**s** *s-Vs.*

hehewo *N* an eyebrow.

hehg; *he* *N* a rival; a wife's

relationship to another wife of the same man; ~a|m *N; Nr (pl)*; ~am*k s-Vt* envy; **chu ~amk** *s-Vs* be jealous or envious; **chu ~am|kam** *N** one who is jealous or envious; ~t *Vt* (of a wife) to receive a rival wife (see App. 4); ~**amthadag** *N* jealousy, envy; rivalry.

hehgig; *he s-N* happiness; *s-Adj,s-Vs* (be) happy; ~a|m *s-Adv* happily, joyfully; ~**chulith/hehgchulith** *Vt* praise.

hehgi*th; he Vt* agree with.

hehiwua; *he V* slide; ~hi*m V*.

hehiwuikud; *he N* a playground slide.

hehiwuisk; *he N* a slide, a sliding place.

hehnig *N* whooping cough.

hehogi *s-Vs* be cool (temperature); ~h *Vp;* ~h|him *V;* ~th/~jith *Vt;* ~th|a|kud *N* a cooler.

hehotakud *N* a fan.

hehpch'ed *s-Adv* in winter (lit. in the cold); ~kam *s-N* winter.

hehpi; *he s-Adj* cold (of temperature only); ~chu *s-N* something cold; ~h *Vp;* ~h|him *V;* ~jith *Vt;* ~th *Vs*.

hehwachuth; *he N* the bluejay.

hejel; *he'e Adj* emphatic (my, your, his, etc.) own; *Adv* alone; independently; *N* self; *Vs* be alone; ~i|g *Vs* be alone; ~ko *Adv* alone, by oneself; by myself; by yourself, etc.; *Vr* seclude oneself; ~ **memdatham** *N* an automobile; any self-propelled vehicle.

hejel e-eshatham *N* tumbleweed, Russian thistle (*Salsola kali*) (lit. something that sows itself).

hek; *he N* an armpit; ~po *N;* ~sh|ch *Vts* hold (something) under the arm; ~shp* *Vt* grasp (something) under the arm.

¹**hekaj,__kaj** *Prep* by means of, with; on account of, because of; for (a specified reason or purpose): **hekaj g uhs** or **g uhskaj**=*by means of a stick; Conj* because; since.

²**hekaj** *Vt* use, make use of.

heki/heki__ *CE* unspecified time; past time; loss of time, substance or direction: ~**huchij**/~**hukam** *N** something old; ~ **huh/hu** *Adv* already; some time ago; long ago; ~th *Adv* when.

hekia *Adj* pure; whole, entire; ~gi*th Vt* renew; ~**kam** *N** anything unique, one of a kind; someone or

something completely of one nature, quality, substance, etc.

Hekia S-ap'ekam Gewkthag *N* the Holy Spirit.

hekith/hikith *Adv* sometime; when; ever; **pi** ~ *Adv* never.

heli*g, he,* ~i *Vt* spread to dry; ~ch *Vts*.

hem- See **M-**.

hema *Adj* a, an; one; *Pron* one; someone; *Adv* at a time before another (specified) time: **hema tako**=*(on) the day before yesterday;* ~ch*uth Vt* mistake for another; **hegai** ~ *Pron* the other one.

hemajim *s-Adv* gently; kindly; sympathetically; humanely; ~a *s-Vs;* ~a|kam *N** a gentle, kind, sympathetic, or humane person; ~a|ta|lig *N* gentleness; kindness; sympathy, humaneness.

hemajkam; *he* (dist) *N* a person; people; ~ch*uth Vt* treat like a human; **gawul mahs** ~ *N* a foreigner; another people or nation; **nahnko mahs** ~ *N (pl)* various kinds of people; nations; ~**ta/hemajta** *N* created people. See App. 3.

hemako; *he Adj,N* (a) one; ~ch*uth Vt* unite; ~**thag** *N* unity.

hemapath, hemapai; *he Vt* gather, collect; ~**as** *Vs;* ~**ch** *Vts*.

hemho *Adv* once.

hemho wa *Adv* certainly, necessarily.

hemiap *Adv* in one place.

hems *Adv* probably; **tp** ~ *Adv* maybe.

hemu/~ch *Adv* now, at present; soon; ~ch|kam *N** something new or up to date; ~ **tash** *Adv* today.

heni- See **NI-**.

henihopt *V* hiccup; sniffle.

heosig *N* a blossom, a flower; *s-Vs* be flowery (lit. and fig.).

heosi*th; he Vt* decorate, adorn; ~a *N;* ~a|kud *N* decoration, adornment; ~a|s *Vs*.

heo*t,* ~**tap** *V* bloom, produce flowers; ~a *N;* ~a|him *V*.

het *N* red or white earth; ocre for coloring; ~**magi** *s-Vs* be red; ~**math** *Vt*.

hetasp; *he Adj, N* (a) five; (a) fifth.

heu'u/hau'u *Adv* yes.

hew__ *CE* air current: ~**kon*** *Vt* blow on; ~**mk;** ~**kk*** *V* (of a being) to become chilled; ~**shan*** *Vt* sniff for (as a scent).

hewagi*th* *Vt* smell; **chu ~a|dag**
s-Vs have a keen sense of smell.
hewaji*th*/**hewbaji***th* *Vt* cool, chill;
relieve (pain).
hewastk; *he s-Vs* be able to endure
wind and cold.
hewbagig† *N* rest, relaxation.
hewbagim *s-Adv* restfully.
hewbagi*th*† *Vt* cause to rest; *Vr* rest.
hewbaji*th* See HEWAJITH.
hew*ed* *V* (of the wind) to blow; **~o**
V stop blowing.
hewel *N* air; wind; natural gas; any
substance of a gaseous nature;
~chu*th* *Vb* make wind for (as
with a fan); **~hog** *Vs* be breezy
or windy; **~hog|i***th* *Vt* fan;
~i|m *s-Adv* windily; breathily,
voicelessly; **~i|m|a** *s-Vs;*
s-gewk ~, siw ~ *N* a cyclone.
hewel-ch-ed u'uwhig *N* the dwarf
cowbird (*Molothrus ater obscurus*).
hewel-e'es *N* the parry penstemon
plant (*Penstemon parryi*).
hewel-mohs *N* the western kingbird.
hewel-neoktham *N* a radio (lit. a
speaker by air).
hewest *s-Vs* be chapped; **~sith** *Vt*
cause to be chapped.
hewgia *Vt* smell (around) for;
~ma|him *Vt;* **~med** *Vt.*
hewgig/hewgithag *N* the sense of
smell.
hewgithag See HEWGIG.
hi See HI'I.
_hi_ See _HIM.
hi _ *CE* urine: **~a** *N* urine; **~uw**
s-Vs to smell of urine.
hia *N* a sand dune; **~sh|ch** *Vts* have
(someone or something) buried;
~sh*p*** *Vt* bury; submerge.
hi'a, hia, hi, hia'i *V* urinate;
~m|chuth *s-Vt;* **~med*** *V;* **~m***k*
s-V; **ta-~m|a** *s-Vs* be diuretic.
hiabog; *h* *Vt* dig up, excavate.
Hiakim; *h* *N* a Yaqui tribesman.
hialwui *N* poison; **~math** *Vt*
poison.
hiani *N* a tarantula.
hia tatk *N* the sand-root plant
(*Ammobroma sonorae*) (lit. sand
dune root).
higi, hig *Adv* how about.
hiha'ini/hihi'ani *N* a grave; a
graveyard.
hihi'ani See HIHA'INI.
hihij *N* intestines, bowels; a hose;
~ga *N* tripe.
hihitsh *Vt* slice.

hih*k*, **~i, hihika** *Vt* clip; mow; cut
(grain, etc.); **~a** *N* a plant cutting;
the act of cutting; **~a|kud** *N*
clippers; a mower; **~i***th* *Vtb;*
~tham *N* one who clips; a barber.
hihlo; *hi* *N* thread; **~dath** *Vt* thread.
[<Sp *hilo*]
hihnath; *hi* *Vt* yell to.
hihnk, hihin*k*, **~i, hihinnak** *V* yell;
bark; yelp; howl; blow a horn or
whistle; **~o'|i***th* *Vt* yell at; bark at;
boo at.
hihoin, hihoinak; hioppash (*dist*) *Vt*
bewitch; **~a** *N* the act or an
instance of bewitching; witchcraft;
~tham *N* one who bewitches; a
witch; a warlock.
hihtpadag; *hi* *N* braid.
hihtpag; *hi* *Vt* braid.
hihw__; *hi* *CE* a sore or bruise: **~og**
N a sore on the body; a bruise on a
plant; **~sith** *V* cause a sore or boil;
~thag *N* a sore; a boil.
hihwai; *hi* *N* the sunflower
(*Helianthus*); a strip of squash for
storage.
hi'i, hi on (the) one hand ... on the
other; for one: **Heg at hi gm hu wo
hih, t ith hi ia hu wabsh-o
thakath**=*That one, for one, will
drive off, and this one, in contrast,
will just stay here;* **Nt hi-o hih**=*I, for
one, will leave;* **Nt hi-o m-oi**=*I, for
another, will go with you;* **Heg
hi'i?**=*How about that one?*
hiji; ~wo *V imperative only* move,
get out of the way.
hik; *hi* *N* the navel; the center; **~aj**
N the umbilical cord; **~po** *N.*
hik__; *hi* *CE* cut: **~shan*** *Vt* trim,
cut in strips; serrate; **~shan|i** *Vs;*
N; **~shp*** *Adv* asunder, in parts;
~tani *N* a gulley; **~won** *Vt* cut
jaggedly, serrate; **~wona** *N*
serration.
hikiwigi; *h* *N* the Gila woodpecker
(*Centurus uripygialis*).
hikshpi *V* drizzle, rain lightly.
hikuch*k*, **~i; hikkumi'a***k*, **~i** *Vt* cut;
~a *N* the act of cutting or
circumcizing; something cut or
someone circumcized; circumcision;
~a|kud *N* an implement for
cutting (as a saw); **~a|s** *Vs;* **pahl ~**
Vt circumcize.
hikug *V* (of a tree) to drop its
blossoms; **~t** *V* form fruit; **~thag**
N a saguaro cactus button.
Hi-lihpih; *hi* — *li* *Adj* Filipino; of or

relating to the Filipino people or their language; *N* a Filipino person or the language.

hilio; *hi* *N* a blacksmith. [<Sp *herrero*]

him, hih, hihhim, hihm; *hi* *V* move along; progress; walk; (of anything that progresses, as time, opportunity, experience) to pass; *Vt* conduct (as one's affairs); obey; observe; follow (as laws, customs, etc); **a'ai e** ~**chchul***ith* *Vr* pace the floor; walk to and fro; **ab** ~ *V* approach, come; *Vt* concern; ~**ch|chul** *N* a parade; ~**ch|chulith** *Vt* march; ~**chuth** *Vt* cause to move, etc.; maintain; administrate; **gm hu** ~ *V* go, leave; **heb hu** ~ *V* go somewhere unknown to the speaker; become lost; (euph.) to die; **heb hu** ~**kam** *N** one who has gotten lost; **heb hu** ~**tham** *N** one who is lost; **heki** ~ *V* become lost; lose one's place; go wrong; **heki** ~**chuth** *Vt* lead astray; confuse; trick; return; ~**him** *V* wander, amble; ~**im***k* *s-V* want to go; ~**kam** *N* one who has gone to (a place); ~**s** *Vs* be a route; **ta'i** ~ *V* return, go back; ~**tham** *N* one who is going to (a place).

[1]**___him** *suffix added to non-stative verbs and gerunds to form verbs of motion of the same transitivity* go along (doing something): AHGAHIM, MAHKHIM.

[2]**___him** *suffix added to verbs formed by* [2]**___t** *to form intransitive verbs* begin (if completed action) or continue (if incompleted action) to become (a specified condition): AP'ETAHIM, SHOPOLKAHIM.

himith; *hi* *Vs* be able to walk; ~**t** *Vp* learn to walk.

himlu *V* *as spoken to a young child* walk.

himthag; *hi* *N* a way of life; a culture; a custom or practice; traditions; *Vs* be able to walk; *s-Vs* be a good walker.

himto, himttog *Vp* leave or arrive.

___hin, ___hish *suffix added to combining elements to form transitive verbs* strike (in a specified manner): SHONIHIN.

hinwal *N* a grass mat.

hiopch *N* the body louse (*Pediculus*); a termite.

hiowichu*th* *Vt* soak underground.

hipig *Vt* spread open to dry; ~**a** *N* food for drying.

hip___ *CE* spray: ~**shun*** *Vt* spray (often with the mouth); ~**shun|am***k* *Vt*.

Hi-suhs *N* Jesus. [<Sp *Jesus*]

[1]**hithod; *hi*** *N* cooked food; a (specified) cooked food: **huawi chuhkug** ~=*cooked venison*.

[2]**hithod; *hi*** *Vt* cook; ~**a** *N;* ~**a|kud** *N* a cooking vessel, a pot, a pan.

hitpod; *hi* *Vt* operate on; cut open (an animal).

hi'ush; *hi* *N* the bladder.

hiw *Vt* rub; ~**chul***ith* *Vt* rub (a notched percussion instrument); ~**chulith|a** *N* the act of rubbing (such a stick), particularly as used in ceremonial treatment of an illness (see App. 3.); ~**chulith|akud** *N* a notched stick used as a percussion instrument; ~**kon** *Vt* shave; scrape; smooth; ~**kon|a** *N;* ~**kon|a|kud** *N* a scraper (utensil); a razor; ~**mun** *Vt* grate (lit. only); ~**mun|a** *N;* ~**mun|a|kud** *N* a grater (utensil); ~**shan*** *Vt* scrape smooth; ~**shan|a** *N;* ~**shan|a|kud** *N* a plane (tool); a file (tool).

hi wa/hi-a *Conj* unless.

hiwchu; *hi* *N* the groin; the side of the body; ~**-wegi**, ~**-wepegi** *N* the black-widow spider (lit. a creature with a red groin).

hiwi*g* *Vt* depend on; trust; have confidence in; ~**a** *N* someone to depend on; ~**ith** *Vdt* loan; *Vtinf* allow; **si** ~**a** *N** someone dependable; a champion.

hiwithchuls *s-N* canaigre, dock, wild rhubarb (*Ruminex hymenosepalus*).

hiwium† *Vt* shave (the skin).

hiwk; *hi* *s-Vs* be rough or coarse; ~**a** *Vp* break out in bumps; ~**a|dag/**~**a|lig** *N* measles; ~**a|hi***m* *V;* ~**chu** *N* a file (tool).

hiwsh *Vt* gird (up).

ho See WO.

[1]**___ho** (**___o** after any consonant) *suffix added to intransitive verbs to form intransitive perfective verbs* (of an action or condition) to cease or reverse a process: GI'IHO, MAHSO.

[2]**___ho** (**___ko** after *k*, **___o** after other stops, stem vowel length lost) *suffix added to adjectives of number to form adverbs* a (specified) number of

times: HEMHO, GOKKO [<gohkko],
HA'AKKIO [<ha'akia *and* ho],
CHUHTHPO.
hoa; h N a basket; a coil basket; ~**bad**
N a basket no longer used; ~**bd|ag**
Vs (of a story) to be finished in the
telling; ~**t** V; ~**t|a** N basketry.
hoan, h Vt search for; search through;
~**ith** Vtb search for (something) for
(someone).
hoas-ha'a; h — ha N a plate or dish.
hobinod; ho Vt wrap; ~**ag** N the art
of wrapping; a device for wrapping or
enclosing.
hobinol; ho Vs be wrapped.
[<hobinod + __ i]
ho-e-juh/ho-ni-juh/ni-juh Adv an
expression of agreement: yes; okay.
__**hog** (with shortening of long vowel
in the stem) *suffix added to
non-stative verbs to form* **1.** *stative
verbs of the same transitivity* be
expected to (do): MAKIHOG; **2.**
*s-class stative verbs of the same
transitivity*: be tired of (doing):
S-ta-NEITHHOG.
hogi; ho N* leather, hide; ~**dag** Vs
be saddled; ~**dath** Vtp saddle; put
leather on; ~**dath|ch** Vts; **huawi**
~, **sihki** ~ N buckskin; ~**mag** Vs
be saddled.
hohag; h Vt haul; ~**ch** Vt; ~**chug**
Vt; ~**him** Vt go along loading (as
in a moving vehicle).
hohalimagi s-Adj,s-Vs (be) hollow;
~**chu** s-N.
hohhi; ho N the mourning dove
(*Zeraidura macroura*).
hohhi-e'es N the California poppy
(*Eschscholtzia californica*);
the Desert gold poppy
(*E. glyptosperma*); the Mexican
gold poppy (*E. mexicana*)
(lit. mourning dove plants).
hohho'ith s-Vt enjoy; like; admire;
appreciate; care for; *s-Vcmpl* ᐟ
appreciate; ~**a** N; ~**a|chuth** Vt;
~**a|dag** N pleasure, enjoyment;
admiration; appreciation; **pi** ~ Vt
not enjoy, etc., dislike; **pi** ~**a|chuth**
Vt displease.
hohlwiki N a snail shell.
hohni__; ho CE a wife: ~**chuth** Vt
marry off (a male); ~**g** N one's
wife; ~**g|a|m** N one who has a
wife; ~**med*** V; ~**mk** s-Vt; ~**t**
Vt (of a man) to marry; Vr (pl) (of a
couple) to get married; ~**t|a** N a

marriage, a wedding; Nr a bridge;
~**t|a|m** N a married man; Nr (pl)
a married couple; ~**t|a|mk** s-Vt (of
a man) to want to marry; s-Vr (pl)
(of a couple) to want to get married;
wo-ha-~**t|a|m** N an engaged man;
wo-~**t|a** Nr one's fiancée;
wo-~**t|a|m** Nr (pl) an engaged
couple.
hoho'i N a porcupine.
hoho'ibad N the filaree plant
(*Erodium cicutarium*).
hohokimal N a species of small
yellow butterfly (unidentified).
hohowai N the jojoba or goatnut
plant; the fruit of this plant
(*Simmondsia chinensis*).
hohowo Vt sniff.
Hohpih N a Hopi tribesman.
hoht__; ho CE speed, haste: ~**am**
s-Adv quickly, fast; ~**k** s-Adj, s-Vs
(be) quick, fast; ~**k|ith** s-Vt; s-Vr
hurry, rush; ~**ma|gith** s-Vt hurry
(up), rush.
ho'i; ho (dist) N a thorn; a sticker; (a)
cactus; ~**bad** N a needle; ~**bad|jeg**
N the eye of a needle; ~**dag**
s-Adj,s-Vs (be) thorny; ~**kkan***
Vt puncture; ~**pig** Vt; ~**sh|ch**
Vrs be punctured or stuck with
thorns; ~**shp*** Vt prick or pierce.
ho'ige'elith See HO'IGE'ITH.
ho'ige'ith/ho'ige'elith s-Vt pity; ~**a**
N; **ab** ~ Vt thank; **ab** ~**a|m**
s-Adv thankfully; ~**a|dag** N
thankfulness; ~**a|dag/**~**a|lig** N
blessing; kindness; mercy; ~**a|hun**
Vr pray; ~**a|hun|a** N a prayer, a
supplication; ~**a|m** s-Adv
mercifully.
¹**hoin** Vt greet.
²**hoin, hoik'e; ho** V move, stir.
ho'ip, -o'ip Conj not until.
[<*contraction of* wo *and* ip]
ho'ith Vdt share with.
ho'ithkam; ho N the ironwood tree
(*Olneya tesota*).
ho'iumi† Vt nail; pin.
hokkad; ho N the cactus wren
(*Heleodytes brunneicapillus*).
holiw; ho V roll up; ~**k** Adj
rolled-up; Vs be rolled up; ~**ka|th***
Vt roll up, fold up.
holwuikud N a swing.
homi N the inside of basketry coils.
hon; ho N the body (excluding the
head); ~**chk*** Vt lean against with
the body; ~**chk|wua*** Vt push

along with the body; ~**gew** *V;*
~**gith** *Vr* shake oneself; wiggle;
~**hain*** *Vt;* ~**shp|a|dag** *N* one's
body; ~**wua*** *Vt* walk beside; press
against.
ho-ni-juh See HO-E-JUH.
ho'ok; ho *N* a witch or monster.
~**-wah'o** *N* the nightblooming
cereus (*Cereus greggi*) (lit. a witch's
tongs).
ho'okemhun *Vt* flatter; ~**a|dag** *N*
flattery.
ho'oma; ho *N* a favorite; a charm,
something that brings good luck;
~**chuth** *Vb* make a charm or lucky
arrow, etc., for.
ho'onma; ho *N* a rib (of the body).
hothai; ho *N* a stone; gravel; a rock; a
cement floor; a charm; ~**chuth** *Vt*
petrify (lit. and fig.); stupefy; ~
shahmt *N* cement.
hothodk *Vs* be dented.
hotsh† *Vt* send; ~**a** *N* an emissary;
an apostle; ~**tham** *N* a dispatcher.
hottk *s-Vs* be swift.
howij *N* a banana; a fruit of the
banana yucca; ~**-je'e** *N* the banana
yucca plant (*Yucca baccata*).
howi__ *CE* ingressive breath: ~**chk***
Vt breathe in; ~**chk|wua*** *Vt* suck
in with the breath; choke on; ~**shim**
s-Adv greedily; ~**shla** *N* a greedy
person; ~**shp*** *Vt* gulp (food).
hu See HUH.
huai See HUAWI.
hua-mihlia/fa-mihlia *N* a family.
[<Sp*familia*]
Huan; h *N* John. [<Sp*Juan*]
huashomi; h *N* a buckskin bag;
a wallet; a medicine bag;
a pocketbook.
huawi/huai *N* the mule deer
(*Odocoileus hemionus*); ~ **chuhkug**
N venison; ~ **mad** *N* a fawn.
huch/huhch; huhch *N* a claw; a hoof;
a fingernail.
huchgam *N* a small red and gray bird
(unidentified).
huchin; hu *Vr* stumble, stub one's
toe.
huchwuag; hu *Vr* stub one's toe.
huda; hu *N* a side; particularly, a side
of the midriff.
hudaweg; hu *Vt* discuss; give
attention to; bother; **ab** ~ *Vt* annoy,
bother; **pi** ~ *Vt* ignore.
hudukath; hu (*dist*) *Adv* in the
evening; each evening.

¹**huduni, huhuduk; hu** *V* descend;
(of the sun) to set or sink; (of
pressure, as in a tire) to go down.
²**huduni/~g** *N* sunset; west; evening;
night; ~**him** *V;* ~**ko** *Adv;*
~**ko|dag** *s-Vs* be slanting
downward; ~ **tahgio/~tgio** *Adv*
west; westward; ~**th** *Vr* continue
an activity until sundown.
hudunig See ²HUDUNI.
hudunk *Adv* tonight; in the evening;
N evening.
huduntgio See ²HUDUNI.
hudwua *V* become frightened or
upset; ~**kch** *Vs* be afraid or upset.
hug, huh, huhuge; hu *V* end; am
~**ith** *V* complete a ritual number
of repetitions (see App. 3); **eda**
~**kam** *N** half; ~**kam** *Conj* until;
as far as.
hug__ *CE* eat: ~**chuth** *Vdt* cause to
eat (usually white clay) (see App. 3);
~**i** *N* food.
hugiog; hu *Vt* destroy; spend; use
(up); ~**a** *N* destruction; use;
~**a|him** *Vt*.
hugith__; hu *CE* edge; side: ~**a|g** *N*
an edge; a side; ~**d-an** *Prep* by,
beside.
huh, hu *CE indicates remoteness or
nonfactualness:* **heb** ~ *N*
someplace unknown to the speaker;
ia ~ *Adv* way over here; ~ **wo**
Adv hopefully, it is hoped (that),
one hopes (that).
huhch See HUCH.
huhk; hu *s-Adj,s-Vs* (be) warm; ~**a**
Vp; ~**a|him** *V;* ~**a|jith** *Vt* make
warm, warm (up); ~**a|lith** *Vt* warm
(a person or animal); ~**chu** *N*.
Huhlio Mashath *N* July. [<Sp*julio*]
huhl matagiwua† *Vr* tumble.
huhm; huhume; huhum *V* become
empty of liquid.
huhni *N* corn; an ear of corn;
~**-wa'ug** *N* a variety of prickly pear
cactus (*Opuntia*).
huhpan, huppan, huppad, huhpsh
Vt remove, pull out (as a thorn);
uproot.
huhud *Vt* lubricate, oil; anoint;
grease; ~**a** *N* lubrication; an
anointing; the act of lubricating;
something lubricated; ~**a|kud** *N*
oil; grease, lubricant; linament.
huhuda-wuhpkam† *N* the black-eyed
pea (*Leguminosae*) (lit. side-eyed
ones).

huhug, ~**e** *Vp* perish; die; disappear; ~**a|m** *N* (*pl*) those who are gone or have died; ~**e|tham** *N** temporary or temporal entity; ~**him** *V;* **pi ha** ~**e|tham** *N** a permanent or eternal entity.

huhu⎵ *CE* menstruation: ~**ga** *N* menstruation of humans or dogs; ~**ga kih** *N* a menstrual house, ~**ga|t** *V* menstruate; ~**math** *Vt* (of a menstruating woman) to touch with implied resulting danger. See App. 3.

huihlsa *N* force; law; ~**math** *Vtinf* force; *Vcmpl* demand. [<Sp *fuerza* force]

Huiwis *N* Thursday. [<Sp *jueves*]

hujed *Adv* from over there; from a remote place.

hujud; hu'u *N* a black lizard (unidentified).

huk *N* lumber; pine (any member of the pine family, *Pinaceae*).

huk⎵; hu *CE* a hook: ~**itsh** *Vt* slash; claw; ~**shad|kam** *N* something that hooks; a species of thorny bush (unidentified); ~**shan/**~**shom** *Vt* scratch; rake; ~**shan|a** *N* the act of scratching; ~**shan|a|kud** *N* an implement for scratching; a rake; a scratch; ~**sh|ch** *Vts;* ~**sh|ch|i|m** *Nr** something hooked together; ~**sh|ch|i|m** **wainomi** *N* a chain; ~**sh|ch|i|m** **wainomidath** *Vt* chain; ~**shp*** *Vt* hook; pinch; ~**shp|a** *N;* ~**shp|a|kud** *N* a hook, a clasp.

Hulio† *N* a Jew. [<Sp *judio*]

hulkath, hulkai *V* bud.

humukt; hu *Adj,N* (a) nine; (a) ninth.

⎵**hun** *suffix added to nouns and gerunds to form transitive or reflexive verbs* apply: BITHHUN, HO'IGE'ITHAHUN.

huni⎵ *CE* corn: ~**ga; hu**~**ga** *N* a bunion, a corn; ~**med*** *V* go grocery shopping (lit. go to get corn).

hupalwini *Vt* curl.

Husi *N* Joseph. [<Sp *José*]

hu'u; hu *N* a star.

hu'udagi; hu *N* a bumblebee.

hu'uith, huhu'ith, huhu'ith *Vt* chase; round up; ~**a** *N* a roundup.

hu'ul/hu'uli (*infm*); **huhhu'ul** *N* one's maternal grandmother; one's great-aunt on this side; ~**i|m** *N;* ~**-keli;** ~**kekel** *N* one's great-uncle on this side; ~**keli|m;**

~**-kekeli|m** *N;* ~**-oks;** ~**-o'oki** *N* one's great-aunt on this side; ~**-oksi|m;** ~**-o'oki|m** *N*. See App. 4.

hu'ul-nahgi; hu~ *N* a moth (lit. grandmother's skirt).

huwith *s-Vs* be thrifty.

I

i *indicates a specific point in an action, or a specific thing, place, time, number, direction, etc.:* **am** ~ *Adv* right then, at that time; ~ **ha'asa** *V* stop, cease, quit; ~ **hih** *V* start to go; **ia** ~ *Adv* right now, at this time; ~ **wah** *V* enter.

¹⎵**i,** ⎵**'i** *suffix added to verbs* **1.** *to show non-continuous action:* BEI, THAHIWUA; **2.** *to form combining elements:* THAHL⎵.

²⎵**i,** ⎵**'i** *suffix added to adjectives to form adverbs* more: BA'ICH I.

³⎵**i** See ³⎵A, ¹⎵S.

⁴⎵**i** See ⁴⎵A.

⁵⎵**i** *suffix used in the formation of certain plural nouns:* O'OKI (for which see OKS).

ia *Vp* gather cactus fruit; ~**med*** *V*.

iag⎵; i'ag⎵ *CE* sacrifice: ~**chulith** *Vt* make (a propitiatory sacrifice); ~**chulith|a** *N* the act of sacrificing; a sacrifice; ~**chulith|a|kud** *N* an altar; ~**t|a** *N* propitiatory giving, a propitiating gift; a ceremonial article for the harvest ceremony. See App. 3.

i'ajed *Adv* from here; from now on.

iajith; i'ajith *Vt* surround; swarm over.

ialhim *V* walk with a limp.

iapta; i'apta *N* a hammock.

iatto⎵; i'atto *CE* deceit: **chu** ~**mk** *s-Vs;* ~**gig** *N* a lie; deceit; ~**gith** *Vt* lie to; deceive; ~**gith|a** *N;* ~**mk** *s-V;* ~**m|kam** *N** a liar.

iawu/~**a; i'awu/**~**a** *Vt* pour; spill; dump; (of fruit) to develop after the flowering stage; ~**a** *N;* ~**a|kud** *N* a container to pour from; ~**i** *N;* ~**i|kud** *N* a container to pour into; ~**i|s** *Vs*.

ibhonis *Vs* be breathless.

igwua; 'i *V* (of particles, leaves, feathers, hair, etc.) to fall off or out.

ih *Intj* an exclamation of surprise or disbelief: Oh!

__ih (__i after *j*, *l*, *s*) *suffix added to nouns of relationship to show informal address as in a child's speech:* BABIH (for which see BAHB), WOJI (for which see WOSK), HU'ULI (for which see HU'UL).

ihab *Adv* at this point, here.

ihamhu*n* *Vt* hinder; delay; ~**a** *N* hindrance; delay.

ihbam, ~**k,** ~**muk; ihbk,** ~**k,** ~**ko'o** *V* get out of breath.

ihbhai *N* the prickly-pear cactus or its fruit, Indian fig (*Opuntia*); nopal; ~**magi** *s-Vs*.

ihbhei; *'i* *N* (a) breath; **si i** ~**wua*** *V* sigh; ~**wua*** *V* take a breath.

ihbhe*ni*, *'i* *V* breathe.

ihbthag; *'i* *N* the heart; the inner life; a fruit bud.

ih*'e*, **i'i__, ih'i** *Vt* drink; (of a plant) to absorb (moisture); (of a machine) to use (gasoline, oil, etc.); ~**chuth** *Vt* water (stock); give a drink to; ~**him** *Vt;* ~**thag** *N* a drink; *s-Vs* be habituated to strong drink; ~**to,** ~**ttod** *Vtp* drink (up); ~**toi** *N* that which is all drunk up.

ihg, *'i* *V* (of something small, as the seeds of a plant) to fall; ~**ith** *Vt* shake (as seeds or water) from a plant.

ih'in *V* prepare for danger.

ihkowi *N* a yam or a sweet potato; the hog potato or manroot (*Ipomoea pandurata*).

ihm *Vt* greet or call by a kinship term.

ihma/~'a, im *Adv* here facing away.

ihma'a See IHMA.

ihmigi *N,habN* a kin relationship; *hasN* an in-law.

ihmki *N* soot.

ihna/~'a, in *Adv* here facing across.

ihna'a See IHNA.

ihnagi/nahgi *N* a skirt of ancient style.

ihnam, ~**k,** ~**muk; ihnk,** ~**k,** ~**ko'o** *Vp* develop a craving (especially for meat); ~**chu***th* *Vt;* ~**kam;** ~**koi** *N;* ~**thag** *N* such a craving.

ihs*ith*, *'i* *Vtb* give (particles, as seeds) to in a container.

ihswigi; *'i* (*dist*) *N* any species of hedgehog cactus (*Echinocereanae*).

iht, i'ita; *'i* *Vt* scoop (up) (as dirt or seeds); ~**a** *N;* ~**a|chug** *Vt* carry (gathered particles); ~**a|kud** *N* a scoop (implement).

ihtha/~'a, ith *Pron* this, this one; he; she; it.

ihtha'a See IHTHA.

ihtham/itham *Pron* these; they or them (nearby).

ihug *N* the devil's claw plant (*Proboscidea parviflora* and other varieties); a pod of this plant.

ihwagi *N* an edible green for humans; ~**m** *s-Adj,s-Vs* (be) green.

ihwith *V* make fire with a fire stick.

ihya/~'a *Adv* here; here facing this way.

ihya'a See IHYA.

i'ibhunig *N* a sprout of a plant.

i'ibtog *V* breathe convulsively.

i'ihog *V* cough; ~**ig** *N* tuberculosis.

i'im, ~**k,** ~**muk; i'ik,** ~**k,** ~**ko'o** *s-V* want to drink; ~**kam;** ~**koi** *s-N* an excessive drinker; a wino.

i'ipudttham *N* a dressmaker.

i'iwegih *Vp* (of a plant) to sprout.

i'iwonig *N* a twig.

ikus; *'i* *N* cloth; a cloth or rag; ~**t** *Vt* weave (cotton).

im See IHMA.

__imk (__am*k* after *t, th, m*) *suffix added to non-stative verbs to form non-stative verbs of the same transitivity* want to (do): s-HIMIMK.

in See IHNA.

iolagi*th*; **i'olagi***th* *Vt* stir, mix.

ioligam *N* the manzanita shrub (*Arctostaphylos*).

Ioligam *N* Kitt Peak mountain in south-central Arizona.

iolith; i'olith *Vt* fry.

i'oma† *s-Vs* be healthy.

i'omko† *s-Adv* on or at the right.

i'oshan *Vr* clear the throat.

i'owi *s-Adj, s-Vs* (be) sweet or tasty; ~**h** *Vp;* ~**h|him** *V;* ~**jith** *s-Vt* sweeten; ~**m** *s-Adv* sweetly.

ip/op *Conj,* until after.

ipud; *'i* *N* a dress or shirt.

iskli; *'i/i* **cheshajkud;** *ch* *N* a ladder. [<Sp *escala*]

is-kohbli *N* a chisel. [<Sp *escoplo*]

I-spahnia *N* Spain. [<Sp *españa*]

is-pahyo; *'i* —*pa* *N* a sword or spear. [<Sp *espada*]

is-paula; *'i* (*dist*) *N* baking powder.

ispul; *'i* *N* a spur on a horseman's heel or on a male fowl. [<Sp *espuela*]

istliw; *'i* *N* a stirrup. [<Sp *estribo*]

is-tuhhua *N* a stove. [<Sp *estufa*]

I-tahlia *N* Italy. [<Sp *italia*]

ith See IHTHA.

'__ith *suffix added to intransitive verbs to form stative verbs* be able to: MELITH.

²_ith See _GITH, _JELITH.
itham See IHTHAM.
ithani *Adv* now, at this season.

J

¹_j *suffix added to adjectives to form stative verbs* be (in a specified condition): GE'EJ.
²_j (_d *before any preposition which begins with* a *or* e) *suffix added* **1.** *to nouns to show that there is a possessor which was not previously expressed:* **kihj g Huan** (but **Huan kih**)=*John's house;* **am kihd-ed g Huan** (but **am Huan kih ed**)=*in John's house;* **2.** *to certain prepositions to show that there is an object which was not previously expressed:* **am wehmaj g Huan** (but **am Huan wehm**)=*with John.*
_jed See AMJED.
je'e; jehj *N* one's mother; (*pl*) parents; (*pl*) a plant that bears a (specified) fruit.
je'es/je'esi (*infm*); **jehjes** *N* an uncle senior to one's mother; **~i|m** *N* one who has such an uncle; **~-oks;** **~-o'oki** *N* an aunt by marriage to such an uncle; **~-oksi|m; ~-o'oki|m** *N.* See App. 4.
jeg; hje *N* outside; a clearing; an opening; *Vs* be open; **~a** *Vp* (of as a door) to open; **~a|him** *V* (of as a door) to open; **~ko** *Adv* in the open.
_jeg *suffix added to nouns to form nouns* an opening or passage: HO'IBADJEG, KIHJEG. [<jeg]
jegda; jeh~ *N* a clearing; a racetrack.
jegel*ith*; *je* *Vt* make room for.
jegos; *j* *N* a storm.
jegwoni *N* the act of oozing out; **~,** **jegwosh;** *je* *V* ooze out.
jehg *N* mesquite-pod flour.
jehjegt *s-Vt* knit. [<jeg]
jehjena *N* the act of smoking (as a cigarette).
jeh*k*, **~i, jejka** *Vt* taste.
jehka'ich; *je* *Vr* suffer the consequences, get one's due; be struck with calamity; *Vt* bring calamity to; play a prank on.
jehkch *Vt* look for the tracks of.
jehkig *N* the sense of taste; flavor.
jehni, jehj*en*, **~i, jejjen** *V* smoke

tobacco; **~g***ith* *Vt* address or speak to (lit. cause to smoke); *Vr* confer; **~gith|a** *N* a meeting; a discussion; **~gith|a|kud** *N* a meeting place; **~gith|tham** *N* a speaker; *Nr* a councilman; one who confers; **~k|tham** *s-N* one who smokes, a smoker; **~kud** *N* a meeting house; a smoking-room; **~mk/~k** *s-Vs* like to smoke.
jejewk *s-Vs* be spotted or striped.
jejewuakhi*m* *V* trot.
jeki_ *CE* track: **~amed; ~op*** *Vt* go tracking.
_jel*ith* (_jith when the passive is formed by ²_jith; _ith after g, n, p, and 'ok; _chuth after _chutha, and replacing ¹_t and ²_t) *suffix added to transitive and ditransitive verbs to indicate that there is a beneficiary* do for or on behalf of: MAHKJELITH, ME'AJITH, KU'AGITH, HOANITH, KUHPITH, KUHPI'OKITH, APCHUTHACHUTH, KIHCHUTH. [<kihtchuth]
jew *s-Vs* be rotten, spoiled, or decayed; be leavened; **~a** *Vp* rot; spoil; decay; become leavened; **~a|him** *V;* **~a|j***ith* *Vt* rot, spoil, decay; **~a|jith|a** *N;* **~a|jith|a|s** *Vs;* **~a|jith|a|kud** *N* yeast, leaven; **~a|lig** *N* something rotten, spoiled, or leavened; **~am uhw** *s-Vs* be rotten smelling, etc.; **~o** *Vp* cease giving off odor.
jewakag; jejewhakag *N* the king snake (*Lampropeltis getulus*).
jewed; *je* *N* soil, earth; real property; estate; a country; the earth or world; **~gim** *s-Adj,s-Vs* (be) earth-colored; **~-heosig** *N* (*pl*) earth-flowers (reputed to be an aphrodisiac); **~-ho'ithag** *Vt* the puncture-vine plant (*Tribulus terrestris*) (lit. ground thorn); **~ kahchim** *N* the earth; **~o** *Adv* on the ground; **~pig** *Vt* remove earth from (something); **~ u'ujig** *N* an earthquake.
jewho; *je* *N* a gopher.
jiawul; *ji* *N* a devil or demon; the barrel cactus (*Echinocactus cavillei, Ferocactus acanthodes*, and *wislizenii*); **~kih** *N* hell (lit. the devil's house); **~ wuhi** *N* a television (lit. the devil's eye). [<Sp *diablo* devil]
Jiawul *N* Satan, the devil. [<above]
jiia See JIWIA.

jiosh; *ji* *N* a god; ~**chuth** *Vt* deify;
~**chutha** *N* deification; ~**thag** *N*
the quality or character of being
divine, divinity. [<Sp *dios* god]
Jiosh *N* God. [<above]
jisk; jijsi *N* an aunt junior to one's
mother; ~**am;** ~**m** *N;* ~**keli;**
~**kekel** *N* an uncle by marriage to
such an aunt; ~**-kelim;** ~**kekelim**
N. See App. 4.
¹__**jith** (__**th** imperfective, __**i**
perfective; __**chuth** replacing final
¹__*t* and ²__*t*) *suffix added to verbs
to form causative verbs* cause (to
reach a specified state):
SHOPOLKATH.
²__ **jith** *suffix added to certain
transitive verbs to form passive
reflexive verbs* undergo, experience:
KE'IJITH.
³__**jith** See __JELITH.
jiwa See JIWIA.
jiwhia__ *CE* arrive: ~**s** *Vts* be
extended to; ~**thag** *N* an arrival.
**jiwia/jiia/jiwa, jijiwhia; thatha,
thaiwe** *Vp* arrive.
__**jj** *suffix added to adjectives of
quantity* (*except* one) *to indicate all
or part of a particular group:*
ha'akiajj hegam a'al=*a number of
those children* (but **ha'akia a'al**=*a
number of children*); **waikajj hegam
haiwani**=*three of those cows;*
he'esijj hegai pilkani?=*how much
of that wheat?;* **wehsijj**=*all of it.*
judumi; *ju* *N* a bear; a tractor;
gew-ch-ed ~ *N* a polar bear;
~ **mad** *N* a bear cub.
judwua; *ju* *V* bounce; land on one's
feet; ~**him** *V* jump along.
¹**juh** See WUA.
²**juh, jujju** *Vp* (of the sun) to reach a
(specified) position, usu. to designate
time of day; ~**k, jujju** *N,Adv* (at)
the time indicated.
juhagi; *j* *s-Vs* be resilient; be bouncy.
¹**juhk,** ~**i, jujku** *V* rain; ~**i** *N* rain;
~**i|g** *s-Vs.*
²**juhk;** *ju* *s-Adj,s-Vs* (be) deep (in
measure or complexity); ~**a** *Vp*
become deep, deepen; ~**a|him** *V;*
~**a|lig** *N* depth; ~**a|m** *s-Adv*
deeply (in measure or complexity);
~**chu** *N;* ~**o** *Adv* in a deep place.
juhkam See WUA.
Juhkam; *j* *N** a Mexican; **s-wadag** ~
N a Mexican laborer who enters the
U.S. illegally, a wetback (lit. a wet
Mexican).

juhkch; *j* *habVts* have on or wear.
juhni See WUA.
¹**juhpin/wi'inim** *N* the north; ~
tahgio *Adv* north, northward.
²**juhpin** *V* soak in, sink.
jujju See WUA, JUHK.
jujk__ *CE* rain: ~**ith** *Vt;* ~**u** *s-Vs*
be rainy.
jujul; *hu'u* *s-Adj* zigzag, crooked;
~**chu** *s-N;* ~**i|m** *s-Adv*
crookedly, zigzaggedly; ~**i|wua|him**
V run jerkily; ~**k** *s-Vs.*
juk__ *CE* rain: ~**i|to; jujkitog** *V;*
~**shp*** *Vt* rain on.
jukiabig; *j* *N* a rainy season.
Jukiabig Mashath *N* July (lit. rainy
season month).
julashan/nulash† *N* a peach. [<Sp
durazno]
jumadk; *'uju* *Vs* be humpbacked.
jumal; *'uju* *Adv* in a low position,
rank, or place; ~**k** *Vs;* ~**k|a|th***
Vt lower; ~**k|chu** *N* something
or someone low in position; an
underling.
jun See WUA.
¹**juni;** *ju* *N* (a) dried saguaro cactus
fruit.
²**juni** *habN* (an) activity.
³**juni** *habN* any given kin relationship;
hasN used in direct and indirect
questions: **K has d m-juni?**=*What
relationship is he to you?*
jupij; *'uj* *s-Adv* quietly; ~ **him** *s-V*
sneak; ~ **ne'e** *s-V* (of a person) to
hum or sing quietly; ~ **neok** *s-V*
whisper.
jushadk; *'uj* *Vs* be loose (not tight);
~**a** *Vp;* ~**ahim** *V;* ~**ath*** *Vt*
loosen.
jushal; *'uj* *Adv* quietly.
jusukal; *j* *N* a large black lizard
(unidentified).

K

k See KU__.
-k- (after certain nouns considered
negative, **-t-** before *a*, **-ch-** before *e*)
*a connector between nouns and
prepositions where ownership is not
stated:* **kih-t-ab**=*at a house* (but
ni-kih-ab=*at my house*);
kahon-ch-ed=*in a box* (but
ni-kahon-ed=*in my box*).
¹__**k** *suffix added to non-stative verbs
to form non-stative verbs of action,
viewed as completed or to be*

completed. ▶ Verbs thus formed are used: **1.** *in adverb clauses* when, when about to: **Ha at nei am himk**=*He saw them when he left;* **Ha at nei am-o himk**=*He saw them when he was about to leave;* **2.** *in forming the suffix* ²_*kam.*

²_**k** *suffix added to the head or main word of stative clauses (stative verbs, nouns, pronouns, prepositions, and adverbs of place) to support the non-present tense suffixes* _*ahim* and _*th:* **Am o kihkahim**=*He was living there;* **Am at-o kihkath**=*He will be living there;* **Do ni ahmokahim**=*He was my boss;* **Dat-o hegaikath**=*He will be the one;* **Ith at-o t-thahmkath**=*He will be over us;* **No am amaikahim?**=*Was he there?*

▶_**th** may drop after ²_*k,* and must be deleted before ¹_*m:* **Am at-o kihk**=*He will be living there;* **kihkam**=*an inhabitant or dweller.*

³_**k** *suffix added to adjectives to form stative verbs* be (in a specified condition): GAWULK.

⁴_**k** *suffix added to nouns to form stative verbs and adjectives* (be): S-ONK.

_**ka** See _GA.

ka'a_; kahk_ *CE* one's paternal grandmother or great-aunt: ~**bad** *N* the same deceased; ~**mad** *N* the relationship of a woman's son's child to her and her peers; a grandchild, grandnephew, grandniece, etc.; ~**ma-je'e;** ~**mad-ha-je'e;** ~**mad-ha-jehj** *N* a woman's daughter-in-law or mother-in-law, etc.; ~**ma-jehjim;** ~**mad-ha-jehjim** *Nr (pl);* ~**md|a|m** *N* one who has such a grandchild, etc.; *Nr (pl).* See App. 4.

¹**ka'al** *N* the gall bladder; ~ **shuhthagi** *N* gall (lit. only).

²**ka'al** *N* the white-oak tree.

kah *Vt,Vcmpl* hear; understand.

kahba; k *N* a cloak or cape. [<Sp *capa*]

kahch; wehch; we'ewech *Vs* lie lifeless, exist over an area: **Bihugig o eda am kahch eda**=*At that time there was famine over the area;* ~**i|m** *N* something that lies or exists in a particular place, as the earth or the heavens; *Adj* lying lifeless; non-contagious.

kahchk *N* a lake; a sea; **ge** ~ *N* an ocean.

kahio; k *N* a leg; ~**gith** *V* shake one's leg.

kahiobin, k, kk *Vt* cross (as a road; or one thing with another, as the legs); ~**s** *Vs* be crossed; be intersected.

¹**kahk** *habVs* (of something, as chili) to have a (specified) taste; **pi has** ~, **pi ab hu ha** ~ *Vs* be tasteless (lit. only).

²**kahk/gagih** (*infm*); ~**a'ak** *N* one's paternal grandmother; one's great-aunt on this side; ~**-keli:** ~**-kekel** *N* one's great-uncle, etc., on this side; ~**-keli|m,** ~**-kekeli|m** *N;* ~**-oks;** ~**-o'oki** *N* one's great-aunt etc., on this side; ~**-oksi|m;** ~**-o'oki|m** *N.* See App. 4.

kahkag *V* (of a raven or crow) to caw or crow.

kahkam *s-Vs* have big cheeks.

kahlisa; ka *N* a jail. [<Sp *cárcel*]

kahm; hka *N* a cheek of the face.

kahma; ka *N* a quilt. [<Sp *cama* a bed; a bedstead]

kahmbo; ka *N* a camp. [<Sp *campo*]

kahnia/kahnu; ka *N* cane; sorghum; ~**g** *s-Vs.* [<Sp *caña*]

kahnu See KAHNIA.

kahon; k *N* a box; a fort. [<Sp *cajón* box]

ka-hui *N* coffee; coffee beans. [<Sp *café*]

kahui-thihla; k —thi *N* a coffee pot. [<Sp *cafetera*]

kahw; ka *N* a badger.

kahwal/kahwul; ka *N* a sheep; ~ **chuhkug** *N* mutton; ~ **mad** *N* a lamb; ~ **wopo** *N* wool. [<Sp *cabra* goat]

kahwul See KAHWAL.

kahya; ka *N* a street. [<Sp *calle*]

kai; ka *N* a seed or pit; semen; ~**ch|ka** *N* seed or grain set aside for planting; ~**ch|ka|t** *Vt* save (seed) for planting; ~**j** *N* the seed of (saguaro unless specified); ~**pig** *Vt* harvest (grain); scrape (corn) from the cob.

¹**kai_; kakai_** *CE* hear: ~**chug** *Vt* listen to habitually; ~**chuth** *Vt;* ~**chuth|ch,** ~**chuth|k** *Adv* within earshot; ~**mk** *Vt;* ~**m|kam** *s-N** an inquisitive person.

²**kai_** *CE* sound: ~**jelith** *Vtb, Vbcmpl* say for (someone's) benefit; ~**jelith|amk** *Vbinf;* ~**lig** *N* news

or word about; ~**lith** *Vt* cause to make a sound; *Vr* announce oneself; make oneself heard; ~**thag** *N* a sound; *V* make a sound; *Vt* spread (a rumor); *Vr* announce oneself with a sound; ~**thag|him** *V;* ~**thag|im** *Adv* noisily; ~**thag** **o'ohana** *N* a letter of the alphabet.

_ka'i/_kai *suffix added to non-stative verbs to form non-stative verbs* (do) and go: BEKA'I.

kaiham; kakaim *Vt* listen to; heed; obey; ~**a** *N* a hearing; **chu-~** *s-Adv* interestedly; **chu** ~**a** *s-Vs* be of an interested nature; **chu** ~**a|kam** *s-N** one who has an interested nature; **ta** ~ *s-Adv* interestingly; **ta** ~**a** *s-Vs* be interesting to hear; **ta** ~**a|kam** *s-N** someone or something interesting to hear.

¹kaij *Intj* an expression of contempt: **Kaij, ahpim am sha'i pi ha'ichu amichuth**=*Contemptible, you understand absolutely nothing (PNT* John 12:49).

²kaij, chei/che'e__, kakithaj/chech'e, cheh'i *habVt, Vinf, habVcmpl* say.

kaikia shuhshk *N* a sandal.

kaimagi *s-Adj,s-Vs* (be) pepper-colored or spotted; ~**chu** *s-N*.

kais; ka *s-Adj,s-N* (the) rich, (the) wealthy; ~**chuth** *Vt;* ~**chuth|a** *N* the acquisition of wealth; acquired wealth, riches; ~**i|m** *s-Adv* richly; ~**t|a|lig** *N* wealth, material possessions.

kaishagi; ka ~ *N* the crotch (of a person).

kaishch *Vts* have or hold between the legs; ~ **g kawiyu** *V* ride bareback.

¹_kaj *suffix added to nouns to form adverbs* in a similar or like manner: BANKAJ.

²_kaj See HEKAJ.

kakaichu *N* a quail; particularly, the Gambel's quail (*Callipepla gambelii*).

kakaist *N* a cactus rib cage.

kaka-wuathi *N* a peanut. [<Sp *cacahuate*]

kakke *Vtcmpl* ask (for information): **Ab ani kakke mat hebaijed i hih**=*I asked him where he came from;* ~**i** *N* a question.

kak-luhji *N* a cockroach. [<Sp *cucaracha*]

kakpsith *Vt* give a physical examination to; ~**a** *N* a physical examination.

kaksipul *N* the bells on a clown-dancer's costume.

ka-lihna; k—li *N* a chain. [<Sp *cadena*]

kalioni; ka *N* a stallion. [<Sp *garañón*]

kalistp *N* a species of paloverde (unidentified).

kalit; k *N* a wagon. [<Sp *carreta*]

kalshani; ka *N* underpants. [<Sp *calzones<calzón*]

kal-sihtho; ka—si *N* a sock; a stocking; an innertube. [<Sp *calcetín* a sock]

kal-tuhji; ka—tu *N* a cartridge; a bullet. [<Sp *cartucho*]

¹_kam *suffix* (formed from ¹_*k* and ¹_*m*) *added to verbs to form nouns:* one who has done or will do a (specified) action: BEIKAM.

²_kam *suffix* (formed from ²_*k* and ¹_*m*) *added to stative verbs, nouns, and prepositions to form nouns* one (who is characterized by that which is specified): GEWKTHAGKAM.

³_kam; _koi *suffix added to verbs of* want *to form nouns* one who suffers a lack of: TONOMKAM.

kam__; kakam__ *CE* a cheek: ~**po** *N* a sideburn; ~**sh|ch** *Vts* have in one's mouth; ~**shp*** *Vt* put in one's mouth.

ka-mihyo *N* a camel. [<Sp *camello*]

kamish; k† *N* a shirt; an undershirt; a T-shirt. [<Sp *camisa* a shirt]

kammialt/kambialt; ka (*dist*) *Vt* change (as a shirt); exchange or trade; ~**a** *N* an exchange or trade; the act of exchanging; ~**a|kud** *N* a device for changing gears, phases, etc.; a gearshift. [<Sp *cambiar* to change]

ka-mohthi *N* a yam or sweet potato. [<Sp *camote*]

kam'on, ka *Vt* debate with; argue with.

kampani; ka *N* a bell; the uvula; a bell housing. [<Sp *campanilla* a small bell]

kanaho; ka *N* a boat; **ge'e** ~ *N* a ship. [<Sp *canoa* a canoe]

ka-nahsti; k—na *N* a loose-woven basket. [<Sp *canasta*]

kanjel/kanjul; ka *N* a candle; a lamp; an electric light. [<Sp *candela* a candle]

ka-nohwa *N* a trough; a canoe. [<Sp *canoa* a canoe]

kan-tihna *N* a saloon or bar; a night

club; a refreshment stand. [<Sp *cantina*]

kapad; '*ak* *Vs* lie flat; be flopped down; ~**thag** *s-N* flatness; ~**wua*** *Vp* flop down; dance a leaping dance.

kapani*th*, *k* *Vt* strike together loudly.

kape, *k* *V* make a clapping sound.

kapijk; '*ak* *Adj,Vs* (be) narrow; (as of the waist of a garment) (to be) gathered in.

kapsi*th*; *ka* *V* make a clapping noise.

kashadkath, kashadkai; '*ak* *Vr* spread the legs.

kaska-lohn *N* the sand verbena (*Abronia villosa*). [<AmSp *cascarón* filled with confetti]

kastigal *Vt* punish. [<Sp *castigar*]

Ka-tohliga *N*** a Catholic. [<Sp *católico*]

kawad; *ka* *N* a war shield.

kawadk; *ka* *Vs* be flat.

kawhai*n*, **kawhaish;** *ka* *Vt* quarrel or argue with; make a crunching noise.

kawijk; '*ak* *Vs* be in a narrow course or line.

kawiyu; *k*, *kka* *N* a horse; ~ **mad** *N* a foal; a colt; a filly. [<Sp *caballo*]

kawk; kawpk *s-Adj,s-Vs* (be) hard or solid; (be) difficult (to do); (be) strict; (be) callous; ~**a** *Vp;* ~**a|him** *V;* ~**a|th*** *Vt;* ~**chu** *s-N.*

kawnim; *ka* *s-Adv* crunchily.

kawud; '*ak* *s-Adv* closely; short (measure): **S-kawud g wulshpi**=*Tie him up short* (as a horse on a short rope); ~**k** *Vs;* ~**ka** *Vt* gather; *N* an association, an organized group.

ka-wuiya *N* one who runs about naked.

kawulk; '*ak* *N* a hill.

kch (**ch** after any consonant); **k** (to agree with completive verbs) *Conj* and. ▶Also connects various types of clauses: if...then; It is (a person) who, or (thing) that: **Do Jiosh ch ab ni-mahkch g gewkthag**=*It's God who gives me strength;* also suffixed to verbs to form adverb clauses: when; while; about to; following.

___**kch** (___**ch** after any consonant) *suffix added to non-stative verbs to form stative verbs with the same transitivity* have or (reflexive) be (in a specified state or condition): NAHTOKCH, WAKONCH.

kedkoli*th*; *ke* *Vt* tickle (lit. only).

kedwua *V* ejaculate semen; ~**thag** *N* semen.

ke'e, kei, *k,* **keh'i** *Vt* bite.

kegch*uth*; *he* *Vt* beautify; repair; improve; cleanse; clean.

keh'el See KEH'ITH.

keh'elith See KEH'ITH.

kehg; *he* *s-Adj* good, nice; beautiful, pretty; *s-Adv* completely; ~**a** *Vp;* ~**ahi***m* *V;* ~**aj** *s-Vs;* ~**chu** *s-N.*

Kehg S-hehpijig Mashath‡ *N* November (lit. pleasant cold month).

keh'i See KE'E.

kehi___ (**kei___** before voiceless consonants); **kekei** *CE* an action with the feet: ~**ch***k* *Vt* kick; ~**chk|wua*** *Vt;* ~**hi***n* *V* kick; perform a traditional dance; ~**hin|a** *N* (a) traditional dance; ~**hin|a|kud** *N* a traditional dance ground; ~**hin|tham** *N* a dancer of traditional dance; ~**homi***n* *Vt* weaken an adversary by singing and dancing (see App. 3); **i** ~**kon*** *Vt* incite; encourage; ~**juni** *Vt* eliminate someone's (illness); ~**kkan*** *Vt* kick with repeated blows; ~**kon*** *V* trip, stumble; ~**sh|ch** *Vts* have under foot; ~**shp*** *Vt* step on; pace the measurement of; ~**shp|a** *N* a pace; a yard (measure); a mile†; ~**shun*** *Vt* crush under foot; ~**wi***n* *Vt* thresh (grain).

keh'ith, keh'eli*th*, **keke'eli***th* *s-Vt* hate; scold; rebuke.

¹**kehk; chuhch; chu'uchuch** *Vs* (of something) to be standing; ~**a|m;** ~**i|m** *N.*

²**kehk; gegok** *Vs* (of a person or animal) to be standing; **ab wui** ~ *Vts* be standing facing; be opposing; ~**hi***m* *V* take a step or steps, move along; **sipud** ~; '*is* ~ *Vs* be stooped; **wabsh** ~ *Vs* be anxious.

kehkud *N* the place in which or where one stands; a role, position, or office; one's office room; a place for placing or standing (something); ~ **ed** *Prep* in place of, instead of.

kehsh, kei, keksha; chuhcha *Vt* erect; stand up or make erect; appoint or elect (to be); ~**a;** ~**i** *N* something erected; an appointee; an electee; an apostle; ~**a|him;** ~**him** *Vt;* ~**a|kud;** ~**kud** *N* a stand, a holder.

kei See KEHSH, KE'E.

ke'i; *ke* *N* a bite or sting; ~**jith** *Vtb;* *Vr* get bitten.

ke'ith___; *ke* *CE* hate: **chu** ~**a|m**

Adv hatefully; **chu** ~a|m|kam *N**
a hateful person; **ta** ~a|m *s-Adv*
meanly or rudely; **ta** ~a|m|a; *ke*
s-Vs be mean or rude.
keki___; gegoki___ *CE* stand: **ab wui**
~**wua** *Vtp* stand facing; come to a
stop facing; oppose; **sipud** ~**wua;**
si'ispud ~**wua** *Vp* stoop; ~**wua***
Vp stand; stop; take office; *(sing*.)
(of one person in a vehicle) to stop;
(pl) (of more than one person in a
vehicle) to stop.
¹**keli; kekel** *N** an adult male; the
male of any animal; *(pl*.) a group of
adults which includes males; *CE*
one's uncle by marriage to one's
(specified) aunt; a (specified)
great-uncle; ~ **bahsho** *N* a Casaba
melon; ~**ga** *N (infm)* one's husband
(lit. one's old man); ~-**huch;**
~-**huhch** *N* the curve-billed
thrasher (*Toxostoma curvirostre*) (lit.
old man's toenail).
²**keli; kekel** *N* an uncle senior to one's
father; ~**m;** ~**im** *N;* ~-**oks;**
~-**o'oki** *N* an aunt by marriage
to such an uncle; ~-**oks|i|m;**
~-**o'ok|i|m** *N*. See App. 4.
kelimai *N* an elder, an older person.
keli*w***; *ke* *Vt* shuck (corn).
keshkud; *ke* *N* a back scratcher (the
implement).
keshwua, keshwup; *kk* *Vt* stand;
stop.
___**ki;** ___**ki___** *CE* evidently,
obviously: **Kuki am thaha**=*He's*
evidently there: **Natki-o juh?**=*Is it*
obviously going to rain?
kia/~p *N* a while; **ho'ip** ~ *Conj* not
until; ~/~ **koi** *Intj* an expression
used to prevent or stop an activity
temporarily: Wait! Not yet!; **wabsh**
~/**hash** ~ *Adv* still, even to this
time.
___**kia** (___**k** before ___**pa**) *suffix added*
to pronoun combining elements of
quantity to form adjectives of
quantity indicating number a
number (of): **ha'akia**=*that number*
(of): **ha'akpa**=*that number of*
places; **he'ekia**=*how many.*
ki'agani; ki'ago *V imperative only*
wait.
kia koi See KIA.
¹**kih** *Vs* be dwelling or residing.
²**kih; *hki*** *N* a house; a dwelling;
where one lives, home, a residence; a
building; a wall; a container; a room;
~**chu***th* *Vtb* build for (someone);

draw a line around and for (a patient)
to contain ceremonial healing power
(see App. 3); **ikus** ~ *N* a tent; ~**jeg**
N a doorway; a passageway through
a fence or wall; ~**jeg|o** *Adv* at a
doorway; **lial** ~ *N* a purse or wallet;
~**mk** *s-V* become homesick;
~**m|thag** *s-N* homesickness; ~**t**
Vt build; ~**t|a** *N* building or
construction; the act of building;
~**t|a|him** *Vt;* ~**thag** *N* a home
and property; a neighborhood;
one's means of subsistence;
one's estate.
kiheh; ki~ *N* an in-law who is one's
spouse's peer relative; ~**m** *N*.
kihhim *N* a village; a group of
villages.
kihkam *N* an inhabitant; a dweller;
a villager; a citizen; population;
miabithch ~ *N* a neighbor;
wehm-~ *N* one's spouse; one's
family.
kihshath; *hk* *Vt* ambush; ~**a** *N* an
ambush.
kihsho; *k* *N* cheese. [<Sp *queso*]
ki'i___; kih~ *CE* an action of the
teeth: ~**hin*** *Vt* bite off; ~**kkan***
Vt chew on; ~**kon*** *Vt* gnaw
clean; ~**mu***n* *Vt* gnaw on; ~**sh|ch**
Vts; ~**sh|chug** *Vt;* ~**shp*** *Vt*
grasp in the teeth; ~**shp|a|kud** *N*
pliers; tweezers; ~**shun*** *Vt;* ~**wih**
N chewing gum; ~**win*** *Vt* chew
(up); ~**win|a** *N*.
kikkiadag *Vs* (of a house) to be
abandoned.
kiohod; kikihod *N* a rainbow.
ki'omi *Vr* get discouraged; give up.
kiot *Vt* rustle (livestock).
___**kkan,** ___**kkad,** ___**kkash** *suffix*
added to combining elements to form
transitive verbs strike vigorously (in
a specified manner): MO'OKKAN.
___**kkio** See HO.
klahwo/lahwos; *l* *N* a nail
(carpentry). [<Sp *clavo*]
Klihsto *N* Christ; ~ **mahsithag tash**
N Christmas; ~ **wohohchuththam**
N a Christian, a believer in Christ.
[<Sp *Cristo*]
___**ko,** ___**o** *suffix added to nouns to*
form adverbs of place in, on, or at a
place: s-TONIKO, JEWEDO.
koa; *k* *N* the forehead, brow; a cliff,
bank, or dropoff; ~**chk*** *Vt* lean the
forehead against; peep over;
~**chk|wua*** *V* peek; ~**dag** *N*
bangs on the forehead; ~**po** *N* hair

or bangs on the forehead; ~wua*
V put the forehead (against); bow low.
ko'a, huh/hug, huhuga, huhgi Vt
eat; ~th|ma Vt appear to eat.
koabith; k; kk Vt hem.
koadag; k N a hem.
koaw; k Vt tie together; ~gi'a N a
string of beads, shells, etc.; ~gith
Vt string (beads, etc.); ~gith|a N
beadwork.
koawul; k N any species or edible
fruit of the wolfberry (Lycium).
kodog, ko V rumble or gurgle; ~ith
Vt cause to rumble or gurgle.
kohathk N something dried and
burned.
kohba; k; kko N a drinking glass.
[<Sp copa]
kohji; k N a pig; a javelina, a peccary;
~chuhkug N pork; ~ mad N a
shoat. [<MexSp coche]
kohkod N a goose; ~ mad N a
gosling; ~-oipij/hoho'ibad N
alfileria (Erodium cicutarium)
(lit. goose's awls or needles).
kohlo'ogam; koklo'ogam N a
whippoorwill.
kohm N the hackberry tree (Celtis
reticulata).
kohmagi; ko s-Adj,s-Vs (be) gray;
(be) dim; (be) dull in thought or
understanding; ~chu s-N;
~m s-Adv dimly.
Kohmagi Mashath N February‡;
January† (lit. gray month).
kohmagi-u'us N arrowweed (Tessaria
sericia).
kohmch Vts have in the arms.
kohmhai N (a) mist, (a) fog; ~wua
V; ~wua|dag/~wua|gi Vs.
kohmk, ~i, kokme; hko Vt embrace,
hug.
kohntpul/kohtpul; ko/hk N a cicada
or locust.
kohsh, koi, koksho; hk V sleep.
kohsi___ CE sleep: ~g N sleep;
~mk s-V; ~m|thag N sleepiness;
~th Vt; ~th|a N; ~th|a|kud N
something that induces sleep, a
sleeping pill.
kohsk; ko s-Vs be sleepy-headed.
kohths N a legendary monster.
kohtpul See KOHNTPUL.
kohwih; ko† N a beaver.
kohwli N copper. [<Sp cupre]
kohwog; ko s-Vs be full from eating;
~chuth Vt.
kohwoth; ko Vp become full from
eating.

kohya N a horse collar. [<Sp collera]
¹koi Adv before; not yet.
²koi Connective Phrase that is, I
mean, in other words.
³koi See KOHSH, MUHK.
ko'i See MUHKI.
ko'ijith See ME'IJITH.
ko'ithag See MUHKITHAG.
ko'ito Vtp eat up, devour; ~hi|med*
Vt.
kokaw N the staghorn cactus or its
edible bud (Opuntia versicolor or
O. arborescens versicolor).
kok'o See MUMKU.
kokodki N a sea shell.
kokoho‡/~a† N the burrowing owl
(Speotito cunicularia).
kok'oi N a ghost; a spirit of the dead.
kok'otham ha-kih N a hospital.
koksikud N a hotel or motel; a
nightgown or pajamas.
koksim V go along falling asleep.
koktha See ME'A.
kokthai See ME'A.
kolbiwua Vt juggle.
kolhai; k; kk N a fence; a corral;
~ chuhchim N a fence post; ~dag
N the fence or wall (of an area);
Vs; ~dath Vt fence (in);
~dath|ch Vts have (something)
fenced; ~t V; ~t|a N; ~t|a|s Vs;
wainomi ~ N a barbed-wire fence.
[<Sp corral yard, corral]
kolig; ko V clatter or rattle; ~him V.
kolwahtho N a necktie. [<Sp
corbata]
kologith; ko Vt rattle; ~a N;
~a|kud N a rattle.
komad; 'ok Adv (of a plant, ants, or
of moving creatures seen from a
height) in a spread out or creeping
position; ~k Vs (of a plant, etc.) to
be in a spread out position; ~ka|th*
Vt flatten; ~wua* Vt cause to be
low or flat.
¹komal; k N one's child's godmother;
one's godchild's mother; ~i|m N;
Nr (pl). [<Sp comadre]. See
App. 4.
²komal; k N a griddle. [<AmSp
comal]
³komal; 'ok Adj flat, level; thin or
shallow (lit. only); (of clouds, etc.)
thin or fleecy; ~i|m Adv flatly, in
a flat manner; thinly; shallowly;
~k Vs; ~k|a V; ~k|a|him V;
~k|a|th* Vt; ~k|chu N.
komalk-mo'okam N the Gila
woodpecker.

komba-nihya *N* a business company.
[<Sp *compañia*]
kom-bihsh *Vt* confess. [<Sp *confeso*
I confess]
komchkahi*m Vt* go along carrying in
the arms.
komi; h*ko; h**kko N* the lower back; a
shell covering the back of a turtle,
bug, etc.; ~**kam** *N* someone or
something with a back or shell
covering; a beetle.
komi__/kom__; ko~ *CE* the back; a
shell covering; a scab: ~**shad** *V*
stretch one's back; take a nap;
~**sh|ch** *Vts;* ~**shp*** *Vt* load on
one's back; ~**shp|a|dath** *Vdt;* ~**tp**
Vt crack the shell of. ▶Occurring
with *kom__:* ~**kch'ed** *N* a turtle;
~**pig** *Vt.*
kommo'ol *N* a millipede.
kompal; ko *N* one's child's godfather;
one's god-child's father; ~**i|m** *N;*
Nr (pl). [<Sp *compadre*]. See
App. 4.
__kon, __kosh *suffix added to*
combining elements to form transitive
and reflexive verbs indicating that an
action occurs in a specified manner
along a surface: **ma'ikon**=*glance*
off; **thapkon**=*slip;* **chelkon**=
scratch.
kont-lahtho *N* a contractor. [<Sp
contratante]
ko'o See MUHK.
ko'oi See KO'OWI.
ko'ok; ko *s-Vs* be painful, be aching;
(of food) be hot or biting; *s-N* pain;
~**ajig** *s-Vt* harm with occult power;
~**am** *s-Adv* painfully; ~**am**
iattogith *Vt* betray; ~**em|hu***n Vt*
hurt (someone's) feelings; ~**thag** *N*
a pain, an ache.
ko'okmadk *N* the blue paloverde tree
(*Cercidium floridum*, Legume
family).
Ko'ok Mashath‡ *N* May (lit. painful
month).
ko'okol *N* a chili pod; chili powder;
a'al ~**/u'us** ~ *N* wild chili
(*Capsicum annuum*); ~ **hithod** *N*
prepared chili; ~**math** *Vt* add
prepared chili to.
ko'okoth *s-Vt* take offense at; object
to; resent; **ta** ~**ama** *s-Vs* be
sarcastic.
ko'omash *V* to play a girl's game with
sticks; ~**a** *N* the game so played;
~**a|kud** *N* a stick for this game.

ko'owi/ko'oi; koh~ *N* a rattlesnake;
a'agam ~ *N* the small rattlesnake
called the sidewinder (lit. a horned
rattlesnake).
ko'owi-tahtami *N* the senna plant
(*Cassia*) (lit. rattlesnake teeth).
kop*k; k V* clop; pop; explode; thunder
sharply; have a brainstorm; ~**hi***m*
V; ~**i** *N* a popping sound; an
explosion; sharp, cracking thunder.
kopnihi*m; k V* (of as a car) to go
along with a popping sound.
kopnim *Adv* with a snapping or
popping sound.
koponi; ko *Vt* cause to explode.
koponthakud *N* an instrument for
making a popping noise; the
locoweed plant (*Astragalus*).
kopoth; 'ok *Adj* swollen; ~**k** *Vs;*
~**k|a** *Vp;* ~**k|a|hi***m V;* ~**ka|th***
Vt inflate; ~**k|chu** *N;* ~**kth|a|kud**
N baking powder.
kopsith; k *Vt* cause to explode.
kosh; k; kk *N* a nest; a placenta or
afterbirth; **ha'ichu** ~**dag** *N* a
container or case for something, a
cassette; **nowi** ~**dag** *N* a glove.
koshodk; 'ok *Vs* be puffed up; be
ballooned; be foamy; (of as bread) to
be risen; ~**a|hi***m V;* ~**a|th*** *Vt;*
~**th|a|kud** *N* baking powder.
koshwa; k *N* a skull; a numskull, a
blockhead, a stupid person.
kosin; k; kk *N* a kitchen. [<Sp
cocina]
kos-nihlo; k — *ni N* a cook. [<Sp
cocinero]
koson; k *N* the pack rat or wood rat
(*Neotoma*).
kostal; k; kk *N* a bag; a handbag.
[<Sp *costal*]
koswul; k; kk *N* a cocoon.
kotdobi *N* the jimsonweed plant
(*Datura stramonium*).
kotoni; k; kk *N* a shirt. [<Sp *cotorina*
jacket]
kots; ko *N* a religious cross; ~**ith** *Vt*
make the sign of the cross on. [<Sp
cruz a cross]
kotwa; k *N* the shoulder of a person or
animal.
kow, kohko*w, ko,* ~**i** *V* dig in a hard
place.
kowgith; ko *s-Vs* be nourishing.
kowk; kowpk *s-Adj,s-Vs* (be) thick;
(of terrain) (to be) high; ~**a** *Vp;*
~**a|th** *Vt* cause to puff up; cause to
rise (as bread).

kownal; *ko* N a governor; a president;
a political official; a king; a queen;
a prime minister; (a) government;
~ ahithag N a fiscal year; ~t V;
~t|a|lig N a domain; a kingdom; a
country; ~ thaikud N a throne; the
seat of government.
kownith V kick; rattle.
ko-yahl N a horse collar. [<Sp *cuello*
collar]
koyata *Adj* dun-colored; ~dag *s-Vs.*
ku__, k *CE* (may be deleted if it does
not end a word) *independent clause
introducer* and: **Kuni** (or **Ni**) **am
chikpan**=*And I'm working there;*
Kup (or **P**) **hebai chikpan**=*And
where do you work?;* **K hebai
chikpan**=*And where does he work?*
kuadagi; *k*; *kk* N a species of ant with
long black legs (unidentified).
kuadk N a chant used for diagnosing
illness.
ku'ag *Vt* get firewood; ~a N;
~a|med; ~op* V; ~a|mel|imk;
~op|imk V; ~i N firewood; ~ith
Vb get firewood for (someone);
~ith|a|med; ~ith|op* Vb; ~pa*
Vt arrive bringing (specified)
firewood.
kualtho N a quart. [<Sp *cuarto* quart]
Kuapa; *k* N a Cocopa Indian.
kuathi; *k*; *kk* N a twin. [<Sp *cuate*]
kuathlo Huhlio N the fourth of July.
[<Sp *cuatro (de) julio* July four]
kuawith See AGSHP.
kuaya N a town square. [<Sp *cuadro*]
kubjuwi; *ku* *s-Adj,s-Vs* (be) brown or
gray; ~chu *s-N.*
kubswua V puff out smoke.
kuchdwua *Vt* dodge.
kuchul; 'uk *Adj* convex; ~k *Vs* be
convex; ~k|chu N; ~ u'umam N
an ant with convex thighs.
__kud *suffix added to gerunds to form
nouns* a device or material with
which, or place in which, to perform
(a specified action):
CHEPOSITHAKUD, TOHAJITHAKUD.
kudat N the gilded flicker
(*Colaptes chrysoides*).
kudshani *s-Vs* be smoky.
kudut; *ku* *Vcmpl* worry; *Vt* trouble,
worry; disturb; *Vr* be troubled; be
conscience-stricken; worry.
kuduwich See KUL-WICHIGAM.
kug; *ku* N a tip, an end; ~wua* V
(of an animal) to bump a tip.
kugi__ See KUHG.

kuh__ *CE* scorch: ~shp* V get
scorched and stick to a pan; ~shp|ith
Vt allow to get scorched and stick to
a pan.
¹kuhag; kukag N a roast (food).
²kuhag; kukkag *Vt* roast on a stick;
~ith *Vtb.*
kuhb__; *ku* *CE* extraneous material in
the air: ~honi V make smoke;
~hon|ta|kud N smoke-producing
material; ~s N dust; (a) fog; smoke;
(a) vapor; ~s|i|g *s-Vs* be dusty or
smoky; ~s|math *Vt* dust with
powder; **s-wadagi** ~s N steam; ~s
wo'iwua; ~s wohpiwua V raise
dust hurrying along; ~thag N dust
raised by travel.
kuhchki; *k* N a burning stick.
kuhg/kugi__, kuhhug N,CE an edge
or end; ~wua*; **kukugiwua** *Vp*
come to an end.
kuhgam; 'uku *Adv* backward, in
reverse.
kuhgia N (an) erection.
kuhgit; *hu* *Vp* end; ~a|him V end.
kuhgith, *hu*; *k*, *kk* *Vt* cause to end,
end; make a point on.
kuhgkim *s-Adv* with a whirring,
fluttering, whistling, or vibratory
sound.
kuhi N the sound of neighing,
crowing, cawing, screeching (as of
an owl), or blowing (as of a horn).
kuhigam N a species of a black bird
(unidentified).
kuhijith; kukuijith *Vb* make music
for; sound a siren for; *Vt* call (an
animal).
kuhjegi; *ku*; *kku* N a mirage; a heat
wave (as on the road).
kuhk V roar; ~o *Vp.*
kuhkpadag N bush muhly
(*Muhlenbergia porteri*).
kuhkpi N a war trophy enclosed in a
bundle. See App. 3.
kuhkta; *ku* N a hanging shelf.
kuhkwul N the elf owl (*Micrathene
whitneyi*).
kuhm, kuhkum, *k*, ~i *Vt* chew;
crunch.
kuhmikud; *ku* (dist) N a corncob.
kuhna N a blanket hammock. [<Sp
cuna cradle]
kuhp, ~i, kukpa; kuhkp, ~i *Vt*
close; confine; seal; trap; shut in;
contain; ~a N a dam; a dike;
~a|ch*uth* *Vt* confine; ~a|dag N a
door; a gate; a lid; a trap door; that

which seals, a seal; ~a|him *Vt;* ~ch
Vts; ~i *Vs* be closed, etc.; ~i|k
N an enclosure; a diked-in place;
~i|'ok* *Vt* open; ~i|'ok|a *N;*
~i|'ok|a|s *Vs;* ~i|'ok|ch *Vts;*
~i|'ok|ith *Vtb* open for (someone);
~jelith/~ith *Vtb* close for
(someone).

kuhpag *N* longleaf ephedra; mormon
tea (*Ephedra trifurca*).

kuhpi'okud; k *N* an implement for
opening, an opener; **pualit** ~ *N* a
doorknob.

kuhshath/kuhshth__; k *Vt* in
hunting, to chase (game); ~a *N* a
chase; ~amed* *Vt.*

kuhsjim *N* a species of large orange
bird (unidentified).

kuhst__ *CE* thirst: ~a|lig *N* thirst-
endurance; ~k *s-Vs* be able to
endure thirst.

kuht; k *V* light a fire or a cigarette,
etc.; ~pa *Vt* treat with heat.

kuhthagi; hk *N* a firebrand or torch.

kuhthch *Vs* have a torch burning.

kuhthshp, kuhthshap, ~i *Vt* sear or
treat with a hot point.

kuhu, k, kk *V* make the sound of
neighing, crowing, cawing,
screeching (as of an owl), or the
blowing of a wind instrument;
~tham *N* a musician; a band (of
musicians).

kuhwith; ku *N* the pronghorn
antelope (*Antilocapra americana*).

kuhwo; ku *N* a bucket. [<Sp *cubo*]

kui; ku (*dist*) *N* the mesquite tree, the
honey mesquite (*Prosopis glandulosa*
or *P. juliflora*); ~g *Vs; s-Vs.*

ku'ibad; ku; hkku *N* a saguaro rib
with crosspiece for harvesting
saguaro cactus fruit.

kuichuth *s-Vt* express disapproval of,
boo, razz.

kuigam *N* the phainopepla bird
(*Phainopepla nitens*).

kuiji *N* traucoma.

kuikud; ku; kku *N* a wind instrument
or musical horn; a whistle; **wahpk** ~
N a flute; a wind instrument.

ku'inhog__; ku *CE* an extension:
~ith *Vt* add to or make an
extension on; annex; add; *Vb*
assume control for; ~itha *N* an
extension; an annex; ~s *Vs* be
extended.

kuint; ku *Vt* count; measure; ~a *N*
the act of counting; accounting; that
which is counted; ~a|dag *N* a

measurement; any number in a series;
size; a chapter; ~a|kud *N* a device
for keeping count; a gauge; a meter; a
measuring tape or ruler; ~a|tha|m
N an accountant; one who counts, a
counter; **mashath** ~a|kud *N* a
calendar; ~ta ~a|m|a *s-Vs* be
countable, etc.; **uhs** ~a|kud *N* a
measuring stick; a ruler; a yardstick.

kuishani, kuishad; ku *V* cry out;
groan, moan; sob; whine, whimper;
grumble.

ku'ishom; ku *Vt* hook together.

kuitas; ku *N* a firecracker.

kuiwo *Adv* downstream; in the west;
~jed *Adv.*

ku'iwona; ku *N* boiled food; the act of
boiling food.

ku'iwoni; ku *V* boil; ~th *Vtb* boil
for (someone).

kuk chehethagi *N* the paloverde tree
(*Ceridium microphyllum*).

kukpaikud *N* a jail or prison.

kuksho wuhplim *N* the columbine
plant (*Aquilegia canadensis*); the
larkspur plant (*Delphinium parishii*)
(lit. those who are tied at the throat).

kukuwith ha-hahth *N* the black-eyed
Susan or yellow daisy plant
(*Rudbeckia hirta*) (lit. pronghorn
antelope lily).

kulani; ku; kku *N* medicine;
medication; **e bab'etham** ~ *N* a
pill; ~kaj kegchuth *Vt* disinfect;
~math *Vt* medicate; treat for a
disease. [<Sp *curar* to cure]

kulgiwagi; ku *s-Adj* curly; ~ bahi *N*
a bony tail; ~chu *s-N.*

kulshani *N* a cross.

ku-luhji; ku; kku—lu *N* a bonnet.
[<Sp *cucurucho* a cloak with a hood]

kulwani; ku *s-Vs* (of hair) to be curly
or kinky.

kul-wichigam; ku—pi *N* the
curved-bill thrasher (*Toxostoma
curvirostre*).

kummun *Vt* smoke (as a ham); blow
smoke on. See App. 3.

kun; hku *N* a husband; ~am *N* one
who has a husband; ~chuth *Vt*
marry off (a female); ~ma *s-Vs*
have need of a husband; ~ma|kam
N a marriageable female; ~t *Vt*
(of a woman) to marry; ~t|a *N* a
man just married, a groom; ~t|am
N; ~t|amk *Vt* (of a woman) to
want to marry; **wo-ha-**~t|am *N* an
engaged woman; **wo-**~t|a *N* a
fiancé.

kup__ CE close one or both eyes: ~sh|ch V; ~shp* Vp close one or both eyes, blink, wink.

kupal; 'uk Adj overturned; upside down; leaning over; Adv back side up.

kupkkia, ~sh V blink and grimace.

kuppiad; ku; kku N a shovel.

kusal; kuksa'al; kukssa'al N a spoon; a trowel; silverware. [<Sp cuchara spoon]

kushathk; 'uk Vs be dry; be stiff; be cramped; ~ath* V get cramps; get old and stiff.

kusho; k N the back of the neck.

kusho thagshpa N the act of grasping the back of the neck at the sight of a tarantula. See App. 3.

kushpo N the hair on the back of the neck.

¹kushul; k s-Vs be syrupy.

²kushul; k; kk N jam or jelly; hihij ~ N saguaro cactus fruit jam; ~t Vt thicken (a liquid); make into jam.

kushwi'ot; k Vt shoulder (a load); ~a N a burden on the back; ~a|chug Vt; ~a|chuth Vdt load (a burden) onto (someone's back); ~a|jelith Vtb; ~ch Vts.

kusta; k N a tendon in the neck.

kuswo; k N the neck; ~dag N a collar; ~oh'o N a cervical vertebra.

ku'ukpalk N the purslane or pursley plant (Portulaca oleracea).

ku'ul† N gruel.

kuwijk; uku Vs have a dome or peak.

kuwithchuls N the screwbean, tornillo, or screwpod mesquite tree (Prosopis pubescens, Legume family).

L

__la suffix added to nouns and verbs to form nouns (a person or animal) with an abnormal part or function: MO'OLA, SI'ILA.

la'a__; l CE a hook; a trap: ~shp* Vtp hook; trap; clamp; ~shp|a N; ~shp|a|kud N a hook; a trap; a clamp; ~shp|a|med* Vt; ~sh|ch Vts. [<Sp lazo trap, lasso]

lahbis; l N a pen; a pencil. [<Sp lapiz pencil]

lahmba; la N a lamp. [<Sp lámpara]

lahnis; l/lahnsa; la N a spear; a club. [<Sp lanza lance, spear]

lahnju; la N a ranch. [<Sp rancho]

lahnsa See LAHNIS.

lahst Vt harrow; ~a|kud N a harrow; ~math Vt go over with a harrow. [<Sp rastra]

lahwos See KLAHWO.

lai; hla N a king or ruler. [<Sp rey]

lanjeki; la N the lentil plant or its seed (Lens culinaris). [<Sp lenteja]

lasan/lason N a ration. [<Sp ración]

lason See LASAN.

lawait; l Vt drag; ~a N; ~chug Vt drag along. [<Sp trabar to fasten or shackle]

ledo'osh; lelidosh N* an immoral person.

lepithwua V slip (on a smooth or wet surface).

lial; li (dist) N money; a bit: gohk lial=two bits; gi'ik lial=four bits; chuhthp lial=six bits. [<Sp real coin]

liat; li N a rawhide lariat. [<Sp reata]

lichintog s-Adj,s-Vs (of an animal) (to be) rust-brown or charcoal gray. [<Eng lichen]

__lig see ²DAG.

ligpig Vt deprive of. [<Sp rico rich]

lihbih; li N an orphan; a dogey. [<Sp lepe a stray calf]

lihma; li (dist) N a whetstone. [<Sp lima a file]

lihmhun; li Vt sharpen; cleanse.

lihntha; li N a horse rein. [<Sp rienda]

lihso; l N a prisoner; ~chuth Vt take as a prisoner. [<Sp preso]

lihwa; li; lli N a coat; a jacket. [<Sp abrigo]

li-juhwa N lettuce. [<Sp lechuga]

li-mihtha/m — li; l — mi/mi-lihtha N glass; a glass bottle. [<Sp limeta]

li-mohn N a lemon. [<Sp limón]

limoshan, limoshad; li Vt appeal for a donation from; ~a N a donation, the act of appealing for a donation; ~a|med* Vt. [<Sp limosnear]

lohba; l N dry-goods. [<Sp ropa clothes]

lohgo; l N* a demented or insane person; one who acts in a foolish manner; ~chuth Vt; ~dag Vs; N insanity. [<Sp loco mad, crazy]

lohmba; lo N a Jew's harp. [<Sp birimbao]

lohna; l N canvas; a piece of canvas; ~ wako N a canvas water bag. [<Sp lona canvas]

lohnji; lo N (a) lunch. [<AmSp lonche <Eng]

lomaidag: *l N* a horse saddle made of grass, a grass saddle; *Vs.* [<Sp *lomo* the back of an animal]

lomaidath; *l Vt* put a grass saddle on. [<above]

losalo; *l N* in the Catholic religion, a string of beads for praying, and as the collection of prayers said and counted by these beads, a rosary; ~t *Vr* have a rosary service; ~t|a *N* a rosary service. [<Sp *rosario*]

lothai; *l CE* judge: ~t *Vt* judge; hold a legal hearing for; contest in a lawsuit; sue; argue with; ~t|a *N* the act or process of judging; a court trial; ~t|a|kud *N;* ~t|a|kud kih *N* a courthouse or courtroom; ~thag/~sig *N* a judgment; ~t|tham *N* a judge. [<Sp *rodear* to encircle]

Luhgas; *l N* Luke. [<Sp *Lucas*]

luhlsi *N* candy. [<Sp *dulce*]

Luhnas *N* Monday. [<Sp *lunes*]

luhya; *lu Adj* gray (of a horse); unpredictable; ~chu *N;* ~g *s-Vs* be gray. [<MexSp *grulla* ash-colored (of a horse)]

lunag; *l Vr* connect. [<Sp *unir*]

M

m See M__, [4]__M, AMAI.

m-/hem- *CE* you (*sing. object only*); your (*sing.*): **m** (or **hem**) -neith=*sees you;* **m** (or **hem**) -kih=*your house*.

m__, m *CE* introduces all noun, adjective, and adverb clauses, and infinitive phrases: **Bo kaij matsh-o hih**=*He said he would go;* **Tachchua ani mant-o hih**=*I want to go;* **S-mahch ani mat hebai hih**=*I know where he went;* **Hegai mo am chikpan o d ni-nawoj**=*The one who's working there is my friend;* **Matp-o juh, nt pi-o hih**=*If it rains, I won't go.*

[1]__**m;** *suffix added* **1.** *to non-stative verbs to form nouns* one (who does a specified action) (completed action marked by [1]__ *k,* incompleted action marked by __ *th*): BEIKAM (completed action), BEHETHAM (incompleted action); **2.** *to stative verbs to form nouns* one (who has a thing, experience, or relationship): WONAMIM, ALITHKAM, KIHKAM, GOHKKAM.

[2]__**m** *suffix added to verbs, nouns, and stative verbs to form adverbs* in a (specified) manner, -ly, -ishly: S-GEWKAM, S-BAGAM, s-chu AMICHUTHAM.

[3]__**m,** __**muk;** __**k,** __**kko'o** *suffix added to stative verbs to form intransitive verbs of completed action* want (to ingest fluid): TONOM. [<muhk, ko'ok]

[4]__**m, m** *CE* you (*pl. subject only*); they, someone: **S-mahch ani mamt hema hih**=*I know that one of you went there;* **Kum** (or **M**) **haschu neith**=*And what do you see?*

__**ma** *suffix added* **1.** *to nouns to form stative verbs:* S-A'ALMA; **2.** *to adjectives to form adjectives:* S-CHUKMA; **3.** *to verbs to form verbs of the same transitivity* appear or seem (to do or be): KO'ATHMA, S-WOHOHMA.

machchud; *ma N* a stone on which grain is ground, a mortar. [<Sp *metate* a flat stone used for grinding corn, etc.]

machgai/machga; *ma N* an acquaintance.

machma *CE* know: **hab hi** ~ *s-Vs* seem to know; **ta** ~ *s-Vs* be desirable to know.

machpod; *m N* a finger (usu. the thumb).

machwinag; *ma Vs* (of a tree) to be branched.

machwithag; *ma N* a wing feather. See App. 3.

mad; *hma N* a female's offspring; a nephew or niece by a younger sister or a female cousin of younger ancestry; a godchild; the fruit of a plant; ~am/~kam *N; Nr* (pl); ~-ohg; ~-ha-ohg *N* one's brother-in-law or cousin by marriage who is father of this nephew or niece; the reciprocal relationship; ~-ohgam; ~-ha-ohgam *N* someone who has such a relative; ~-o'ogam; ~-ha-o'ogam *Nr* (see App. 4.); ~pig *Vt* pick (fruit or vegetables, esp. corn, squash, cantaloupe) from the plant; ~wua See MAHMDHO.

__**mad,** __**ma**__ *suffix added to nouns to form nouns indicating the relationship of a lower generation relative to the specified relationship group:* WOSMAD.

madkam See MADAM.

madt, mma; hma *Vt* bear (offspring); (of corn, squash, or cantelope plants) to bear (produce); ~**ahi**m *V* approach birth.

__**mag** *suffix added to nouns to form stative verbs* be (in an applied state): HOGIMAG.

magajith; m *V* wave the hand.

magew *V* wave the hand.

__**magi** *suffix added to nouns to form s-class stative verbs* be like: S-O'ODMAGI, S-IHBHAIMAGI.

magkan, magkad, magkash; ma *Vt* break through, make a hole through, perforate.

magkas; ma *Vs* be broken through, be holey.

Ma-hahwi *N* a Mohave Indian.

¹**mahch, mai, mamche** *Vt* learn; investigate; find out; **pi ap s-chu** ~ *s-Vs* be corrupt; **s-ap** ~ *s-Vt* know well; memorize.

²**mahch; m** *s-Vts* have knowledge of; be aware of; *s-Vt* know; *s-Vrs* have knowledge; have special skill; have occult knowledge; ~ **ch ahg** *Vtr* acknowledge; affirm; ~**chu**li*th* *Vdt* introduce to; make known to; ~**i**|**g** *N* knowledge; ~**i**|**m** *s-N** a knowledgeable person; *s-Adv* knowledgeably; ~**i**|**m**|**chu***th* *s-Vt;* ~**i**|**m**|**i**|**g** *N* studies; ~**i**m*k* *s-Vt;* **pi** ~ **ch ahg** *Vtr* deny.

Mahgas; m *N* Mark. [<Sp *Marcos*]

mahgina; m; mma *N* a car, an automobile; ~ **kahio** *N* a wheel; ~ **shuhshk** *N* a tire; ~**thag** *N* a motor. [<Sp *máquina* machine]

mahhagam *N* a fan-palm tree.

mahk, ~i, mamka *Vdt* give; **ab** ~**i**|**dag** *N* an award; ~**ch** *Vdts;* ~**him** *Vdt* distribute to; ~**i**|**g** *N* a gift presented to; the act of giving to; ~**i**|**g**|**dag** *N* a gift belonging to; ~**i**m*k* *s-Vdt;* ~**jeli***th* *Vdtb* give (something) to (someone) for (someone else); ~**s** *Vts* have something which is given to.

mahkai; ma *N* a medicine man; a doctor.

Mahltis *N* Tuesday. [<Sp *martes*]

mahm; ma *N* one's father (in a clan of the buzzard moiety); ~**gam** *N.* See App. 3.

mahmad ha-mahkai *N* a pediatrician.

mahmdho/madwua *V* (of humans) to give birth.

mahmsh *N* an animal tick; a castor bean.

mahniko; ma *N* a cripple; ~**dag** *Vs* be crippled; be physically abnormal; ~**kam** *N** a cripple.

mahs; m *CE* have a certain appearance: *habVts* be (look, appear, seem) like; *habVs* be a (specified) color; *habAdj* this or that kind of; *s-Adj,s-Vs* (be) bright or radiant; (be) clear; ~**chu** *habN;* ~**i** *Vp* emerge, appear (as a newborn or as the sun at dawn); dawn; ~**i**|**g** *N* the dawn of day, morning; ~**i**|**jit***h* *V* endure through the night (lit. to cause the day to dawn); ~**i**|**kam** *N* a (new-, first-, second-, last-, etc.) born person or animal; ~**it***h* *Vt* bring forth; give birth to; color; *Vr* be brought forth, etc.; ~**ith**|**a** *N;* ~**i**|**thag** *N* the birth or emergence of; ~**ith**|**a**|**kud** *N* paint; dye; pigment; ~**ith**|**chu***th* *Vtb* color for (someone); ~**ko** *Adv* in plain sight; clearly; ~**o** *Vp* fade; **pi** ~**it***h* *Vt* cause to disappear; ~**t** *V* make tracks (lit. only); ~**t**|**a**|**g** *N* color; ~**t**|**a**|**him** *V;* **wepo** ~ *Adj,Vrs* (be, look, appear, seem) alike.

mahsho; m *Adj,Vs* (be) trained; (be) tamed or broken (as a horse); ~**chu***th* *Vt* train; tame; ~**kam** *N* a trained or tamed animal. [<Sp *manso* tame]

mahth *N* one (*used in counting*); *Prep* except; ~**o** *Conj* only if.

mahwua; hm *Vt* put a hand in or on; intrude.

mai See ¹MAHCH.

¹**ma'i; ma** *N* a nephew or niece by an older sister or a female cousin of older ancestry; ~**kam** *N; Nr* (*pl*); ~**-ohg;** ~**-ha-ohg** *N* one's brother-in-law or cousin by marriage who is father of this nephew or niece; the reciprocal relationship; ~**-o'ogam;** ~**-ha-o'ogam** *Nr* (*pl*). See App. 4.

²**ma'i; ma** *N* a pit roast; ~**kud;** **mam** ~**kud** (*dist*) *N* a roasting pit.

ma'i__; ma *CE* an action with something held or thrown: ~**chk** *Vt* hit with a thrown object; ~**chk**|**wua*** *Vt* knock out with a thrown object; ~**hin*** *Vt;* ~**kkan*** *Vt* pelt; ~**kkan**|**a** *N* an instance of pit-roasting; ~**kon*** *Vt* bounce; *Vr* visit briefly; ~**n** *Vt* cover (food) in a roasting pit; ~**sh**|**ch** *Vts;* ~**shp*** *Vtp* cover (lit. and fig.);

~**shp|a** *N* the act of covering; a sweetheart (see App. 3); ~**shp|a|dag** *N* a fixed covering such as a roof; ~**shp|a|hi**m *Vt;* ~**shp|a|kud** *N* a lid or other such removable cover; ~**shp|i** *Vs;* ~**shp|i|'ok*** *Vt* uncover; ~**shp|i|'ok|a** *N;* ~**shp|i|'ok|a|s** *Vs;* ~**shun*** *Vt* crush with something held or thrown.

maihogi; *ma N* a centipede.

maim, ~**k; maik,** ~**k** *Vp* get indigestion; ~**ch**u**th** *Vt;* ~**thag** *N* indigestion; *s-Vs* be prone to indigestion.

main; *ma N* a woven straw mat; ~**t|a|tham** *N* a mat weaver.

maki *CE* give: **chu** ~**ma** *s-Vs* be of a generous nature; ~**hog** *Vts* be expected to give; **ta** ~**ma** *s-Vs* be desirable to give.

makkumi *N* a large edible green caterpillar (unidentified).

mako; *m Vt* connect; couple; hitch together; shackle; ~**dag** *N* connection; *Vs;* ~**dath** *Vt;* ~**dath|ch** *Vts;* ~**d|pi|'ok*** *Vt* disconnect; ~**g** *Vs*.

Ma-liia; *M — l N* Mary. [<Sp *María*]

maliom‡/malioni†; *ma N* a foreman; a superintendent; a boss. [<Sp *mayordomo* majordomo, steward]

malioni See MALIOM.

ma-lohma; *m — lo N* an acrobat; a circus; acrobatics; a tightrope walk. [<Sp *maromo* somersault; an acrobatic performance]

mal-sahna See MANI-SAHNA.

mamadhod; *m (dist) N* mildew, mold; algae; scum; ~**ag** *Vs* be moldy, mildewy, or scummy; ~**magi** *Adj* algae-colored.

mamche *V* investigate. [<mahch]

mamhadag *N* a branch (of a plant).

mamhadt *V* (of a plant) to grow a branch.

mammasig *Vs* be branched.

manayo; *m (dist) N* an untamed or unbroken horse. [<Sp *manada* herd, flock]

maniadag; *m Vs* be hobbled or handcuffed.

maniadath; *m Vt* hobble; handcuff; apply brakes to, brake; ~**a|kud** *N* a hobble or handcuff.

mani-sahna/mal-sahna *N* an apple. [<Sp *manzana*]

manjekih *N* lard. [<Sp *manteca*]

manthi-gihya ‡ *N* butter; ~**math ‡** *Vt* butter. [<Sp *mantequilla*]

mashath; *m N* the moon; a moon; a month; ~ **ab** *Adv* during a (specified number of) month(s); ~**ga** *N* a menstrual period; the end of gestation.

mashcham**;** *ma (dist) Vdt,Vtinf, Vtcmpl* teach; *Vtr* study; take up (as a study); ~**a** *N;* ~**a|kud** *N* a school; ~**a|thag** *N* a lesson; a doctrine; a teaching; ~**ch**u**th** *Vt* cause to learn, educate; ~**tham** *N* a teacher; *Nr* a student.

mashwua *N* a wrist.

mashwuag *s-Vs* (of moonlight) to be bright.

masit; *m N* a machete. [<Sp *machete*]

maskal; *m N* a bandana; silk. [<Sp *máscara* a mask or disguise]

maskogith; *m Vt* clarify; *Vr* reveal one's powers or intentions; reveal oneself.

masma *Adj* similar to, -like: **ban masma**=*similar to a coyote, coyote-like; Adv* in a (specified number of) way(s): **waik masma**=*in three ways;* **ha'akia masma**=*in that/those (specified number of) way(s);* **he'ekia i masma**=*in some* (or what) *number of ways;* **hab** ~ *Adv* similarly to that (specified) or this (demonstrated); *Vts* be similar to; **hab** ~...**has i** ~ *Correl. Conj* the same...as: **Ab amt-o si pihk e elithath wehs ha-wui g hemajkam hab masma mam has i masma hejel e-wehhejed si pihk elith**=*You are to have the same concern for all people as you have for yourself (PNT 796);* **has** ~ *Adv* in a certain way; (not) any way; **has i** ~ *Adv* somehow; how.

matai; *ma (dist) N* ash, ashes; cinders; ~ **iawuikud** *N* an ash dump; ~**magi** *s-Adj,s-Vs;* (be) ash-colored; ~**thag** *N* an ash (as on a cigarette); a cinder; *Vs*.

__math *suffix added to nouns to form transitive verbs* apply or add (something) to: KO'OKOLMATH, MIHSHMATH.

Ma-tiias *N* Matthew. [<Sp *Matías*]

matk; *m N* the palm of the hand.

matog, *m Vt* unravel; disassemble; solve.

maw__; *ma CE* the hand: ~**a|gi**th *V* wave the hand; ~**sh|a|p** *Vt* put one's hand in; take responsibility for; not to lift a finger (in negative, fig.); interfere with; *Vr* lock the fingers;

~sh|ch *Vts* have one's hand in
(lit. and fig.); be promiscuous.
mawith; maipith; *mma N* a lion;
a puma, a cougar; ~ mad *N*
a lion cub.
maw tatk *N* the broomrape herb
(*Orobanche*).
ma-yahthi; *m — ya/*wainomi
kolasham *N* a green fruit beetle.
me'__/mu'__; koktha__, kokththa__
CE kill: ~a|md|am, ~o|kam;
~a|md|am, ~i|o|kam *N;*
~a|med, ~op; ~a|med, ~i|op* *N.*
me'a/mu'a (u can replace the *a* here in
all these forms), mea, mem'a,
mea'i; koktha, kokththa *Vt* kill;
murder; ~; ~i *N* one's prey; chu
~dag *s-Vs* be good at hunting; chu
~mk; chu ~imk *s-Vt;* hejel e ~
V commit suicide; ~hog *Vts;*
~jith *Vtb; Vr;* ~kam *N* a killer;
~kud *N* a lethal weapon or
anything used as such; an implement
for slaughtering; a place for killing
or slaughter; ~kud kih *N* an
execution chamber; a slaughterhouse;
~mk; ~imk *s-Vt;* ~to *Vt.*
med, meh, memda, mehl; wohpo'o,
woppo, wohpo'i (*dist*) *V* run;
drive; (of the wind) to blow; flow;
eda i ~ *V* do a dance in which the
participants run together into the
middle; ~tham *N* one who runs,
a runner.
__med, __mmed (both with singular
subjects); __op, __oppo (both
with plural subjects) *suffix added
to combining elements to form
transitive verbs* go (to do or get):
me'amed=*go to kill;* me'op=(of a
plural subject) *go to kill;*
kokthaimed=*go to kill* (a plural
object); kokthaiop=(of a plural
subject) *go to kill* (a plural object);
hunimed=*go to get groceries.*
mehe, mei; memhe, memhei *V* burn
(lit. only).
mehi *N* (a) fire.
mehi-nihlo *N* (*joc.*) a cook who burns
food.
mehith, mehmheith *Vt* burn; ~akud
N an incinerator; a burner; a pan for
holding hot coals, a brazier; ~thag
N a burnt or charred part.
mehk; 'eme *Adj* distant; *Adv* far;
~jed *Adv* from far.
mehkoth *Vt* remove far away; *V* (of
time) to go on and on; ~am *s-Adv*
far away, distantly.

mei *Vp* burn; ~hig *Vs* be burned;
~him *V; Vr* contract venereal
disease; ~tto *V* burn completely,
burn up, burn down.
me'i__; ko'i__ *CE* kill: ~jith *Vtb;
Vr.*
¹mel *N* the act of running.
²mel, ~iw, ~opa; wo'i, ~w, ~opa
Vp (of water, wind, a runner or
driver) to arrive; ~nam *Vtp* meet
(someone) while running; ~nod *Vp*
turn while running; return.
¹mel__ *CE* run; blow; flow: ~chk*
Vt run into, collide with;
~chk|wua* *Vt* run over, run down;
knock down; ~pig *Vt* deprive of
the ability to run; ~to, ~ttog *Vp*
finish running; (of the wind) to cease
blowing.
²mel__, me~; wohpo'i__, woppo'i__
CE run: ~chuth *Vt* cause to run;
drive (a vehicle); ~chuth|a *N* a
race; ~chuth|a|dag *Vs* be able to
drive; *s-Vs* be good at driving;
~chuth|tham *N* one who drives, a
driver; *Nr* one who runs, a runner;
~im|chuth *s-Vt;* ~imk *s-V;*
~i|th *Vs* be able to run; ~i|thag *N*
the ability to run; *s-Vs* be good at
running; ~i|th|kam *N;* ~i|th|t *V.*
melhog *N* the ocotilla plant, also
called candlewood, coachwhip, or
vine cactus (*Fouquieria splendens*).
melith; *me Vt* invite to a sing,
healing, ceremony, or a story-telling;
~a *N.*
meliwig *N* a meeting place.
meliwkud; *me N* a place where the
runners end a race, a finish line.
melomin *Vt* cultivate with a disk.
memelchutha *N* diarrhea.
memelkud *N* a place for running,
a track.
mia; *mi Adv* near, nearby; *Vs* be
near or nearby; ~jed *Adv* from
nearby; ~ko *Adv* at a nearby place.
miabith, mmi; *mi Vt* come nearer to,
approach; ~ch, ~k *a dependent
verb which functions like the
preposition* near (to) *in English;* ta
~ama *s-Vs.*
Mialklos *N* Wednesday. [<Sp
miércoles]
mihl *Adj,N* a thousand. [<Sp *mil*]
mihnas; *m N* a mine. [<Sp *minas*
<*mina* a mine]
mihsa/mihsh; *m N* a table. [<Sp
mesa]
Mihsh; *m N** a Protestant; ~ kih *N*

a Protestant church; ~**math** *Vt*
preach to; lead in worship or church
mass (lit. apply the mass or
communion to); *Vr* worship or
attend mass. [<Sp *misa* (Catholic)
mass]
mihstol/mihtol; m *N* a cat; a
caterpillar tractor; ~ **mad** *N* a
kitten. [<Sp *muixo, mizo⌐micho* cat]
mihtol See MIHSTOL.
mihya *N* a mile. [<Sp *milla*]
mihyu† *N* a coin valued at five U.S.
cents, a nickel.
mikithwuikud *N* the stones for a
girl's game; jacks.
milgan See MIL-GAHN.
mil-gahn/milgan *N* a person of the
white race, an Anglo (southwest
U.S. sense only). [<Sp *Americano*
an American]
mi-lihtha See LI-MIHTHA.
milini/miloni *N* a muskmelon. [<Sp
melones<*melón*]
miloni *N* a melon. [<above]
mimb-lihyo *N* the fruit of the quince
tree; ~**je'e** *N* a quince tree. [<Sp
membrillo]
mi-nuhlo See MI-NUHTHO.
mi-*n*uhtho/mi-*n*uhlo *N* cooked tripe,
hominy, and hoof bones. [<Sp
menudos giblets]
mi-*n*uhto *N* a minute. [<Sp *minuto*]
mischini; mi *Adj* wild; uncivilized; ~
ha'ichu thoakam chehgitha *N* a
zoo (lit. a wild animal exhibition).
[<Sp *mesteño* wild, untamed]
mi-yohn *N,Adj* a million.[<Sp *millón*]
__mk See __IMK.
moashan *N* a hump.
moh *Vt* gather (seed).
mohg *N* straw; husks or hulls; grounds
of coffee or tea.
mohjo; mo *N** one who is maimed or
lacking a limb. [<Sp *mocho*
maimed]
Mohmli *N** a Mormon. [<Eng
Mormon]
mohnthi; mo ‡ *Vr* play cards; ~**kud**
N a playing card. [<Sp *monte* a
card game]
moho *N* bear grass (*Nolina
microcarpa*).
moho__ *CE* itch: ~**gih** *Vp;*
~**gih|him** *V;* ~**gith; mo** *s-V* itch;
~**gith|chuth** *s-Vt.*
mohon, m *Vt* thresh; pulverize; ~**a**
N; ~**a|kud** *N* a thresher for wheat
and beans; ~**a|s** *s-Vs;* ~**i** *s-Adj,*
s-Vs (be) granular.

mohs/~i (*infm*); *m* *N* the relationship
of a woman's daughter's child to the
woman and her peers, a grandchild,
great-nephew, great-niece, etc.;
~**im** *N; Nr* (*pl*); ~**ohg/moi-ohg**
(*infm*); ~**-ha-ohg** *N* a woman's
son-in-law or man's mother-in-law,
etc.; ~**-ohgam; ~-ha-ohgam** *N;*
~**-o'ogam; ~-ha-o'ogam** *Nr* (*pl*).
See App. 4.
mohsi See MOHS.
mohto, momtto; m *Vt* bear; carry on
the head or in a vehicle; ~**i** *N* a
burden or load; a responsibility;
~**'ith** *Vdt* burden with; commit
(a responsibility) to; accuse of;
~**i|s** *Vs.*
moihun; mo *Vt* soften; plow;
cultivate; ~**a** *N;* ~**a|s** *Vs.*
moik; mo *s-Adj,s-Vs* (be) soft, tender,
flexible, pliable; ~**a** *Vp;* ~**a|him**
V; ~**a|jith** *Vt* soften; tan (a hide);
~**am** *s-Adv used with intransitive*
verbs softly; ~**a|th|a** *N;* ~**chu**
s-N; **wabsh i** ~ *s-Vs* be debilitated.
moima; mo *s-Adv used with transitive*
verbs softly.
moi-ohg See MOHS-OHG.
moisha; mo *Vr* limber up; exercise.
momoikantham *N* a tanner.
monjel; mo *N* a bandana. [<Sp
mantel altar cloth, tablecloth]
Month-lai *N* California. [<Sp
Monteréy]
¹mo'o *N* (a) hair of the head; *s-N*
much hair.
²mo'o; mohm/~i *N* the head (of the
body); a postage stamp; the part of
a motor above the head gasket;
the front part of a vehicle; ~ **am**
himtham/~ am kehsha *N* a head
man; ~**bad** *N* the mounted head of
an animal; an animal head used as a
hunter's disguise; ~**bd|am** *N* a
hunter; ~**chk** *Vt* lean the head
against; show the head above;
~**ch|kud** *N* a pillow; ~**chkud**
hobinodag *N* a pillowcase;
~**chk|wua*** *Vt;* **gahi** ~**gith** *Vr*
shake the head as a negative response
or in disapproval; ~**gew** *V* have
head tremors; ~**gith** *Vr* shake the
head; ~**hain*** *Vt* hit with the head;
~**kkan*** *Vt* bunt or butt with the
head; ~**kon*** *Vt* hit with the head;
~ **ko'okthag** *N* a headache; ~**la**
N a person or animal with an
abnormal head; ~**shap** *Vts* be
pressing against with the head; have

near the head; **shel** ~**gi***th* *Vr* nod the head as a positive response; ~**sh|ko** *Adv* at the head end; ~**t** *V* grow hair; ~**tk** *N* the scalp; ~**win** *V* (of a deer) to clean the antlers.

MO'OBDAM

mo'ochwig; *m N* a toad.
mo'okat; moh~ *V* pop the head out; sprout.
mo'okwad; *m N* a tadpole.
mo'otad, mo'omtad *V* poke the head out.
mo'otadk *N* the broomrape or cancer-root plant (*Orobanche ludoviciana*).
mo'owhani *N* the hedgehog cactus (any species of *Echinocereus*).
moshogi; *m N* a woman who has a continuing extramarital sexual relationship with a man, a mistress.
mu'a, See ME'A.
mualig *V* (of a person) to spin or dance.
muda__; *'um CE* a tassle: ~**gew, mugew** *V* (of grain) to undulate; ~**thag** *N* the tassle of a plant; ~**tht** *V* (of a plant) to produce a tassle.
muhadagi; *m s-Adj,s-Vs* (be) greasy; (be) brown; ~**chu** *s-N*.
muh*k*, ~**i, mumku; ko'o, koi, kok'o, koh'i** *Vp* die; cease giving off light, become eclipsed.
muhki; ko'i *N** a dead person or animal, a corpse; ~**hi***m* *V* advance toward one's death, be dying; ~**thag** *N* one's dead.
muhkig *N* death; ~**a|m** *s-Adj* deathly.
muhkith; *m Vr* get or be killed (lit. be caused to die).
muhks *Vs* be numb; be necrotic.
muhla; *m N* a mule; ~ **tahtami** *N* corn on the cob (lit. mule teeth); ~ **wanimedtham** *N* a species of

spider (unidentified) (lit. mule leader). [<Sp *mula* mule]
muhni *N* any kind of bean or beans; **mams** ~ *N* a pinto bean; pinto beans.
muhs *N* the vagina.
muhsigo; *m N* a musician; *V* make music. [<Sp *musica* music]
muhthag *N* a wound.
muhwal; *mu N* an insect; a fly; a bee; ~**biht** *N* a punctuation mark (lit. fly feces).
muhwij; *'um Vs* be oblong; be thin and long; be irregular; be jagged; be triangular.
muhyo; *m N** a mute person. [<Sp *mudo*]
mu'i; *mu Adj* many; much; *Pron* many; much; ~**j** *Vs;* ~**jj** *Pron;* ~**k|ko** *Adv* often; ~**k|pa** *Adv* at many places; ~**th|a** *Vp* multiply; ~**th|a|hi***m* *V;* ~**th|a|jith** *Vt* multiply; ~**th|a|jith|a|s** *Vs.*
mukchiwitham *N* a dragonfly.
mukiagam *N* a daredevil; daring.
mukialig *N* an invalid.
mukihog *V* be expected to die.
mukima *s-Adj* deathlike; expecting to die; ~**kam** *s-N* readiness for death.
mul*in;* omin *Vt* break by bending; ~**i|g** *N.*
mumki__; kok'oi__ *CE* sick: asugal ~**thag** *N* diabetes; ~**ch***uth;* ~**ch***uth* *Vt;* kahchim ~**thag** *N* an illness caused by breaking a taboo (see App. 3); **oimmedtham** ~**thag** *N* a contagious disease; ~**thag** *N* (an) illness or disease.
mumku; kok'o *Vs* be sick; *Vp* get sick; ~**tham** *N* a patient, a sick person; **asugal** ~**tham** *N* a diabetic. [<**muhk** *and* **ko'o**]
mummu *Vt* shoot at; *Vr* practice shooting; get shot at; ~**dag** *N* a wounded animal; a wound; *Vs* be wounded.
mumsha *N* plantain.
__**mun** *suffix added to combining elements to form transitive verbs* manipulate (in a specified manner): THAGIMUN, SIHMUN.
muspo *N* the pubic hair of a female.
mu'u, muh, mummu, muh'i *Vt* wound.
mu'uhug; mu'umuhug *s-Vs* be sharp-edged.
mu'uk; mu'umk *s-N* a peak; a point; *s-Vs* be sharp or sharp-pointed; ~**a** *Vp;* ~**a|hi***m* *V;* ~**a|jith** *Vt* hone;

~am *s-Adv* sharply; with a high pitch; ~a|th* *Vt* sharpen; ~sig *N* a razor blade; ~thag *N* sharpness.

mu'umka *V* become pimply; ~dag *Vs; N* a pimple; ~th* *Vt* make bumpy.

N

n＿ *CE clause introducer which* 1. *begins questions requiring Yes and No answers:* Napt s-ap koi?=*Did you sleep well?;* 2. *begins reason clauses* (requiring *pi* to form positive statements, and *pi pi* or *ge* to form negative statements) because: S-hehpith o no pi juhk=*It's cold because it's raining;* S-toni o no pi pi juhk (or no ge juhk)=*It's hot because it isn't raining.*

na＿ *CE* (requires *a* and ³＿*s*) *independent clause introducer* perhaps, maybe: Na'as juhk=*Maybe it's raining;* Na'anis-o hih=*Maybe I'll go.*

na'ana *Adv* once upon a time, long ago.

naggia; nahngia *V* hang; *Vt* hang, suspend; *Vr* be suspended; *N* a hammock; i ~ *V* droop; ~kch *Vts;* ~kud *N* a device for hanging something; a hanger; a clothesline; a clothes hanger.

nahagew; nahngew *V* (of certain animals) to flap the ears.

nahagio; *n N* a mouse; an earring.

nahgi See IHNAGI.

nahj oimmedtham *N* a phosphorescent light seen at night over marshy ground, a will-o'-the-wisp.

nahj*ith*, *ntha*; *n Vb* make a fire for (someone).

¹nahk *s-Vts* like the taste of.

²nahk; nahnk *N* an ear; ~ ki'itpag *Vt* advise; ~ ko'okthag *N* an earache.

nahkag *N* a species of prickly pear cactus (*Opuntia*).

nahnko *Adj* various; *Adv* variously, in variance with the norm; ~ ahg *Vt* ridicule, make fun of; ~git*h Vt* ridicule; tease; joke with; misuse; waste; ~gith|a *N* the act of ridiculing, etc.; a joke; ~gith|tham *N* one who ridicules; a joker; a tease; ~gsi|m *s-Adv* jokingly;

~ mahs *Adj,Vs* (be, look, appear, seem) varied in appearance.

nahsh*p*, *nha*, ~i *Vt* fold; turn; *Vt* multiply (a specified number of times).

nahs*ith Vt* rake; ~a|kud *N* a rake (tool).

nahth, nai, nantha *V* make a fire; ~a *N* a fire; the act of firemaking; ~a|kud *N* a fireplace; an oven; ~ch *Vs*.

nahto, nattod *Vtp* accomplish, complete, finish; establish; prepare; make ready; make (build; create; earn, as money); manufacture; *Vr* finish; ~gig *N* an accomplishment; a completion; a preparation; creation (abstract only); ~i *N* a finished product, a creation; a building; earnings; ~i|s *Vs* be finished; ~kam *N* a maker, builder, or manufacturer; ~kch *Vts* have in a finished condition; *Vrs* be ready.

Nahwaho *N* a Navajo Indian.

nai See NAHTH.

naipijju See NAWOJ.

nak＿; *hn CE* the ear: ~pig *V* mark or cut the ear of (an animal); ~pig|a|s *Vs* be marked or cut on the ear; ~pi|thag *N* an earmark (on an animal); ~po *N;* ~sh|ch *Vts* be attentive to the prospect of receiving secret information, keep/have an ear out for (lit. to have one's ear against); ~wua|dag *Vs* listen well (lit. to have earwax).

nakog, *n*, ~i *V* suffice; *Vt* endure; tolerate; *Vrinf* can, be able; get ready; manage; *Vr* maintain or continue with a (specified) pursuit; ab ~ *Vr* plead; ~ahim *Vt;* chum ~ *Vrinf* try; i ~it*h Vtb*.

nakosh; *n Adj,Vs* (be) foolish; ~dag *N* foolishness.

nakosig; *n s-Adj,s-Vs* (be) noisy; (be) boisterous; *s-N* (a) noise; ~am *s-Adv* noisily; boisterously.

Nakshad *N* a Mohave Indian.

nakshel; *na N* a scorpion.

nalash *N* an orange. [<Sp *naranja*]

＿nam *suffix added to intransitive verbs to form transitive verbs* meet (while performing a specified action): WO'INAM (see under ²MEL). [<namk]

namk, nanmek, nanammek, ~i *Vt* meet, encounter; comply with (a specified obligation or the price of goods received); encounter and presumably gain spiritual power from

(usu. an animal); ~a|m *N;* ~chuth
Vt; ~him *Vt;* ~s *Vs* be adjoined.
namki; *n N* a meeting.
namkig *s-Adj,s-Vs* (be) expensive,
valuably, or precious; ~am *s-Adv*
expensively, valuably, preciously;
~chu *s-N.*
namkith *Vdt* pay; repay; compensate;
~a *N* (a) payment, etc. (in
reference to the payer); the act of
paying; ~a|dag *N* (a) payment, etc.
(in reference to the payee); a price;
wage or wages; a reward; **s-ko'ok**
~a|dag *N* (a) punishment, (a)
penalty; **s'ko'okam** ~ *Vt* punish;
penalize.
nan'aipijju See NAWOJ.
nanakumal *N* a bat (animal).
nanawuk *V* glow; glitter; sparkle;
flicker.
nantha See NAHTH.
napad; 'an *s-Adj* sprawled; ~k *Vs*
be sprawled, dilapidated, or in a poor
state; ~wua *V* sprawl.
nasi-yohn *N* a nation. [<Sp *nación*]
naw *N* a species of cactus
(unidentified).
¹nawait *N* wine; saguaro cactus wine.
²nawai*t,* **naupait** *V* make wine;
~a|kud *N* an olla or earthen jar
for making ceremonial wine in.
nawash; *n N* a pocket knife. [<Sp
navaja]
nawijju; *na N* a ceremonial clown.
nawm, ~k, ~muk; **nawk,** ~k, ~ ko'o
V get intoxicated or drunk; ~chuth
Vt; ~ki; ~koi *N* a drunkard.
nawoj; naipijju; nan'aipijju ‡/nawuj;
naupuj; nan'aupuj† *N* a friend;
a brother; a sister; a cousin; ~im;
~gim *N* one who has a friend, etc.;
Nr (pl) those related; ~m|a *s-Vs*
be friendly; ~m|a|kam *N** a
friendly person; ~t *Vt* befriend;
~thag *N* (a) friendship;
acquaintance.
nea, ~'a; *ne V* look, see; **pi** ~ *Vs*
be blind; **pi-**~dag *N* blindness;
pi-~tham *N** one without sight,
a blind person; ~tham *N* one
with sight.
nead *Vdt* beg from.
neahim *Vt* wait for; expect; look for.
neal; *ne Vt* visit expecting a gift or
a meal; ~i|g *N;* ~i|med* *Vt;*
~imkam *s-N* a beggar; ~kam *N*
one who waits for something free.
ne'e, nei, nen'e, neh'i *Vt* sing; *V*
make music; ~tham *N* a singer.

¹neh; *ne connective word or phrase
(sometimes used adverbially) to
call for attention or indicate the
conclusion of a topic* look, see, so
you see; so then; finally; **Neh, pi ant
am hu wo hih**=*Look, I'm not going
to go there;* **Neh, t gam hu wahawa
hih**=*So you see, he left.*
²neh, nen__, **nenena** *Vp* wake up;
~him *V* wake up, wake, awake,
awaken.
nehbig *N* a legendary monstrous snake.
nehnchuth See THA'ICHUTH.
¹nehni; neni__; *ne N* a tongue;
~wua* *Vt* lick.
²nehni See THA'A.
nehnihim See THA'IHIM.
nehn__ *CE* sight: ~t *V* gain sight;
~thag *N* sight, the ability to see;
s-Vs be alert.
nehol; *ne N* a slave; a servant.
nehpod; *ne N* the lesser nighthawk
(*Chordeiles acutipennis*).
ne'i; *ne N* a song; (a piece of) music;
(pl) a concert, concerts; ~chuth *Vb*
sing or play music for (someone);
~him *V;* ~kud *N* a place for
singing; a concert hall; ~med* *V;*
~t *V* compose music; ~thag
s-Vs; ~to *V.*
ne'ibijim See NE'IBIM.
ne'ibim/ne'ibijim *Vt* run around;
pass, overtake.
neijig *s-N* (a) disaster; (a) calamity;
(a) tragedy; (a) foreboding.
ne'iopa See THA'IWUNI.
neith, ne, nne *Vt,Vcmpl* see;
discover; visualize; realize; perceive;
Vt experience; ~a *N* the act of
seeing; something seen, a sight; (an)
experience; **ab** ~ *Vt* look at; ~ **ab
amjed** *Vdt* realize (a gain) from;
~a|him *Vt* examine, look over;
watch; ~a|kud *N* a mirror;
am-absh ~ *Vt* merely observe;
~a|mk *Vt;* **chu** ~am *Adv*
curiously; **chu** ~amadag *s-N*
curiosity; **chu** ~amk *s-V* stare; be
curious; **chu** ~amkam *s-N** a
starer or one who is curious; be
~agam *s-Adj* ominous; **ta** ~am
s-Adv presentably; **ta** ~am|a
s-Vs; **ta** ~am|a|kam *s-N**
someone or something presentable;
ta ~hog *s-Vts* be undesirable to
see; be tired of seeing; **ta** ~hogim
s-Adv undesirably in appearance;
tonolithch ~ *Vt* foresee; see by
revelation.

nem *N* the liver; ~**aj** *N* liver.
nena *N* (in one's) sight or view (fig.
and lit.); ~**dt** *V* (of an animal) to
acquire sight.
nenashan; ne *V* look; investigate;
become alert; ~**am|chuth** *s-Vt;*
~**amk** *s-V;* ~**i** *s-Vs* be alert; be
early-waking.
nenchuth; ne *Vt* cause to have
sight.
nen'e See THA'A.
nen'eith See NEN'OITHK.
nenhog; ne *V* look around.
nenida‡ *Vt* wait for.
nen'oithk/nen'eith *s-Vt* guard
against.
neok, nne, ~**i; ne, nne,** ~**i** *V* talk;
~**imk** *s-V;* ~**ith** *Vb;* **juhkam-**~
V speak Spanish; (of the dead) to be
non-haunting as a result of Christian
baptism (see App. 3); **pi e mahch ch**
~ *Vs* be delirious (lit. speak
without knowing); **s-gogsim-**~ *V*
use offensive language (lit. speak
dog-like); **s-hewelim** ~ *V* talk
formally; ~**sith** *Vt* imitate speech
or supposed speech of (a person,
coyote, etc.); ~**tham** *N* a speaker; a
talker; an electronic speaker.
ne'okchutha *N* an imitative sound.
ne'oki *N* (a) language; (a) speech;
a word; a message.
ne'owin *Vt* argue or talk seriously
with; ~**a** *N* an argument; the act of
arguing.
nepodk; 'ene *Vs* be loaf-shaped.
¹ni *Conj* neither, nor, not even.
[<Sp *ni*]
²ni See **¹__ni.**
ni- (n- before *n, t,* or *th*)/**heni-** *CE*
me; my; myself; my own: **ni-kih** or
heni-kih=*my house.*
¹__ni, ni (n before *t*) *CE* I: **Kuni** (or
Ni) **am chikpan**=*And I'm working
there;* **Nap s-mahch mani am
chikpan**=*Did you know I'm
working there?*
²__ni *CE* you (imperative).
niawul; ni *N* a devil or demon.
Niawul *N* the Devil, Satan.
niosh *Intj* an expression of dismay:
oh, my God! [<Sp *dios*]
¹nod/tohta heosig *N* the prickly
poppy (*Argemone platyceras*).
²nod; hno *Vp* turn; bend; return; ~**a**
Vp get dizzy; ~**a|gam** *N** a rabid
animal; ~**agig** *s-Vs* be dizzy-
causing; *N* rabies; ~**ag|s** *Vs* be

turned, bent, or curved; **shelkam** ~**a**
Vr panic; get frightened.
__nod *suffix added to intransitive
perfective verbs to form other
intransitive perfective verbs* turn
(while performing the specified
action): WO'INOD (see under ²MEL).
[<nod]
nodagith; nohnogith *Vt* answer; pay
(something) back, return (what is
owed); get revenge (for); cause
to turn.
nohnhoi See NOWI.
Noji-wihno *N* Christmas Eve;
~ **mashath** *N* December (lit.
month of the blessed night). [<Sp
Nochebuena Christmas Eve]
nolawt, no *Vdt* buy; buy from; ~**a** *N*
a purchase; shopping; a buy; ~**a|kud**
N a store or shop; ~**tham** *N* one
who buys, a buyer, a shopper.
nonha *N* an egg; ~**t** *V* lay an egg
(lit.); conceive.
nonoig *Vt* stir.
nowi; nohnhoi *N* a hand; an arm;
~**-bebhe** *Vt* shake hands with;
chum ~**; chu'uchum** ~ *N* a finger;
~**gith** *V* shake the arm; ~**kaj** *Adv*
by hand; ~ **kalit** *N* a wheelbarrow;
~**kud** *N* a sleeve; ~**po** *N.*
nowiyu; no *N* a castrated bull, a steer.
[<Sp *novillo* a young bull]
nu'a, nua, nua'i *Vt* rake together.
nuhkuth *Vt* tend, take care of; guard;
protect; ~**a** *N* a ward, charge, or
responsibility; the act of caring for
or protecting; **pi ap** ~ *Vt* neglect;
abuse; **pi ap** ~**adag** *N* neglect;
abuse; ~**tham** *N* a caretaker;
a foster parent; a guard; a
protector.
nuhmilo; nu *N* a number. See
App. 6. [<Sp *número*]
nu'i__ *CE* a pushing or forcing action:
~**chk** *Vt* push on; ~**chk|wua*** *Vt*
push along or away; push down or
topple; force; ~**chk|wu|i** *N* an
instance of pushing along;
~**chk|wu|i|kud** *N* a thimble; ~**him**
Vt; ~**himtham kalit** *N* a wheelbarrow; a pushcart.
nulash† *N* a peach. [<Sp *durazno*]
nunuwi-jehj *N* ragweed (*Ambrosia*)
(lit. vulture mothers).
nuwi; nu *N* the turkey vulture
(*Carthartes aura*); any vulture (lit.
only); ~**opa** *N* the black vulture
(*Coragyps atratus*).

O

¹o *Conj* or. [<Sp]

²o See A_

_o See _KO.

oag; o'ag *N* the brain; a nerve; marrow.

Oam Mashath *N* April‡; March† (lit. yellow and orange month).

oam; o'am *s-Adj,s-Vs* (be) brown, orange, or yellow; a penny; ~**a** *Vp;* ~**a|him** *V;* ~**a|jith** *Vt;* ~**a|jith|a** *N* something browned; particularly, a deep-fried pancake, a pop-over; toast; a waffle; ~**chu** *s-N.*

oan; o'an *Vt* erase, wipe off; do away with; ~**a** *N* an erasure; ~**a|kud** *N* an eraser; ~**a|s** *Vs;* **gm hu wabsh** ~ *Vt* absolve, excuse, forgive; ~**ith** *Vtb.*

obga; 'o *N* an enemy; ~**thag** *N* enmity, hate, hostility.

od, oh, oh'oda *Vt* gather (fruit), harvest; ~**a** *N* a harvest of fruit; ~**tham** *N* one who or that which harvests, a harvester.

ogol; 'o *N* one's father in the bear clan; ~**gam** *N.* See App. 3.

¹oh *Intj* an expression of dismay: oh.

²oh; o'o *N* the back (of the body); ~ **ko'okthag** *N* a backache; ~**shad** *N* a tiger; a jaguar; ~**shan*** *Vr* relax; stretch (lit. stretch the back).

ohaggel *N* a phantom-like creature. See App. 3.

Ohbathi *N* an Opata Indian.

ohbgam *N* a small tree of the paloverde species.

Ohbi *N* an Apache or Navajo Indian; historically, any hostile tribesman; ~**-mad** *N* a gecko lizard.

ohche'ew; 'o *Vt* find, locate; ~**i** *N* a find.

ohchwigi; 'o *N* an inchworm (member of the family *Geometridae*).

ohg; 'o *N* one's father; ~**a|m** *N.*

ohgig; 'o *s-Adj,s-Vs* (be) left (direction); ~**chu** *s-N;* ~**ko** *s-Adv* on the left; ~**kam** *s-N*** a left-handed person.

ohhoth *s-Vt* discard; reject; abandon; divorce; ~**a** *N* a discard, a reject, a throwaway; *Nr* a divorce; ~**a tapial** *N* a writ of divorce; divorce papers; ~**a|chuth** *s-Vdt;* ~**amk** *s-Vt;* **ta** ~**am|a** *s-Vs* be undesirable; **ta** ~**am|a|kam** *s-N*** someone or

something undesirable; **ta** ~**am|chuth** *s-Vt* cause to be disinterested, bore.

oh'ith *Vt* remind of sadness by mentioning the dead; (by the appearance of an animal) to forewarn of death. See App. 3.

¹ohla; 'o *N* gold. [<Sp *oro*]

²ohla; 'o *N* an hour: **Do hetasp ohla**=*It's five o'clock;* **Do hemako eda hugkam ohla**=*It's one thirty;* ~**-ab** *Adv* during (a specified number of) hour(s); ~**-ch-ed** *Adv* at (a specified time). [<Sp *hora* hour]

oh'o *N* a bone; **chini** ~ *N* a beak; **wabsh** ~ *N* a bony or skinny person or animal.

oh'og *N* a tear from the eye.

ohso; 'o *N* a scythe; a sickle. [<Sp *hoz* sickle]

oht; o'otta *V* drip; leak.

ohtk *N* the flesh beside the backbone; ~ **tatai** *N* sinews beside the backbone.

oi *Adv* soon; now; on time.

oi wa *Conj* yet; but.

oimmed; oiopo *Vs* be walking around or about; wander; travel; be present (outside or in an open place); (of a contagious disease) to spread; ~**tham;** ~**kam** *N* a wanderer; a traveler.

oimmelig *N* travel; a trip; a habitat; a favorite place much visited, a stamping ground.

oipij See OWIJ.

¹oith, 'o *Vt* follow; accompany; ~**a|chug/chug** *Vcmpl,Vinf* think; *Vt* follow around; think over; think about; await a chance at; ~**ahim** *Vt* follow; *Vcmpl* think; consider; ~**am** *Prep* during; behind; ~**amk** *s-Vt;* ~**ch,** ~**k** *Vt a dependent verb which functions like the preposition after in English* (be doing a specified action) after or following; ~**ch|jed** *Prep* from behind; **i** ~**ahim** *Vt* think about; consider; ~**k|a|m** *N* one that follows, a follower.

²oith; 'o; 'o *CE* a field: ~**ag** *N* a field; a farm; ~**a|j** *N;* ~**bad** *N;* ~**kam** *N* a farmer; a field owner.

oiwichuth See OIWIGITH.

oiwigith/oiwichuth *Vt* cause to hurry.

oiwith *V* hurry; arrive soon or on time.

_ok/_k *suffix added to non-stative verbs to form non-stative perfective*

participles having done: NEITHOK.
__'ok See __PI'OK.
okokoi; '*o** N** the white-winged dove
(*Zenaida asiatica*).
oks; o'oki N** an adult female; a lady or
a woman; *CE* an aunt by marriage
to a (specified) uncle; a (specified)
great-aunt: ~**ga** N** (*infm*) one's wife
(lit. one's old lady); ~**t** V** (of a
female) to become old. See App. 4.
oksi/ogih (*infm*); **'***o** N** an aunt senior
to one's father; ~**-keli;** ~**-kekel** N**
an uncle by marriage to such an aunt;
~**-kelim** ~**-kekelim** N;* ~**m** N.**
See App. 4.
okstakud N** a mushroom; a toadstool.
ola; '*o;* **'***o** N** a puck for field hockey;
a tumor; ~**s** N** a sphere; a ball; a
globe; a lump; *Adj* spherical, round;
lumpy; *s-Vs;* ~**s|im** *s-Adv*
spherically; in a coiled manner; ~**s**
pilkan N** Pima wheat (lit. spherical
wheat); ~**t** *Vtp* roll up; bundle up;
coil (up); ~**t|ahi***m* Vt.**
olapap See OLOPA.
ol-gihya N** a fork; a pitchfork. [<Sp
horquilla a small pitchfork]
olhin See OL-NIHYO.
olhoni; '*o** N** a maverick. [<Sp
huérfano an orphan]
ol-nihha See OL-NIHYO.
**ol-nihyo/ol-nihha/olhin; o'ol-nihnio/
o'ol-nihniha/o'olhin** N** an
adobe oven; a portable furnace or
stove. [<Sp *hornillo* kitchen stove]
olopa/olapap; '*o** N** a kidney; ~**j** N**
kidney.
ol__; '*o** *CE* hook: ~**shap** *Vts* (of a
latch) to be hooking (something);
~**sh|ch** *Vts;* ~**shp*** Vt** hook (as a
doorlatch); ~**shp|a** N;* ~**shp|a|him**
Vt; ~**shp|i** *Vs;* ~**shp|i|'ok*** Vt**
unhook; ~**shp|i|'ok|a** N;*
~**shp|i|'ok|a|s** *Vs;* ~**shp|i|'ok|ch**
Vts.
omin See MULIN.
omina N** a medicinal stick. See
App. 3.
omlik; '*o** *Adj,Vs* (be) humped; (be)
humpbacked; (be) bumpy.
on; '*o** (*dist*) N** salt; ~**a|med*** V;* ~**k**
s-Adj,s-Vs (be) salty; ~**k|a** *Vp;*
~**k|a|hi***m* V;** ~**k|chu** *s-N;* ~**ko**
Vp lose saltiness; ~**ko|hi***m* V;**
~**k|thag** *s-N* saltiness; ~**magi**
s-Adj,s-Vs (be) salt-colored; ~**math**
Vt salt; ~**pig** *Vt.*
ongoi N** sage-brush (*Artemisia*);
leaves of this plant used for seasoning
and for medicine.

onk ihwagi N** saltbush (*Atriplex
elegans, A. polycarpa, A. wrightii*);
nettleleaf goosefoot (*Chenopodium
murale*).
onk kui N** the tamarack tree (*Tamarix
aphylla*) (lit. a salt tree).
onk washai N** salt grass (*Distichlis*).
O'obab N** a Maricopa Indian.
o'od/o'ohia N** grit; sand; gravel;
a crystal (mineral); ~**kith** *Vt*
crystalize (a mineral); ~**magi**
s-Adj,s-Vs (be) gritty, sandy or
gravelly; ~**magi|chu** *s-N.*
o'odopiwis/o'odopiwa N** a sparrow.
o'ohadag N** a picture, drawing, or
painting; *Vs* be drawn, be painted;
be written.
o'ohan/o'ohon; o''ohan/o''ohon *Vt*
write; draw; paint; print; make a
design on; *Vr* register one's name
(as in voting, census, etc.); ~**a|s**
Vs; ~**ch** *Vts;* ~**ith** *Vtb* write to;
draw for; ~**tham** N** a writer; a
painter; a printer; one who draws,
a drawer.
o'ohana/o'ohon N** handwriting;
a piece of writing; a treatise; a
composition; an essay; the act of
writing; a drawing (picture); a book;
a letter (for correspondence); **kaithag**
~ N** any letter of the alphabet.
o'ohia See O'OD.
o'ohon See O'OHANA, O'OHAN.
o'oi; o''oi *s-Adj,s-Vs* (be) striped;
~**chu** *s-N.*
o'oith† *Vt* hunt; ~**tham** N** a hunter.
o'osith *Vt* percolate; put through
a strainer, strain; ~**a|kud** N**
a strainer.
o'othham; o''thham N** a person; a
human; a tribesman; ~**ag** *Vs* be
populated; be at home; ~ **ap'ethag**
N** Indian rights; human rights;
~**chuth** *Vt* treat like a human;
~**thag** N** human dignity or worth;
personality; Indianness; humanity;
wabsh ~ N** a layman or common
person; a local person.
O'othham N** a Papago or Pima
Indian; the Papago or Pima language;
~ **hemajkam** N** the Papago people;
~**kaj/~aj** *Adv* in the Papago or
Pima language.
op See IP.
__op See __MED.
opojk; '*o** *Adj,Vs* (be) humped.
opon; '*o** N** patata, patota, a winter
plant used for edible greens
(*Monolepis nutalliana*).
oshkon; '*o** *Vt* scrape, bruise.

owgam; 'o *N* a species of bush (unidentified).

owi; 'o *N* an opponent; the opposition.

owich; 'o *Vt* light (as a cigarette); **~k** *N* a lit cigarette.

o-wihspla; 'o —pi *N* a bishop. [<Sp *obispo*]

owij; 'o/oipij *N* an awl.

ownag; 'o *N* a collarbone, a clavicle.

P

¹**__p** *CE added to combining elements showing time or source* if, assuming (that), is it the case that: **Nt-o ha'ichu ei matp-o juh**=*I'll plant something if it rains.*

²**__p, p/ap** *CE added to combining element a__* you (*sing. subject*): **Napt am hih mapt hebai s-himim?**=*Do you go where you wanted to go?;* **Ia ap ni-neith**=*You see me here.*

³**__p** See ¹**__**PA.

¹**__pa, __p** *suffix added to adjectives of number to form adverbs* in so many (specified) places: HEMIAP, MU'IKPA, HA'AKPA.

²**__pa, __pad, __pash** *suffix added to nouns to form transitive verbs of motion* arrive carrying or bringing: KU'AGPA. [<u'apa]

pad; 'apa *Adv* badly; evilly; *Adj* bad; evil; spoiled, deteriorated; **~aj** *Vs;* **~chu** *N;* **~chuth** *Vt* spoil; wreck; damage; deplete; **~chuth|a** *N* spoilage; wreckage; damage; depletion; **~chuth|a|s** *Vs;* **~hog** (see ELITH); **~ma** *s-Vs* be lazy; **~ma|chuth** *s-Vt;* **~ma|dag** *s-N* laziness; **~ma|kam** *s-N** one who is lazy; a layabout; **~t** *V* spoil; deteriorate; **~talig** *N* deterioration; **~tham** *N.*

pahl; pa *N* a minister; a priest or Father; an evangelist; a prophet; any religious leader or guru; *Adj* religious; **~-wakon** *Vt* baptize. [<Sp *padre* father]

pahla; p *N* a shovel. [<Sp *pala*]

pahn *N* bread; **s-i'owi ~** *N* (a) cake (lit. sweet bread); **sitdoi ~** *N* toast; **~t** *V,Vt* bake; **~t|a|kud** *N* an oven; **~t|a|kud kih** *N* a bakery; **~t|tham** *N* a baker. [<Sp *pan* bread]

pahtho; p *N* a duck; **~ mad** *N* a duckling. [<Sp *pato* duck]

Pahwlo *N* Paul. [<Sp *Pablo*]

pako'ola; p *N* a ceremonial clown. [<Sp <Yaqui the pascola dance of the Yaquis]

Palasi *N* a member of the Jewish Pharisee party. [<Eng *Pharasee*]

pal-mihtho *N* a palomino horse; **~g/thag** *s-Vs* be palomino-colored. [<Sp *palomito*]

pa-lohma; p —lo *N* a pigeon. [<Sp *paloma*]

pa-nahl *N* a bee; **~ sit'ol** *N* honey (lit. bee syrup). [<Sp *panal* honeycomb]

pa-nihtha; pa —ni‡ *N* a handkerchief. [<Sp *panuelito* dim. of *panuelo*]

pa-nohji *N* unrefined sugar. [<Sp *panoche*]

papa See PAPALI.

papali/papa *V imperative only* eat (speaking to a child).

papa-lohthi *N* the blade of a fan, propeller, or windmill; a kite. [<Sp *papalote* kite; windmill <Aztec *papalotl*]

paplo *N* a pigeon. [<Sp *paloma*]

pasam; papsama (*dist*). *Vr* see the town, window-shop; **~a** *N* window-shopping; **~amed*** *V;* **~chuth** *Vt* take to see the town, etc. **~tham** *N* a window-shopper. [<Sp *pasar* to while away (the time)]

pas-tihl *N* baked goods; a pie; **~t** *V,Vt* bake. [<Sp *pastel* pie, pastry]

paw-lihna *N* a godfather. [<Sp *padrino*]

pa-yahso; pa —ya *N* a clown; **~chuth** *Vr* clown, act like a clown. [<Sp *payaso*]

pegi See PEJ.

pegih an expression of agreement or conclusion: OK, sure; well then.

pehegi *s-Adj* easy; trifling; having little value or importance; **~chu** *s-N;* **~chuth** *s-Vt;* **~m** *s-Adv* easily.

pehegia *Adv* supposedly.

pej/pegi *connective phrase used in correcting or expanding a statement* I mean, what I mean is; in fact.

pen *indicates an attempt of the speaker to remember something* What was (it)?; I thought (it was . . .): **Shah'o pen chehgig?** =*What was his name?;* **Pen okis hab chehgig Huan**=*I thought his name was Juan,* or *Wasn't his name Juan?*

pi *Adv* not; **~ ha** *Adv* not at all, not in any way; **~ mahch ch e ahg** *Vt* deny, repudiate; **~ oi** *Adv* late.

pi- *a prefix which negates, or gives a negative character to, a noun:* pi-AP'EKAM, pi-GEWKTHAG.

pi'a *Adv* no; ~**jed** *Adv* from nowhere.

piach† *Vs* be absent; be non-existent.

pialhai*n*; *pi*; *hpi* *V* trip, stumble.

piast; *pi N* a celebration; a party; *Vr* celebrate; party; ~**a** *N* celebrating; ~**a|med*** *V;* ~**ch***uth* *Vt* amuse. [<Sp *fiesta*]

pias-tihlo; *pi — ti N* a master of ceremonies or a person in charge of a celebration, an emcee. [<Sp *fiestero*]

pi'ata *V* disappear; ~**ch***uth* *Vt;* ~**dag** *N* disappearance.

pig-ab *N* a pickup (truck). [<Eng] __**pig** *suffix added to nouns to form transitive verbs* remove from: JEWEDPIG.

pihba; *p N* a tobacco pipe. [<Sp *pipa*]

pihch*uth* *Vt* waste (someone's) time (*with* someone *considered the object, that is,* waste the time of [someone]); cause trouble for (someone).

pihgo; *p N* a pickaxe. [<Sp *pico*]

pihhu*n*, **pihhush;** *pi Vr* finish work; adjourn; recess; retire; ~**a** *N* (an) adjournment, recess, or retirement.

pihk See CHU'IG, ELITH.

pihla; *pi N* a bucket, a pail. [<Sp *pila* basin]

pihlas *N* a pear tree; a pear; ~**im** *s-Vs* be pear-shaped. [<Sp *peras* <*pera*]

pihnia *N* a fine-toothed comb. [<Sp *peine*]

pihnto; *pi Adj* with spots, spotted; ~**chu** *s-N;* ~**g/dag** *s-Vs*. [<Sp *pinto*]

pihpchul *Adj* concave.

pihsh; *p (dist) N* a dollar (of any country); particularly, a U.S. dollar; **Juhkam** ~ *N* a Mexican peso. [<Sp *peso* peso]

pihthag *N* effort; trouble; a waste of time.

Pihwlo *N* Peter. [<Sp *Pedro*]

pi'ich*uth*, *p Vt* challenge; dare; doubt the ability of; ~**a|dag** *N* a challenge or dare.

pikchul*ith* *Vt* take a picture of, photograph; ~**a|kud** *N* a camera; ~**a|thag** *N* a photograph. [<Eng *picture*]

pil-gihtho; *pi — gi N* a parrot. [<Sp *periquito*]

pilin; *p N* a bridle; a bit (for a horse). [<Sp *freno*]

pilkani *N* wheat (*Triticum*). [<Sp *trigo*]

Pilkani Bahithag Mashath† *N* May (lit. wheat harvest month).

pi-lohn *N* a treat; sweets. [<Sp *pilón* conical sugar loaf]

pi-lohtha *N* a ball for playing. [<Sp *pelota*]

pilsa; *pi N* a blanket. [<Sp *frazada*]

pim *Adv* not.

pi-mianthi *N* black pepper; ~**math** *Vt* put pepper on, pepper. [<Sp *pimienta*]

pi-nohl *N* a meal made of parched seeds. [<Sp *pinole*] __**pi'ok/__'ok,** ~**i** *suffix added to verbs that express a state or condition resulting from an action to form perfective verbs* undo (a specified action): YAHWIDPI'OK, WUL'OK.

pion *N* a worker. [<Sp *peon*]

pipchumagi *s-Adj,s-Vs* (be) freckled; ~**chu** *s-N*.

pisal; *p N* a measure (linear and weight); ~**t** *Vt* weigh (lit. only); ~**t|a** *N;* ~**t|a|kud** *N* a scale for weighing, scales. [<Sp *pesar* to weigh]

pisin; *p N* a bison, a buffalo. [<Sp *bisonte*]

pis-tohl; *pi — to N* a pistol, a handgun; ~ **koshdag** *N* a holster. [<Sp *pistola*]

pi-to'ichu *N* a gecko lizard.

piu *N* the sound an arrow makes; ~**gim** *s-Adv* with a whirring sound. [Imitative]

plahnja; *la Vt* iron; ~**kud** *N* an iron; ~**tham** *N* one who irons, an ironer. [<Sp *plancha* an iron]

plahtha *N* silver. [<Sp *plata*]

plihntha *N* something left as security for a loan, collateral, security; ~**t** *Vt* pawn; ~**t|a|kud** *N* a pawnshop. [<Sp *prenda* a security, a pledge]

plohmo; *l N* lead (the metal). [<Sp *plomo*] __**po (__wo** after vowels, with shortening of long vowel in the nouns) *suffix added to nouns to form nouns* hair (of the specified body part): ESHPO. [<wopo]

podoni; *po V* thump; ~**ch***uth* *Vt;* ~**m** *s-Adv* in a thumping manner; ~**tham** *N* a thumper.

pohlwis *N* blasting powder. [<Sp
polvos <*polvo* powder]
pohmpo *N* a device for pumping; a
pump. [<Eng probably through
southwest Sp]
pohtol *N* a bronco. [<Sp *potro* a foal]
poshol; popsho'ol *N* boiled food; ~t
Vt boil (food). [<Sp *posole* <Aztec
pozolli]
pot-lihya; *li* *N* a pasture. [<Sp
potrero]
pualit; *pu* *N* a door. [<Sp *puerta*]
puhl *N* a swimming pool. [<Eng
pool]
puhlo; *p* *N* a cigar. [<Sp *puro*]
puhst† *N* a saddle. [<Sp *fuste*]
puinthi; *pu* *N* a bridge (to afford
passage for vehicles, etc.).
[<Sp *puente*]
puiwlo; *pu* *N* a city; a town.
[<Sp *pueblo*]
pulato; *p* *N* a bowl; a platter.
[<Sp *plato* plate, dish]

S

s-__ *a prefix added* **1.** *to s-class words
to indicate the positive:* **S-ap'e o**=*It's
good* (but **Pi o ap'e**=*It isn't good*);
2. *to verbs of ability to indicate the
intensive:* **S-melithag o**=*He's good
at running* (but **Pi o s-melithag**
=*He's not good at running*); **3.** *to
verbs of existence to indicate
abundance:* **Am o s-kuig**=*Mesquite
are abundant there.*
¹__s (__i after *p, n,* and combining with
d as *l*) *suffix added to active verbs
and gerunds to form stative verbs* be
in a (specified) state as a result of
action: NAHTOIS, KUHPI, HOBINOL.
²__s *suffix added to pronoun
combining elements of quantity to
form adjectives of quantity indicating
amount in various senses:* **Ha'as
ant bei g o'od**=*I got so/that much
sand;* **He'es apt bei?**=*How much did
you get?;* **He'esko apt hih?**=*How
far did you go?*
³__s/s *CE added to combining
elements indicating that the speaker
does not know if what he is saying is
true:* **Kus** (or **S**) **has-o e juh**=*I
wonder what he will do;* **Kus hab-o e
juh**=*I wonder if he will do it;* **Kunis
hu s-mahch mat-o s-ni-hohho'i**=*I*

don't know if she will like me; **Pi ani
mahch mas juh**=*I didn't know if it
had rained* (but **Pi ani mahch mat
juh**=*I didn't know that it had
rained*).
sahgo; *sa* *N* a blouse; a sweater. [<Sp
saco a loose-fitting coat; a sport coat]
sahnto; *sa* *N* a religious picture; an
image or a person represented by an
image. [<Sp *santo* saint]
Sahnto *N* a Catholic; *Adj* Catholic;
~ **kih;** ~ **kihki** *N* a Catholic
church. [<above]
sahwano; *sa* *N* a bedsheet. [<Sp
sábana]
sahyo; *s* *N* a rival. [<Sp *adversario*
foe]
sai ed† *V* become ashamed.
sai eda† *Adv* shamefully.
Sajusi *N* a member of the Jewish
Sadducee party. [<Eng *Sadducee*]
sal-tihn; *sa* *N* a frying pan. [<Sp
sartén]
s-chu See CHU.
S-gevk Mashath† *N* April (lit. strong
month).
¹__sh/sh *CE added to combining
elements indicating assumption
reportedly, presumably, they say,
it is said:* **Kush** (or **Sh**) **am
chikpan**=*And he reportedly works
there;* **Am ash kih mash am d
Chehthagi-Wahia**=*He reportedly
lives at the place called Green-Well.*
²__sh, __i *suffix added to stative verbs
to form causative verbs:* put or place
(in the specified stance): KEHSH,
THAHSH.
³__sh a reduction of __*shp* when __*ch*
follows.
sha *Conj indicates that the
proposition is contrary to fact or not
wholly true:* if (as is not the case);
Adv somewhat, to some degree or
extent, a little; (for) a short time,
awhile, barely.
sha'adk/sha'alk; *sha* (*dist*)
s-Adj,s-Vs (be) forked or cleft; (be)
divided; *N* a prominence between
clefts; a branch or protrusion; a
division or section of an organization;
~**a** *Vp;* ~**a|him** *V;* ~**ath*** *Vt.*
sha'aligi; shashaligi *N* a forked brace
for carrying a basket.
sha'awai; *sh* *Vdt* buy; buy from.
shaba See WABSHABA.
shabani, shabke; *sha* *V* make a
splashing sound or clapping sound, clap.

shah___ See ¹HAB.

shahchu See HA'ICHU.

shahd *N* the amoreuxia plant or its edible root (*Amoreuxia*).

sha heg wepo See WEPO.

shahgig; *hsh N* a canyon; a ravine; a gorge.

shahgith; *hsha*; '*asha Prep* between; among; si ~ *Prep* in the midst of, amid.

shahk, shashke *Vt* take a handful of; ~*ith Vt* give a handful of; ~*u'a Vt* carry in the palm; ~*uch Vts* have in the palm.

shahkim; *hsh N* a halter for a horse. [<Sp *jaquima* rope headstall]

shahko See HASKO.

shahkum *Vt* catch; grasp.

shahmt *N* adobe; an adobe brick; (a) brick.

shahmug *Vt* shake; *V* make a noise.

shahm*uni V* make a sound; rustle; ~m *Adj* noisy; *Adv* noisily; pi ~g *Vs;* pi ~m *Adj* noiseless, quiet; still.

shahmuth, *sha Vt* shake (as a blanket); drive away, shoo (away).

shahshagi*th Vt* mix or combine (ingredients).

shahshani *V* groan; ~kam *N* a groaner.

shahth, shai, shashtha; *sha (dist) Vt* herd or drive a herd of (animals); chase away (an animal); ~a *N;* ha ~kam *N* a drover, a herder.

Shahwai *N* Saturday. [<Sp *sábado*]

shahwai___; *sh CE* fiber: ~thag *N* fiber in a plant stalk (as maguey) used for making rope.

shai See SHAHTH.

¹sha'i/sha___wa'i *Adv an intensive* extremely, very; pi ~ *Adv an intensive* not, not at all: Pi o sha'i mahch=*He doesn't know at all.*

²sha'i, *sha N* grass; brush; waste, trash; ~ch*uth Vt* hang (as an article on a clothesline); ~chuth|a *N;* ~jith *Vr* get stuck, get hindered; ~wua* *V* get stuck.

shaj___; *sha CE* scrape, chip: ~kon* *Vt* scrape; chip (off); ~kon|a *N* a chip; the act of chipping; ~kon|a|kud *N* a scraper (tool).

shakajtha; *sh N* the comb of a bird.

shakal; '*ash (dist) Adv* side by side; in line; ~k *Vs* be spread apart from a common point; ~k|a *Vp;* ~k|a|him *V;* ~k|a|th* *Vt* spread (something) apart; ~wua *V* stagger, wobble.

shaliw; *sha N* trousers, pants; hogi ~ *N* chaps (lit. leather pants). [<Sp *jaripero*]

___shan, ___shad, ___shash *suffix added to combining elements to form transitive verbs* rub, scratch (in a specified manner): CHEKSHAN.

shapij; '*ash Adj* narrow or oblong; ~k *Vs; N* a variety of squash (unidentified); ~k|a *Vp;* ~k|a|him *V;* ~k|a|th* *Vt;* ~ko *Adv.*

shapol; '*ash Adj* aspherical, out of sphere, oblong; ~k *Vs;* ~k|a *Vp;* ~k|a|him *V;* ~k|a|th* *Vt* make aspherical; ~k|chu *N.*

shashani; *sh (dist) N* a blackbird; s-chuk ~ *N* any black bird; s-oam ~ *N* an oriole (*Icteridae*); s-wegi ~ *N* a red-winged blackbird (*Agelaius phoeniceus*).

shashawk; *sh (dist) V* echo (lit.); ~im *Adv* in an echoing manner, echoingly.

shashkaj; *sh (dist) N* a mirage.

shaw; *sha V* rattle; ~ikud *N* a rattle.

shawad; '*ash (dist) Adj* thick (in diameter); ~k *Vs;* ~k|a *Vp;* ~k|a|him *V;* ~k|am *Adv* thickly.

sha___wa'i See ¹SHA'I.

shawant; *sh V* go on a roundup; look for livestock, usu. cattle; *Vt* look for (specified animals); ~a *N;* ~a|med* *V,Vt.*

shawoni; *sha N* soap; ~math *Vt* apply soap to, soap. [<Sp *jabón* soap]

shegoi/shegih; *she (dist) N* the creosote bush (*Larrea tridentara*), also known locally as greasewood.

sheh'e; *sh N* a wolf.

Shehl *N* a Seri Indian.

shehpij; *she N* one's relative in his own generation but younger if a brother or sister, or of younger ancestry if a cousin; one's relative of his fourth ascending generation, a great-great-grandparent; ~i|m *N; Nr (pl).* See App. 4.

shehsha *N* an arrow shaft.

shel; *hshe N* permission; a permit; a license; a right; ~ch*uth Vr* get ready; ~ him *V* go continually; go in a straight line; ~ him|tham *N* someone or something that goes continually; ~wua *V* practice shooting; ~wui|thag *N* ability to shoot; s-*Vs* be good at shooting.

¹shelam *Adv* always; continually.

²**shelam** *V* question; ~**adag** *Vs;*
~**tham** *N* a questioner.
shelin, shelsh; *hshe Vt* straighten;
~**a** *N* an arrow shaft; ~**a|kud** *N*.
shelini; *hshe s-Adj,s-Vs* (be) straight;
~**m** *s-Adv* straight; ~**th** *Vt*
instruct.
shelkam *Adv* almost.
shemach*uth; sh Vr* act boldly or
meanly without regard to possible
punishment; ~**adag** *N* boldness;
meanness; ~**tham** *N** a bold or
mean person.
s-hiwk-wainomi *N* an implement for
filing, a file.
shoak, shosha, shoshshak; shoani *V*
cry; **si** ~ *V* wail.
shobbiad; shoshobiad *N* a doll.
shodobin *Vs* be crowded; ~**ch***uth*
Vt bother, pester; crowd.
shohba; *sho N* a joint of the body.
shohbi*th; sh Vt* hinder, restrain;
forbid; correct; *Vtinf* forbid; ~**a**
N; ~**adag** *N* (a) hindrance; (a)
restraint; (a) correction; ~**ch** *Vs*.
shohm*m; hsho Vt* sew; darn; ~**a** *N*
something sewn or darned; a seam;
the act of sewing or darning; ~**jeli***th*
Vtb; ~**tham** *N* a sewer or
darner; a seamstress.
shohni See SHONTPAG.
shoh'o; *sh N* a grasshopper.
shoh'o-kahio *N* a carpenter's square
(lit. a grasshopper's leg).
shohs See A-LOHS.
shohshoba; *hsh N* a bracelet, a
wristband.
shohshomakud; *hsh N* a sewing
machine.
shohshomiththam; *sh N* a
seamstress; a tailor.
shohshon *N* an ancestor. [<shon]
shohwua; *sho V* blow one's nose.
¹**sho'ig;** *hsho Adj* humble, modest;
poor; *Adv* humbly, modestly; *Vs*
be humble, modest, or poor; **ab i**
~**thag** *N* humility; modesty;
~**ch***uth Vt* impoverish; cause
to suffer; *Vr* humble oneself;
apologize; grieve; suffer; ~**chuth|a**
N an apology; ~**chuth|a|dag** *N*
ill-fortune; suffering;
impoverishment; ~**kam** *N*
a poor person; a humble or modest
person; ~**thag** *N* suffering;
poverty; humble station.
²**sho'ig** *Intj* an expression of sympathy
or shock: how awful!, etc.
shoiga; *sho N* a domestic animal; a pet.

shomaig; *sho V* catch (a) cold;
~**chuth** *Vt;* ~**ig** *N* a cold; ~**kam**
N.
shon; *hsho N* a base or foundation;
the trunk or stump (of a plant); the
source or beginning; an ancestor;
~**chuth** *Vb;* ~**kam** *N* a spring
(of water); ~**wua*** *V* begin;
~**wui|chuth** *Vt* begin.
shonchki; *sho N* a war club; an axe; a
tomahawk.
shoni CE an action of the hand or of
something held: ~**ak|a** *N* a log cut
for use; ~**ak|a|m** *N* a woodcutter;
~**chk;** ~**ak** *Vt* chop down;
~**chk|wua** *Vt* move (someone or
something) by striking it; bat (a ball);
~**hin*** *Vt* hammer; hit with a
hammer or the fist; ~**hin|a** *N;*
~**hin|a|kud** *N* a hammer; ~**kkan***
Vt pound on; beat; box (with); club;
~**kon*** *Vt* strike, hit; ~**shun*** *Vt*
crush with the hand; ~**wi|kud** *N* a
pestle; ~**win** *Vt* reduce to small bits
(as grain) by pounding; ~**win|a** *N*.
shonigiwul; *sho N* a ball used in a
racing game. See App. 3.
shonthal; *sho N* a soldier. [<Sp
soldado]
shontpag; *sho/***shohni** *V* pound;
knock; *Vt* pat; pound; knock.
shontsig *N* chopped firewood.
shontsi*th Vdt* chop (wood) for;
~**a** *N*.
sho'odkath, sho'odkai; *sho Vr*
frown; grimace.
sho'owa *N* a bull snake.
shopol; '***osh Adj* short (in measure);
~**im** *Adv* for a short time; ~**k**
Adj,Vs (be) short; ~**k|a** *Vp;*
~**k|a|him** *V* (begin, continue) to
become short; ~**k|a|th*** *Vt* shorten;
~**k|chu** *N;* ~**k|th|a|s** *Vs*.
Shopol Eshabig Mashath *N* August
(lit. short crop month).
shosha *N* nasal discharge; ~**ki** *N* the
act of crying; ~**ki|m***k s-V;* ~**ki|t***h*
Vt cause to cry.
shoshkthag *N* a nostril.
showichk *N* a narrow passage; a
gorge; a canyon; a ravine; *Vs*.
**shp** (***sh** before _***ch**), _**shap**,
_**shshap,** _**shpi** *suffix added to
combining elements to form transitive
verbs* **1.** make contact with, or hold
in or against (a specified body part):
THAGSHP, HEKSHP; **2.** apply
(something) to: BITHSHP; **3.** (of rain,
etc.) to fall on: JUKSHP.

shuhg; *shu* *N* a mockingbird.
shuhshk; *shu* (*dist*) *N* a shoe; a tire; a
wheel rim; ~ **chuchkathakud** *N*
shoe polish; ~**dag** *Vs* be shod;
~**dath** *Vt* put a shoe on; shoe (a
horse); **kaigia** ~ *N* a sandal;
kawiyu ~ *N* a horseshoe; **mahgina**
~ *N* a tire; ~**-wakch** *N* the
baccharis plant (*Baccharis
sarathroides*) (lit. shoe wetting).
¹shuhth† *N* the vagina.
²shuhth; *hshu* *Adj,Vs* (be) full of
liquid; ~**ahi*m*** *V;* ~**ch** *Vts.*
shuhthagi; shuhshugi (*dist*) *N* water;
liquid; a pond.
shuhthagi u'uwhig *N* a crane, heron,
or other water bird.
shuhthags *Vs* be filled.
shuhthath; shuhshuth *Vt* fill (up).
shuhthgim *Adv* in or to every part,
throughout.
shuhthk *Adj* full.
shuh'uwad *N* the tansy mustard
(*Descurainia pinnata*).
shulig See GEHSH, ²WUA.
___shulig See ²___WU.
___shun, ___shud, ___shush *suffix added
to combining elements to form
transitive verbs* crush (in a specified
manner): MA'ISHUN.
shuwijel; *shu* *N* a saddle blanket.
[<Sp *sudadero*]
si *Adj* real, genuine; ultimate; of good
character; precise, very: **heg si tash
ed**=on that very day; *Adv* quite,
very, intensely, really; completely.
si'ad *V* (of the sun) to rise.
siakam *N* a hero; one who has endured.
si'al *N* the east; ~ **kehk** *Adv* before
dawn; ~ **tahgio/~tgio** *Adv* east,
eastward; ~ **wecho** *Adv* in the east.
si'al___, *si* *CE* morning: ~**i|g** *N* (a)
morning; ~**i|m** *Adv* tomorrow;
~**math** *Adv* in the morning, each
morning.
sialt *V* bet.
si'altgio See SI'AL.
siant; *si* (*dist*) *Adj,N* (a) hundred; (a)
hundredth; ~ **ahithag** *N* a century.
[<Sp *ciento*]
siawogi *N* a comet, a falling star, a
meteorite; a warning of danger.
sibiyo; *s* *N* a hoe.
sigal; *s* *N* a cigarette. [<Sp *cigarro*]
sih___ *CE* an action with a hook or
blade for pulling: ~**chk** *Vt* hook;
~**chk|wua*** *Vt* hook and toss
(as a bale of hay); ~**kon/~mun**
Vt hoe; mash.

sihbani; *s* *V* sprinkle, drizzle.
sihki *N* the white-tailed deer
(*Odocoileus virginianus*);
~ **chuhkug** *N* venison; ~ **mad**
N a fawn.
sihl; *si* *N* a saddle; ~ **at;** ~ **a'at** *N*
the back of a saddle; ~ **mo'o;**
~ **mohmi** *N* a saddle horn or
pommel.
sihngo; *si* *Adj* five; one of the sticks
used in the game of GINIS; *N* (a)
five; a coin worth five cents, a nickel.
[<Sp *cinco* five]
sihnju; *si* *N* a buckle; a cinch; a saddle girth; ~**dag** *Vs* be buckled or
cinched; ~**dath** *Vt* buckle (up),
cinch (up). [<Sp *cincho* saddle girth]
sihnto *N* a belt. [<Sp *cinto*]
sihon See SIHOWIN.
sihowin/sihon; *si* *Vt* stir; rummage
through; investigate.
Sihpud; *si* *N* the anus.
sihs/ si'ihe/si'ihegi (*infm*); *si* *N* one's
relative of his own generation but
older if a brother or sister, or of older
ancestry if a cousin; one's relative
of his fourth descending generation,
a great-great-grandchild; ~**im** *N*.
See App. 4.
sihsh; *si* *N* an elbow.
sihsh*p*, ~**i, sishshap;** *si* *Vt* nail; pin;
screw; bolt; ~**a** *N;* **ab** ~ *Vt*
fasten; ~**a|kud** *N* a straight pin; a
safety pin; a tie pin; a broach; a tack;
a bolt; a screw; **tohb k ab** ~ *Vt*
fasten with a screw.
sihskim *V* make a lapping or pattering
sound.
sihski*th* *Vt* sift; ~**a** *N;* ~**a|kud** *N* a
device for sifting, a sifter.
sihwotha; *s* *N* a feather on one's head;
a ray of light.
si'i, sih, sis'i, sih'i *V,Vt* suck, nurse
at the breast; ~**chu*th*** *Vt* nurse
(the young); ~**kud** *N* a baby bottle,
nursing bottle; ~**la** *N* a person or
animal that drinks excessively.
si'ihe See SIHS.
si'ihegi See SIHS.
sijki*th*; *si* *Vt* rattle.
sikod; *si* *Adj* round; circumscribed.
si koktha *Vt* cause to cry.
sikol; 'is *Adj,Vs* (be) circular, round;
Adv around; ~**chu** *N;* ~ **i**
kekiwua *V* turn around; **i** ~**kath**
Vt circle around; *Vr* turn in a
circle; ~**im** *Adv* circularly, in a
coiled manner; ~**k** *N* a circle; ~**k|a**
Vp; ~**k|ahi*m*** *V;* ~**ka|th*** *Vr*

coil; *Vt* make circular or curved; ~k|th|ah**i***m* *V*.

sikul; *s N* one's relative in his own generation but younger if a brother or sister, or of younger ancestry if a cousin; one's relative of his fourth ascending generation; a great-great-grandparent.

sil-wihsa *N* (a) beer. [<Sp *cervesa*]

simin-jihlo *N* a cemetery. [<Sp *cementerio*]

simito; *s N* a bread bun.

simnolt; *si V* flee, run away.

simudkaj; '*is V* grimace.

sinat See SINOT.

sini'oliga *N* an internal pain.

sinot/sinat; *si N* a Mexican girl. [<Sp *señorita*]

sin-tahwo *N* a cent. [<Sp *centavo*]

sipshud; *s Vt* cause to exude.

sipud; '*is Adv* in a stooped or squatting position; ~k *Vs* bent at the hips.

sipuk; *p* (*dist*) *N* the Arizona cardinal (*Richmondena cardinalis*); any bird of the cardinal species.

sipulk; '*is Vs* be in a pile; ~ath* *Vt* pile.

sip*uni***;** '*is V* break open and exude fluid.

sisidchelig *Vs* be serrated.

sisiki *N* the sparrow hawk (*Falco sparverius*).

sisloni *N* cracklings, fried pork fat. [<Sp *chicharrones*<*chicharrón*]

siswua *V* salivate, spit; ~dag *N* saliva, spit; ~math *Vt* spit on.

sitdoi *N* any roasted food except meat.

___**sith** *suffix added to non-stative verbs to form non-stative transitive verbs* mimic: NEOKSITH.

sitholim *Adv* in a coil.

sit'ol; *s N* syrup.

siw *Adj,Vs* (be) bitter; ~chu *N*.

si-wahyo *N* barley. [<Sp *cebada*]

siwani *N* a chief medicine man.

siwat/~o; *s N* a goat; a kid under a year old; ~-huhch *N* a crowbar (lit. a goat hoof); ~mad *N* a kid or young goat. [<Sp *chivato* a kid between six months and one year old]

siwato See SIWAT.

si-wihnia *N* a winch.

siwithchulis *N* the wild rhubarb, canaigre, dock (*Rumex hymenosepalus*).

siwk, *si V* make a simmering sound; sputter in the heat.

siwol *N* an onion. [<Sp *cebolla*]

siwuliki See SIWULOGI.

siwulogi/siwuliki; '*isi N* a whirl of wind, a dust devil; a twister, whirlwind, tornado, or cyclone.

sohba *N* soup. [<Sp *sopa*]

sohla *N* a soft drink or soda pop. [<Sp *soda*]

so-nohla *N* Sonora, Mexico. [<Sp]

spulwam *N* alfalfa.

___**stk** *suffix which forms s-class stative verbs* be able to endure (that which is specified): S-BAMUISTK, S-EDASTK, S-HEWASTK.

suhna; *s* (*dist*) *N* a fig; ~ je'e *N* a fig tree (*Ficus carica*). [<Yaqui *chuúna*]

suklatog *Vs* be dark brown. [<Sp *chocolate*]

sulij/shulij *N* an endearing term for a baby boy or young male.

T

t- *CE* us; ourselves, each other; our; our own.

[1]___**t** (___**ta**___) *suffix added to nouns to form verbs* **1.** create, build, make: KIHT; **2.** bear young or fruit: MADT; **3.** grow a part, as hair, feathers, etc.: A'ANT, MO'OT; **4.** form a relationship with: KUNT; **5.** become: KOWNALT.

[2]___**t, t** *CE added to pronoun combining elements to indicate contemporary time, any time from recent past through future:* **Kut** (or **T**) **am hih**=*And he went there;* **Am ant-o hih**=*I will go there;* **Pi apt ni-ahgi mapt am hih**=*You didn't tell me you went there.* ▶___**t** *is omitted before* ___*s, and in incompleted action unless it is conditional or future:* **Pi ani mahch mas-o juh**=*I don't know if it's going to rain;* **Am o him**=*He's going there;* **Kutp juhk?**=*Is it raining?;* **Tki-o juhkath**=*It will evidently be raining.*

[3]___**t** *suffix added to intransitive verbs to form other intransitive verbs* learn to: BAHNIMEDT.

ta *precedes transitive verbs to form combining elements showing a characteristic of an undergoer of the action:* S-ta AMICHUTH.

___**ta** *after certain verbs* (___**t** *if final,* ___**h** *after vowels,* ___**u** *after uk,* ___**ka** *after ajij, and otherwise usually* ___**a** *after consonants*) *suffix added to stative verbs to form intransitive* *perfective verbs* reach (a specified state or condition): AP'ET, TOHAH, OAMA.

tachchu/~a/tatchua *Vt,Vinf,Vcmpl* wish; *Vt,Vinf* want, need, like, love; **ab si** ~ *Vt* love; **~i** *N* will, desire; necessity; **~ith** *Vtb* want for (someone); *Vtinf* want; **~i|thag** *N* a need, desire; love; **~ith|ch** *Adj* beloved; **~tham** *N* one who loves, a lover.

tachchua See TACHCHU.

tad; hta *N* a foot of a person or animal, or of measure; **~agith** *Vr* shake the foot; **~gew** *V* kick or swing the foot, have a twitch of the foot; **~po** *N;* **~pod** *N* a toe.

tadai; *t* *N* the roadrunner (*Geococcix californianus*).

tadan, tadannek; hta *Vt* spread out flat; **~chu** *N* something wide; **~i** *Adj,Vs* (be) spread out; (be) wide; **~ih** *Vp* become wide; **~ih|him** *V.*

tadnim; hta *s-Adv* in a widespread manner, widely.

tahgio; '**ata** *Prep* in front of, before, in the way of, in the direction of: (do) to; (happen) to.

tahhath__ *CE* emotion or feeling: **~ag** *Vs* have a (specified) emotion or feeling; *s-Vs* be interesting; be fun; **~am** *s-Adv* enjoyably, amusingly; **~chuth** *Vt* amuse; **~kam** *N* a (specified) emotion; someone who has a (specified) emotion; **ap ~kam** *s-N* (a) joy; a joyful person; an amusement; a pleasure.

tahlk *N* a sack. [<Sp *talega*]

tahngih; *ta* *N* a tank. [<Sp *tanque*]

tahnhadagi *N* trash.

tahni, tai, tahanne *Vdt* ask for; **~g** *N* a request; **~med*** *Vdt.*

tahpalo; *t* *N* a shawl. [<Sp *tapadora*]

tahpan, tapsha; *t, t* *Vt* split; divide; crack; **~ch** *Vts;* **~i** *Vs; N* a split; a division; a crack; **~jelith/ tahpjelith** *Vtb.*

tahpath *Vtb* divide for.

tahpna *N* a division, a part.

tahsa; *t* *N* a drinking cup. [<Sp *taza*]

tahtam, t *Vt* touch; feel; pet.

tahtami *N* a tooth; ~ **ko'okthag** *N* a toothache; ~ **mahkai** *N* a dentist (lit. a tooth doctor).

tahtchulith *Vt* reach; cause to touch.

tahtk; ta *Vt* feel; lay hands on; *V* become conscious; come to one's senses; *Vr linking* feel; *s-Vrs*

be patient; **ab i e** ~ *Vr* become wholesome; **has** ~ *Vr* feel disturbed.

tahtkag *N* the sense of feeling; awareness.

tahtko *N* a jaw.

tahtshakud; ta *N* a comb; an implement for splitting.

tahum; *t* *N* burlap.

tahwlo; ta *N* a border of a field. [<Sp *tabla*]

¹**tai** *N* (a) fire; a match for starting a fire.

²**tai** See TAHNI.

ta'i *Adv* back; up; to the north; **~bim, ~bij**im *Vt* go around.

taimun *Vt* chop into kindling; **~i|g** *N* kindling.

taiwig; ta *N* a firefly.

tako *Adv* yesterday; **d hema** ~ *Adv* (the) day before yesterday.

takui; *t* *N* the soaptree or soapweed yucca plant (*Yucca elata*).

talwin; ta *V* make rope.

tam__ *CE* tooth: **~hain*** *Vr* have the teeth set on edge with a bitter taste.

tamal, ta *N* a tamale. [<Sp <Aztec *tamálli*]

tamblo; ta *N* a drum. [<Sp *tambor*]

tamhog *s-Vts* consider a nuisance.

tamhon *Vt* scrape off flakes from.

tamiam, m† *Vt,Vtinf* wait for.

tamko *N* a stick for removing fruit from organ pipe cactus.

tamsh *N* a gum of the mouth; ~ **sha'ada** *N* a space from a lost tooth.

tamtol *N* a sparrow.

tanglo; ta *N* a spool; a spinning top.

tanja-lohn *N* a tangerine. [<Sp *tangerina*]

tapaho; *t* *N* a blinder; **~dag** *Vs;* **~dath** *Vt.* [<Sp *tapaojo*]

tapial; *t* *N* paper; a piece of paper; tar paper for building; a legal writ; **kakkei** ~ *N* a questionnarie; **o'od** ~ *N* sandpaper. [<Sp *papel* paper]

¹**tash** *Adv* for a (long) time.

²**tash** *N* time of day; daytime; time; **has** ~ *Adv* some day; **~kaj** *Adv* during a (specified number of) day(s); **kuint g** ~ *Vt* time; *V* count the time; **~-mahhag** *N* the Arizona lupine (*Lupinus sparsiflorus arizonicus*); ~; *t* *N* a day; a clock, watch, sundial, or other timepiece; the sun; any sun.

tasho *Adv* clearly, distinctly; so as to leave no doubt; **~gith** *Vt,Vdt*

clarify, explain; illustrate; reveal;
Vt expose to the sun, sun; ~gith|a
N clarification; explanation;
illustration; revelation; the act of
clarifying, etc.; ~gith|a|s *Vs;*
~gith|tham *N.*
tatai *N* a tendon; a sinew.
tatal/~i (*infm*); *ht N* an uncle junior
to one's mother; ~i|m/~ka|m *N;*
~-oks; ~-o'oki *N* an aunt by
marriage to such an uncle; ~-oksi|m;
~-o'oki|m *N.* See App. 4.
tataniki *N* thunder; ~m *Adv* with a
thundering sound.
tatchua See TACHCHU.
tatk *N* the root of a plant; ~ch*uth Vt*
root; ~kam *N;* ~pig *Vt;* ~t *V*
root.
tatshagi *N* the saltbush (*Atriplex
elegans*).
tawago See TA-WAHGO.
ta-wahgo/tawago *N* tobacco. [<Sp
tabaco]
tehrr *N* a prairie dog. [Imitative]
__tgio *CE occurs with words for
points of the compass* __ward:
si'altgio=*eastward.* [<tahgio]
[1] **__th** *suffix added to adverbial
elements of time to form indefinite
adverbs of time:* HEKITH.
[2] **__th** *suffix added to verbs to indicate
that a condition or incompleted
action is not past tense.* ▶ **__th** is
deleted in present tense except
before *ch,* may also be deleted after
[2] __*k.*
[3] **__th, __i** *suffix added to intransitive
perfective verbs which express a
change of state or condition to form
transitive verbs* cause (a specified
change): SHAPOLKATH.
[1]**tha'a** *s-Vts* be sparing of; **chu** ~thag
s-Vs be selfish, thrifty, or stingy;
chu ~tham *s-Adv* selfishly.
[2]**tha'a, thah, thath'e, thah'i; nehni,
nen'e** *V* fly; jump; (of a bird, plane,
etc.) to leave the ground, take off;
ha'ichu ~tham *N* something that
flies; **uhg** ~tham *N* an airplane.
tha'al† *N* a mother.
thag *N* caliche.
[1]**__thag** (__**tha** before __*j,* __**th** before
prepositions beginning with a vowel)
*suffix added to nouns and verbs to
form nouns* someone or something
belonging to or related to: ALITHAG.
[2]**__thag** (__**dag** after [2]__*a*) *suffix
added to verbs and gerunds* **1.** *to
form stative verbs* be able to:

MELCHUTHADAG; **2.** *to form nouns*
ability to: MELITHAG.
thag__; tha *CE* an action with the
hands: **e** ~tpagtham *N* a piano;
~him *V (pl)* feel one's way along;
~kon/~kuan† *Vt* drop; wipe;
~kon|ith *Vtb;* ~shch *Vts;* ~shp*
Vt touch; press on; play (an
instrument with strings or keys);
~shp|a *N;* ~shun* *Vt;* ~tpag
Vt press on.
thagi__; tha *CE* an action with the
hands: ~mu*n Vt* massage; knead;
~muna *N* a massage; the act of
massaging, etc.; ~o*n Vt* wipe;
~shpakud *N (pl)* a key of a
musical instrument; any instrument
with strings or keys; ~to* *Vt*
discard; leave; omit; release; yield;
~to|kch *Vts.*
thagio'ith *Vt* take care of, support.
thaha; d *Vs* be sitting; (of a vehicle)
to be sitting†; be or be present; be
residing or living; (as an official) to
be incumbent; (as a star in the sky, or
a patch on clothing) to be situated;
sipud ~; **si'ispud** ~ *Vs* be
squatting.
thahi__; thadhai__ *CE* sit: **sipud**
~wua; **si'ispud** ~wua *V* squat;
~thag *Vs;* *s-Vs* be skilled at
riding an animal; ~th|t *Vp* learn
to sit; ~th|t|ahim *V;* ~wua*
Vp sit.
thahithag; htha *N* a tuber; a handle.
thahiwua; thahthhaiwua *N* a
kangaroo rat.
thahk; hth *N* the nose.
thahm; 'atha *Prep* above or over (in
position or authority); on top of; **i** ~
Prep after; ~jed *Prep* from
above; ~juhk *Adv* at noon; *Vs* be
noon; ~kahchim *N* heaven; the
heavens.
thahpi *Intj* an expression of lack of
knowledge about something: who
knows? I don't.
**thahpiu*n; tha Vt* smooth; iron; ~a
N; ~a|kud *Vt* smooth.
[1]**thahpk** *N* an Indian wheat
(*Plantago*); the chia plant (*Salvia
columbariae*).
[2]**thahpk; hth** *s-Adj,s-Vs* (be) smooth;
(be) slippery; (be) naked or bare;
~am *s-Adv* smoothly; ~chu *s-N.*
thahsh, thai, thathsha; hth, thathsh
Vt put or place; appoint to office;
~ch *Vts.*
thahth; ~a'ath *N* an aunt senior to

one's mother; a godmother; ~kam
N one who has such a relative;
~-keli, ~-kekel *N* an uncle by
marriage to such an aunt; ~-keli|m;
~-keki|m *N*. See App. 4.
thai See thahsh.
thai___; *tha*; *ththa CE* sit: ~chug *V*
go along in a sitting position; ride on
an animal or in or on a vehicle;
kownal- ~**kud** *N* a seat of
government, the seat or office of a
government official; ~**kud** *N* a
chair; a seat; a dwelling; ~**sh** *Vt*
cover (something) by sitting on it;
repress; ~**sh|ch** *Vts;* ~**shun*** *Vt*.
tha'ichshp *V* appear from nowhere,
pop up.
tha'ich*uth***; thath'aich***uth***; nehnch***uth***
Vt throw; fly.
tha'ihi*m***, thath'ehim; nehnihi***m***,
nen'ehim** *V* go along jumping.
tha'im*k* *s-V* want to fly.
tha'ithag, thath'eithag; nen'eithag
Vs be able to fly; *s-Vs* be good at
flying, jumping, or bucking.
thaiw See JIWIA.
tha'iwu*ni***, tha'iwush; ne'iopa** *V* rush
out; rush past; escape; *Vt* alert;
warn.
thak___; *hth CE* nose: ~**po** *N;*
~**wua** *V*.
thakam; *d (dist)* *N* a dweller (at a
specified place).
thakosh; *th Vt* muzzle (an animal).
___tham *suffix added to non-stative
verbs to form nouns* one (who does
an action): SHELAMTHAM. [<²___th
and ¹___m]
thapithwua, ~**p** *V* slip, slide.
thash___ *CE* pile; set up: ~**wua*** *Vtp*
pile; set up; ~**wui|s** *Vs*.
thatha See JIWIA.
thath'e; nene'e *V* (of an animal) to
buck; ~**i|thag** *s-Vs* be good at
bucking; **si** ~ *V,Vcmpl* complain.
thathge/thathgi___ *Vt* wrestle;
~**chuth** *Vr* struggle.
thathpk-washai *N* side oats.
¹**thoa;** *th Vs* be alive, have life;
ha'ichu ~**kam** *N* an animal; ~**kam**
N a living creature.
²**thoa;** *th Vp* get well; *s-Vs* be
healthy; ~**jig** *N* health; ~**jith** *Vt*
heal; ~**jith|a** *N*.
tho'ag; *htha N* a mountain.
thoahi*m* *V* (of thunder) to rumble;
hum.
thoajk; *th s-Vs* be wild; timid; afraid;
~**am** *s-N* an untamed animal;
a wild person.

thoakag/thoakthag; *th N* (a) life;
a soul; a lifetime.
thoakthag See THOAKAG.
thohm, thohtho*m***,** *th*, ~**i** *V* copulate,
have sexual intercourse.
thohththa *Vt* do something to.
thohwai *Intj* an expression of
readiness for an activity: ready! now!
tho'i *Adj* raw; ~**g** *Vs* be raw.
tho'ibia, thotho'ibiad *Vt* save,
rescue; deliver; ~**kam;** *tho N* a
savior, a rescuer; a deliverer; ~**thag**
N salvation; deliverance.
thomig *N* a week; *Adv* for a
(specified number of) week(s). [<Sp
domingo Sunday]
Thomig *N* Sunday. [<above]
thotholim *s-Adv* calmly; in a
self-controlled manner; ~**a/~k**
s-Vs; ~**a|t** *Vp;* ~**a|t|ahim** *V;*
~**chuth** *Vt* calm; ~**thag** *s-N*
calmness; self-control;
self-discipline.
tiampo; *ti N* (a) time. [<Sp *tiempo*]
tianna/chiantho; *ti/ch N* a store.
[<Sp *tienda*]
tih *N* tea. [<Eng]
tihha *N* a washer for a bolt.
tihna; *t N* a tub. [<Sp *tina*]
tihtili *N* a talking doll; a puppet. [<Sp
títere]
ti-kihla *N* wine. [<Sp *tequila*]
ti-lahnthi; *ti___la N* suspenders. [<Sp
tirantes]
tlahmba; *la N* a tramp. [<Sp *trampa*]
tlohgih; *lo N* a truck. [<Sp *troque*]
___to, ___tod, ___ttod *suffix added to
non-stative verbs and to verbal
combining elements ending with*
¹___*i (def.* 2) *to form verbs of
completed action* finish: KO'ITO,
THAGITO.
¹**toa** *N* the oak tree (*Quercus*).
²**toa** See CHEHK.
to'a, toa, ~**w, toa'i** *Vt* pour; ~**kch**
Vts have (something) poured. See
also ²CHEHK.
toaya; *t N* a towel. [<Sp *toalla*]
tobaw; *t N* a species of hawk
(unidentified).
tobtham *N* a hunt caller, leader of
the hunt.
todk; *to V* snore; growl; roar; *N* a
horsefly.
todwin; *to Vt* irritate; disturb.
toha; tohta *s-Adj,s-Vs* (be) white; *N*
a dime; ~**h** *Vp* become white;
~**jith** *Vt* whiten; bleach;
~**jith|a|kud** *N* a substance used for
whitening; face powder; bleach;

~-komikam N (a) cake (lit.
something white-backed); ~ma
s-Adv brightly, with a bright hue.
tohawes N the brittlebush plant
(Encelia farinosa).
tohb Vt wring; twist.
tohbi; to N the cottontail rabbit.
tohdai Intj an expression showing that
one is resigned to a consequence: so,
so then, etc.
tohlo; t N a bull. [<Sp toro]
Tohmog N the Milky Way
constellation.
tohmthag N (a) late fruit.
tohn; hto N a knee; an axle.
tohnk; 'oto N a dike, bank, or dam;
a hill; a wave of water; ~ath* Vt
dike, bank, or dam up; cause to form
a wave; ~tha N the act or an
instance of diking, etc.; dike-work.
tohnto; to N a pervert; a fool; a
degenerate; Adv perverted; foolish;
degenerate; ~chuth Vt pervert;
degenerate; ~dag Vs; ~m s-Adv
pervertedly; foolishly; degenerately;
~m|th|ad|dag N perversion,
foolishness; degeneracy. [<Sp tonto
a fool, stupid person]
tohono N (a) desert; the south.
Tohono O'othham N the Desert
People, the Papago people.
tohta heosig See NOD.
tohwa; to N a turkey; ~ mad N a
turkey poult.
to'ith Vtb set out or aside for
(someone); bet.
toka; t N field hockey; ~da N field
hockey; ~him V go to play field
hockey.
tokayo; t N a namesake. [<Sp
tocayo]
tokih N raw or absorbent cotton;
cotton string; any material made
of cotton.
tokithhud; t N a spider; ~ chuaggia
N a spider web.
toliant; to Vt aggravate. [<Sp torear]
tol-nihyo N a nut for a bolt. [<Sp
tornillo a screw]
to-mahti N a tomato. [<Sp tomate]
to-mohli; t—mo N an automobile.
[<Sp automóvil]
ton__; hto CE knee: ~hain* Vt;
~wua* V kneel; bump the knee.
tondam Adj brilliant; shining; Adv
brilliantly.
¹toni s-N heat (temperature); ~ko
s-Adv in the heat.
²toni; ho s-Adj,s-Vs (be) hot
(temperature); ~h Vp (of weather,

food, etc.) to get hot; ~h|him V;
~jig s-N a fever; ~jith/~th Vt
heat (up); ~m s-Adv hotly (lit.
only).
toniabkam N (a) summer.
tonlig; to (dist) N (a) light (lit. and
fig.).
tonod, hon V shine; twinkle.
tonolith, hon; t, hon Vt shine onto;
give light to; ~ch Adv by
revelation; i ~ Vt enlighten.
to'olwad N (an) off-season fruit; ~ag
Vs be (an) off-season fruit.
tonom, ~k, ~muk; tonk, ~k,
~kko'o Vp get thirsty; ~chuth
Vt; ~kam; ~koi N* a thirsty
person or animal; ta ~ma s-Vs be
no relief from thirst; ~thag N
thirst.
to'owagi; ht s-Adj,s-Vs (be) faded.
topithk; 'oto s-Adj,s-Vs (be) askew.
tosi'igo† N bacon. [<Sp tocino]
tosiw; t N the western meadowlark
(Sturnella neglecta).
toskoni; t V swell, become swollen.
tothkesh; to V jerk with fright.
tohsith; to Vt alarm, startle; frighten;
i ~ Vt alert.
totoni N an ant; a'al ~ N a small
ant; a'anam ~ N a feathered ant;
chuchk ~ N a black ant; uhw ~
N an odorous ant; wepegi ~ N a
red ant.
totp__ CE simmer: ~k V simmer,
be at or just below the boiling point;
~sith Vt cook by simmering.
totshagi N foam from the mouth;
bubbles.
towash; t† N a handkerchief; a towel.
Tuhlgo; tu N a Jew. [<Sp Turco
Turk]
tuhngo; tu N an overgarment
extending below the waist or over the
skirt, a tunic. [<Sp tunica]
tuhwo; tu N a tube; a lamp chimney.
[<Sp tubo]

U

__u See ²__T.
u'a Vt carry; ~pa* Vt bring; arrive
carrying.
uam; u'am s-Adj,s-Vs (be) soiled or
dirty; (be) polluted; (be) vile; ~chu
s-N; ~hun Vt soil, dirty; pollute.
udawhag N the cattail plant (Typha
angustifolia).
ugijith/ujugith; 'u Vt shake; rock.

uhdwis *N* a grape; ~-**gakithag** *N* a raisin; ~-**je'e** *N* a grape vine (lit. only). [<Sp *uvas* <*uva* grape]

uhg; '*u* *Adv* in a high place (lit. and fig.); up; ~**chu** *N* a chief, a head man; a director; a chairperson; a chairman; ~**k** *Adj,Vs* (be) high up (lit. only); ~**k|a** *Vp* rise; ~**k|a|him** *V*.

uhhum See UHPAM.

uhimal; '*u* *N* a large velvet-covered ant, the cow killer (*Dasymutilla occidentalis*).

uhksh; '*u* *N* the calf of a leg; ~**a** *N* a wall or fence used as a windbreak.

uhli; '*u* *N* rubber; asphalt roofing. [<Sp *hule*]

uhpad; '*u* *N* the cat's-claw bush of the legume family (*Acacia greggii*).

uhpam/uhhum *Adv* back to an earlier place or condition.

¹**uhpio;** '*u* *N* a skunk.

²**uhpio;** '*u* *N* a willow tree; the English walnut tree.

uhs; '*u* *N* a tree; a bush; a stick; a crutch; wood; (*pl.*) a wood, woods; forest timber; *Adj* wooden; ~-**bawi** *N* (*pl*) the black-eyed pea (*Leguminosae*) (lit. tree bean); ~-**jewedbad** *N* the lotebush (*Condalia lycioides*); ~-**kokmagi** *N* the arrowweed or arrowwood plant (*Pluchea sericea*).

uhsh; '*u* *N* the stinger of an insect; an arrowhead.

uhw; '*u* *s-Adj,s-Vs* (be) odorous or smelly; ~**a** *Vp* give off an odor; enter estrus; ~**a|him** *V* continue giving off an odor; be in estrus; ~**a|ith** *s-Vt* become repulsed by; ~**a|i|thag** *s-N* disgust; ~**a|ith|chuth** *Vt* disgust; repulse; ~**a|lig** *N* an odor; estrus; ~**chu** *s-N;* ~**math** *Vt* perfume; ~**o** *Vp* stop giving off an odor; terminate estrus.

Uhwalig Mashath† *N* November (lit. mating odor month).

ui See BEHE.

u'i See BEHI, BEI.

uiwi; '*u* *V* expel gas through the anus.

ujugith See UGIJITH.

ulin, '*u; h'u* *Vt* hold (something) out; *Adj* of a (specified) characteristic; ~**ch** *Vts* have (something) held out; be detaining; **gahi i** ~ *Vt* tilt; ~**ig** *Vs* be dwelling or abiding; (of a skill or aptitude) to be abiding (in its possessor); ~**ith** *Vtb;* ~**k|a|him** *V*.

ulinihogig‡ *N* rest; relaxation.

ulinihogith; *h'u* ‡ *Vt* cause to rest; *Vr* rest.

ulinithag; '*u* *N* talent.

ulu__; '*u* *CE* rock, sway: ~**gith** *Vt* rock (a baby); ~**kud** *N* a cradle.

um; '*u* *N* a thigh.

umug *N* the sotol plant (*Dasylirion wheeleri*).

upulig *N* a wart.

us__; '*u* *CE* a stick: ~**kon** *Vt* hook; fork; gore; ~**kon|a** *N;* ~**kon|a|kud** *N* a scoop; a fork.

usaga; '*u* *N* a gavel; a hockey stick; ~**kam** *N* a presiding officer; a judge; a hockey player.

ushabi; '*u* *N* resin, sap, or pitch; ~**thag** *N* resin, sap, or pitch of a specified plant; *Vs* have resin, etc.

utko; '*u* *N* a stalk of the mountain yucca plant; ~-**jehj** *N* the mountain yucca plant (*Yucca schottii*).

¹**u'u** *N* a rifle shell; a war arrow.

²**u'u** See BEHE.

u'uhig See U'UWHIG.

u'umhaidath *Vt* put a head on (an arrow).

u'uwhig/u'uhig *N* a bird.

__uw *suffix added to combining elements to form intransitive verbs have a* (specified) *odor:* BITUW, HI'UW.

uwi; '*u* *N* a female; a woman; ~**chuth** *Vt* make one a woman; alter to feminine behavior; ~**ga** *N* a sister; ~**mk** *s-V* want a woman; be girl-crazy.

uwikwuad; '*u* *N* a sissy; a coward; an effeminate male; ~**ag** *Vs*.

W

wa/-a *indicates shared knowledge or expectation:* **Kut am-o wa hih**=*He'd go there as we know;* **Nt-o wa ep m-nei**=*I assume I'll see you again.*

wa'akih; wahpakih *N* the mound of an ancient dwelling.

wa'akpan/w'apkan *Vt* sprinkle with liquid.

wa'apkan See WA'AKPAN.

wa'athk; wa'awapathk *Vs* be naked; be smooth.

wabsh/hash (**wa__absh/ha__ash**) *Adv* just, only, merely; *Adj* mere.

wabsh chum/hash chum *Adj*

precedes any indefinite form any or
any__ whatever; ~ **has**, ~ **haschu**
Pron anything; ~ **has masma** *Adv*
anyway; ~ **hebai** *Adv* anywhere;
~ **hedai** *Pron* anyone; ~ **he'ekia**
Adj any number of; ~ **he'es** *Adj*
any amount of; ~ **hekith** *Adv* any
time.
wabshaba/hashaba/shaba *Conj* but.
wachchui; *p* (*dist*) *Vt* bathe; *Vr*
bathe; swim; ~**mk** *s-Vr*.
wachiho; *p N* a wooden bowl. [<Sp
batihoja a gold or silver beater, a
sheet-metal worker]
wachki; *p N* a reservoir; a pond.
wachp *V* dive into water.
wa chum *Conj* though, although,
even though.
wachum, ~**ok**, ~**muk**; **wachk**, ~**k**,
~**ko'o** *Vp* drown; submerge; dive;
sink.
wachumtham *N* a diver; the mud hen
or coot (*Fulica americana*).
wadag; *p s-Adj,s-Vs* (be) wet.
wadagi *N* (a) juice; ~**th** *Vt* wet.
wag; *hpa N* a hole.
wagima; *pa s-Vs* be industrious;
~**kam** *s-N** an industrious person
or animal; ~**m** *s-Adv* industriously.
wah*g*, ~**i**, **wapga** *Vt* moisten; soak;
irrigate; ~**a** *N* cement; dough.
wahhigam; wapahigam *N* a species
of slender water snake (unidentified).
wahia See WAWHIA.
wah*k*, ~**i**; **wapke**; **wahp***k*; ~**i**, **wapke**
V enter; sink in (lit. only); ~**im***k*
s-V; ~**ith** *Vt* bring in; take (into);
insert; ~**ith** **chehanig-ch** ed *Vt* take
to court, bring legal suit against; ~**s**
Vs be (in); be inserted or entered
(in).
wahks See WAHKUS.
wahkus/wahks; *hpa N* a rug; a floor;
a mat; a bedroll; a sleeping bag.
wahl *N* a rifle shell. [<Sp *bala*]
wahlko; *pa N* a boat; a trough; **ge'e** ~
N a ship. [<Sp *barco* boat, ship]
wahlthi; *pa N* a bucket. [<Sp *balde*]
wahm *Adv* especially.
wahmug *N* a mosquito.
wahmul *N* a swamp.
wahmuth *Vt* arouse to action;
promote (as a cause).
wahngo; *pa N* a financial institution,
a bank. [<Sp *banco*]
wahn-ohg See WAJELHO.
wah'o *N* tongs; saguaro rib tongs used
for harvesting cactus buds and fruit;
~**sith** *Vt* wedge.

[1]**wahpai** *N* a saguaro cactus rib.
[2]**wahpai** *N* the container for the game
of GINIS.
wahpk *N* bamboo, cane, or reed.
wahs *N* a species of plant used for
pink dye (unidentified).
wahshaj *Adv* over there.
wahshan *Adv* up there; way over there
to one side.
wahso; *p N* a can. [<Sp *vaso* a
drinking glass]
wahud *s-V* sweat.
wahul__ *CE* sweat: ~**ch***uth* *s-Vt;*
~**thag** *N* sweat; *s-Vs*.
wahw *N* one's father in a clan of the
buzzard moiety; ~**gam** *N*. See
App. 3.
wahyo; *p N* a yellowish-brown horse;
~**dag**/~**g** *s-Vs*.
wa'i, **-a'i** *Adv* only, solely,
exclusively; just; exactly: **Do wa'i
gi'ik tash mat am e cheh**=*It's been
exactly four days since he was put
away* (*PNT John 11:39*); *Correl.
Conj* not only . . . but also: **pi heg-a'i
kch-abshaba ihtha ehp**=*not only
that but this also.*
wa'i*g*; *hpa Vt* get a liquid (usu.
water); ~**amed**; ~**op*** *Vtb;*
~**amed|am**; ~**o|kam** *N;* ~**i** *Vt*
household water; the act of getting
water; ~**ith** *Vtb;* ~**kud** *N* a
container for water; a pitcher; a
bucket or pail; a pot or olla;
~**pa*** *Vt*.
waik; '*awa Adj,N* (a) three; (a) third.
waikka; *pa N* a ditch.
Waik-tash *N* Wednesday.
waila *Vt,Vr* dance; ~**kud** *N* a dance
floor; ~**thag** *N* a dance. [<Sp *baile*
a dance]
wainomi; *pa N* (a) metal; an iron; a
knife; *Adj* metalic, of metal; **aj** ~
N a telephone wire; ~**-kalit** *N* a
railroad car; a train; ~**-kohlasham**
N the green June beetle
(*Ruteliinae*); **s-jehjeg** ~ *N* a
screen (as for a door or window).
wai*th*, *hpa*, *ppa Vt* call, summon;
invite; ~**a** *N* the act of calling, etc.;
one who is called, etc. ~**a|dag** *N* an
invitation; a summons; a calling (as
to the ministry); ~**tham** *N* a caller
or summoner; an inviter.
waiwel *N* the cockleburr weed
(*Xanthium*).
wajelho; *p*/**wahn-ohg** *N* the whiptail
lizard (*Cnemidophorus*).
wajuk *N* a goldfinch.

wakaig; *p N* the mud hen or coot (*Fulica americana*).

wakch *Vts* have (something) soaking.

wak'e; *p Vt* milk; squeeze.

wakial; *p N* a cowboy. [<Sp *vaquero*]

wakimagi; *pa s-Vs* be ragged; be frayed; ~**him** *V.*

wako; *p N* a water gourd; a canteen.

wakodk See GAKODK.

wakola; *p N* flood debris.

wakolim See WAKOLIW.

wakoliw/wakolim *N* the south; ~ **thahgio** *Adv* south, in the south; ~ **wui** *Adv* south, southward.

wakon; *p Vt* wash; *V* (*pl*) wash clothes; *Vr* wash oneself; ~**a** *N;* ~**a|dag** *N* the activity of washing; a baptism; ~**ch** *Vs* be washed; ~**i** *N;* ~**ith** *Vtb;* ~**tham** *N* a launderer; a baptizer; the dock or curlyleaf plant (*Rumex crispus*).

wakui___; *p CE* diarrhea: ch**uth** *Vt* cause to have diarrhea; ~**thag** *N* diarrhea.

wakumagi; *p s-Adj,s-Vs* (be) rusty; (be) rust-colored; ~**chu** *s-N;* ~**thag** *N* dry remains; rust.

walaho† *Vt* play cards. [<Sp *barajo* first person sing. of *barajar* to mingle or mix]

walin; *p N* a barrel. [<Sp *barril*]

walit; *p N* a digging bar. [<Sp *barrote* thick bar or rail]

wa-lohn *N* a gallon. [<Sp *galón*]

wamad; ham (*dist*) *N* any non-poisonous snake; **chuk** ~ *N* the black racer snake; **wegi** ~ *N* the black racer snake (lit. a red snake).

wamig, ham, ~**i, hpa** *V* rise from lying, get up, arise.

wamigith, ham; wahpagith, wappagith *Vt* raise from lying.

wani___ *CE* a pulling or influencing action: ~**chk*** *Vt* pull on; influence; ~**chk|wua*** *Vt* pull along, wrench away; win the opinion or allegiance of; ~**med,** ~**mmed** *Vt* lead, guide; ~**med|tham** *N* a leader or guide; ~**mun, wapanimun** *Vt* pull pieces or strands from; ~**'on, wapni'osh** *Vt* stretch; ~**'ontham** *N* an accordian.

wanjel; *pa N* a flag. [<Sp *bandera*]

wan-nihha/wan-thihha; *pa — ni/thi N* a pan. [<Sp *bandeja*]

want *CE* rip: ~**p** *Vt* wrench apart; tear; ~**shp*** *Vt* tear; rip.

wan-thihha See WAN-NIHHA.

wapkon *Vt* launder.

wapshud *N* a blister.

washa *N* a covered basket; a suitcase; a woven storage case; a box†.

washai/washa'i *N* grass.

Washai Gakithag Mashath *N* September (lit. dry grass month).

washomi; *p Vt* dip out; ~**ch** *Vts;* ~**i** *N* a drink; ~**ith** *Vtb;* ~**wua*** *Vt* mix by dipping and pouring.

wathathk; '**ap** *Vs* be shiny; be bald.

watksh *N* a sand lizard.

watopad *V* get worms.

watopi; *p N* a fish; a worm; ~ **hithod** *N* a sardine; a salmon; **memhetham** ~ *N* a glowworm, a larva of certain species of the Phengodida family; **shuhthagi-ch-ed** ~ *N* a fish; **wamad** ~ *N* an eel.

watto; *p N* an overhead man-made shelter, a ramada.

wa'u, ~**p** *Vp* get wet; ~**ch,** ~**chchek** *Vt* soak; ~**sig;** *p s-Adj,s-Vs* (be) dewy or damp; ~**sim** *s-Adv* in a damp condition, damply; ~**sith** *Vt* dampen; ~**thag** *N* dampness; dew; *s-Vs* be damp.

wa'ug; *p N* a straw; a stalk; a chaff, a stem.

waw; ~**pai** *N* bedrock; a cliff; a rock.

wawan; wawpan *Vt* lead; ~**i** *Vs* be lying in a line.

wawhia/wahia; waipia *N* a well.

wawini; wawpini *V* quench the thirst; ~**g** *s-Vs* be thirst-quenching.

wawli; *pa N* a trunk; a valise. [<Sp *baúl*]

wawnadag; wawpnadag *N* a ridge pole; a line.

wawnim; wawpnim *N* an arrangement or series, a row; a verse.

wawuk; waupuk *N* a raccoon.

wechij; *p Adj* new; young; fresh; ~**him** *V;* ~**ith** *Vtp.*

Wechij Ahithag *N* New Year.

wecho; '**ewe/p** *Prep* under; ~**kam** *N* an underling; ~**thag** *N* underclothes; an undershirt; a T-shirt; undershorts, underpants.

wechun; *p Vt* burden.

[1]**wegi** *N* red clay.

[2]**wegi;** *p s-Adj,s-Vs* (be) red; ~**chu** *N;* ~**h** *Vp;* ~**h|him** *V;* ~**ma** *s-Adv* brightly; in a red or red-hot state; ~ **uhs;** ~ **u'us** *N* the tamarix shrub or tree (*Tamarix*) (lit. red stick).

wehbig See WEHGAJ.

[1]**wehch;** *p* (*dist*) *s-N* a pound

(weight); *s-Adj* heavy; burdensome; *s-Vs* be heavy, etc.; ~**chu** *s-N;* ~**him** *V;* ~**thag** *N* (a) weight.
²**wehch** See KAHCH.
wehgaj/wehbig; '*ewe Prep* around, behind.
wehhejed; we'ewejed *Prep* on behalf of, for; for the counter-benefit of; for the purpose of; ~**kam** *N* (a) benefit to.
wehm/~aj; '*ewe Prep* with; **ab e** ~**jim/ab e** ~**kam** *N* a team; ~**aj** *Vts* be with; **e** ~ *Adv* together; in a group of (a specified number); ~**jim/~kam** *N* a companion; an associate; a fellow member; ~ **kihkam** *N* a spouse; a spouse or spouses and his/her or their children (lit. co-dweller).
wehmaj See WEHM.
wehmkal; *pe N* a clan companion; a totem. See App. 3.
wehmt; *pe Vt* help; marry; ~**a** *N;* ~**a|dag** *N* help; **pi am hu i e** ~ *Vr* disagree; ~**tham** *N* a helper.
wehnag; *p N* a relative of one's own generation; a brother; a sister; a cousin; ~**a|m** *N; Nr (pl)*; ~**s** *Vts* (of nonliving things) to be together.
wehnath; *p Vt* assemble (parts); combine (ingredients); add; ~**ch**, ~**k** *a dependent verb which functions like the English preposition* with; ~**ch** *Vts* have in an assembled, etc., condition; *Vrs* be in an assembled, etc., condition.
wehog See ELITH.
wehoh See WOHOH.
wehoh__ See WOHOH.
wehpeg *Adj,Adv* first; ~**at** *V* become the first; ~**kam** *N* the first (one).
wehs *(pl); p (dist) Adj* all; each, every; both; *Pron* all; both; ~**chu** *N* all of one's possessions; ~**ig** *Vs* be of sound mind or in good mental health; ~**ijj** *Pron* all of (a group or substance); both of; ~**ko** *Adv* everywhere; ~**ko|jed** *Adv* from everywhere; *Prep* from everywhere in; **pi** ~**ig|kam** *N* a victim of mental or emotional disorder; a retardate; ~ **tashkaj** *Adv* every day; daily; *Adj* everyday; daily.
welgim; *pe*† *s-N* one shrewd at bargaining.
Welgim; *pe*† *s-Adj* Jewish; Hungarian; Russian; of or relating to the Jewish, Hungarian, or Russian

people or their languages; *s-N* a Jew; a Hungarian; a Russian; the Hebrew, Hungarian, or Russian language.
wenog *Adv* then, at that time.
wepegith *Vr* go to the movies. [<wegi *and* __ith]
wepgih *N* lightning; a battery; a flashlight; a motion picture, a movie, the movies; electricity; *Adj* electric. [<wegi]
wepo; '*ep Adj* even or level; equal, (the) same; alike; *Adv* alike; *Correl. Conj* as...as: **Huan o wepo s-ap hab wua g e-chikpan mo hi g Husi**=*John does his work as well as Joe; Vrs* be alike; ~**dag** *Vs* have characteristics similar (to what is specified); *s-Vs* be level; ~**dag|im** *s-Adv* evenly; **i** ~**t** *Vt* do the same as, imitate; **sha heg** ~ *Vinf,Vcmpl* appear, seem.
west-mahm; *p Adj,N* (a) ten; (a) tenth.
wewa'ak/wewkam/wewa'am; *p Adj,N* (a) seven; (a) seventh.
weweg *V* drone; hum; whir; buzz; ~**im** *s-Adv*.
wewkam See WEWA'AK.
wewkud; *p N* a sling shot; a bullroarer.
¹**wia;** *pi s-Vt* ruin; wear.
²**wia;** *pi' Vt* hunt; stalk.
wi'a, wia; *pi, wia'i Vt* leave (something) behind; ~**him** *Vt* sneak up on; save up bit by bit; ~**m** *s-Vt* want to be left, leave (something).
Wialos *N* Friday. [<Sp *viernes*]
wiapo *N* the pubic hair of a male.
wiappo'oge'el/wiappoi; wihpiop *N* a boy, a young man.
wiappoi See WIAPPO'OGE'EL.
widut; *pi Vt* swing; wave; flutter; **sikol** ~ *Vt* twirl.
widwua; *pi Vt* stir, beat.
wiha; *hpi N* the penis.
wihbam *N* milkweed (*Asclepiadaceae*); the gum of this plant; chewing gum.
wihbi *N* milk.
wihgi *N* a pin feather; the down of a bird.
wihgith *V* hold a harvest ceremony; ~**a** *N* a harvest ceremony; a prayer stick decorated with bird-down for use in this ceremony.
wihkol; *pi N* one's relative of the great grandparent generation; one's relative of the great grandchild

generation (Ko-lohthi dialect); ~i|m
N. See App. 4.

wihnam; *p s-Adv* with difficulty,
difficulty.

wihni, wihpin**, p,** ~i *Vt* lick with the
tongue.

wihnim; *pi N* a singer and dancer in
the harvest ceremony.

wihnk; *pi s-Adj,s-Vs* (as of meat) to
be tough; (be) attached tightly; (be)
difficult; (be) tight; ~a|hi**m** *V;*
~a|th* *Vt* tighten; ~ch**u** *s-N.*

wihnui; *p (dist) N* whiskey; **a'ud-**~
N agave wine. [<Sp *vino* wine]

wihog; *pi N* a bean pod;
~-**babhaijith** *N* the stag beetle
(*Lucanidae*); ~-**mad** *N* a beetle that
feeds on mesquite beans; ~**thag** *Vs.*

wihol; *pi (dist) N* a pea.

wihonagi; *pi s-Vs* be ragged.

wihos; *pi N* vomit, regurgitation;
~ch**uth** *Vt.*

wihot**;** *pi V* vomit, regurgitate.

wihpedho *N* a testicle; ~**pi**g *Vt*
castrate.

wihpsh *N* a wasp; a hornet; any
wasp-like insect.

wihs; *p s-Vs* be ragged.

wihshad; *pi N* one's relative of the
great grandchild generation; one's
relative of the great grandparent
generation (Ko-lohthi dialect);
~**kam** *N; Nr (pl).* See App. 4.

wihthakud; *pi N* an oblong stone
used to grind grain.

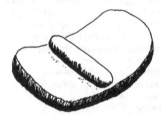

WIHTHAKUD

wi'i, wih, wip'i, wih'i; *hpi V* stay,
remain or be left; ~s *Vs* be left over
or remaining.

wi'i__ *CE* a current of air or water:
~**chk*** *Vt* wash or blow against;
~**chk|wua** *Vt;* ~**hin*** *Vt* wash
away with water; ~**kon*** *Vt* erode.

Wi'ihanig Mashath *N* October (lit.
left-over gathering month).

wi'ikam; wihpkam *(dist) N* a
remnant; a survivor; **hejel** ~ *N* a
widow or widower; an orphan.

wi'in; *p Vt* flood; ~**og** *N* a
water-borne object; ~**thag** *N*
a flood.

wi'inim See JUHPIN.

wi'ishani; wipishani *N* a small wash,
rivulet.

wi'ith**;** *p Vtb* leave (something) for
(someone).

wi'ithag; *hpi N* a leftover.

wijin; *p Vt* twist; ~**a** *N* (a) rope; (a)
cord (string); ~**at** *V* make a rope;
~i *s-Adj,s-Vs* (be) wrinkled.

wikla; *p Vdt* owe; **ab** ~**t** *Vdt* go into
debt to (someone) for (a specified
amount); ~**dag** *N* (a) debt; a bill
(amount owed).

wilant; *p V* hold a wake; keep watch
for cattle; ~**a** *N* a funeral wake; a
vigil for trapping stock. [<Sp *velar*
to watch, be vigilant]

wil-gohgih/wil-gohthi *N* an apricot or
apricot tree. [<Sp *albaricoque* an
apricot]

wil-gohthi See WIL-GOHGIH.

__**win** *suffix added to combining
elements to form transitive verbs* rub
or scratch (a surface) or pulverize (a
substance) (in a specified manner):
CHELWIN, KEHIWIN.

wi-nahl *N* vinegar. [<Sp *vinagre*]

wini__ *CE* action of the lips: ~**kon***
Vt lick; ~**kon|tham** *Nr* that which
is licked (as an ice cream cone);
~**um** *Vr* lick the lips.

winma *s-Adv* with difficulty,
difficultly.

winogim; *p s-Adv* in a swaying or
weaving manner.

winthani; *pi N* a window. [<Sp
ventana]

wio-lihn; *pi N* a violin. [<Sp *violin*]

wi'omi *Vdt* drain (a liquid) from.

wipi'a; wipi'__ *Vt* hunt; stalk;
~**md|am;** ~**o|kam** *N* a hunter;
~**med*** *Vt* go hunting.

wipih *N* a breast, an udder; a nipple;
~-**si'itham** *N* the common
primrose plant (*Primula vulgaris*)
(lit. breast sucker).

wipismal *N* the hummingbird; the
black-chinned hummingbird
(*Archilochus alexandri*); the Costa's
hummingbird (*A. costae*).

wipnoi *N* the branched pencil cholla
cactus (*Cylindropuntia ramosissima*);
the desert Christmas cactus (*C.
leptocaulis*); the bush cholla cactus
(*C. arbuscula*); the edible bud of any
of these.

wisag See WISHAG.

wishag/wisag; *p N* the sharp-shinned hawk, the chicken hawk (*Accipitridae striatus*).

wishbad; *p N* a deceased ancestor.

wisig-lihtha; *p N* a bicycle. [<Sp *bicicleta*]

wisilo; *p N* a calf; ~ **chuhkug** *N* veal. [<Sp *becerro*]

wisit *Vt* visit. [<Sp *visitar*]

witkwua *Vt* roll up (as a sleeve).

wi'ushanig; *pi* (*dist*) *N* a ripple of sand.

wiw *N* wild tobacco, desert tobacco (*Nicotiana trigonophylla*).

wiwa *N* the pancreas.

wi-yohthi; *pi — yo N* an acorn; ~ **je'e** *N* an oak tree. [<Sp *bellota* an acorn]

[1]wo/ho, (-o after consonants; w__ -o sentence initially) *indicating future tense or willingness* will; would: **Am ant-aha wo hih**=*Then I'll go there;* **Want-o hih**=*I'm going to go.*

[2]wo (-o after consonants) *the imperative plural indicator:* **Am g haha wo hihim**=*Go there then.*

wo'__ See MEL.

__wo See __PO.

wogsha; *po N* a quiver, an arrow case; a step child, an adopted child.

wo-ha-hohntam; *ho N* a fiancé.

wo-ha-kuntam; *ku N* a fiancée.

wohg; *po N* a road; a path; a trail; the course of (a heavenly body, etc.); **~ith** *Vt* instruct in the ways of life; **~ith|a** *N* any such instructions, the act of so instructing; **wainomi-** ~ *N* a railroad.

wohiw *Vt* singe.

wohk; *hp N* the stomach; the abdomen; the belly; the hull of a ship or boat; ~ **ko'okthag** *N* a stomach ache.

wohla; *p Vr* play ball; have a party.

wohlih; *p Adj* hornless; dehorned; cropped; *N* a hornless (etc.) animal; **~chuth** *Vt* dehorn.

wohlim *s-Vs* be cropped.

wohni, wohpon, *p,* **~i** *Vt* pick; harvest; uproot (plants).

wohoh/wehoh *Adv* truly, indeed, in fact; *Vs* be the truth; **ab ~chuth** *Vt* believe in; **~chuth** *s-Vt,* *s-Vcmpl* believe; **~chuth|a** *N* what one believes, a belief; the act of believing; **~chuth|a|dag** *N* faith; **~chuth|tham** *N* a believer; **~'i** *Adv* very; **~kam** *N* truth; fact;

someone or something genuine; **~kam|chuth** *Vt,Vcmpl* testify; acknowledge; prove; affirm; certify; *Vinf* prove; **~kam|chuth|a** *N* testimony; acknowledgment; proof; affirmation; certification; **~m** *s-Adv* truly; indeed; **~ma** *s-Vs* seem to be true or real; **pi ~kam** *N* an unpremeditated untruth; a falsehood.

wohp, woppo *Vp* camp; stay overnight.

wohpo'i__ See MEL__.

wohpo'o See MED.

wohppo'ith *Vdt* deprive of, take away from; **~a** *N* deprivation; **~a|dag** *s-Vs* be of a grasping nature.

wohshag; *p N* a pocket. [<Sp *bolsa*]

wohth, woi, woptha *Vt* lay down; put in writing; sign (one's name); **~ch** *Vts* have in a reclining position, etc.

wohtha; *p†N* a boot. [<Sp *bota*]

woi See WOHTH.

wo'i See MEL.

wo'i__; wohpi__ *CE* in a prone position: **~chug** *Vt;* **~him** *V* move in a prone position, roll over; **~kud** *N* a place to lie down; a bed; **~wua*** *Vp* lie down; flow out flat.

woikchuth; *po Vr* boast, show off.

woikima; *po s-Vs* be boastful, be proud; **~thag** *N* boasting, boastfulness; pride.

woikshanimkam; *po s-N* a braggart; a proud person; a show-off.

wo'isheg *V* wait.

woiwis; *opo N* an ox. [<Sp *bueyes* oxen]

wojgi See WOSK.

woji See WOSK.

wok__; *p CE* the belly or abdomen; **~jith** *Vr* shake oneself; belly-dance; **~sh|ch** *Vts;* **~shp*** *Vt.*

wonami; *p N* a hat. **~m** *N.*

[1]wo'o; wohp; wo'owop *Vs* (of things that can move, as people, animals, or liquid) to be lying flat; be in the uterus.

[2]wo'o; *p N* a natural pond.

wo'olakhim/woshthakhim *V* trot.

wo'oshani; woposhani *N* a watershed; (a) lowland.

wo'otk *N* a valley.

wopishul *N* a centipede.

wopiwul; *hp N* a caterpillar.

wopo *N* (a) hair of the body; fur; **~pig** *Vt.*

wopsi See WOSK.

woptha See WOHTH.

wosho; *p N* a rat.

wosk/woji/wojgi (*infm*); *p*/**wopsi**
(*infm*) *N* one's paternal
grandfather; one's great-uncle on this
side; ~**k|a|m** *N* one who has such a
relative; ~**-keli;** ~**-kekel** *N* one's
great-uncle on this side; ~**-keli|m;**
~**-kekeli|m** *N;* ~**-oks;** ~**-o|oki**
N one's great-aunt on this side;
~**-oksi|m;** ~**-o'oki|m** *N.* See App. 4.

woskud See WOSUN.

wosmad; *p N* the relationship of
a man's son's child to the man
and to his peers, a grandchild,
great-nephew, great-niece; ~**am** *N;*
N (*pl*). See App. 4.

wosma-je'e; wopsmad-ha-je'e;
wopsmad-ha-jehj *N* a man's
daughter-in-law; a woman's
father-in-law, etc.; ~**m** *N.*
See App. 4.

wosma-jehjim; wopsmad-ha-jehjim
Nr (*pl*) those mutually related as
daughter-in-law, father-in-law. See
App. 4.

wosun, *ps,p Vt* sweep; ~**a** *N*
refuse; the act of sweeping;
~**a|kud/woskud; wopskud** *N* a
broom or brush.

wothalt *V* vote; ~**a** *N* an election.
[<Sp *votar* to vote]

wothwua *Vt* lay down.

wotoni; *p N* a button; ~**dag** *Vs;*
~**dath** *Vt* button. [<Sp
botones<*botón*]

wowoit; wohppoit *N* an aunt junior to
one's father; ~**kam** *N* one who has
such an aunt; ~**-keli;** ~**-kekel** *N* an
uncle by marriage to such an aunt;
~**-keli|m;** ~**-kekeli|m** *N.* See
App. 4.

¹_wu/_wua, _**wup** *suffix added to
combining elements to form verbs of
completed action* **1.** bump or put (a
specified body part against
something): TONWUA; **2.** take a
particular position or stance:
KEKIWUA; **3.** put in a particular
position: KESHWUA.

²_wu/_wua, _**wup** (all with
singular objects); _**shulig** (with
plural objects) *suffix added to
transitive verbs to form causative
verbs* move (in a specified manner):
HONCHKWUA.

³_wu/_wua, _**wup** *a suffix added
to nouns to form verbs* become.

¹wua/wui_, juh/juni_, jujju, juhni

habVt do, perform; *habVr* engage
in a (specified) activity, to happen;
habVtinf cause; **ab** ~ *habVt* apply
(as a patch); attach; put on (as
clothes); **gawul** ~ *Vt* change; **gm**
hu ~ *habVt* discard; do away with;
i ~ *habVt* destroy, do away with;
move (something); ~**kch** *Vts* have
on (as clothes or a harness), wear;
mahsko ~ *Vt* reveal; make clear;
nahnko ~ *Vt* treat variously or
deviously; *Vr* engage in trifling
activities, fritter one's time away;
s-ap ~ *Vt* properly dispose of (as a
deceased person); **s-ko'okam** ~ *Vt*
harm. ▶ Occurring with *wua_:*
~**tham** *habN* a doer, performer, or
maker (used with present tense only).
▶ Occurring with *wui_:* ~**jith**
habVtb; **wabsh** ~ *habVinf,*
habVcmpl pretend. ▶ Occurring
with *juni_:* ~**chug** *habVt* carry
on a (specified) activity; ~**him**
habVt; ~**hog** *habs-Vr* liable
to happen; ~**mk** *habs-Vt* want
to do. etc.; ~**s** *habVs;* ~**sith**
Vt imitate the actions of;
~**sith|tham** *N* an imitator; ~**th**
habVtb. ▶ Occurring with *juh:*
_**kam** *habN* a doer or performer
(used for past or future tense only).

²wua, hpp, wua'i; shulig, hul *Vt*
place or put down; throw away; **heb**
hu ~ *Vt* lose; **heki** ~ *Vt* waste;
~**kch** *Vt.*

_**wua** See ¹_WU, ²_WU, ³_WU.

wuua__ *CE* celebrate a girl's puberty:
~**a** *N* a girl's puberty celebration;
(the) afterlife; ~**a|dag** *s-Vs* be
a good singer for a girl's puberty
celebration; ~**a|med*** *V* go to
a girl's puberty celebration;
(euphemistically) to die, hence, to
pass away or pass on; ~**ith** *Vr* take
part in a girl's puberty celebration;
~**tham** *N.*

wuahawua; wuashulig *Vt* remove,
take off; tear down.

wuakithalig† *N* a jacket; a coat;
a sweater.

wual; ap *N* a soldier. [<Sp *guardia*]

wuanthi; *p N* a glove. [<Sp *guanta*]

wud, d, d__ *CE* be *linking:* **Shahchu**
o wud? =*What is it?; Do* **kalit**=*It's a
wagon.*

wudakud; *p* (*dist*) *N* a rope or strap
to tie, as a sling for a broken arm;
kakio ~ *N* a garter.

wuddag; *pu* *N* a bandage; a sore or wound.

wuhan, wupash *Vt* awaken, wake (up).

wuhd, wupda; *hpu* *Vt* rope or tie (up); **alast k** ~ *Vt* tie up; hogtie.

wuhi (wui__ before voiceless consonants); **wuhpui** *N* an eye; ~**ga** *N* an eyeglass; ~**gew** *V* have a twitch in the eye; ~**gith** *V* blink; raise the eyebrows; **hemako** ~**kam** *N* a one-eyed person; a television set; ~**kon** *Vt* glance at; ~**po** *N* an eyelash.

wuhio; *hp* *Adv* face to face.

wuhiosha; *hp* *N* a face; a mask.

wuhlith; *pu* *Vtb* rope for (someone).

wuhlo See WUHLU.

wuhlu/wuhlo; *p* *N* a donkey; a bench; a funnel; ~**-ihbthag** *N* a spirit level (lit. a burro heart); ~**-ki'iwia** *N* oatmeal (lit. burro chewings). [<Sp *burro* donkey]

wuhpiostakud *N* the parry penstemon plant (*Penstemon parryi*).

wuhpui mahkai *N* an ophthalmologist.

wuhsh *V* rust; ~**thag** *N* rust.

wuhshani, wushke; wuwhag, ~**i** *V* emerge; exit; resign; appear; go to the outhouse; ~**g** *N* things that emerge (as plants, music, smoke, etc.); *N* an emergence; **gahi** ~ *Vt* pass through; experience; undergo; **ta'i** ~ *V* exit backwards.

wuhshath, sh; wuwhasith *Vt* bring out; deliver; celebrate; give birth to, bear (young)†; ~**a** *N;* **gm hu i** ~ *Vt* expel.

wuhshkam *N* one who emerges; (*pl*) ancestors of the Papago and Pima (lit. those that emerge from the earth). See App. 3.

wuhshthag; wupshthag *N* a plant.

¹wui See WUA.

²wui/~j; 'uwu *Prep* to; toward; **ab** ~ *Prep* against; ~**chuth** *Vdt* cause to inherit; hand down (as clothes) to; *Vtb* designate for (someone); ~**chuth|a** *N;* ~**chuth|a|him** *Vr* amble lazily, schlep; ~**kam** *N* one's due; a right; (a) punishment; an inheritance.

wuichuth *Vr* race.

wuithag *s-Vs* be skilled at racing.

wuichwig *N* a sty on the eyelid.

wuihum *N* lightning; a streak or flash of lightning.

wuij See WUI.

wuilodag See WUILOG.

wuilog/wuilodag *s-Adj,s-Vs* (be) albino.

wul; *pu* *Vs* be tied together; **ali** ~**kud** *N* a cradle board; ~**kud** *N* a rope or device for tying; ~**sh|ch** *Vts* have (someone or something) bound, trapped, tied, roped, hindered, restricted, or as a debtor; *Vrs* be bound, trapped, tied, roped, hindered, restricted or in debt; ~**shp*** *Vt* bind (lit. and fig.); tie, rope, hinder, restrict; trap; apply (brakes), brake; *Vr* incur a debt; ~**shp|a** *N;* ~**shp|a|dag** *N* a debt; ~**shp|a|kud** *N* a trap; a device for hindering motion, a brake; ~**shp|i** *Vs* be tied.

wulim; *hp* *N* a bale; a bundle.

wuliwga *N* a target for archery practice.

wul'ok, *pu;* *hpu* *Vt* untie.

wupaj *N* a yucca shoot.

wus__ *CE* exhalation: ~**chk** *Vt* blow on; ~**chk|wua*** *Vt* blow away.

wusot; *p* *Vt* blow on (usu. for ceremonial treatment of a disease); ~**a** *N* an instance of ceremonial treatment or cleansing; **chu** ~**a|thag** *s-Vs* be able to perform ritual cures. See App. 3.

Y

yahntha; *ya* *N* a tire. [<Sp *llanta*]

yahwi; *ya* *N* a key; a lock; ~**dag** *Vs* be locked; ~**dath** *Vt* lock; ~**dath|ch** *Vts* have (something) in a locked condition; ~**d|pi'ok*** *Vt* unlock; ~**d|pi'ok|a|s** *Vs.* [<Sp *llave* a key]

yehwa *N* a yoke for an animal; ~**dag** *Vs* be yoked; ~**dath** *Vt* yoke; ~**d|pi'ok** *Vt* unyoke; ~**d|pi'ok|a|s** *Vs.* [<Sp *yugo*]

yuhngih *N* an anvil; a rail; an iron tool for splitting wood. [<Sp *yunque* an anvil]

yuhs *Vt* use. [<Eng]

Abbreviations and Symbols

adj./ective
adv./erb
conj./unction
correl./ative
intj.   interjection
n./oun
prep./osition
pron./oun
v./erb
v.i.   intransitive verb
v.t.   transitive verb
†   marks words that are used only in Pima.
‡   marks words that are used only in Papago.
*   (1) marks words that in Papago or Pima are prefixed with s-, *hab-*, etc.;

(2) marks words that are used in phrases. It is necessary to refer to the Papago/Pima—English Dictionary for use of these words. Some shorter phrases are given here.

~   stands for the main-entry word. For example, under the main-entry **east** are the two subentries **in the** ~, and ~**ward**, which mean **in the east** and **eastward** respectively.

NOTES:

A comma separates variant forms.

Words in SMALL CAPITALS are cross references. For example, under the main-entry **blow** is the subentry CRUSH **with a** ~; for this phrase it is necessary to look under **crush.**

Plants and animals are entered under the generic word. For example, a **bull snake** is listed under **snake,** and the **hedgehog cactus** is listed under **cactus.** However, commonly identified items like **Gila monster** and **sparrow** will be found under these common names.

English—Papago/Pima Dictionary

A

a *article* g*; hema
abandon *v.t.* kikkiadag*; ohhoth*
abdomen *n.* wohk
abide *v.i.* ulinig*; ulinkahim*
ability *n.* __thag*; doubt the ~ of
pi'ichuth
able *adj.* nakog*; __thag*; be ~
__ith
abnormal *adj.* mahnikodag*
about *prep.* ab; am hu'i
above *prep.* thahm; from ~
thahmjed
absent *adj.* ha'ichug*; piach*
absolve *v.t.* gm hu wabsh oan
absorb *v.t.* ih'e*
abundance *n.* s-*
abundant *adj.* s-*; ~ly *adv.* ba'ama*
abuse *v.t.* pi ap nuhkuth; *n.* pi ap
nuhkuthadag
accept *v.t.* behe; he'eni*
accessible *adj.* apkog*
accompany *v.t.* oith
accomplish *v.t.* nahto; ~ment *n.*
nahtogig
accordian *n.* wani'ontham
account *n.* ~ant *n.* kuintatham;
~ing *n.* kuinta; on ~ of hekaj
accusation *n.* abchuth*; abchutha
accuse *v.t.* abchuth*; gagda; ~r *n.*
abchuththam; ~ of *v.t.* abchuth;
chu'ichigchuth; mohto'ith
ache *v.i.* ko'ok*; *n.* ko'okthag
acknowledge *v.t.* mahch ch ahg;
wohohkamchuth, wehohkamchuth;
~ment *n.* wohohkamchutha; ~
one's IDENTITY
acorn *n.* wi-yohthi
acquaintance *n.* nawojthag; an ~
n. machgai, machga
acquire *v.t.* behe; behi*; behi__*;
edagith; edagith*
acquisitive *adj.* edagith*
acre *n.* ahgli
acrobat *n.* ma-lohma; ~ics *n.*
ma-lohma

across *prep.* aigo; gahi; gahi*;
gahiobs*; FROM ~
action *n.* arouse to ~ wahmuth*
activity *n.* chichwidag; juni*
add *v.t.* ku'inhogith; __math*;
wehnath; in ~ition ehp
address *v.t.* jehnigith
adjoin *v.t.* namks*
adjourn *v.i.* pihhun; ~ment *n.*
pihhuna
adjust *v.t.* ap*; apchuth; ~ment *n.*
apchutha
administrate *v.t.* himchuth
admiration *n.* hohho'ithadag
admire *v.t.* hohho'ith*
adobe *n.* bith; bith*; (an) ~ brick *n.*
shahmt; ~ oven *n.* ol-nihyo*
adorn *v.t.* heosith; heosith*; ~ment
n. heosithakud
affirm *v.t.* mahch ch ahg;
wohohkamchuth, wehohkamchuth;
~ation *n.* wohohkamchutha
afraid *adj.* ehbith*; hudwua*; thoajk*
after *prep.* i thahm; oithch*; ~birth
n. kosh; UNTIL ~; ~ward(s) *adv.*
hahawa, haha
again *adv.* ehp
against *prep.* ab wui
agave *n.* a'ud*
age *n.* ahith__*
aggravate *v.t.* toliant
aggravation *n.* bagatalig
agree with *v.t.* hehgith
ahead of *prep.* ba'ich; ba'ichkam*
air *n.* hewel; ~plane *n.* uhg
tha'atham
alarm *v.t.* tothsith
alas *intj.* ai
albino *adj.* wuilog*
alert *v.t.* i tothsith; tha'iwuni; *adj.*
nenashan*; nehnthag*
alfalfa *n.* spulwam
alfileria *n.* hoho'ibad; kohkod-oipij
algae *n.* mamadhod; ~-colored *adj.*
mamadhodmagi
alike *adj.* wepo; wepo*; *adv.* wepo
alive *adj.* thoa*
all *pron.* wehs; wehs*; *adj.* ge;

wehs; **at** ~ ha*; ~ **day** ge tash;
~ **there is** al i wehs
allegiance n. **win the** ~ **of**
wanichkwua
allow v.t. (with infinitive) hiwigith
all right adj. ap'e*; ap'et*
almost adv. chum alo, chem alo;
shelkam
alone adj. hejel*; adv. hejel*;
hejelko
along prep. an
also adv. ehp; epai; hab-a ehp; **not
only...but** ~ wa'i*
although conj. chum as, chem as;
wa chum
alveolar adj. ha'apaga*; ha'apapig*
always adv. chum hekith, chem
hekith; shelam
amble v.i. himhim; wuichuthahim
ambush v.t. kihshath; n. kihshatha
amid prep. si shahgith
among prep. eda; shahgith
amount n. ha'a___*; ² ___s*; **any** ~ **of**
wabsh chum he'es, hash chum he'es
amuse v.t. piastchuth; tahhathchuth;
~**ment** n. tahhathkam*
amusingly adv. tahhatham*
an article g*; hema
ancestor n. shohshon; shon; wishbad
and conj. kch*; ku___*
angel n. anghil
anger v.t. bagachuth; baga*; n.
bagatalig; **one easily** ~**ed** bagatam;
bagwul
Anglo n. mil-gahn, milgan
animal n. ha'ichu thoakam; **domestic**
~ n. shoiga
angry adj. baga*
ankle n. chekosh*; chekwo; ~ **rattle**
n. chekoshda
annex v.t. ku'inhogith; n.
ku'inhogitha
announce v.t. amog; amog*; ~
oneself kailith; kaithag*;
~**r** n. amogtham
annoy v.t. ab hudaweg
anoint v.t. huhud; **an** ~**ing** n.
huhuda
another pron. one ~ e*; e-*
answer v.t. nodagith
ant n. kuadagi*; totoni; uhimal*;
black ~ n. chuchk totoni;
feathered ~ n. a'anam totoni;
odorous ~ n. uhw totoni; **red** ~ n.
wepegi totoni; **small** ~ n. a'al totoni
antelope n. **pronghorn** ~ n.
kuhwith
antler n. mo'owin*

anus n. at; at*; sihpud
anvil n. yuhngih
anxious adj. kehk*
any pron. ha'i*; adj. g*; hab*;
ha'i*; wabsh chum, hash chum; ~
AMOUNT **of; not** ~**where** pi hebai;
pi heba'i; ~ NUMBER **of;** ~**one**
pron. hedai*; wabsh chum hedai,
hash chum hedai; ~**one's** pron.
hedai*; ~**thing** pron. has; wabsh
chum has, hash chum has; ~ TIME;
~**way** adv. wabsh chum has
masma, hash chum has masma;
~**where** adv. wabsh chum hebai,
hash chum hebai
Apache Indian n. Ohbi
apologize v.i. sho'igchuth
apology n. sho'igchutha
apostle n. kehsha; hotsha†
appeal v.t. bahmuth; n. bahmuth*;
bahmutha; ~ **a** CASE **to;** ~**er** n.
bahmuththam; ~ **to** v.t. bahmuth
appear v.t. sha heg wepo; v.i.
ap'ema*; ap'etama*; ___ma*; mahsi*;
wuhshani; ~ **alike** mahs*; ~**ance**
n. mahschu*; ~ **from nowhere**
tha'ichshp; ~ **like** mahs*
apple n. ablis†; mani-sahna,
mal-sahna
apply v.t. ___hun*; ___math; wua*; ~
(brakes) v.t. wulshp
appoint v.t. keksh*; ~**ee** n.
chekchim; kehsha; ~ **to office**
thahsh
appreciate v.t. hohho'ith*
appreciation n. hohho'ithadag
apprehend v.t. an behe
approach v.t. miabith; v.i. ab him
appropriately adv. ap*
approval n. apchutha
approve v.t. ap*; apchuth
apricot n. wil-gohgih, wil-gohthi
April n. Oam Mashath‡; S-gevk
Mashath†
apron n. bahsho*; bahshodag
apt adj. amichuth*
argue v. ~ **with** v.t. kam'on;
kawhain; lothait; ~ **seriously with**
v.t. ne'owin
argument n. ne'owina
arise v.i. wamig
Arizona n. Al-Shonk; ~ CARDINAL
arm n. nowi; **have in the** ~**s**
kohmch; ~**pit** n. hek; hek*; **shake
the** ~ nowigith
around adv. sikol; prep. wehgaj,
wehbig
arouse to ACTION

arrange v.t. ap*; apchuth; ~ment
n. apchutha; wawnim
arrest v.t. an behe
arrival n. jiwhiathag
arrive v.i. aha*; himto; jiia; jiwa;
jiwia; ²mel*; ~ carrying v.t. u'apa;
~ carrying or bringing v.t. __pa;
~ soon or on time oiwith
arrow n. hapot; ho'omachuth*;
u'umhaidath*; ~ case n. wogsha;
~head n. uhsh; ~ shaft n.
shehsha; shelina; WAR ~;
~weed/~wood n. uhs-kokmagi
arroyo n. aki; akithag*
as conj. masma*; ~...as correl.
wepo
ash n. matai; mataithag; ~-colored
adj. mataimagi*; ~ dump n.
matai iawuikud; ~es n. matai;
ROAST in ~es
ashamed adj. elith*; become ~ sai ed†
ask v.t. kakke*; ~ (a question) of
v.t. chu'ichk; ~ for v.t. tahni;
tahnimed
askew adj. topithk*
asleep adj. fall ~ koksim*
asphalt roofing n. uhli
aspherical adj. shapol; shapol*
assemble v.t. wehnath; wehnath*
associate n. wehm*
association n. kawudka
assume v.t. elith*; ¹__p*
astray adv. LEAD ~
asunder adv. hikshp
at prep. ab; am; eda*; ohla-ch-ed*; ~
(a place) prep. __ko
attach v.t. __dath*; wihnk*; wua*
attention n. give ~ to hudaweg
attitude n. chegitoithag
August n. Shopol Eshabig Mashath
aunt n. chuhchudam*; hakit*; je'es*;
jisk*; ¹keli*; ²keli*; oks*; oksi*;
tatal*; thahth*; wowoit*; GREAT-~
automobile n. hejel memdatham;
mahgina; to-mohli; ~ tire n.
mahgina shuhshk; ~ wheel n.
mahgina kahio
avenge v. ag__*
awake v.i. nehhim
awaken v.t. wuhan; v.i. nehhim
aware adj. mahch*; ~ness n.
tahtkag
away adv. THERE facing ~
awe n. elitha*; be in ~ of elith*
awhile adv. sha
awl n. owij
axe n. hahsa; shonchki
axle n. tohn

B

baby n. ali; ali*; sulij; ~ bottle n.
si'ikud
baccharis n. shuhshk-wakch
back n. chuhk*; komi__*; oh*; adv.
ta'i; ~ache n. oh ko'okthag; ~ and
forth aigo*; gahi; lower ~ n.
komi; ~ scratcher n. keshkud; ~
side up kupal; ~ward adv. kuhgam
bacon n. ha-mohn; tosi'igo†
bad adj. pad; pad*; ~ly adv. pad
badger n. kahw
bag n. kostal; sleeping ~ n.
wahkus, wahks
bake v.t. pahnt; pas-tihlt*; v.i.
pahnt; ~r n. pahnttham; ~ry n.
pahntakud kih
baking n. pahnta; ~ POWDER
bald adj. wathathk*
bale n. wulim
ball n. bohl; olas; pi-lohtha; play ~
bohl; wohla
ballooned adv. koshodk*
bamboo n. wahpk
banana n. howij; ~ YUCCA
band n. giwud; giwud*; kuhutham
bandage n. wuddag
bandana n. maskal; monjel
bangs n. koadag, koapo
bank v.t. tohnkath; tohnktha*; n.
koa; tohnk; wahngo
baptism n. wakonadag
baptize v.t. pahl-wakon; ~r n.
wakontham
bar n. kan-tihna; digging ~ n. walit
barber n. hihktham
bare adj. thahpk*; ~ly adv. sha;
RIDE ~back
bark v.i. hihnk; n. elithag; ~ at
v.t. hihnko'ith; remove ~ from
elpig
barley n. si-wahyo
barrel n. walin; ~ CACTUS
base n. shon; shonchuth*
bashful adj. elith*; ~ness n. si
elithadag
basis n. on the ~ of ab
basket n. giwho*; hoa; hoa*; homi*;
washomi*; begin a ~ atchuth;
bottom of a ~ at; coil ~ n. hoa;
hoa*; covered ~ n. washa;
loose-woven ~ n. hashda;
ka-nahsti; ~ry n. hoata
bat v.t. shonichkwua; n. nanakumal
bathe v.t. wachchui; v.i. wachchui;
wachchuimk*

battery *n.* wepgih
battle *v.t.* cheggia; *n.* cheggiadag;
~**field/ground** *n.* cheggiakud;
~**ship** *n.* cheggiakud wahlko
bayonet *n.* chu'akkad*
be *v.i.* chu'ig*; ___dag; ___g*;
ha'ichug*; ___j*; ³ ___k*; ⁴ ___k*;
kahch*; ___mag*; ___magi*; ¹ ___s*;
thaha*; wud*; ~ **alike** mahs*;
~ **like** mahs*; ~ **in** wahks; ~
together wehnags; ~ **with** wehmaj.
See also WAS *and* WILL
bead *n.* STRING **of** ~**s;** ~**work** *n.*
koawgitha
beak *n.* chini oh'o
beam *n.* **upright support** ~ *n.*
chetondag, che-tondag
bean *n.* muhni; CASTOR ~; lima ~ *n.*
hawol; **orange tepary** ~ *n.* o'am
bawi; **pinto** ~ *n.* mams muhni; ~
pod *n.* wihog; wihogthag; **tepary**
~ *n.* bawi; **white tepary** ~ *n.*
tohta bawi; **wild tepary** ~ *n.*
ban-bawi
bear *v.t.* ahgachug*; madt*; mohto;
___t*; *n.* judumi; ~ **cub** *n.* judumi
mad; ~ GRASS; **polar** ~ *n.*
gew-ch-ed judumi; ~ (**young**) *v.t.*
wuwhasith
beard *n.* eshpo
beat *v.t.* gew; shonikkan; widwua
beautiful *adj.* kehg*
beautify *v.t.* kegchuth
beaver *n.* kohwih; ~**tail** CACTUS
because *conj.* hekaj; n___*; ~ **of**
prep. hekaj
become *v.i.* ___him*; ___t*
bed *n.* wo'ikud; ~**rock** *n.* waw;
~**roll** *n.* wahkus, wahks; ~ **sheet**
n. sahwano
bee *n.* muhwal; pa-nahl
beer *n.* sil-wihsa
beetle *n.* komikam; wihog-mad*;
fruit ~ *n.* ma-yahthi; **green June**
~ *n.* wainomi kohlasham
befall *v.t.* ab wui gehsh
before *prep.* hema*; koi; tahgio
befriend *v.t.* nawojt
beg *v.i.* neal*; ~ **from** *v.t.* nead;
~**gar** *n.* nealimkam*
beget *v.t.* alitht
begin *v.t.* shonwuichuth; *v.i.*
shonwua; ~**ning** *n.* alijk*; shon
behalf *n.* **on** ~ **of** ___jelith*;
wehhejed
behind *prep.* oitham; wehgaj,
wehbig; **from** ~ *prep.* oithchjed
belch *v.i.* hadwuag
belief *n.* wohohchutha, wehohchutha

believe *v.t.* wohoh*; wohohchuth,
wehohchuth; ~**r** *n.*
wohohchuththam, wehohchuththam
belittle *v.t.* pi ha'ichuchuth
bell *n.* kaksipul*; kampani; ~
housing *n.* kampani
belly *n.* wohk; wok___*; ~-**dance**
v.i. wokjith
beloved *adj.* tachchuithch
belt *n.* giwud; giwud*; sihnto
bench *n.* wuhlu, wuhlo
bend *v.i.* nod; nod*; sipudk*. See
also BENT
benefit to *n.* wehhejedkam
bent *adj.* gakodk; gakodk*
beside *prep.* hugithd-an
bet *v.t.* to'ith*; *v.i.* sialt;
betray *v.t.* gagda; ko'okam iattogith;
~**er** *n.* gagdatham; ko'okam
iattogiththam
between *prep.* shahgith
bewitch *v.t.* hihoin; hihoin*
beyond *prep.* ba'ich
bicycle *n.* wisig-lihtha
big *adj.* ge; ge'e; **get** ~ ge'etha;
~**horn** LAMB; ~**horn** SHEEP; **just so**
~ alha'as
bill *n.* wikladag
bind *v.t.* gishshum*; wulshch*;
wulshp
bird *n.* u'uhig; u'whig; BLACK~;
black ~ *n.* s-chuk shashani;
kuhigam*; BLUE~; **pyrrhuloxia** ~
n. bichpod; **water** ~ *n.* shuhthagi
u'uwhig
birth *n.* mahmdho*; madwua*;
approach ~ madtahim; **give** ~ **to**
mahsith; wuwhasith; **the** ~ **of**
mahsithag
bishop *n.* o-wihspla
bison *n.* pisin
bit *n.* pilin; **a** ~ **of** al chum; **the last**
~ al i wehs
bite *v.t.* ke'e; ke'i*; ~ **off** *v.t.*
ki'ihin
bitter *adj.* siw; siw*
black *adj.* chuk*; ehkegchu*; ~**bird**
n. shashani; ~ BIRD; ~**en** *v.t.*
chukujith; ~-**eyed** PEA; ~-**eyed**
Susan *n.* kukuwith ha-hahth; ~
person *n.* ehkegchu*; ~ **phoebe**
n. gihsupi; ~**smith** *n.* hilio;
red-winged ~**bird** *n.* s-wegi
shashani; ~ VULTURE; ~-**widow**
SPIDER
bladder *n.* hi'ush
blade *n.* papa-lohthi
blame *n.* chu'ichig; ~ **for** *v.t.*
chu'ichigchuth

blanket *n.* chedhum†; che'ewhuith*; che'ewhuithadag; pilsa; ~ **hammock** *n.* kuhna; SADDLE ~
blasting POWDER
bleach *v.t.* tohajith; *n.* tohajithakud
bleed *v.i.* e'edobad*
bless *v.t.* ho'ige'ith*; ~**ing** *n.* ho'ige'ithadag*
blind *adj.* nea*; pi-neatham; ~**er** *n.* tapaho; tapaho*; ~**ness** *n.* pi-neadag
blink *v.i.* kupkkia; kupsh; wuhigith
blister *n.* wapshud
blockhead *n.* koshwa
blood *n.* eh'ed; ~ **vessel** *n.* edhaithag
bloom *v.i.* heot; heot*
blossom *n.* heosig; hikug*
blouse *n.* sahgo
blow *v.t.* kuhi*; kuhu*; *v.i.* hewed*; med*; ¹mel__*; ~ **against** *v.t.* wi'ichk; wi'ichkwua*; ~ **away** *v.t.* wuschkwua; CRUSH **with a** ~; ~ **on** *v.t.* hewkon; wuschk; wusot*; ~ **a** WHISTLE or HORN
blue *adj.* a-nihlmagi*; chehthagi*; ~**bird** *n.* chehthagi-u'uwhig; ~**ing** *n.* a-nihl; a-nihl*; ~**ish** *adj.* chehthagim; ~**ishly** *adv.* a-nihlmagim; ~ **jay** *n.* hehwachuth; **light** ~ *adj.* chedhaiwagi; chedhaiwagi*
boar *n.* keli*
boast *v.i.* woikchuth; ~**ful** *adj.* gimaima*; woikima*; ~**fully** *adv.* gimaim*; ~**fulness** *n.* gimaimadag; woikimathag; ~**ing** *n.* gimaimadag; woikimathag
boat *n.* kanaho; wahlko
bobcat *n.* gewho
body *n.* chuhkug, chuhhug; hon*; ~ **hair** *n.* wopo; wopopig*; ~ LOUSE; SIDE **of the** ~
boil *v.t.* ku'iwona*; ku'iwonith; *v.i.* ku'iwoni; *n.* hihwsith; hihwthag; ~**ed** FOOD; ~ **(food)** *v.t.* posholt
boisterous *adj.* nakosig*; ~**ly** *adv.* nakosigam
bold *adj.* ha'ahama*; shemachuththam; ~**ly** *adv.* shemachuth*; ~**ness** *n.* shemachuthadag
bolt *v.t.* sihshp; *n.* sihshpakud
bone *n.* oh'o
bonnet *n.* ku-luhji
bony *adj.* gaki*; **a** ~ **tail** *n.* kulgiwagi bahi; kulgiwagichu*
boo *v.t.* kuichuth*; ~ **at** *v.t.* hihnko'ith

book *n.* o'ohana
boot *n.* chew shuhshk; wohtha
booty *n.* behi; ehsig
border *n.* chekshani; ~ **of a field** tahwlo; ~ **patrolman** *n.* s-wadag-jujkam chi-lihhi
bore *v.t.* ohhoth*
born *adj.* mahsikam*
boss *v.t.* chehani; *n.* ahmo; maliom‡; malioni
both *pron.* wehs; *adj.* wehs; ~ **of** wehsijj
bother *v.t.* an hudaweg; shodobinchuth
bottle *n.* BABY or nursing ~; GLASS ~
bottom *n.* at; FLAT-~**ed;** ~ **of a** BASKET or JAR
bounce *v.t.* ma'ikon; *v.i.* judwua
bouncy *adj.* juhagi*
boundary *n.* chekshani, chekshna; **make a** ~ **for** chekshan*
bow *v.i.* gehsh; *n.* gaht; gatwua*; ~ **low** koawua
bowels *n.* hihij
bowl *n.* bihkud; pulato; **wooden** ~ *n.* wachiho
box *v.t.* cheggia; cheggia*; *n.* kahon; shonikkan; washa; ~**er** *n.* cheggiatham; ~**ing** MATCH; ~**ing** RING
boy *n.* wiappo'oge'el, wiappoi
brace *n.* sha'aligi; ~**let** *n.* shohshoba
brag *v.i.* gimaihun; woikimhun; ~**gart** *n.* gimai; woikshanimkam
braid *v.t.* hihtpag; *n.* hihtpadag
brain *n.* oag; **have a** ~**storm** kopk; kopk*
brake *v.t.* maniadath; wulshp; *n.* wulshpakud
branch *n.* mamhadag; mamhadt*; sha'adk, sha'alk; ~**ed** *adj.* machwinag*; mammasig*
brand *v.t.* chepos__*; cheposith; *n.* cheposig; ~**ing** IRON
brave *adj.* chechojim*; ~**ery** *n.* cheojthag; ~ **man** *n.* si cheoj
brazier *n.* mehithakud
bread *n.* pahn
break *v.t.* hahlmath*; mulin*; ~ **in pieces** hain; hain*; ~ **off** *v.t.* haishan*; ~ **open and exude fluid** sipuni; ~ **out in bumps** hiwka; hiwkahim*. *See also* BROKEN
breakfast *n.* gegosig
breast *n.* bahsho; wipih
breath *n.* banuw*; ihbam*; ihbhei; ihbheiwua*; ~**ily** *adv.* hewelim*; ~**less** *adj.* ibhonis*

breathe *v.i.* ihbheni; ~ **convulsively** i'ibtog; ~ **in** *v.t.* howichk
breech strap *n.* ataio___*; ataiodag
brick *n.* shahmt; **a** ~ *n.* shahmt; **an** ADOBE ~
bride *n.* hohnita
bridge *n.* puinthi
bridle *n.* pilin
bright *adj.* mahs*; mashwuag*; tohama*; ~**ly** *adv.* tohama*; wegima*
brilliant *adj.* tondam; ~**ly** *adv.* tondam
bring *v.t.* u'apa; ARRIVE ~**ing;** ~ **forth** mahsith; mahsith*; mahsitha*; ~ **in** *v.t.* wahkith; ~ **out** *v.t.* wuwhasith; wuwhasitha*
brittlebush *n.* tohawes
broach *n.* sihshpakud
broil *v.t.* ga'a
broken *adj.* hahaisig*
bronco *n.* pohtol
broom *n.* wosunakud, woskud; ~**rape** *n.* maw tatk; mo'otadk
brother *n.* nawoj; nawoj*; wehnag; ~**in-law** *n.* mad-ohg*; ma'i-ohg*
brow *n.* koa
brown *adj.* kubjuwi*; muhadagi*; oam*; suklatog*
bruise *v.t.* oshkon; *n.* hihwog
brush *n.* gagkata; sha'i; woskud, wosunakud
bubbles *n.* totshagi
buck *v.i.* thath'e; tha'ithag*; *n.* keli*
bucket *n.* kuhwo; pihla; wahlthi; wa'igkud
buckhorn cholla CACTUS
buckle *v.t.* sihnjudag*; sihnjudath; *n.* sihnju
buckskin *n.* huawi hogi; ~ **bag** *n.* huashomi
bud *v.i.* hulkath; *n.* hawpalithag*; FRUIT ~
buffalo *n.* pisin; ~ **gourd** *n.* adawi
bug *n.* **stink** ~ *n.* bititoi, bitikoi
build *v.t.* kih*; kihchuth*; kiht; nahto; **a** ~**ing** *n.* kih; nahtoi; ~**er** *n.* nahtokam
bull *n.* tohlo; **castrated** ~ *n.* nowiyu; ~**roarer** *n.* wewkud; ~ SNAKE
bullet *n.* kal-tuhji
bumblebee *n.* hu'udagi
bumpy *adj.* mu'umkath*; omlik; omlik*
bun *n.* simito
bundle *n.* wulim; ~ **up** *v.t.* olat; olatahim*
bunion *n.* huniga

bunt *v.* ~ **with the head** mo'okkan
burden *v.t.* mohto'ith; wechun; *n.* kushwi'ot*; mohtoi; ~**some** *adj.* wehch*
burlap *n.* tahum
burn *v.t.* kohathk*; mehi-nihlo*; mehith; mehith*; *v.i.* mehe; mei; mei*; ~**er** *n.* mehithakud; STOP ~**ing;** ~ **up** *v.i.* hagito; ~ up/down *v.t.* meitto
burrowing OWL
burst *v.t.* hain; hain*
bury *v.t.* hiashp; hia*
bush *n.* uhs; ~ **muhly** *n.* kuhkpadag
business *n.* chikpan; **a** ~ *n.* komba-nihya
but *conj.* eda; oi wa; wabshaba, hashaba, shaba
butt *v.* ~ **with the head** mo'okkan
butter *v.t.* manthi-gihyamath; *n.* chihno-oag†; manthi-gihya‡; ~**fly** *n.* hohokimal*
buttock *n.* atapud; ~**s** *n.* at; atshnig*
button *v.t.* wotonidag*; wotonidath; *n.* wotoni; **saguaro** CACTUS ~
buy *v.t.* nolawt; sha'awai; *n.* nolawta; ~**er** *n.* nolawttham; ~ **from** *v.t.* nolawt*; sha'awai*
buzz *v.i.* weweg; wewegim*
by *prep.* ab*; hugithd-an

C

cactus *n.* ho'i; naw*; **barrel** ~ *n.* jiawul; **branched pencil cholla** ~ *n.* wipnoi; **buckthorn cholla** ~ *n.* cheolim‡; **bush cholla** ~ *n.* wipnoi; **cholla** ~ *n.* hanam; **desert Christmas** ~ *n.* wipnoi; **fish-hook** ~ *n.* ban-chepla; ~ **fruit** *n.* ia*; **hedgehog** ~ *n.* ihswigi; mo'owhani; **organ-pipe** ~ *n.* chuchuis; **prickly-pear** ~ *n.* gisoki*; ihbhai; nahkag; ~ **rib cage** *n.* kakaist; **saguaro** ~ *n.* hahshani; **saguaro** ~ **button** *n.* hikugthag; **saguaro** ~ **fruit** *n.* bahithaj*; juni; **saguaro** ~ **fruit jam** *n.* hihij kushul; **saguaro** ~ **rib** *n.* ku'ibad; wahpai; **saguaro** ~ **wine** *n.* nawait; **senita** ~ *n.* chehmi; **staghorn** ~ *n.* kokaw; **strawberry** ~ *n.* bahban ha-ihswigi; **teddybear cholla** ~ *n.* hadshadkam; **Thornber's** ~ *n.* ban-mawpai; **vine** ~ *n.* melhog; ~ WREN

cake *n.* s-i'owi pahn; toha-komikam
calamity *n.* jehka'ich*; neijig*
calendar *n.* mashath kuintakud
calf *n.* haiwani mad; uhksh; wisilo;
MOOSE ~
caliche *n.* thag
California *n.* Month-lai; ~ POPPY
call *v.t.* ahg; ihm*; waith; waitha*;
a ~ing *n.* waithadag*;
~ (an animal) *v.t.* kuhijith; ~ by
name chehg; ~er *n.* waiththam
callous *adv.* kawk*; ~ly *adv.*
kawkam
calm *v.t.* thotholimchuth; *adj.*
thotholim*; ~ly *adv.* thotholim*;
~ness *n.* thotholimthag*
camel *n.* chew-kuswokam; ka-mihyo
camera *n.* pikchulithakud
camp *v.i.* wohp; *n.* kahmbo
can *modal auxiliary* nakog; *n.*
wahso
canaigre *n.* hiwithchuls*;
siwithchulis
cancer-root *n.* mo'otadk
candle *n.* kanjel, kanjul; ~wood *n.*
melhog
candy *n.* luhlsi
cane *n.* kahnia*; wahpk
cannon *n.* cheggiakud; ge'e gawos
canoe *n.* ka-nohwa
canteen *n.* wako
canvas *n.* lohna; ~ WATER bag
canyon *n.* shahgig; showichk
capably *adv.* ap*
cape *n.* kahba
captive *n.* behi
capture *v.t.* behijith*
car = AUTOMOBILE
card *n.* playing ~ *n.* mohnthikud;
walahokud†; play ~s mohnthi;
walaho†; play ~s with mohnthi;
walaho†
cardinal *n.* sipuk; Arizona ~ *n.*
sipuk
care *n.* elithadag*; ~ for *v.t.*
hohho'ith*; ~ful *adj.* gihug; ~less
n. chuhugia; ~taker *n.*
nuhkuththam; take ~ of nuhkuth;
thagio'ith
carpenter's square *n.* shoh'o-kahio
carry *v.t.* behichug; ~chug*;
ihtachug*; komchkahim*; u'a*;
ARRIVE ~ing; ~ in a vehicle mohto;
~ in one's grasp gi'achug; ~ on
v.t. wua* (under *Occurring with*
juni__); ~ on one's back chuhk; ~
on the head mohto
cartridge *n.* kal-tuhji
Casaba melon *n.* keli-bahsho

case *n.* [1]__p*; appeal a ~ to ab wui i
gehsh
cassette *n.* ha'ichu koshdag
castor bean *n.* mahmsh
castrate *v.t.* wihpedhopig
cat *n.* mihstol, mihtol; ~bird *n.*
chew-chinikam; ~'s-claw *n.*
uhpad; ~tail *n.* udawhag
catch *v.t.* shahkum; ~ up to/with
v.t. aihim
caterpillar *n.* makkumi*; wopiwul; ~
tractor *n.* mihstol, mihtol
cathedral *n.* ge'e cheopi
Catholic *n., adj.* Ka-tohliga; Sahnto;
~ CHURCH
cattle *n.* haiwani
cause *v.* __chulith*; __chuth*;
__jith*; wua*
cave *n.* cheho
caw *v.i.* kahkag; kuhi*; kuhu*
cease *v.t.* ha'asa; __ho*; *v.i.* i ha'asa
celebrate *v.t.* wuwhasith; *v.i.* piast
celebration *n.* piast; piast*;
wuwhasitha*
cement *n.* hothai shahmt; ~ floor *n.*
hothai
cemetery *n.* simin-jihlo
cent *n.* oam; sin-tahwo; fifteen ~s
n. gihnisi
center *n.* hik; in the ~ of [2]eda*
centipede *n.* maihogi; wopishul
century *n.* siant ahithag; ~ plant *n.*
a'ud
ceremonial DANCE
cereus *n.* ho'ok-wah'o
certainly *adv.* hemho wa
certification *n.* wohohkamchutha
certify *v.t.* wohohkamchuth
chaff *n.* wa'ug
chain *v.t.* hukshchim wainomidath;
n. hukshchim wainomi; ka-lihna
chair *n.* thaikud; ~person/man *n.*
uhgchu
challenge *v.t.* pi'ichuth; *n.*
pi'ichuthadag
champion *n., adj.* si hiwiga
chance *n.* chahnsa; await a ~ at
oithachug
change *v.t.* gawul wua; kammialt*
chant *n.* kuadk*
chapped *adj.* hehewini*; hewest*
chaps *n.* chapa-lihya
chapter *n.* kuintadag
character *n.* chu'ichig; ~istic *adj.*
wepodag*; of good ~ si
charcoal *n.* chuhd__*; ~(-)gray
adj. lichintog*
charge *n.* nuhkutha; press ~s against
gagda

charm *n.* ho'oma; ho'omachuth*;
hothai
chase *v.t.* hu'uith; *n.* kuhshtha; ~
away (an animal) *v.t.* shahth; ~
(game) *v.t.* kuhshath;
kuhshthamed*
cheat *v.t.* banmath
check *n.* chahgih
cheek *n.* kahkam*; kahm
cheese *n.* kihsho
chest *n.* bahsho; ~ hair *n.* bashpo
chew *v.t.* ki'iwin; kuhm; ~ing GUM;
~ on *v.t.* ki'ikkan; ~ up *v.t.*
ki'iwin; ki'iwina*
chicken *n.* chuchul; baby ~ *n.*
chuchul mad; cooked ~ *n.* chuchul
hithod; live ~ *n.* chuchul; ~ pox
n. chuchul ha-hihiwthag; uncooked
~ *n.* chuchul chuhkug
chickpea *n.* galwash
chief *n.* uhgchu; *adj.* ge'e
child *n.* ali; ali*; adopted ~ *n.*
wogsha; ~hood *n.* alichuth*;
~ishly *adv.* a'alim; step ~ *n.*
wogsha
chili *n.* add prepared ~ to
ko'okolmath; ~ pod *n.* ko'okol;
~ powder *n.* ko'okol; prepared ~
n. ko'okol hithod; wild ~ *n.* a'al
ko'okol, u'us ko'okol
chilicote *n.* bahwui
chill *v.t.* hewajith; hewbajith;
hewmk*
chimney *n.* chimi-nihya; LAMP ~
chin *n.* esh
China *n.* Chihno ha-jewedga
Chinese *n.,adj.* Chihno*
chip *v.t.* chepin; chepwinag*
chisel *n.* is-kohbli
choke on *v.t.* howichkwua
cholla CACTUS
choose *v.t.* gawulkath
chop *v.t.* shontsith*; ~ down *v.t.*
shonichk; ~ into kindling taimun;
~ped FIREwood
chorizo *n.* cho-lihsa
Christ *n.* Klihsto; ~ian *n.* Klihsto
wohohchuththam; ~mas *n.* Klihsto
mahsithag tash; ~mas CACTUS;
~mas Eve *n.* Noji-wihno
church *n.* cheopi; Catholic ~ *n.*
Sahnto kih; large ~ *n.* ge'e cheopi;
Protestant ~ *n.* Mihsh kih
cicada *n.* kohntpul, kohtpul
cigar *n.* puhlo
cigarette *n.* sigal; light a ~ kuht; lit
~ *n.* owichk
cinch *v.t.* sihnjudag*; sihnjudath; *n.*
sihnju

cinder *n.* mataithag; ~s *n.* matai
circle *n.* sikolk; ~ around *v.t.* i
sikolkath; TURN in a ~
circular *adj.* sikol; sikol*; ~ly *adv.*
sikolim
circumcision *n.* hikuchka
circumcize *v.t.* hikuchk*; pahl
hikuchk;
circumscribed *adj.* sikod
circus *n.* ma-lohma
citizen *n.* kihkam
city *n.* puiwlo
claim *v.t.* ahgalith*
clamp *v.t.* la'a__*; la'ashp; *n.*
la'ashpakud
clan *n.* e wehmjim, e wehmkam; ~
companion *n.* wehmkal; ~ names
See App. 3
clap *v.i.* kape*; kapsith*; shabani
clarification *n.* tashogitha
clarify *v.t.* maskogith; tasho*;
tashogith
clasp *n.* hukshpakud
clatter *v.i.* kolig; kolig*
clavicle *n.* ownag
claw *v.t.* hukitsh; *n.* huch, huhch
clay *n.* bith; bith*; red ~ *n.* wegi
clean *v.t.* kegchuth; ~se *v.t.*
kegchuth; lihmhun
clear *adj.* mahs*; a ~ing *n.* gagka;
jeg; jegda; ~ (land) *v.t.* gagkat;
~ly *adv.* mahsko; tasho; ~-voiced
adj. ba'itk*
cleave *v.t.* sha'adk*
cleft *n.* sha'adk*
clever *adj.* amichuth*; ~ly *adv.* chu
amichuththam; ~ness *n.*
amichuthadag
cliff *n.* koa; waw
climb *v.t.* cheshaj; cheshaj*; *n.*
cheshajig
clip *v.t.* hihk; hihk*; ~pers *n.*
hihkakud
cloak *n.* kahba
clock *n.* tash
clop *v.i.* kopk; kopk*
close *v.t.* kuhp; kuhp*; kuhpjelith*;
adj. abai*; ~ an EYE/the eyes; ~ly
adv. kawud*; ~-mouthed *adj.*
chinishch
closet *n.* chekkud
cloth *n.* ikus
clothe *v.t.* enigadath; enigadathch*
clothes *n.* eniga; dirty ~ *n.*
bihtagiga; ~ hanger *n.* eniga
naggiakud; ~ line *n.* eniga
naggiakud; SUIT of ~; wash ~ wakon
cloud *n.* chewagi; ~y *adj.*
chewagig*

clover *n.* owl ~ *n.*
clown *v.i.* pa-yahsochuth; *n.*
pa-yahso; ceremonial ~ *n.*
nawijju; pako'ola
club *v.t.* shonikkan; *n.* lahnis;
WAR ~
coachwhip *n.* melhog
coarse *adj.* hiwk*; ~ly *adv.*
chedkam*
coat *n.* lihwa; wuakithaligt
coccoon *n.* koswul
cockleburr *n.* waiwel
cockroach *n.* kak-luhji
coconut *n.* chahngo-mo'o
coffee *n.* ka-hui; ~ beans *n.* ka-hui;
~ grounds *n.* mohg; ~ pot *n.*
kahui-thihla
coil *v.t.* olasim*; olat; sikolim*; *v.i.*
sikolkath; *n.* sitholim*
cold *adj.* hehpi*; *n.* hewastk*; a ~
n. shomaig*; shomaigig; catch (a)
~ *n.* shomaig
collar *n.* kuswodag; ~bone *n.*
ownag; HORSE ~
collateral *n.* plihntha
collect *v.t.* hemapath; hemapath*
collide with *v.t.* melchk
color *v.t.* mahsith; mahsithchuth*;
n. mahs*; mahschu*; mahstag
colt *n.* kawiyu mad
columbine *n.* chuchul-i'ispul,
kuksho-wuhplim
comb *n.* shakajtha tahtshakud;
fine-toothed ~ *n.* pihnia
combine *v.t.* wehnath; wehnath*; ~
(ingredients) *v.t.* shahshagith
come *v.i.* ab him; ~ to one's SENSES
comet *n.* siawogi
comforter *n.* che'ewhuith*;
che'ewhuithadag
command *v.t.* chehani; *n.* chehanig
commit *v.t.* mohto'ith*
companion *n.* wehm*; CLAN ~
compensate *v.t.* namkith
compensation *n.* namkith*
compete *v.i.* chichwi; chichwi*; ~
with *v.t.* bijimith; chichwi
competition *n.* chichwithag
competitive *adj.* chichwithag*
competitor *n.* chichwitham
complain *v.t.* si thath'e; *v.i.* si
thath'e; ~er *n.* si thath'etham
complete *v.t.* nahto; ~ly *adv.*
kehg*; si
completion *n.* nahtogig
comply with *v.t.* namk
compose MUSIC
composition *n.* o'ohana
composure *n.* chegitoithag

concave *adj.* pihpchul
conceive *v.i.* nonhat
concern *v.t.* ab him; *n.* elitha*; pihk
elithadag; have ~ for pihk elith; ~
oneself (about) pihk elith
concert *n.* ne'i*; ~ hall *n.* ne'ikud
conclude *v.t.* elith*
condition *n.* apko*
conduct *v.t.* him*
confer *v.i.* jehnigith; jehnigiththam*
confess *v.t.* kom-bihsh; *v.i.*
chu'ichig-ahg
confidence *n.* have ~ in hiwig
confine *v.t.* kuhp; kuhp*; kuhpachuth
conflict *n.* cheggiadag; ~with *v.t.*
cheggia
confuse *v.t.* heki himchuth
connect *v.t.* gi'is*; lunag; mako;
~ion *n.* makodag
conquer *v.t.* thahm i cheshaj
conscience *n.* have a clear ~ pi
elith; ~-stricken *adj.* kudut*
conscious *adj.* tahtk*
consequence *n.* suffer the ~s
jehka'ich
consider *v.t.* oithahim; i oithahim;
constipate *v.t.* bihim*
constipation *n.* bihimthag
constrict *v.t.* giwudk*; giwulk*
contain *v.t.* kuhp; ~er *n.* chekkud;
iawuakud*; iawuikud*; kih; ~er for
storage *n.* ba'ihamakud; ba'iham*
contaminate *v.t.* bith*; bithhun
contest *v.t.* lothait*; *n.* chichwithag;
~ant *n.* chichwitham
continue *v.t.* aha*; ___chug*; ___him*;
~ with *v.t.* nakog*
continually *adv.* shelam; GO ~
contractor *n.* kont-lahtho
control *n.* assume ~ for (someone)
ku'inhogith; assume ~ of behe
convex *adj.* chepodk*; kuchul;
kuchul*
cook *v.t.* baha*; bahi*; bahijith;
hithod; hithoda*; ~ed *adj.* bai___*;
baikam
cool *adj.* hehogi*; hewajith,
hewbajith; ~er *n.* hehogithakud
cooperative *adj.* chekaithag*
coot *n.* wachumtham; wakaig
copper *n.* kohwli
copulate *v.i.* thohm; ~ with *v.t.*
hahbiw
coral bean *n.* bahwui
cord *n.* wijina; umbilical ~ *n.* hikaj
corn *n.* ga'iwesa*; huhni; a ~ *n.*
huniga; ~cob *n.* kuhmikud; ~ on
the cob *n.* muhla tahtami
corner *n.* chuhl

corona-de-Cristo = CROWN-of-
thorns
corpse *n.* muhki
corral *n.* kolhai
correct *v.t.* shohbith; shohbith* *adj.*
ap*; ap'e*; ~ion *n.* shohbithadag;
~ly *adv.* ap*
corrupt *adj.* mahch*
cotton *n.* tokih; desert ~ plant *n.*
ban-tokiga; ~ material *n.* tokih; ~
string *n.* tokih; ~tail RABBIT;
~wood tree *n.* mohmli auppa
cougar *n.* mawith
cough *v.i.* i'ihog
council *n.* e jehnigiththam; ~man
n. jehnigiththam
count *v.t.* kuint; kuint*; *n.*
kuintakud*; ~able *adj.* kuint*;
~er *n.* kuintatham; ~ the TIME
country *n.* kownaltalig; a ~ *n.*
jewed
couple *v.t.* mako; *n.* hohni__*
course *n.* chekith*; wohg*; set a ~
for chekshan*
court *n.* ~house/room *n.*
lothaitakud kih; take to ~ wahkith
chehanig-ch ed; ~ trial *n.* lothaita
cousin *n.* chuhchud*; hakimad*;
hakima-je'e*; mad*; ma'i-ohg;
nawoj; nawoj*; wehnag
cover *v.t.* chehmo'o; ma'in*; ma'ishp;
thai__*; *n.* ma'ishpakud; ~ with a
blanket *n.* che'ewhuith;
che'ewhuith*
cow *n.* haiwani; ~boy *n.* wakial; ~
killer *n.* uhimal; dwarf ~bird *n.*
hewel-ch-ed u'uwhig
coward *n.* chu ehbiththam;
uwikwuad; uwikwuadag*; ~ly *adj.*
chu ehbiththam
coyote *n.* ban; in a ~-like manner
bankaj; C ~ moiety *n.* apapa*;
apkih*; ~ TOBACCO plant
crack *v.t.* hain; hain*; *n.* tahpani;
~lings *n.* sisloni
cradle *n.* ulukud; ~ board *n.* ali
wulkud
cramp *v.t.* kushathk*; *n.*
kushathkath*
crane *n.* shuhthagi u'uwhig
crave *v.t.* ihnam*
crawl *v.i.* bahni__*; ~er *n.*
bahnimedtham
create *v.t.* nahto
creation *n.* nahtogig; nahtoi
creature *n.* thoakam
credit *n.* chu'ichig; give ~ for
abchuth
creep *v.i.* bahni__*
creosote bush *n.* shegoi, shegih

cricket *n.* chukugshuad
cripple *n.* mahniko; ~d *adj.*
mahnikodag*; mahnikokam
criss-cross *v.t.* gahiobin
criticism *n.* ahgadag*
crooked *adj.* gakodk; gakodk*;
jujul*; ~ly *adv.* jujulim*
crop *v.t.* wohlim*; *n.* e'es; ~ped
adj. wohlih; wohlih*
cross *v.t.* gahiobin; gehsh*;
kahiobin*; *n.* kotsith*; kulshani; ~
over *v.t.* gahi cheshaj; religious ~
n. kots
crotch *n.* kaishagi *
crow *v.i.* kahkag; kuhi*; kuhu*;
~bar *n.* siwat huhch, siwato huhch
crowd *v.t.* shodobinchuth; shodobin*
crown *n.* gihko‡; gihkoa†;
~-of-thorns *n.* ahgowi
crudely *adv.* gogsim*
crunch *v.t.* kuhm; *v.i.* kawhain*;
~ily *adv.* kawnim*
crush *v.t.* __shun; ~ (grain) *v.t.*
edmun; ~ with a blow gewishun; ~
with the hand shonishun
crusted *adj.* cheodagi*
crutch *n.* uhs
cry *v.i.* shoak; shosha*; ~baby *n.*
a'alimakam; cause to ~ si koktha;
~ out *v.i.* kuishani; STOP ~ing
crystal *n.* o'od, o'ohia; ~ize *v.t.*
o'odkith, o'ohiakith
cultivate *v.t.* moihun; moihun*; ~
with a disk melomin
culture *n.* a ~ *n.* himthag
cup *n.* tahsa
curiosity *n.* neith*
curious *adj.* neith*; ~ly *adv.* chu
neitham
curl *v.t.* hupalwini; ~y *adj.*
kulgiwagi*; kulwani*
curry FAVOR
curve *v.t.* gakodk; gakodk*;
sikolkath*; sikolkthahim*
cushion *n.* a looped ~ *n.* hakko,
hakko'o; hakko*
custom *n.* himthag
cut *v.t.* hihk*; hik__*; hikuchk;
hikuchk*; a ~ting *n.* hihka; ~
open *v.t.* hitpod*
cyclone *n.* siwulogi, siwuliki

D

daily *adj.,adv.* wehs tashkaj
daisy *n.* ~ plant *n.* ban-chinishani;
yellow ~ *n.* kukuwith ha-hahth
dam *v.t.* tohnkath; tohnktha*; *n.*
kuhpa; tohnk

damage *v.t.* padchuth; padchuthas*;
n. padchutha
damp *adj.* wa'usig*; wa'uthag*; ~en
v.t. wa'usith; ~ly *adv.* wa'usim*;
~ness *n.* wa'uthag
dance *v.t.* waila; *v.i.* mualig*;
waila; *n.* wailathag; ceremonial ~
n. gohimeli; do a SQUAW ~; ~r
n. e wailatham; ~r in a harvest
ceremony *n.* wihnim; ~ floor *n.*
wailakud; RAIN ~; traditional ~ *n.*
kehihina; kehihinakud*
danger *n.* gihug*; ~ous *adj.*
ehbitham; ~ously *adv.* giwul;
PREPARE for ~
dare *v.t.* mukiagam*; pi'ichuth; *n.*
pi'ichuthadag; ~devil *n.* mukiagam
dark *adj.* chuhugam*; chukchu*;
ehkegchu*; *adv.* chukma*; ~en
v.t. chukujith; ~ness *n.*
chuhugam*
darn *v.t.* shohm; shohm*; ~er *n.*
shohmtham; ~ing NEEDLE
date *n.* chukud-shosha
daughter *n.* ~-in-law *n.*
ka'ama-je'e*; wosma-je'e*;
wosma-jehjim
dawn *v.i.* mahsi; *n.* mahsig; before
~ si'al kehk
day *n.* tash; tashkaj*; next ~ ba'ich
tash; some ~ has tash; ~time *n.*
tash
dead *adj.* muhki; one's ~ *n.*
muhkithag
deaf *adj.* chekai__*; ~ness *n.* pi
chekaithag
death *n.* muhkig; muhkihim*;
mukimakam*; oh'ith*; ~like *adj.*
mukima; ~ly *adj.* muhkigam*
debate with *v.t.* kam'on
debilitate *v.t.* moik*
debt *n.* wikla*; wikladag;
wulshpadag; incur a ~ wulshp
decay *v.t.* jewajith; *v.i.* jew*; jewa
deceit *n.* iattogig; ~ful *adj.* iatto__*
deceive *v.t.* iattogith
December *n.* Ge'e S-hehpijig
Mashath; Noji-wihno Mashath
decide *v.t.* ahg*; elith*
decision *n.* elitha*
decorate *v.t.* heosith; heosith*
decoration *n.* heosithakud
deep *adj.* juhk*; ~en *v.i.* juhka;
~ly *adv.* juhkam*
deer *n.* mule ~ *n.* huawi, huai;
white-tailed ~ *n.* sihki
defeat *v.t.* gew; gewito
defecate *v.i.* biht; biht*; bitwua
defecation *n.* bihta
defer to *v.t.* bahbagi

degeneracy *n.* tohntomthadag
degenerate *v.t.* tohntochuth; *n.*
tohnto; *adj.* tohnto; ~ly *adv.*
tohntom*
degree *n.* to some ~ sha
dehorn *v.t.* wohlihchuth; ~ed *adj.*
wohlih
deification *n.* jioshchutha
deify *v.t.* jioshchuth
deity *n.* ha'ichu
delay *v.t.* ihamhun; *n.* ihamhuna
delirious *adj.* neok*
deliver *v.t.* tho'ibia; wuhshath;
~ance *n.* tho'ibiathag; ~er *n.*
tho'ibiakam
demand *v.t.* ab si chehani;
huihlsamath*
demented *adj.* lohgo; lohgo*
demon *n.* jiawul; niawul
dent *v.t.* hothodk*
dentist *n.* tahtami mahkai
deny *v.t.* pi mahch ch ahg
depend *v.* ~able *adj.* si hiwiga; ~
on *v.t.* hiwig; hiwiga*
deplete *v.t.* padchuth; padchuthas*
depletion *n.* padchutha
deprivation *n.* wohppo'itha
deprive of *v.t.* ligpig; wohppo'ith
depth *n.* juhkalig
descend *v.i.* gehsh; huduni;
hudunihim*
desert *n.* tohono; blackthroated ~
SPARROW; ~ broom plant *n.* ahn;
D ~ gold POPPY; D ~ People (i.e.,
the Papago) *n.* Tohono O'othham;
~ lily *n.* ah'at; ~ TOBACCO
design *n.* bibijjim
designate *v.t.* wui*
desirable *adj.* behi__*; ~ to KNOW
desire *n.* tachchui, tachchuithag
destroy *v.t.* hugiog; hugiogahim*
destruction *n.* hugioga
detain *v.t.* ulinch*
deteriorate *v.i.* padt; ~d *adj.* pad;
pad*
deterioration *n.* padtalig
develop *v.i.* iawu*
devil *n.* jiawul; niawul; D ~ *n.*
Jiawul; Niawul; ~'s claw *n.* ihug
devour *v.t.* ko'ito
dew *n.* wa'uthag; ~y *adj.* wa'usig*
diabetes *n.* asugal mumkithag
diabetic *n.* asugal mumkutham
diaper *v.t.* atosha*; *n.* atosha;
atosha*
diarrhea *n.* memelchutha;
wakuichuth*; wakuithag
die *v.i.* huhug; huhugam*; muhk;
muhkihim*; mukihog*; mukima*
diet *v.i.* gi'iho

different *adj.* gawul; gawul* ~iate
v.t. gawulkath; ~ly *adv.* gawul
difficult *adj.* hasig*; kawk*; wihnk*;
~ly *adv.* hasigim*; wihnam;
winma*; **with** ~y wihnam; winma*
dig *v.i.* kow*; ~ **up** *v.t.* hiabog; ~
up and remove *v.t.* ganiwua
dignity *n.* **human** ~ *n.*
o'othhamthag
dike *v.t.* kuhpik*; tohnk*; tohnkath;
n. kuhpa; tohnk; tohnk*
dilapidated *adj.* napadk*
dim *v.t.* chukujith; *adj.* kohmagi*;
~ly *adv.* kohmagim*
dime *n.* toha
dinner *n.* gegosig
dip *v.* ~**per** *n.* ha'u; ~ **out** *v.t.*
wasib; wasib*
direct *v.* **in the** ~**ion of** tahgio; ~**ion**
n. ha'ab*; heki*; ~**or** *n.* uhgchu
dirtily *adv* bihtagim
dirty *v.t.* uam*; uamhun; *adj.*
bihtagi*; uam*
disagree *v.i.* pi am hu i e wehmt
disappear *v.i.* huhug; huhughim*;
pi'ata; pi'atachuth*; ~**ance** *n.*
pi'atadag; **cause to** ~ pi mahsith
disapproval *n.* **express** ~ **of**
kuichuth*
disassemble *v.t.* matog
disaster *n.* neijig*
discard *v.t.* ohhoth*; thagito; wua*;
n. ohhotha
discipline *n.* ha'ichu ahgithadag
disconnect *v.t.* makodpi'ok
discourage *v.t.* ki'omi*
discover *v.t.* chehg; chehg*; neith;
~y *n.* chehgi
discuss *v.t.* ahg; hudaweg; ~**ion** *n.*
ahga; jehnigitha
disease *n.* mumkithag; **contagious** ~
n. oimmedtham mumkithag
disgrace *v.t.* edawua*; *n.* eda__*;
edathag; si elithadag; ~**ful** *adj.*
eda__*; ~**fully** *adv.* eda__*; s-ta
edam, sai eda†
disguise *v.t.* a'agchuth
disgust *v.t.* uhwaithchuth; *n.*
uhwaithag
dish *v.t.* bihs*; *n.* hoas-ha'a; ~ **out**
v.t. bia*
dishonest *adj.* iatto__*
disinfect *v.t.* kulanikaj kegchuth
disinterested *adj.* ohhoth*
disk *n.* CULTIVATE **with a** ~
dislike *v.t.* pi hohho'ith
disobedient *adj.* chekai__*
dispatch *v.t.* ah'ath; ~**er** *n.*
ah'aththam; hotshtham†

display *v.t.* chehgith*; *n.*
chehgithadag
displease *v.t.* pi hohho'ithachuth
distant *adj.* mehk; ~ly *adv.*
mehkotham*
distinctly *adv.* tasho
district *n.* chekshani, chekshna
disturb *v.t.* kudut; tahkt*; todwin
ditch *n.* waikka
diuretic *adj.* hi'a*
dive *v.i.* wachum; ~r *n.*
wachumtham; ~ **into water** wachp
divide *v.t.* sha'adk*; tahpan; tahpan*;
~ **for** *v.t.* tahpath
divination *n.* a'atha
divine *v.t.* a'ath*
divinity *n.* jioshthag
division *n.* sha'adk*; tahpani; tahpna
divorce *v.t.* ohhoth*; *n.* ohhotha; ~
papers *n.* ohhotha tapial
dizzy *adj.* nod*
do *v.t.* chu'ig* (under *Occurring with*
wui__ *and* juni__); ~ **away with**
v.t. wua; ~**er** *n.* chu'ijkam; wua*
(under *Occurring with* juh)
dock *n.* wakontham; = CANAIGRE
doctor *n.* mahkai
doctrine *n.* mashchamathag
dodge *v.t.* kuchdwua
dog *n.* gogs; **many** ~**s** *n.* gogsig*
dogey *n.* lihbih
doll *n.* shobbiad; **talking** ~ *n.* tihtili
dollar *n.* pihsh
-dom *suffix that forms nouns* __dag*
domain *n.* kownaltalig
dome *n.* **have a** ~ kuwijk
donation *n.* limoshan*; limoshana
donkey *n.* wuhlu, wuhlo
door *n.* edpa*; kuhpadag; pualit;
~**knob** *n.* pualit kuhpi'okud; ~
mat *n.* chemhonakud; ~**way** *n.*
kihjeg
doubt *n.* tasho*
dove *n.* **mourning** ~ *n.* hohhi;
white-winged ~ *n.* okokoi
down *n.* wihgi; ~**stream** *adv.*
kuiwo; kuiwo*; ~**ward** *adv.* agshp
drag *v.t.* chewaimed; lawait; ~ **along**
v.t. lawaitchug
dragonfly *n.* mukchiwitham
drain *v.t.* wi'omi*
draw *v.t.* o'ohan, o'ohon; o'ohadag*;
o'ohan*; **a** ~**ing** *n.* o'ohadag;
o'ohana; ~ **a** LINE **on**; ~**er** *n.*
o'ohantham, o'ohontham
dream *v.t.* chehchk*; *n.* chehchki;
one's ~ *n.* chehchkthag
dress *n.* ipud; ~**maker** *n.*
i'ipudttham

drink *v.t.* ih'e; ih'e*; *v.i.* i'im*;
si'ila; *n.* ih'e*; ih'ethag; wasibi;
wasibith*; **excessive** ~er *n.*
i'imkam*; ~ing GLASS; **soft** ~ *n.*
sohla
drip *v.i.* oht
drive *v.t.* melchuth; *v.i.* med;
melchuthadag*; ~ **away** *v.t.*
shahmuth; ~r *n.* melchuththam
drizzle *v.i.* hikshpi; sihbani
drone *v.i.* weweg; wewegim*
droop *v.i.* i naggia
drop *v.t.* thagkon, thagkuan; ~-off
n. koa
drove *n.* shahtha; ~r *n.* ha
shahthkam
drown *v.i.* wachum
drum *n.* tamblo
drunk *adj.* nawm*; ~ard *n.* nawmki
dry *v.t.* gakijith; kohathk*; *v.i.*
hipig; *adj.* gaki*; gaksim*;
kushathk*; ~-**goods** *n.* lohba;
~**ness** *n.* gakithag; SPREAD **to** ~
duck *n.* pahtho; ~ling *n.* pahtho
mad
due *n.* **get one's** ~ jehka'ich; **one's**
~ *n.* wuikam
dull *adj.* kohmagi*
dump *v.t.* iawu; iawu*
dun *adj.* koyata; koyata*
dune *n.* SAND ~
dung *n.* biht
during *prep.* eda; ohla-a*; oitham
dusk *n.* chuk*
dust *v.t.* kuhbsmath*; *n.* kuhb__*;
kuhbs; ~ **devil** *n.* siwulogi,
siwuliki; ~y *adj.* kuhbsig*
dwarf COWBIRD
dwell *v.i.* kih*; ulinig*; ulinkahim*;
~er *n.* kihkam; thakam*; ~ing *n.*
kih; thaikud; ~ **temporarily** chewed
dye *n.* mahsithakud

E

each *adj.* aigojed*; wehs; **on** ~ SIDE
of; ~ OTHER
eagle *n.* ba'ag; ~t *n.* ba'ag mad
ear *n.* nahagew*; nahk; nak__*;
~**ache** *n.* nahk ko'okthag; **have an**
~ **for** chekaithag*; ~**mark** *n.*
nakpithag; ~**ring** *n.* nahagio;
within ~**shot** kaichuthch
early *adj.* uhpam*
earn *v.t.* gew*; nahto; ~ings *n.*
nahtoi
earth *n.* jewed; ~**enware** *n.* bith
ha'a; ~ **flowers** *n.* jewed-heosig;

~**quake** *n.* jewed u'ujig; **red or**
white ~ *n.* het; het*; **the** ~ *n.*
jewed; jewed kahchim
easily *adv.* pehegim*
east *n.* si'al; *adv.* si'al tahgio,
si'altgio; **in the** ~ si'al wecho;
~**ward** *adv.* si'al tahgio, si'altgio
easy *adj.* hauk*; pehegi*
eat *v.t.* hug__*; ko'a; ko'itohimed*;
v.i. gegosith; kohwog*;
kohwoth*; papali*; **appear to** ~
ko'athma; ~ **up** *v.t.* ko'ito
echo *v.i.* shashawk; ~ingly *adv.*
shashawkim
eclipse *v.t.* muhk*
edge *n.* hugithag; kuhg, kugi__
educate *v.t.* mashchamchuth
eel *n.* wamad watopi
effeminate *adj.* uwikwuad*
effort *n.* pihthag
egg *n.* nonha; **lay an** ~ nonhat
eight *n.,adj.* gigi'ik; ~h *n.,adj.*
gigi'ik
ejaculate SEMEN
elbow *n.* sihsh
elder *n.* kelimai; *adj.* ge'e
elect *v.t.* kehsh*; ~ee *n.* kehsha;
~**ion** *n.* wothalta
electric *adj.* wepgih; ~ity *n.*
wepgih; ~ LIGHT
elephant *n.* al-huanthi
elevate *v.t.* cheshaj; cheshaj*;
i cheshajchuth
elf OWL
elongate *v.i.* chewtha
elsewhere *adv.* go'olko; go'olkojed*
embarrass *v.t.* edawua*; ~ing *adj.*
eda__*; ~ingly *adv.* eda__*;
~**ment** *n.* edathag
embers *n.* chuhd__*
embrace *v.t.* kohmk
emcee *n.* pias-tihlo
emerge *v.i.* mahsi; wuhshani;
wuhshanig*; wuhshkam*; ~nce
n. wuhshanig
emissary *n.* ah'atha‡; hotsha†
emotional *adj.* wehs*
employ *v.t.* bahmuth; chikpanachuth,
chikpanachuth; ~er *n.* ahmo
empty *adj.* huhm*
enclosure *n.* kuhpik
encounter *v.t.* namk
encourage *v.t.* gewkemhun;
gewkemhuna*; i kehikon; ~**ment**
n. gewkemhunadag*
end *n.* kuhgitahim; *v.i.* hug;
kuhgit; kuhgitahim; *n.* bahi*;
baik__*; kug; kuhg, kugi__;
kuhgwua*

endure v.t. nakog; v.t. siakam*;
~ **through the night** mahsijith
enemy n. obga
engage v. ~d adj. hohni—*; ~ in
v.t. chu'ij; wua*
enjoy v.t. hohho'ith*; ~ably adv.
tahhatham*; ~ment n.
hohho'ithadag
enlarge v.t. ge'ethajith
enlighten v.t. i tonolith
enmity n. obgathag
enough adj.,adv. ahim
enter v.i. i wah; wahk; wahk*
entire adj. hekia
envious adj. chu hehgamkam; hehg*
envy v.t. hehgamk*; hehgamthadag
equal adj. wepo
-er suffix for comparatives ba'ich i
erase v.t. oan; oan*; ~r n. oanakud
erasure n. oana
erect v.t. kehsh; kehsh*; ~ion n.
kuhgia; ~ly adv. chu'al*
erode v.t. wi'ikon
escape v.i. tha'iwuni
especially adv. wahm
essay n. o'ohana
-est suffix for superlatives wehs
ha-ba'ich i
establish v.t. nahto
estate n. jewed; kihthag
esteem v.t. ha'ichuchuth
estimate v.t. amichuth
estrus n. uhw*; uhwalig
eternal adj. pi ha huhugetham
evangelist n. pahl
even adj. cheped; cheped*; wepo;
adv. chum hems, chem hems; ~ IF;
~ly adv. wepodagim*; ~ TEMPER;
~-tempered adj. bamuistk*; ~
THOUGH; ~ to this time wabsh kia,
hash kia
evening n. chuk*; huduni, hudunig;
hudunk; each ~ adv. hudukath; in
the ~ hudukath; hudunk
ever adv. hekith
every adj. wehs; ~(-)day adj.,adv.
wehs tashkaj; ~where adv.
wehsko; wehskojed*
evidently adv. —ki
evil n. pi-ap'ekam; adj. pad; pad*;
~ly adv. pad; think ~ly padhog*;
think ~ly about padhog*; ~
thinking n. padhog elithadag.
exactly adv. wa'i
examination n. chechgai; physical ~
n. kakpsith*; kakpsitha
examine v.t. chechga; neithahim
excavate v.t. hiabog
exceed v.t. ba'iwichkhim

except prep. mahth
exchange v.t. kammialt, kambialt;
n. kammialta, kambialta
excite v.t. che'owith
exclusively adv. wa'i
excuse v.t. gm hu wabsh oan
execution chamber n. me'akud kih
exercise v.i. moisha
exhibit n. chehgithadag; ~ion n.
chehgithakud; ~ to v.t. chehgith;
chehgith*
exist v.i. ha'ichug; kahch*;
exit v.i. wuhshani; ~ backwards
v.i. ta'i wuhshani
expect v.t. chum*; elith*; —hog*;
neahim; neal*
expedition n. a scouting ~ n.
githahimel
expel v.t. gm hu i wuhshath
expensive adj. namkig*; ~ly adv.
namkigam*
experience v.t. gahi wuhshani; neith;
n. neitha
explain v.t. tasho*; tashogith
explanation n. tashogitha
explode v.t. kopk; kopk*; koponi*;
kopsith*
explosion n. kopki
extend v.t. jiwhias*; ku'inhogs*;
~ to ahas*; ahi—*; ahijith*
extension n. ahijitha; ku'inhogitha
extent n. to some ~ sha
extinguish v.t. chuhsh
extremely adv. sha'i, sha—wa'i
exude v.t. sipshud*
eye n. hehewo; kup—*; wuhi;
wuhi*; ~brow n. hehewo; ~glass
n. wuhiga; ~lash n. wuipo (see
under wuhi); ~ of a needle
ho'ibadjeg; raise the ~brows
wuhigith

F

face v.t. abai*; kehk*; keki—*;
wuhiosha; v.i. ihma*; ihna*; ihya*;
~ powder tohajithakud; ~ to face
wuhio
fact n. wohohkam, wehohkam; in ~
pej, pegi; wohoh, wehoh
fade v.t. to'owagi*; v.i. mahso
faint v.i. chuhugith*; gehsith
fairy-duster n. chuhwi-wuipo
faith n. wohohchuthadag,
wehohchuthadag
fall v.i. gehsh*; ihg*; n. gehsig; ~
off or out v.i. igwua*

falsehood *n.* pi wohohkam, pi wehohkam
family *n.* ge'ejig*; hua-mihlia, famihlia; **one's** ~ *n.* wehm-kihkam
famine *n.* bihugig
famished *adj.* bihugim*
fan *n.* hehotakud; ~ PALM
far *adv.* **as ~ as** hugkam; ~ **away** mehkotham*; **from** ~ mehkjed; REMOVE ~ **away**
farm *n.* oithag; **~er** *n.* oithkam; **~ing** *n.* esha
fast *adj.,adv.* hoht__*
fasten *v.t.* ab sihshp; __dath*; gi'a; gi'is*; ~ **with a screw** tohb k ab sihshp
fat *n.* gihgi*; *adj.* gihg*; gihgchu; gi'i*; **~ten** *v.t.* gi'ichuth
fate *n.* chu'ichig
father *n.* alith*; apapa*; apkih*; kompal*; mahm*; ogol*; ohg*; pahl; wahw*; **~-in-law** *n.* wosma-je'e*; wosma-jehjim*
fatigue *n.* gewkogig
favor *n.* **curry** ~ ban; **~ite** *n.* ho'oma
fawn *n.* huawi mad, huai mad; sihki mad
fear *v.t.* ehbith*; elith*; *n.* ehbithadag; **~ful** *adj.* chu ehbiththam; ehbith*; **~fully** *adv.* ehbith*
feather *v.t.* a'anchuth; *n.* a'an; a'an*; ~ **on one's head** sihwotha; TAIL **~s**; WING ~
February *n.* Chehthagi Mashath†; Kohmagi Mashath‡
feces *n.* biht; bit__*
feed *v.t.* gegos__*; gegosith; **a ~ing** *n.* gegosig
feel *v.t.* tahtam; tahtk; thaghim; *v.i.* tahtk; **hurt (someone's) ~ings** ko'okemhun; **sense of ~ing** tahtkag
fellow member *n.* wehm*
female *n.* oks*; uwi; **adult** ~ *n.* oks; **young** ~ *n.* chehia
feminine *adj.* uwichuth*
fence *v.t.* kolhai*; kolhaidath; *n.* kolhai; kolhai*; uhksha*; **barbed-wire** ~ *n.* wainomi kolhai; ~ **post** *n.* kolhai chuhchim
fever *n.* tonijig*
fiancé *n.* wo ha hohntam; wo-kunta; **~e** *n.* wo ha kuntam; wo-hohnita
fiber *n.* shahwaithag*
field *n.* oith*; oithag; ~ **hockey** *n.* toka; toka*; tokada
fifth *n.,adj.* hetasp
fig *n.* suhna; ~ **tree** *n.* suhna je'e

fight *v.t.* cheggia; cheggia*; *n.* cheggiadag; **~er** *n.* cheggiatham; chu-cheggiadkam; **~ing** *adj.* chu-cheggiadkam
filaree *n.* hoho'ibad
file *v.t.* chelwin; chelwina*; *n.* hiwshanakud; s-hiwk-wainomi
Filipino *n.,adj.* Hi-lihpih
fill *v.t.* shuhth*; shuhthath
filly *n.* kawiyu mad
find *v.t.* chehg*; chehgith*; edagith; edagith*; ohche'ew; *n.* ohche'ewi; ~ **out** *v.t.* mahch
finish *v.t.* nahto; nahto*; __to*; *v.i.* nahto; ~ **line** *n.* meliwkud; ~ **victorious** *v.t.* gewito; ~ WORK
fire *n.* ihwith*; mehi; nahjith*; nahth*; nahtha; tai; **~brand** *n.* kuhthagi; **chopped ~wood** *n.* shontsig; **~cracker** *n.* kuitas; **~fly** *n.* taiwig; **light a** ~ kuht; **~place** *n.* nahthakud; **~stone** *n.* chetto; **~wood** *n.* ku'ag*; ku'agi
first *adj.* wehpeg; wehpegat*; *adv.* wehpeg; *n.* wehpegkam
fiscal YEAR
fish *n.* shuhthagi-ch-ed; watopi; **~-hook** CACTUS
fist *n.* shonihin*
five *n., adj.* hetasp; sihngo
flag *n.* wanjel
flake *n.* tamhon*
flap the WINGS
flashlight *n.* wepgih
flat *adj.* hab__*; kawadk*; komadwua*; komal; komal*; **~-bottomed** *adj.* cheped; cheped*; LIE ~; **~ly** *adv.* habalim*; komalim; **~ness** *n.* kapadthag; **~ten** *v.t.* komadkath
flatter *v.t.* ban*; ho'okemhun; **~er** *n.* ban; **~ery** *n.* ho'okemhunadag
flavor *n.* jehkig
flea *n.* chehpsh
flee *v.i.* ahhimed; simnolt
fleecy *adj.* komal*
flesh *n.* chuhkug, chuhhug; ha'apaga*; ha'apapig*; ohth*
fletch *v.t.* a'anchuth
flexible *adj.* moik*
flicker *v.i.* nanawuk; **gilded** ~ *n.* kudat
flood *v.t.* wi'in; *n.* wi'inthag; ~ **debris** *n.* wakola
floor *n.* wahkus, wahks; CEMENT ~; **pace the** ~ a'ai e himchchulith; **threshing** ~ *n.* alhin
flop down *v.i.* kapad*; kapadwua
flour *n.* chu'i; chu'ig*; MESQUITE- **pod** ~

flow *v.i.* med; ~ **out flat** wo'iwua
flower *n.* heosig
fluid *n.* sipuni*
flute *n.* wahpk kuikud
flutter *v.t.* widut; *v.i.* kuhgkim*
fly *v.t.* tha'ichuth; tha'imk*;
tha'ithag*; *v.i.* tha'a; tha'a*; *n.*
muhwal
foal *n.* kawiyu mad
foam *n.* totshagi*; ~y *adj.*
koshodk*
fog *n.* kohmhai; kuhbs; ~gy *adj.*
kohkaiwuagi*; kohmhai*
fold *v.t.* nahshp; ~ **up** *v.t.*
holiwkath
follow *v.t.* him*; oith; oith*;
oithahim; ~ **around** *v.t.* oithachug;
~er *n.* oithkam
food *n.* bih*; bihugim*; hahaisha*;
hithod*; hugi; sitdoi* **boiled** ~ *n.*
poshol; **ground** ~ *n.* chu'i
fool *n.* golwis; golwis*; tohnto; ~ish
adj. lohgo*; tohnto; ~ishly *adv.*
tohntom*; ~ness *n.* nakoshdag;
tohntomthadag
foot *n.* tad; tad*; **crush under** ~
kehishun; **have under** ~ kehishch;
land on one's feet judwua; ~path
n. aj-wohg; ~print *n.* gohki
for *prep.* hekaj*; __jelith*; wehhejed
forbid *v.t.* shohbith; shohbith*
force *v.t.* huihlsamath*; nu'ichkwua;
n. huihlsa
foreboding *n.* neijig*
forehead *n.* koa; koa*
foreigner *n.* gawul mahs hemajkam
foreman *n.* maliom; malioni
forewarn *v.t.* oh'ith*
forgive *v.t.* gm hu wabsh oan
fork *v.t.* sha'adk*; sha'aligi*;
uskon; uskona*; *n.* ol-gihya;
uskonakud
form *v.t.* WELL-~ed
fort *n.* kahon
forth *adv.* BACK and ~
fortune *n.* abam*, abamthag
foster PARENT
foundation *n.* shon; shonchuth*
four *n.,adj.* gi'ik; ~th *n.,adj.* gi'ik
fox *n.* gaso; **young** ~ *n.* gaso mad
frame of mind chegitoithag
fray *v.t.* wakimagi*
freckled *adj.* pipchumagi*
fresh *adj.* wechij; wechij*
Friday *n.* Wialos
friend *n.* nawoj; nawoj*; ~ly
adj. am__*; amkam;
nawojma*; nawojmakam; ~ship
n. nawojthag

frighten *v.t.* ebkioth; hudwua*; nod*;
tothsith; **become** ~ed **by** ehbith*;
~ing *adj.* ehbith*; ehbithamakam*;
~ingly *adv.* ehbith*
fritter away *v.t.* wua*
frog *n.* babath
from *prep.* amjed; amjed*; ~ **across**
prep. aigojed
front *n.* **in** ~ **of** *prep* bahsho; ba'ich;
tahgio; ~ **of the** NECK; **the** ~ **of**
bahsho
frown *v.i.* sho'odkath
fruit *n.* bahi*; bahithag; mad;
~ BEETLE; ~ **bud** *n.* ihbthag; **dried**
saguaro CACTUS ~; **form** ~ hikugt;
late ~ *n.* tohmthag; **off-season** ~
n. to'oliwad; to'oliwadag*
fry *v.t.* iolith; ~ing PAN
fugitive *n.* ahhimedtham
full *adj.* kohwog*; kohwoth*;
shuhth*; shuhthk
fun *n.* a'aschutha; tahhath__*; **make**
~ **of** hahsig; nahnko ahg; ~ny *adj.*
hehem*
funnel *n.* wuhlu, wuhlo
fur *n.* wopo; wopopig*
furnace *n.* ol-nihyo*
further *adv.* ba'ich i; ba'iwichkhim;
~more *adv.* ehp

G

gain *n.* behi; ~ **on** *v.t.* aihim
gall *n.* ka'al shuhthagi; ~ **bladder**
n. ka'al
gallon *n.* wa-lohn
gallop *v.i.* chu'adkim; halibwua
game *n.* chichwithag
gape *v.i.* ha'athkaj
garlic *n.* ahshos; ~ **clove** *n.* ahshos
garter *n.* kakio wudakud
gas *n.* uiwi*; = GASOLINE; **natural** ~
n. hewel
gasket *n.* HEAD ~
gasoline *n.* a-saithi; gaso-lihn
gate *n.* kuhpadag
gather *v.t.* hemapath; hemapath*;
kawudka; *v.i.* chehm*; ~ **(fruit)**
v.t. od; ~ **in** *v.t.* kapijk*;
~ **(seed)** *v.t.* moh
gauge *n.* kuintakud
gavel *n.* usaga
gearshift *n.* kammialtakud,
kambialtakud
gecko LIZARD
gelatin *n.* gigiwuktham

generosity *n.* chechojimadag
generous *adj.* chechijima*;
chechojimakam; ~ly *adv.*
chechojim*
gentle *adv.* hemajima*;
hemajimakam; ~ness *n.*
hemajimatalig
gently *adv.* hemajim*
genuine *adj.* si
germ *n.* cheawuagi
gestation *n.* **end of** ~ *n.* mashathga
get *v.t.* behe; behi⌐*; edagith;
edagith*; ~ **away** *v.i.,intj.* habba;
~ **out of the way** *v.i.* hiji; ~ **ready**
v.i. shelchuth; ~ **up** *v.i.* wamig;
~ **well** thoa
ghost *n.* kok'oi
gift *n.* mahkig*; mahkigdag*
Gila monster *n.* cheadagi
gird (up) *v.t.* hiwsh
girl *n.* chehia; ~**-crazy** *adj.*
uwimk*; **Mexican** ~ *n.* sinot, sinat
girth *n.* SADDLE ~
give *v.t.* ihsith*; mahk*; maki*; ~ **up**
v.i. ki'omi
glance at *v.t.* wuikon (*see under*
wuhi)
glass *n.* ~ **bottle** *n.* li-mihtha;
drinking ~ *n.* kohba
glean *v.t.* che'ew; che'ew*
glitter *v.i.* nanawuk
globe *n.* olas; ~ **mallow** *n.* gihkota;
hadam-tatk
glove *n.* nowi koshdag; wuanthi
glow *v.i.* nanawuk; ~**worm** *n.*
memhetham watopi
glue *v.t.* hadshp
glutton *n.* banmakam*; ~**ous** *adj.*
banma*; banmakam*; ~**y** *n.*
banmadag*
gnat *n.* chukmug
gnaw *v.t.* ~ **clean** ki'ikon; ~ **on**
v.t. ki'imun
go *v.i.* gm hu him; him*; ⌐med*; ~
along (doing) ⌐him*; ~ **around**
v.t. ba'iwichkhim; bijim; ⌐bim;
ta'ibim; ~ **back** ta'i him; ~ **beyond**
ba'iwichkhim; ~ **blank**
chuhugith*; ~ **continually** shel
him; shel himtham*; ~ **down** *v.i.*
huduni*; ~ **in a straight line** shel
him; ~ **on and on** mehkoth*; ~
past *v.t.* bijim; ⌐bim; START **to** ~;
~ **wrong** heki him
goat *n.* siwat, siwato; ~**nut** *n.*
hohowai; **young** ~ *n.* siwat mad,
siwato mad
god *n.* jiosh; **G**~ *n.* Jiosh; ~**child**
n. komal*; mad; ~**father** *n.*

kompal*; paw-lihna; ~**mother** *n.*
komal*
gold *n.* ohla
good *adj.* ap; ap*; kehg*; **baked** ~s
n. pas-tihl; **the** ~ *n.* ap'ekam*
goose *n.* kohkod
gopher *n.* jewho; ~ **snake** = **bull**
SNAKE
gore *v.t.* agchkwua; uskon; uskona*
gorge *n.* shahgig; showichk
gosling *n.* kohkod mad
gossip *n.* ahgadag*; ~**er** *n.*
chu-ahgimkam; ~**y** *adj.* ahg*
gourd *n.* WATER ~
govern *v.t.* ~**ment** *n.* kownal;
kownal*; ~**or** *n.* kownal
graft *v.t.* gi'is*
grain *n.* kai*; **roasted** ~ *n.* hahki
grand *adj.* ~**child** *n.* ba'a⌐*;
ka'a⌐*; ka'amad*; mohs*;
wosmad*; ~**father** *n.* ba'a⌐*;
bahb*; wosk*; ~**mother** *n.* hu'ul*;
ka'a⌐*; kahk*; ~**parent** *n.* bahb*;
hu'ul*; kahk*; wosk*
granular *adj.* mohoni*
grape *n.* uhdwis; ~ **vine** *n.*
uhdwis-je'e
grasp *v.t.* gi'a; shahkum; CARRY **in**
one's ~
grass *n.* sha'i; washai, washa'i; **bear**
~ *n.* moho; ~**hopper** *n.* shoh'o;
~ **saddle** *n.* lomaidag
grate *v.t.* hiwmun; hiwmuna*; ~**r**
n. hiwmunakud
grave *n.* hiha'ini, hihi'ani; ~**yard** *n.*
hiha'ini, hihi'ani
gravel *n.* hothai; o'od, o'ohia; ~**ly**
adj. o'od*
gravy *n.* at'ol; **saguaro seed** ~ *n.*
kaij at'ol
gray *adj.* chuhhuni*; kohmagi*;
kubjuwi*; luhya*; CHARCOAL ~
grease *v.t.* huhud; *n.* huhudakud;
~**wood** = CREOSOTE BUSH
greasy *adj.* muhadagi*
great *adj.* ge'e; ~**aunt** *n.* bahb*;
hu'ul*; kahk*; wosk*; ~**-grandchild**
n. wihkol*; wihshad*;
~**-grandparent** *n.* wihkol*;
wihshad*; ~**-great-grandchild** *n.*
sihs*; ~**-great-grandparent** *n.*
shehpij*; sikul*; ~**ly** *adv.* ge'e;
~**-nephew** *n.* ba'a⌐*; ka'a⌐*;
ka'amad*; mohs*; wosmad*;
~**-niece** *n.* ba'a⌐*; ka'a⌐*;
ka'amad*; mohs*; wosmad*;
~**-uncle** *n.* bahb*; hu'ul*; kahk*;
wosk*
greed *n.* banmadag*; ~**ily** *adv.*

green 86

howishim*; ~y *adj.* ban*;
banmakam*; behi__*; howishla*
green *adj.* chehthagi*; ihwagim*;
~ish *adj.* chehthagim*; **light** ~
adj. chedhaiwagi; chedhaiwagi*
greet *v.t.* hoin; ihm*
griddle *n.* komal; TORTILLA ~
grieve *v.t.* sho'igchuth
grimace *v.i.* kupkkia*; sho'odkath;
simudkaj
grin *v.i.* he'edkath; he'edkath*
grind *v.t.* chu'a; chuhi__*; ~ **for**
v.t. chu'ith*
grit *n.* o'od, o'ohia; ~ty *adj.*
o'odmagi*, o'odmagichu*
groan *v.i.* kuishani; shahshani; ~er
n. shahshanikam
groceries *n.* chu'imed*
grocery *n.* **go** ~ **shopping**
chuishpamed; hunimed
groin *n.* hiwchu
groom *n.* kunta
ground *n.* COFFEE or TEA ~s; **on the**
~ jewedo; **remove from the** ~
jewedpig; ~ SQUIRREL
group *n.* **in a** ~ **of** e wehm
grow *v.t.* __t*; *v.i.* chewelhim*;
ge'etha; ~th *n.* ge'elig
growl *v.i.* todk
gruel *n.* at'ol; ku'ul†
grumble *v.i.* kuishani
guard *v.t.* nuhkuth; *n.*
nuhkuththam; ~ **against** *v.t.*
nen'oithk*
guide *v.t.* wanimed; *n.*
wanimedtham
guilt *n.* chu'ichig
guitar *n.* gital
gulley *n.* hiktani
gulp *v.t.* ~ **(food)** *v.t.* howishp
gum *n.* ahtha; tamsh; **chewing** ~ *n.*
chihgathih, chihgitha; ki'iwih;
wihbam
gun *n.* cheggiakud; gaht; gatwua*;
gawos
gurgle *v.i.* kodog; kodog*
guru *n.* pahl
gut *n.* edawek

H

habitat *n.* oimmelig
hackberry *n.* kohm
had *v.* __d*; ~ **rather** ba'ich i
s-hohho'ith. *See also* HAVE
hail *n.* chea
hair *n.* kushpo*; ¹mo'o*; __po; BODY

~; CHEST ~; **grow** ~ mo'ot; **nasal**
~ *n.* thakpo; **pubic** ~ **of a female**
n. muspo*; **pubic** ~ **of a male** *n.*
wiapo
half *n.,adj.* eda hugkam; ~-**way**
adv. edawiko
halitosis *n.* banuw*
halter *n.* shahkim
ham *n.* ha-mohn; ~**burger** *n.*
chuhkug shoniwia, chuhhug
shoniwia
hammer *v.t.* shonihin; shonihina*;
n. shonihinakud
hammock *n.* iapta; naggia;
BLANKET ~
hand *n.* mahwua*; nowi; nowi*;
thag__*; ~**bag** *n.* kostal; ~**cuff**
v.t. maniadath; maniadag*;
~**cuff(s)** *n.* maniadathakud;
~ **down to** *v.t.* wuichuth;
wuichutha*; ~**ful** *n.* shahk*;
~**gun** *n.* pis-tohl; **have one's** ~ **in**
mawshch; ~**kerchief** *n.*
pa-nihtha‡; towash; **lay** ~**s on** tahtk;
on the one/other ~ hi'i*; **put**
one's ~ **in** mawshap; **shake** ~**s**
with nowi-bebhe; **strengthen the** ~
of gewkath; **wave the** ~ magajith;
magew; mawagith; ~**writing** *n.*
o'ohana
handle *n.* behikud; gi'a*; gi'adag;
gishshum*; thahithag
hang *v.t.* ahth*; naggia; naggia*;
sha'i*; sha'ichuth*; *v.i.* naggia;
CLOTHES ~**er**; ~**er** *n.* naggiakud
happen *v.i.* wua* (under *Occurring*
with juni__); ~ **to** *v.t.* ab wui gehsh
happily *adv.* hehgigam*
happiness *n.* hehgig*
happy *adj.* hehgig*
hard *adj.* kawk*
harm *v.t.* s-ko'okam wua
harness *v.t.* bibith__*; bibithshp; *n.*
bibithshpadag
harp *n.* ahlpa
harrow *v.t.* lahst; *n.* lahstakud;
lahstmath*
harvest *v.t.* od; wohni; *n.* oh;
~ **ceremony** *n.* iagta*; wihgitha;
~**er** *n.* odtham; ~ **(grain)** *v.t.*
kaipig; **hold a** ~ **ceremony** wihgith;
~ **of fruit** oda; SINGER/DANCER **in a**
~ **ceremony**
hat *n.* wonami; wonamim*
hatchet *n.* al hahsa
hate *v.t.* keh'ith*; *n.* obgathag; ~**ful**
adj. chu-ke'ithamkam; ~**fully**
adv. chu-ke'itham
haughty *adj.* gimaima*

haul *v.t.* ~ **(a load)** *v.t.* hohag; hohag*
have *v.t.* edagith; edagith*; ~ **on** *v.t.* __dag; juhkch; wua*. *See also* HAD *and* HAVING DONE **having done** *perfect participle* __ok* **hawk** *n.* tobaw*; **chicken** ~ *n.* wishag, wisag; **red-tailed** ~ *n.* haupul; **sharp-skinned** ~ *n.* wishag, wisag; **sparrow** ~ *n.* sisiki **he** *pron.* ihtha, ihtha'a **head** *n.* ge'ejig*; ¹mo'o; ²mo'o; ²mo'o*; mo'okat*; mo'otad*; u'umhaidath*; ~**ache** *n.* mo'o ko'okthag; CARRY **on the** ~; ~ **gasket** *n.* mo'o*; ~ **man** *n.* uhgchu **health** *n.* thoajig; wehsig*; ~**y** *adj.* ioma†*; thoa* **hear** *v.t.* chehg; chehg*; kah; ¹kai__*; ²kai__*; kaiham; **a** ~**ing** *n.* chekai__*; kaihama **heart** *n.* ihbthag **heat** *n.* toni*; TREAT **with** ~; ~ **wave** *n.* kuhjegi* **heaven** *n.* thahm kahchim **heavy** *adj.* wehch* **hedgehog** CACTUS **heed** *v.t.* kaiham **heel** *n.* chehmi **heliotrope** *n.* babath ihwagi **hell** *n.* jiawul kih **help** *v.t.* wehmt; wehmt*; *n.* wehmtadag; ~**er** *n.* wehmttham **hem** *v.t.* koabith; *n.* koadag **hen** *n.* mud ~ = COOT **her** *pron.* by ~**self** hejelko; ~**self** *pron.* e*, e-* **herd** *n.* shahtha; **drive a** ~ **of** shahth; ~**er** *n.* ha shahthkam **here** *adv.* ihab; ihya; ihya'a; ~ **facing across** ihna, ihna'a; ~ **facing away** ihma, ihma'a; ~ **facing this way** ihya, ihya'a; **from** ~ i'ajed; **way over** ~ ia huh **hero** *n.* siakam **heron** *n.* shuhthagi u'uwhig **hey** *intj.* hah **hiccup** *v.i.* henihopt **hide** *v.t.* ehsto; ehs*; *n.* hogi **high** *adj.* chuhthk; kowk*; uhg*; *adv.* chehk; ~ **up** *adj.* uhgk; uhgk* **hill** *n.* kawulk **him** *pron.* by ~**self** hejelko; ~**self** *pron.* e*, e-* **hinder** *v.t.* ihamhun; sha'ijith*; shohbith; shohbith*; wulshch*; wulshp; wulshpakud*

hindrance *n.* ihamhuna; shohbithadag **hip** *n.* ~ **joint** *n.* chuhl; **shake one's** ~**s** atgith **hire** *v.t.* chehani **hit** *v.t.* chedeni; gewi__*; gewichk; ma'ichk*; shonihin; shonikon; ~ **with** *v.t.* __hain; ~ **with the head** mo'okon **hitch** *n.* chi-mohn; ~ **together** mako **hobble** *v.t.* maniadag*; maniadath; *n.* maniadathakud **hoe** *v.t.* golwin; sihkon, sihmun; *n.* sibiyo **hog** *n.* ~ POTATO; ~**tie** *v.t.* alast k wuhd **hold** *v.* ~**er** *n.* kehshakud; ~ **out** *v.t.* ulin; ulin* **hole** *n.* magkan*; wag; ~**y** *adj.* magkas* **hollow** *adj.* hohalimagi* **holster** *n.* pis-tohl koshdag **Holy Spirit** *n.* Hekia S-ap'ekam Gewkthag **home** *n.* kih; ~ **and property** *n.* kihthag; ~**sick** *adj.* kihmk*; ~**sickness** *n.* kihmthag* **hominy** *n.* mi-nuhtho* **homosexual** *n.* cheojpa; ge kuhkunaj; ~**ity** *n.* cheojpadag **hone** *v.t.* mu'ukajith **honey** *n.* pa-nahl sit'ol **honor** *v.t.* elith*; ha'ichuchuth; **hoof** *n.* huch, huhch **hook** *v.t.* hukshp; la'a__*; la'ashp; ol__*; olshp; sihchk; uskon; uskona*; *n.* huk__*; hukshadkam; hukshpakud; la'ashpakud; ~ **and toss** *v.t.* sihchkwua; ~ **together** ku'ishom **hop** *v.i.* chu'adkim **hope** *v.t.* huh wo; ~**fully** *adv.* huh wo; **give** ~ **to** gewkath; **have one's** ~ **set on** gewkathch **Hopi tribesman** *n.* Hohpih **horn** *n.* a'ag; kuikud; **blow a** ~ hihnk; ~**ed** *adj.* a'agam; ~**ed** TOAD; ~**less** *adj.* wohlih; wohlih*; **put** ~**s on** a'agchuth **hornet** *n.* wihpsh **horse** *n.* kawiyu; ~ **collar** *n.* kohya; ko-yahl; ~**fly** *n.* todk; **palomino** ~ *n.* pal-mihtho; ~ **saddle** *n.* lomaidag*; lomaidath*; ~**shoe** *n.* kawiyu shuhshk; **untamed/ unbroken** ~ *n.* manayo; **yellowish-brown** ~ *n.* wahyo; wahyodag* **hose** *n.* hihij **hospital** *n.* kok'otham ha-kih

hostility *n.* obgathag
hot *adj.* ko'ok*; toni*; ~ly *adv.* tonim*
hotel *n.* koksikud
house *n.* kih; **meeting** ~ *n.* jehnikud; **menstrual** ~ *n.* huhulga kih
how *adv.* has i masma; ~ **about** higi; ~ **many/much/far, etc.** ha'a__*
however *conj.* eda
howl *v.i.* hihnk
hug *v.t.* kohmk
hull *n.* wohk; ~s *n.* mohg
hum *v.i.* jupij ne'e*; thoahim; weweg; wewegim*
human *n.* o'othham; ~ DIGNITY or WORTH; ~ity *n.* o'othhamthag; ~ RIGHTS; TREAT like a ~
humane *adj.* ~ly *adv.* hemajim*; ~ness *n.* hemajimatalig
humble *adj.* sho'ig; sho'ig*; ~ oneself sho'igchuth; ~ station *n.* sho'igthag
humbly *adv.* sho'ig
humility *n.* ab i sho'igthag
hummingbird *n.* wipismal
humor *n.* a'aschutha; ~ous *adj.* a'as__*; ~ously *adv.* ta a'askim
hump *n.* chuhthk*; moashan; ~backed *adj.* jumadk*; omlik; omlik*; ~ed *adj.* omlik; omlik*; opojk
hunch-backed *adj.* chuwithk*
hundred *n.,adj.* siant; ~th *n.,adj.* siant
hunger *n.* bihugig; bihugimthag; maimthag*
hungry *adj.* bihugim*; bihugimkam
hunt *v.t.* o'oith†; wia; wipi'a; *v.i.* me'a*; *n.* tobtham*; ~er *n.* mo'obdam; o'oiththam†
hurry *v.t.* hoht__*; *v.i.* hoht__*; oiwith; oiwigith*
husband *n.* kun; kun*; mad-ohg*; ma'i*; **one's** ~ *n.* keliga
husks *n.* mohg

I

I *pron.* ahnih; __ni
ice *n.* gew; ~ **pellets** *n.* chea
identify *v.* ahg*
identity *n.* **acknowledge one's** ~ edagith
if *conj.* __p; sha*; **even** ~ chum as hems, chem as hems
ignore *v.t.* pi chegima; pi hudaweg
ill-fortune *n.* sho'igchuthadag

illustrate *v.t.* tasho*; tashogith
illustration *n.* tashogitha
image *n.* sahnto*
imitate *v.t.* i wepot; junisith* (*under* wua)
imitator *n.* junisiththam
immediately *adv.* ha hekaj
immoral *adj.* ledo'osh; ~ WOMAN
importance *n.* ha'ichu*
important *adj.* ba'ichkam*; ha'ichu*; has*
impoverish *v.t.* sho'igchuth; ~ment *n.* sho'igchuthadag
improve *v.t.* ap*; apchuth; kegchuth; ~ment *n.* apchutha
in *prep.* eda; __ko
incant *v.t.* hambthogith; ~ingly *adv.* hambthogim*
inchworm *n.* ohchwigi
incinerator *n.* mehithakud
incite *v.t.* chu'amun; chu'amuna*; i kehikon
incumbent *adj.* thaha*
indeed *adv.* wehoh, wohoh; wohohm*
independently *adv.* hejel
Indian *n.* APACHE ~; COCOPA ~; ~ **fig** = **prickly-pear** CACTUS; MARICOPA ~; MOHAVE ~; NAVAJO ~; ~ness *n.* o'othhamthag; OPATA ~; PIMA ~; SERI ~
indigestion *n.* main*; maimthag; maimthag*
industrious *adj.* wagima*; wagimakam*; ~ly *adv.* wagimam*
infect *v.t.* aha; cheawuagith; ~ion *n.* cheawuagig; ~ious *adj.* cheawuagig*
inflate *v.t.* kopothkath
influence *v.t.* wanichk; *n.* gewkthagkam*
influential *adj.* gewkthagkam
-ing *suffix to verbs* chu__*; __dag*
inhabitant *n.* kihkam
inherit *v.t.* wuichuth*; wuichutha*; ~ance *n.* wuikam
in-law *n.* ihmigi*; kiheh*
innertube *n.* kal-sihtho
inquisitive *adj.* kaimkam; shelmadag*
insane *adj.* lohgo; lohgo*
insanity *n.* lohgodag
insect *n.* muhwal
insert *v.t.* wahkith; wahks*
insides *n.* eda*; edawek
inspect *v.t.* chechga; ~ion *n.* chechga
instead of *prep.* kehkud ed
instruct *v.t.* shelinith; wohg*; ~ion

n. ahgith*; ha'ichu ahgitha; ha'ichu ahgithadag
instrument *n.* thagshpakud*; WIND ~
insufficient *adj.* chum, chem; chum*
intelligibly *adv.* amichuth*
intend *v.t.* ahgch*
intensely *adv.* si
intention *n.* ahga*
interest *v.t.* ~ed *adj.* kaiham*;
~**edly** *adv.* kaiham*; ~**ing** *adj.*
kaiham*; tahhath___*; ~**ingly** *adv.*
kaiham*
interfere with *v.t.* mawshap
interior *n.* eda*
intersect *v.t.* kahiobins*
intestine(s) *n.* edawek; hihij
intoxicate *v.t.* nawm*; ~d *adj.*
gehsith*
introduce to *v.t.* mahchchulith
intrude *v.t.* mahwua
invalid *n.* mukialig
investigate *v.t.* chechga; mahch;
mamche; sihon, sihowin; *v.i.*
nenashan
investigation *n.* chechgai
invitation *n.* waithadag
invite *v.t.* bahmuth; melith*; waith;
waitha*; ~**r** *n.* waiththam
iron *v.t.* plahnja; thahpiun;
thahpium*; **an** ~ *n.* plahnjakud;
wainomi; **branding** ~ *n.*
cheposithakud; ~**er** *n.*
plahnjatham; ~**wood tree** *n.*
ho'ithkam
irregular *adj.* muhwij*
irrigate *v.t.* wahg
irritate *v.t.* baga*; todwin
it *pron.* ihtha, ihtha'a; **by** ~**self**
hejelko
Italy *n.* I-tahlia
itch *v.i.* mohogith; mohogithchuth*;
~**y** *adj.* moho___*

J

jack *n.* ~ RABBIT; ~**s** *n.*
mikithwuikud
jacket *n.* lihwa; wuakithalig†
jagged *adj.* muhwij*
jaguar *n.* ohshad
jail *n.* kahlisa; kukpaikud
jam *n.* kushul; **make into** ~ kushult;
saguaro CACTUS **fruit** ~
January *n.* Gi'ihodag Mashath‡;
Kohmagi Mashath†
Japanese *n.,adj.* Hapo-nihs*
jar *n.* ha'a; nawaitakud*; **bottom of a**
~ at

javelina *n.* kohji
jaw *n.* tahtko
jealous *adj.* chu hehgamkam; hehg*;
~**y** *n.* hehgamthadag
jerk with fright tothkesh
jerky *n.* chuhkug gaki*
Jesus *n.* Hi-suhs
Jew *n.* Hulio; Tuhlgo; ~**ish** *adj.*
Palasi*; Sajusi*; ~**'s harp** *n.*
lohmba
jimsonweed *n.* kotdobi
job *n.* chikpan, chipkan
John *n.* Huan
joint *n.* shohba
jojoba *n.* hohowai
joke *n.* nahnkogitha; ~**r** *n.*
nahnkogiththam; ~ **with** *v.t.*
nahnko*; nahnkogith
jokingly *adv.* nahnkogsim*
Joseph *n.* Husi
joy *n.* s-ap tahhathkam; tahhath___*;
~**fully** *adv.* hehgigam*
judge *v.t.* lothai*; lothait; *n.*
lothaittham; usagakam
judgment *n.* lothaitakud; lothaithag,
lothaisig
judicate *v.t.* gagda
juggle *v.t.* kolbiwua
juice *n.* wadagi
July *n.* Huhlio Mashath; Jukiabig
Mashath; **fourth of** ~ *n.* kuathlo
Huhlio
jump *v.i.* tha'a; tha'ihim*;
tha'ithag*; ~ **along** *v.i.* judwuahim
June *n.* Hahshani Bahithag Mashath
just *adv.* hash, wabsh; wa'i; ~ **a**
LITTLE; ~ SO BIG

K

kangaroo RAT
keep up with *v.t.* aichug
key *n.* yahwi
kick *v.t.* kehi___*; kehichk; *v.i.*
kehi___; kownith
kid *n.* siwat*
kidney *n.* olopaj, olapapaj; **a** ~ *n.*
olopa, olapap
kill *v.t.* me'___*; me'a, mu'a;
muhkith*; ~**deer** *n.* chiwi-chuhch;
~**er** *n.* me'akam; mu'akam
kin *n.* ihmigi*; juni*
kind *adj.* hemajimakam; ~**ly** *adv.*
hemajim*; ~**ness** *n.* hemajimatalig;
ho'ige'itha*; ho'ige'ithadag*; **this or**
that ~ **of** mahs*
kindling *n.* haupul-kosh; taimunig;
CHOP **into** ~

king *n.* kownal; lai; **~dom** *n.* kownaltalig; ~ SNAKE; western **~bird** *n.* hewel-mohs
kinky *adj.* kulwani*
kiss *v.t.* chintath
kit *n.* gaso mad
kitchen *n.* kosin
kitten *n.* mihstol mad, mihtol mad
Kitt Peak *n.* Ioligam
knee *n.* tohn; tonhain*; **bump the ~** tonwua
kneel *v.i.* tonwua
knife *n.* wainomi; POCKET ~
knit *v.t.* jehjegt*
knob *n.* beikud
knock *v.t.,v.i.* shontpag; **~ down** *v.t.* melchkwua; **~ out** *v.t.* ma'ichk*
knot *n.* **tie a ~ in** hahwulith
know *v.t.* mahch*; **be desirable to ~** machma*; SEEM **to ~**; **~ well** mahch*
knowledge *n.* mahch*; mahchig; **~able** *adj.* amichuth*; mahchim*; **~ably** *adv.* mahchim*

L

ladder *n.* iskli
lady *n.* oks
lake *n.* ge'e shuhthagi; ge shuhthagi; kahchk
lamb *n.* **a ~** *n.* kahwal mad; **a bighorn ~** *n.* cheshoni mad
lamp *n.* kanjel, kanjul; lahmba; **~ chimney** *n.* tuhwo
land *v.i.* chuthwua*
language *n.* ne'oki; **use offensive ~** s-gogsim neok
lard *n.* manjekih
large *adj.* ge'e; **~r** *adj.* ge'echu
lariat *n.* RAWhide ~
lark *n.* **horned ~** *n.* chukul-ba'ichuk; **~spur** *n.* chuchul-i'ispul; kuksho-wuhplim
last *adj.* **the ~** BIT
late *adv.* pi oi; **the ~** *adj.* __bad
laugh *v.i.* a'as__*; hehem; **~ at** *v.t.* ash; asim*; **~er** *n.* hehemkam*; **~ing** *adj.* hehemkam*; **~ter** *n.* a'aschutha; hehemthag
launder *v.t.* wapkon; **~er** *n.* wakontham
law *n.* chehanig; huihlsa
lay *v.t.* chehk; chehk*; chehkith; **~about** *n.* padhogmakam*; **~ an** EGG; **~ away** *v.t.* chehkith; **~ down** *v.t.* wohth; wothwua

laziness *n.* padmadag*
lazy *adj.* pad*
lead *v.t.* wanimed; wawan; *n.* plohmo; **~ astray** heki himchuth; **~er** *n.* ge'ejig; wanimedtham; **religious ~er** *n.* pahl
leaf *n.* hahhag
leak *v.i.* oht
lean *v.i.* **~ against** *v.t.* __chk*; **~ing over** *adj.* kupal; **~ness** *n.* gi'ihothag
learn *v.t.* amichuth; chehg; chehg*; mahch; **cause to ~** mashchamchuth; **~ to** *v.t.* ³__t
leash *n.* baiuka
leather *n.,adj.* hogi; **put ~ on** hogidath
leave *v.t.* thagito; wi'a, wi'am; wi'am*; wi'i*; wi'ith*; *v.i.* gm hu him; himto
leaven *v.t.* jew*; *n.* jewajithakud
lechuguilla *n.* a'ud
left *adj.* ohgig*; **~-handed** *adj.* ohgigkam*; **~over** *n.* wi'ithag
leg *n.* kahio; kaishch*; LONG-**~ged; shake one's ~** kahiogith; SHORT-**~ged; spread the ~s** kashadkath
legend *n.* ha'ichu ahgithadag
lemon *n.* li-mohn
lengthen *v.t.* chewthajith; chewthajithas*
lentil *n.* lanjeki
lesson *n.* mashchamathag
letter *n.* kaithag o'ohana; o'ohana
lettuce *n.* li-juhwa
level *adj.* cheped; cheped*; komal; komal*; wepo; wepodag*; *n.* = SPIRIT ~
liar *n.* iattomkam
liberty *n.* ap'ethag*
license *n.* ap'ethag; shel
lick *v.t.* nehniwua; wini__*; winikon
lid *n.* kuhpadag; ma'ishpakud
lie *v.i.* bijims*; iatto__*; wawani*; **~ against** *v.t.* gewishp; **~ down** wo'iwua; **~ flat** kapad; wo'o*; **~ lifeless** kahch; **place to ~ down** *n.* wo'ikud; **~ to** *v.t.* iattogith. *See also* LYING
life *n.* wohg*; **have ~** thoa; **inner ~** *n.* ihbthag; **~time** *n.* thoakag; thoakthag; WAY **of ~**
lift *v.t.* uhg i behe
light *v.t.* owich*; *n.* chuhk*; tonlig; tonolith*; *adj.* hauk*; **~ a** FIRE/CIGARETTE, **etc.; cease giving off ~** muhk*; **electric ~** *n.* kanjel, kanjul; **~-fingered** *adj.* behi__*;

~ning *n.* wepgih; wuihun;
~weight *adj.* hauk*
like *v.t.* hohho'ith*; tachchu,
tachchua; *prep.* chu'ig*; __kaj
-like *suffix that forms adjectives*
__kaj; masma
lily *n.* Mariposa ~ *n.* hahthkos;
Papago ~ *n.* hahth
lima BEAN
limber up *v.i.* moisha
limestone *n.* chemag
limit *n.* chehmo'o*; ~ed *adj.* am
hu'i*
limp *v.i.* gohhim; goikhim; *n.*
ialhim*
linament *n.* huhudakud
line *v.t.* apola__*; *n.* chekshani;
chekshna; chekshshas; wawnadag;
draw a ~ on chekshan; GO in a
straight ~; in ~ shakal; wavy ~s
n. bibijjim; bibolmath*
lining *n.* apoladag; apoladath*
link *v.t.* gi'a
lion *n.* mawith; ~ cub *n.* mawith
mad
liquid *n.* shuhthagi; SPRINKLE with ~
listen *v.* ~ to *v.t.* kaiham; ~ to
habitually kaichug; ~ well
nakwuadag
little *adj.* al; a ~ *adj.* al; *adv.* sha;
only/just a ~ al chum; ~ old *adj.*
al
live *v.i.* thaha*; ~stock *n.* shawant*
liver *n.* nemaj; a ~ *n.* nem
lizard *n.* hujud; jusukal*; gecko ~
n. ohbi-mad; pi-to'ichu; sand ~
n. watksh; whiptail ~ *n.* wajelho
load *v.t.* hohaghim;
kushwi'otachuth*; *n.* kushwi'ot*;
mohtoi
loan *v.t.* hiwigith
locate *v.t.* ohche'ew
lock *v.t.* yahwi*; yahwidath; *n.*
yahwi
locoweed *n.* koponthakud
locust *n.* kohntpul, kohtpul
log *n.* shoniaka*
loincloth *n.* atosha; atosha*
long *adj.* chew; chew*; ~ ago
na'ana; ~-legged *adj.* chu'alk*; no
~er pi ehp
look *v.i.* ap'ema*; ap'etama*; nea;
nenashan; ~ alike mahs*; ~ around
v.i. nenhog; ~ at *v.t.* ab neith;
~ for *v.t.* gahg; gahg*; neahim;
~ for (animals) *v.t.* shawant; ~ like
v.t. mahs*; ~ over *v.t.* neithahim
loop *v.t.* hakkodag*; *n.* hakko*;
~ed *adj.* hakkodag*

loose *adj.* jushadk*; ~n *v.t.*
jushadkath
lose *v.t.* heb hu wua; ~ one's PLACE;
~ WEIGHT. *See also* LOST
loss *n.* heb hu gehsig
lost *adj.* him*. *See also* LOSE
louse *n.* ah'ach; ah'ach*; body ~ *n.*
hiopch
love *v.t.* tachchu*; *n.* pihk elithadag;
tachchuithag; have deep ~ (for), ~
deeply pihk elith; ~r *n.*
tachchutham
low *adj.* jumal*; komadwua*; at a ~
PITCH; ~land *n.* wo'oshani
lower *v.t.* jumalkath
lubricant *n.* huhudakud
lubricate *v.t.* huhud; huhuda*
lubrication *n.* huhuda
luck *n.* abamthag; ho'oma*; ~y *adj.*
ho'omachuth*
Luke *n.* Luhgas
lumber *n.* huk
lump *n.* olas; ~y *adj.* olas; olas*
lunch *n.* chuishpa*; chuishpith*;
gegosig; lohnji
lung *n.* hahaw
lupine *n.* Arizona ~ *n.*
tash-mahhag
-ly *suffix that forms adverbs* __m
lying *adj.* iattomkam; be ~ across
v.t. gahiobs*. *See also* LIE

M

machete *n.* masit
machine *n.* sewing ~ *n.*
shohshomakud
mad *adj.* baga*; ~dening *adj.*
baga*; ~deningly *adv.* baga*
maimed *adj.* mohjo
maintain *v.t.* himchuth
make *v.t.* nahto*; ~ clear mahsko
wua; ~r *n.* nahtokam; wuatham*
male *n.* cheoj; cheoj*; keli*;
effeminate ~ *n.* uwikwuad;
uwikwuadag*; ~ of any (specified)
species *n.* keli*
man *n.* cheoj; cheoj*; ~hood *n.*
cheojthag; ~liness *n.*
chechojimadag; cheojthag; ~ly *adj.*
chechojima*; chechojimakam;
cheoj*
manage *v.t.* nakog*; barely ~ *v.i.*
gehsim
manner *n.* ha'ab*; hab-a ehp*
manroot *n.* ihkowi
manufacture *v.t.* nahto; ~r *n.*
nahtokam

many *pron.,adj.* mu'i; mu'i*
manzanita *n.* ioligam
mar *v.t.* chimkkon
marble *n.* ga-tohthi
march *v.t.* himchchulith
March *n.* Chehthagi Mashath‡; Oam
Mashath†
margin *n.* on the ~ of an
Maricopa Indian *n.* O'obab
Mariposa LILY
mark *v.t.* chekshshas; ~ for
identification *v.t.* cheposith;
chepositha*; ~sman *n.*
gatwuatham
Mark *n.* Mahgas
marriage *n.* hohnita
marrow *n.* oag
marry *v.t.* hohni__*; kun*; wehmt*;
v.t. hohni__*; kun*
Mary *n.* Ma-liia
mash *v.* chuhi__*; sihkon, sihmun
mask *n.* wuhiosha
mass *n.* mihshmath*
massage *v.t.* thagimun; *n.*
thagimuna; thagimuna*
master of ceremonies *n.* pias-tihlo
mat *n.* wahkus, wahks; STRAW ~; ~
weaver *n.* maintatham
match *n.* tai; boxing ~ *n.* cheggia*;
cheggiadag; wrestling ~ *n.*
cheggia*; cheggiadag
Matthew *n.* Ma-tiias
mature *adj.* ge'ehog*; ~ly *adv.*
ge'ehogam*
maturity *n.* ge'el
maverick *n.* olhoni
maxim *n.* ha'ichu ahgithadag
may *modal auxiliary* am hu
May *n.* Ko'ok Mashath‡; Pilkani
Mashath†
maybe *adv.* na__
me *pron.* ahnih; heni-†; ni-
meadowlark *n.* western ~ *n.* tosiw
meal *n.* gegosig
mean *v.t.* ahg*; pej*; *adj.*
ha'ahama; ke'ith*; shemachuththam;
adv. ke'ith*; ~ing *n.* ahga*; ~ly
adv. shemachuth*; ~ness *n.*
shemachuthadag
means *n.* by ~ of *prep.* gahi
wuhshanim; hekaj
measles *n.* hiwkadag, hiwkalig
measure *v.t.* kuint; *n.* pisal; ~ment
n. kehi__*; kuintadag
measuring TAPE, STICK
meat *n.* chuhkug, chuhhug; dried ~
n. chuhkug gaki*; ground ~ *n.*
chuhkug shoniwia, chuhhug
shoniwia; roasted ~ *n.* ga'i

medicate *v.t.* kulanimath
medicine *n.* kulani; ~ bag *n.*
huashomi; chief ~ man *n.* siwani;
~ man *n.* mahkai
meet *v.t.* __nam*; namk; namk*; a
~ing *n.* jehnigitha; namki; ~ing
HOUSE; ~ing PLACE
melon *n.* miloni
melt *v.t.* hahgith; *v.i.* hahg;
~ away *v.i.* hagito
member *n.* __gam*
memorize *v.t.* mahch*
memory *n.* chegitoithag*
menstrual HOUSE
menstruate *v.i.* huhulgat
menstruation *n.* huhulga*
-ment *suffix that forms nouns* __dag*
mental *adj.* wehs*
mercifully *adv.* ho'ige'itham*
mercy *n.* ho'ige'itha*;
ho'ige'ithadag*
mere *adj.* wabsh, hash; ~ly *adv.*
wabsh, hash
mescat acacia *n.* githag
mesquite *n.* kui*; ~ bean *n.*
chepa*; ~-pod flour *n.* jehg
message *n.* ahga; ne'oki
messenger *n.* ah'atha
metal *n.* wainomi; ~ic *adj.*
wainomi; ~ wire *n.* aj-wainomi
meteorite *n.* siawogi
meter *n.* kuintakud
middle *n.* in the ~ edaweso*; in the
~ of edawi; s-eda, si eda
midst *n.* in the ~ of si shahgith
might *modal auxiliary* am hu
mildew *n.* mamadhod; ~y *adj.*
mamadhodag*
mile *n.* kehi__*; mihya
milk *v.t.* wak'e; *n.* wihbi; M~y
Way *n.* Tohmog; ~weed *n.*
ban-wihbam; wihbam
million *n.,adj.* mi-yohn
millipede *n.* kommo'ol
mimic *v.t.* che'isith*
mind *n.* wehsig*
mine *n.* mihnas
minister *n.* pahl
minute *n.* mi-nuhto
mirage *n.* kuhjegi; shashkaj
mirror *n.* neithakud
missile *n.* cheggiakud
missionary *n.* ah'atha
mist *n.* kohmhai; ~y *adj.*
kohmhai*; kohmhaiwuadag*
mistake *v.,n.* ~ for another
hemachuth; make a ~ pihk chu'ig
mistletoe *n.* hahkwod
mistress *n.* moshogi

misuse *v.t.* nahnko*; nahnkogith
mix *v.t.* iolagith; ~ (**ingredients**)
　v.t. shahshagith
moan *v.i.* kuishani
mob *v.t.* bihad
modest *adj.* sho'ig; sho'ig*; ~ly
　adv. sho'ig; ~y *n.* ab i sho'igthag
Mohave Indian *n.* Nakshad; Ma-hahwi
moisten *v.t.* wahg
mold *n.* mamadhod; ~y *adj.*
　mamadhodag*
Monday *n.* Luhnas
money *n.* lial
monkey *n.* chahngo; gogs o'othham
monster *n.* ho'ok; **legendary** ~ *n.*
　kohths
month *n.* mashath; mashath*
moon *n.* mashath
moose *n.* cheshoni; a ~ **calf** *n.*
　cheshoni mad
more *adv.* ba'ich i; ba'iwichkhim;
　ehp; ~over *adv.* ehp
Morman *n.,adj.* Mohmli
morning *n.* mahsig; si'alig; **each** ~
　si'almath; ~glory plant *n.*
　bihbhiag; **in the** ~ si'almath
mortar *n.* chehpo'o*; a ~ *n.*
　machchud
mosquito *n.* wahmug
most *adv* wehs ha-ba'ich i
motel *n.* koksikud
moth *n.* hu'ul-nahgi
mother *n.* je'e*; komal*; tha'al†;
　~-in-law *n.* ka'ama-je'e*;
　mohs-ohg*
motion picture = MOVIE
motor *n.* mahginathag
mound *n.* chuwithk; wa'akih*
mountain *n.* tho'ag
mourning DOVE
mouse *n.* nahagio
moustache *n.* chiniwo; chiniwo*
mouth *n.* chini; chini*; kam___*;
　CLOSE-~ed
move *v.t.* ___gith*; i behe; wuichuth*;
　v.i. chihpia*; (*imperative only*) hiji;
　hoin; ~ along *v.i.* him; himchuth*;
　kehkhim
movie *n.* wepgih; go to a ~ wepegith
mow *v.t.* hihk; hihk*; ~er *n.*
　hihkakud
much *pron.* mu'i; mu'i*; *adj.* mu'i;
　that ~ ahim
mud *n.* bith; bith*; ~ hen = COOT;
　remove ~ from bithpig
mulberry *n.* gohih*
mule *n.* muhla; ~ DEER
multiply *v.t.* mu'ithajith; nahshp*;
　v.i. mu'itha

murder *v.t.* me'a, mu'a
mushroom *n.* okstakud
music *n.* ne'i; **compose** ~ ne'it;
　~ian *n.* kuhutham; muhsigo; **make**
　~ muhsigo; **make** ~ **for** kuhijith;
　play ~ **for** ne'ichuth
muskmelon *n.* milini, miloni
mutton *n.* kahwal chuhkug
muzzle *v.t.* thakosh
my *adj.* ni-, heni-; **by** ~self hejelko;
　~ **own** ni-, heni-; ~self *pron.* ni-,
　heni-

N

nail *v.t.* ho'iumi†; sihshp; *n.*
　klahwo, lahwos
naked *adj.* thahpk*; wa'athk*
name *v.t.* ahg; chehchk; chehgig*;
　n. chehgig; CALL **by** ~; **register**
　one's ~ o'ohan*; ~sake *n.* tokayo
nap *n.* **take a** ~ komishad
narrow *v.t.* aj*; giwudk*; giwulk*;
　adj. aj; kapijk; kapijk*; kawijk*;
　shapij; shapij*
nation *n.* hemajkam*; nasi-yohn
Navajo Indian *n.* Nahwaho; Ohbi
navel *n.* hik; hik*
near *adv.* mia; mia*; *prep.*
　miabithch; ~by *adv.* mia; mia*;
　come ~er to miabith; ~ to *prep.*
　miabithch
necessarily *adv.* hemho wa
necessity *n.* tachchui
neck *n.* ahth*; baiuka; baiukt*;
　kuswo; kusta*; **back of the** ~
　kusho; **front of the** ~ ba'ichu; **have**
　around the ~ baiuk, baiukch; ~tie
　n. kol-wahtho
necrotic *adj.* muhks
need *v.t.* tachchu, tachchua; *n.*
　tachchuithag
needle *n.* ho'ibad; EYE **of a** ~
neglect *v.t.* pi ap nuhkuth; *n.* pi ap
　nuhkuthadag
neigh *v.i.* kuhi*; kuhu*
neighbor *n.* miabithch kihkam;
　~hood *n.* kihthag
nephew *n.* chuhchud*; hakimad*;
　mad*; ma'i*
nerve *n.* oag
nest *n.* kosh
net *n.* chuaggia
never *adv.* pi hekith
new *adj.* hemuchkam*; wechij;
　wechij*
news *n.* ahga; kailig
next *adj.* ba'ich*

nice adj. kehg*
nick v.t. chimkkon
nickel n. a ~ n. mihyu†; sihngo
niece n. chuhchud*; hakimad*; mad*; ma'i*
night n. chuhug; huduni, hudunig; ~ club n. kan-tihna; ENDURE through the ~; ~gown n. koksikud; last ~ adv. chuhug; ~ly adv. chuchkath; the lesser ~hawk n. nehpod
nine n.,adj. humukt
ninth n.,adj. humukt
nipple n. wipih
no adv. pi'a; from ~where pi'ajed; ~where adv. pi hebai, pi heba'i
noise n. che'ithag; nakosig*; ~less adj. pi shahmunim; shahmuni*; make a ~ shahmug
noisily adv. kaithagim; nakosigam*; shahmunim
noisy adj. nakosig*; shahmunim
non-conformist n. golwis; golwis*
non-existent adj. ha'ichug*; piach*
noon n. thahm*; at ~ thahm juhk
nopal n. ihbhai
normal adj. ap; ap*
north n. juhpin, wi'inim; adv. juhpin tahgio, wi'inim tahgio; to the ~ ta'i; ~ward adv. juhpin tahgio, wi'inim tahgio
nose n. thahk; blow one's ~ shohwua; bump the ~ thakwua
nostril n. shoshkthag
not adv. pi, pim; pi sha'i; ~ at all pi ha; pi sha'i; ~ in any way pi ha
notice v.t. chegima*
nourish v.t. gegosith; kowgith*; ~ing adj. kowgith*; ~ment n. gegositha
November n. Kehg S-hehpijig Mashath‡; Uhwalig Mashath†
now adv. hahawa*; hemu, hemuch; ithani; oi; from ~ on i'ajed; right ~ adv. ia i
nuisance n. tamhog*
numb adj. muhks*
number n. ha'a__*; __jj*; nuhmilo; any ~ of wabsh chum he'ekia, hash chum he'ekia
numskull n. koshwa
nurse v.t. si'i; si'i*; v.i. si'i
nut n. tol-nihyo

O

oak n. bitoi; ~ tree n. toa; wi-yohti; wi-yohthi je'e; white-~ tree n. ka'al

oatmeal n. wuhlu-ki'iwia, wuhlo-ki'iwia
obedience n. wehog elithadag
obey v.t. elith*; him; kaiham
object to v.t. ko'okoth*
oblong adj. muhwij*; shapij; shapij*; shapol; shapol*
obsenity n. padhog elithadag
observe v.t. am-absh neith; him
obtainable adj. behi__*
obviously adv. __ki
occur to v.t. ab wui gehsh
ocean n. ge'e shuhthagi; ge kahchk
ocotilla n. melhog
ocre n. het
October n. Wi'ihanig Mashath
odor n. jewo*; __uw*; uwh*; uwhalig; ~ous adj. uhw*
offence n. take ~ at ko'okoth*
offend v.t. che'owith
offer v.t. chehkith*
office n. ~r n. ge'ejig; presiding ~r n. usagakam; take ~ kekiwua
offspring n. alithag*; mad*
often adv. mu'ikko
oh intj. hah; ih; oh
oil v.t. huhud; n. chuk a-saithi; huhudakud
OK adv. ho-e-juh, ho-ni-juh, ni-juh; pegih
okay = OK
old adj. ahithkam*; hekihuchij*; hekihukam*; kushathkath*; ~er adj. ge'echu; ~er person n. kelimai
olla n. nawaitakud; wa'igkud
ominous adj. neith*
omit v.t. thagito
on prep. ab; aigo*; __ko*
once adv. hemho; ~ upon a time na'ana
one n. hemako; mahth; pron. ahg*; hedai*; hegai*; hema; adj. hema; hemako; ~ ANOTHER; by ~self hejelko; for ~ hi'i*; PACE ~self; ~'s hedai*; SECLUDE ~self; ~self pron. e*
onion n. siwol
only adv. wabsh, hash; wa'i; ~ a LITTLE; ~ if mahtho; not ~...but also wa'i*; ~ so BIG
ooze v.i. jegwoni*; ~ out v.i. jegwoni
Opata Indian n. Ohbathi
open v.t. kuhp__*; kuhpi'ok; kuhpi'okud*; v.i. jeg*; adj. jeg*; (an) ~ing n. jeg; ~er n. kuhpi'okud; in the ~ jegko
operate on v.t. hitpod

ophthalmologist *n.* wuhpui mahkai
opinion *n.* chegitoithag; elith*; **win the ~ of** wanichkwua
opponent *n.* owi
opportune *adj.* ap'e*; apkot*
opportunity *n.* ap'ethag; chahnsa
oppose *v.t.* ab wui kehk; cheggia; kehk*
opposition *n.* owi
or *conj.* aha; o
orange *adj.* oam*; **an ~** *n.* nalash
orate *v.t.* amog; amog*; ~r *n.* amogtham
order *v.t.* chehani
organ-pipe CACTUS
oriole *n.* s-oam shashani
orphan *n.* hejel wi'ikam; lihbih; ~ed *adj.* hejel wihkam
other *adj.* aigo*; go'ol; ha'i; hi'i*; **each ~** e*; e-*; t-; **on the ~** SIDE **of;** ~s *pron.* ha'i; **the ~ one** *pron.* hegai hema
ouch *intj.* ana
our *adj.* t-; **by ~selves** hejelko; **~ own** *adj.* t-; **~selves** *pron.* t-
outhouse *n.* wuhshani*
outlast *v.t.* ba'iwichkhim
outside *n.* jeg
oven *n.* nahthakud; pahntakud; ADOBE ~
over *prep.* thahm; **~take** *v.t.* aha; ba'iwichkhim; ne'ibijim, ne'ibim; **~turned** *adj.* kupal
owe *v.t.* wikla
owl *n.* chukud; **burrowing ~** *n.* kokoho‡; kokohoa†; ~ CLOVER; **elf ~** *n.* kuhkwul
own *v.t.* edagith; edagith*; eniga; enigachuth*; *adj.* ge; hejel; **~er** *n.* edagiththam; enigakam; enigat*
ox *n.* woiwis

P

pace *n.* kehi_*; **~ oneself** chekith; **~ the** FLOOR; **~ the** MEASUREment **of**
pack RAT
pail *n.* pihla; wa'igkud
pain *n.* ko'ok*; ko'okthag; sini'oliga; **~ful** *adj.* ko'ok*; **~fully** *adv.* ko'okam*
paint *v.t.* bith*; bithhun; o'ohadag; o'ohan, o'ohon; o'ohan*; *n.* mahsithakud; **a ~ing** *n.* o'ohadag; **~er** *n.* o'ohantham, o'ohontham; **remove ~ from** elpig

pajamas *n.* koksikud
palate *n.* ahtha
palm *n.* matk; shahk*; **fan ~ tree** *n.* mahhagam
palomino HORSE
paloverde *n.* kalistp; kuk chehethagi; ohbgam*; **blue ~** *n.* ko'okmadk
pan *n.* bihkud; hithodakud; wan-nihha, wan-thihha; **deep-fried ~cake** *n.* oamajitha; **frying ~** *n.* bahikam*; sal-tihn
pancreas *n.* wiwa
panic *v.i.* shelkam noda
pant *v.i.* hahawk
pants *n.* shaliw
Papago Indian *n.* O'othham; **the ~ people** *n.* Tohono O'othham
Papago LILY
paper *n.* tapial; **piece of ~** *n.* tapial; SAND~; TAR ~
parade *n.* himchchul
parent *n.* foster ~ *n.* nuhkuththam; ~s *n.* je'e
parrot *n.* chehthagi-u'uwhig; pil-gihtho
parry penstemon *n.* hewel-e'es; wuhpiostakud
part *n.* chu'ithag; ha'ichuthag; shuhthgim*; tahpna; **in ~s** hikshp
party *v.i.* piast; *n.* piast; **have a ~** wohla
pass *v.t.* ba'iwichkhim; ne'ibijim; ne'ibim; *v.i.* him*; **~ageway** *n.* kihjeg*; **~ by** *v.t.* bijim, _bim; **narrow ~age** *n.* showichk; **~ out** *v.i.* chuhugith*; gehsith; **~ through** *v.t.* gahi wuhshani
past *prep.* ba'ich
paste *v.t.* bithshch*; hadshp
pasture *n.* pot-lihya
pat *v.t.* shontpag
patata/patota *n.* opon
patch *v.t.* ab chehk
path *n.* wohg
patience *n.* **have ~** bahbgih
patient *n.* mumkutham; *adj.* tahtk*; **~ly** *adv.* bahbgim*
patrolman *n.* BORDER ~
patter *v.i.* sihskim*
Paul *n.* Pawhlo
pawn *v.t.* plihnthat; **~shop** *n.* plihnthatakud
pay *v.t.* namkith; namkitha*; **~ment** *n.* namkith*; **~ (something) back** nodagith
pea *n.* wihol; **black-eyed ~** *n.* huhuda-wuhpkam†
peach *n.* julashan; nulash†
peafowl *n.* ahdho

peak *n.* mu'uk*; **have a ~** kuwijk
peanut *n.* kaka-wuathi
pear *n.* pihlas; pihlas* **~ tree** *n.*
pihlas
peccary *n.* kohji
peck *v.t.,v.i.* chepwin; chepwin*
pediatrician *n.* mahmad ha-mahkai
peek *v.i.* koachkwua
peel *v.t.* el__*; elpig
peep over *v.t.* koachk
pelt *v.t.* ma'ikkan
pen *n.* lahbis
penalize *v.t.* s-ko'okam namkith
penalty *n.* s-ko'ok namkithadag
pencil *n.* lahbis
penis *n.* wiha
penny *n.* oam*
penstemon = PARRY PENSTEMON
people *n.* hemajkam; hemajkam*;
created ~ *n.* hemajkamta, hemajta
pepper *v.t.* pi-mianthimath; **black** ~
n. pi-mianthi; ~**-colored** *adj.*
kaimagi
perceive *v.t.* neith
percolate *v.t.* o'osith
perforate *v.t.* magkan
perform *v.t.* wua*; ~**er** *n.* wua*
(under *Occurring with* juh)
perfume *v.t.* uhwmath
perhaps *adv.* na__
period *n.* **menstrual** ~ *n.*
mashathga
perish *v.i.* huhug; huhughim*
permanent *adj.* pi ha huhugetham
permeate *v.t.* chehmo'o
permission *n.* shel
permit *n.* ap'ethag; shel
person *n.* hemajkam; hemajkam*;
o'othham; ~**ality** *n.* o'othhamthag;
common, ordinary ~ *n.* wabsh
o'othham; **local** ~ *n.* wabsh
o'othham
perversion *n.* tohntomthadag
pervert *v.t.* tohntochuth; *n.* tohnto;
~**ed** *adj.* tohnto; ~**edly** *adv.*
tohntom*
peso (Mexican) *N* Juhkam pihsh
pester *v.t.* shodobinchuth
pestle *n.* chehpithakud; shoniwikud
pet *v.t.* tahtam; *n.* shoiga
Peter *n.* Pihwlo
petrify *v.t.* hothaichuth
phainopepla *n.* kuigam
Pharisee *n.* Palasi*
phone = TELEPHONE
phosphorescent *adj.* nahj
oimmedtham*
photograph *v.t.* pikchulith; *n.*
pikchulithathag
piano *n.* e thagtpagtham

pick *v.t.* madpig*; wohni; ~**axe** *n.*
ahithkam-tohlo-a'ag; pihgo; ~ **up**
v.t. che'ew*; i behe; ~**up** TRUCK
picture *n.* o'ohadag; **religious** ~ *n.*
sahnto; **take a** ~ **of** pikchulith
pie *n.* pas-tihl
piece *n.* chu'ithag; ha'ichuthag; **pull**
~**s from** wanimun
pierce *v.t.* ho'ishp
pig *n.* kohji
pigeon *n.* pa-lohma; paplo
pigment *n.* mahsithakud
pigweed *n.* chuhugia
pile *v.t.* sipulkath; thashwua;
thashwuis*; *n.* sipulk*
pilgrim *n.* chihpiatham ~**age** *n.*
chihpiathag
pill *n.* e bab'etham kulani; **sleeping** ~
n. kohsithakud
Pima Indian *n.* Akimel-o'othham;
lower ~ **tribesman** *n.*
Chuhwi-Ko'atham
Pima WHEAT
pimple *n.* mu'umka; ~**d** *adj.*
mu'umkadag*
pimply *adj.* mu'umka*
pin *v.t.* ho'iumi†; sihshp; *n.*
sihshpakud; ~ **feather** *n.* wihgi
pinch *v.t.* hukshp; hukshpa*
pine *n.* huk
pinoli *n.* hahki
pipe *n.* pihba; ~ **wrench with chain**
n. chahngo-bahi
pistol *n.* pis-tohl
pit *n.* kai; ~ **roast** *n.* ma'i;
ma'ikkana*; **roasting** ~ ma'ikud;
ma'in*
pitch *v.t.* bahbagi*; *n.* bahbagim*;
at a low ~ bahbagi*; ~**fork** *n.*
ol-gihya
pitcher *n.* wa'igkud
pity *v.t.* ho'ige'ith*
place *v.t.* chehk; chehk*; chehkith;
chekch*; thahsh; thahshch*; wua;
n. kehkud*; __pa*; **give** ~ **to**
bahbagi; **in a high** ~ uhg; **in a low**
~ jumal; jumal*; **in one** ~ hemiap;
in ~ **of** kehkud ed; **lose one's** ~
heki him; **meeting** ~ *n.*
jehnigithakud; meliwig
placenta *n.* kosh
plains tribesman *n.* a'an-wonamim
plan *v.t.* ahg*; elith*; *n.* chu'ichig;
elith*; elithadag*
plane *n.* hiwshanakud
plant *v.t.* es__*; esh; esha*; *n.* e'es;
esha; je'e*; wuhshthag; ~**able** *adj.*
es__*; CROP (**of** ~**s**); ~**ing season**
n. eshabig; ~ **sprout** *n.* i'ibhunig
plantain *n.* mumsha

plaster *n.* bith; bith*; *v.t.* bith*
bithhun; bithshp
plate *n.* hoas-ha'a
platter *n.* pulato
play *v.t.* chel—*; chichwi; chichwi*;
gew*; thag—*; *v.i.* chichwi;
chichwi*; *n.* chichwithag; ~ (a
stringed instrument) *v.t.* chelshan;
chelwin; ~ CARDS; ~er *n.*
chichwitham; ~ground slide *n.*
hehlwuikud; ~ MUSIC for; ~ with
v.t. chichwi
plead *v.t.* ab nakog; ~ to *v.t.*
bahmuth
pleasure *n.* hohho'ithadag;
tahhathkam
Pleides *n.* Chechpa'awi
plentifully *adv.* be'ama*
pliable *adj.* moik*
pliers *n.* ki'ishpakud
plow *v.t.* moihun; moihun*; *n.* gihki
plus *prep.* gamai
pocket *n.* wohshag; ~book *n.*
huashomi; ~ knife *n.* nawash
point *n.* mu'uk*; at this ~ ihab; ~ to
v.t. a'aga
poison *v.t.* hialwuimath; *n.* hialwui
poke *v.t.* chu'amun; chu'amuna*
police officer *n.* cha-lihhi†; chi-lihhi‡
polish *v.t.* chelwin; chelwina*
pollen *n.* chu'i; chu'i wuatham*
pollute *v.t.* uam*; uamhun; ~d *adj.*
oam*
pomegranate *n.* gal-nahyo
pommel *n.* sihl mo'o
pond *n.* shuhthagi; wachki; wo'o
pool *n.* puhl
poor *adj.* sho'ig; sho'ig*
pop *v.i.* kopk; kopk*; kopnihim*;
kopnim* ~-over *n.* oamajitha; ~
up *v.i.* tha'ichshp
poplar tree *n.* mohmli auppa
poppy *n.* California ~ *n.*
hohhi-e'es; Desert gold ~ *n.*
hohhi-e'es; Mexican gold ~ *n.*
hohhi-e'es; prickly ~ *n.* nod; tohta
heosig
populate *v.t.* o'othhamag*
population *n.* kihkam
porcupine *n.* hoho'i
pork *n.* kohji chuhkug; fried ~ fat
n. sisloni
pornography *n.* padhog elithadag
position *n.* in a low ~ jumal; jumal*
positive *adj.* ge
possess *v.t.* edagith; edagith*; eniga;
gain ~ion of edagith; ~ion *n.*
eniga; eniga*; material ~ions *n.*
kaistalig; ~or *n.* edagiththam
postage stamp *n.* mo'o

pot *n.* hithodakud; wa'igkud; ~ter
n. haha'atadkam*
potato *n.* bahbas; hog ~ *n.* ihkowi;
sweet ~ *n.* ihkowi; ka-mohthi; wild
sweet ~ *n.* shahd
poult *n.* TURKEY ~
pound *v.t.* skonikkan; shontpag; *v.i.*
shontpag; *n.* wehch*; ~ on *v.t.*
shonikkan
pour *v.t.* iawu; iawu*; to'a; to'a*;
wasibwua*
poverty *n.* sho'igthag
powder *n.* baking ~ *n.* is-paula;
kopothkthakud; koshodkthakud;
blasting ~ *n.* pohlwis; ~ed *adj.*
chu'i
practice *n.* himthag*
prairie dog *n.* tehhr
praise *v.t.* hehgchulith; hehgigchulith
prank *n.* play a ~ on jehka'ich
pray *v.i.* ho'ige'ithahun; ~er *n.*
ho'ige'ithahuna; ~ing mantis *n.*
bahp-chehpo'ogam
preach *v.t.* amog; amog*; ~er *n.*
amogtham; ~ to *v.t.* mihshmath
precious *adj.* namkig*; ~ly *adv.*
namkigam*
precise *adj.* si
prefer *v.t.* ba'ich i s-hohho'ith*
preparation *n.* apchutha; nahtogig
prepare *v.t.* ap*; apchuth; nahto; ~
for danger ih'in
present *adj.* oimmed*; thaha*; *n.*
mahkig; ~able *adj.* neith*; ~ably
adv. neith*; at ~ hemu, hemuch
president *n.* kownal
press *v.* ~ against *v.t.* honwua; ~
on *v.t.* —chk*; thagshp; thagtpag
presumably *adv.* ¹—sh
pretend *v.t.* wua* (under *Occurring
with wui*—)
pretty *adj.* kehg*
prey *n.* one's ~ *n.* me'a, mu'a
price *n.* namkithadag
prick *v.t.* ho'ishp; ~ly-pear CACTUS
pride *n.* gimaimadag; woikimathag
priest *n.* pahl
prime minister *n.* kownal
print *v.t.* o'ohan; o'ohon; o'ohan*;
~er *n.* o'ohantham, o'ohontham
prison *n.* kukpaikud; ~er *n.* lihso;
lihsochuth*
prize *n.* gehgewi, gehgthag
probably *adv.* hems
proceed past *v.t.* bijim
proclaim *v.t.* amog; amog*; ~er *n.*
amogtham
prod *v.t.* chu'amun; chu'amuna*
progress *v.i.* him; himchuth*
prominence *n.* sha'adk*

promiscuous *adj.* chehpa'awidag*;
mawshch*; ~ly *adv.* chehpa'awim
promise *v.t.* ah'ath*
promote *v.t.* wahmuth*
prone *adj.* wo'i__*
pronghorn ANTELOPE
pronunciation *n.* che'ithag
proof *n.* wohohkamchutha
properly *adv.* ap*
property *n.* real ~ *n.* jewed
prophet *n.* ah'atha; pahl
propitiatory *adj.* iag__*
protect *v.t.* nuhkuth; nuhkutha*; ~or
n. nuhkuththam
Protestant *n.,adj.* Mihsh; ~ CHURCH
proud *adj.* woikima*;
woikshanimkam*; ~person *n.* gimai
prove *v.t.* wohohkamchuth,
wehohkamchuth
puberty *n.* chuhwua*; wuag__*
puck *n.* ola
puff *v.* ~ out SMOKE; ~ up *v.t.*
koshodk*; kowkath*
pull *v.t.* wanimun*; ~ along *v.t.*
wanichkwua; ~ on *v.t.* wanichk; ~
out *v.t.* huhpan*
pulse *n.* chuwithani; chuwithani*
pulverize *v.t.* mohon; ~ (grain) *v.t.*
edwin
puma *n.* mawith
pumpkin *n.* hahl
punctuation mark *n.* muhwal-biht
puncture *v.t.* chu'akkanas*;
ho'ikkan; ho'ishch*; ~ vine *n.*
jewed ho'ithag; ~ wound *n.*
chu'akkana
punish *v.t.* kastigal; s-ko'okam
namkith; ~ment *n.* s-ko'ok
namkithadag; wuikam
puppet *n.* tihtili
puppy *n.* gogs mad
purchase *v.t.* nolawt; sha'awai; *n.*
nolawta
pure *adj.* hekia
purpose *n.* ahgch*; for the ~ of
wehhejed
purse *n.* lial kih
purslane *n.* ku'ulpalk
pursley = PURSLANE
push *v.* ~ along *v.t.* nu'i*;
nuichkwua; ~ away *v.t.*
nu'ichkwua; ~cart *n.* nu'ihimtham
kalit; ~ down *v.t.* nu'ichkwua; ~
on *v.t.* nu'ichk
put *v.t.* chehk; chehk*; chehkith;
thahsh; thahshch*; ~ down *v.t.*
wua; ~ on *v.t.* __dath*; wua*; ~
on (a shoe) *v.t.* cheka; cheka*
pyrrhuloxia *n.* bichpod

Q

quail *n.* kakaichu Gambel's ~ *n.*
kakaichu
quarrel with *v.t.* kawhain
quart *n.* kualtho
queen *n.* kownal
question *v.i.* shelam; *n.* chu'ichki;
kakkei; ASK (a ~) of; ~er *n.*
chu'ichktham; ~ing *adj.*
chu'ichktham; ~naire *n.* kakkei
tapial
quick *adj.,adv.* hoht__*
quiet *adj.* pi shahmunim; shahmuni*;
~ly *adv.* jupij*; jushal
quilt *n.* che'ewhuith*;
che'ewhuithadag; kahma
quince *n.* mimb-lihyo; ~ tree *n.*
mimb-lihyo je'e
quit *v.t.* ha'asa; *v.i.* i ha'asa
quite *adv.* si; not ~ chum alo, chem
alo
quiver *n.* wogsha

R

rabbit *n.* black-tailed jack ~ *n.*
chuk chuhwi; cottontail ~ *n.* tohbi;
jack ~ *n.* chuhwi; white-tailed
jack ~ *n.* toha chuhwi
rabid *adj.* nodagam
rabies *n.* nodagig
raccoon *n.* wawuk
race *v.i.* wuithag*; *n.* menchutha*;
black ~r SNAKE; run a relay ~ with
bijimith; ~track *n.* jegda
radiant *adj.* mahs*
radio *n.* hewel-neoktham
rag *n.* ikus; ~ged *adj.* wakimagi*;
wihinagi*; wihs*
ragweed *n.* nunuwi-jehj
raider *n.* githaihimdam
raiding *adj.* githaihimdam
rail *n.* yuhngih; ~road *n.*
wainomi-wohg; ~road car *n.*
wainomi-kalit
rain *v.i.* juhk; jujk__*; juk__*; *n.*
juhki; ~bow *n.* kiohod; ~ dance
n. chelkona*; ~ lightly hikshpi;
~ on *v.t.* jukshp; ~y *adj.*
juhkig*; ~y season *n.* jukiabig
raise *v.t.* cheshaj; i cheshajchuth;
cheshaj*; ~ from lying wamigith;
~ (offspring) *v.t.* ge'elith
raisin *n.* uhdwis-gakithag
rake *v.t.* golwin; hukshan, hukshom;
nahsith; *n.* hukshanakud;
nahsithakud; ~ together *v.t.* nu'a

ram n. ¹keli*
ramada n. watto
ranch n. lahnju
rank n. in a low ~ jumal; jumal*
rash n. chedkalig
rasp n. chelwinakud
rat n. wosho; kangaroo ~ n.
thahiwua; pack ~ n. koson; wood
~ n. koson
ration n. lasan, lason
rattle v.t. kologith; sijkith; v.i.
kolig; kolig*; shaw; n. kologitha;
kologithakud; shawikud; ANKLE ~;
~snake n. ko'oi; ko'owi
raven n. hawani
ravine n. aki; shahgig; showichk
raw adj. tho'i; tho'i*; ~hide n.
haiwani elthag; ~hide lariat n. liat
ray of light n. sihwotha
razor n. hiwkonakud; ~ blade n.
mu'uksig
razz v.t. kuichuth*
reach v.t. a'ahe*; aha*; chehmo'o*;
cheka; tahtchulith
ready adj. nahtokch*; nakog*; intj.
thohwai; GET ~
real adj. si; wohohma*; ~ly adv. si
realize v.t. neith; neith ab amjed*
reason n. ahgch*; hab*
rebuke v.t. keh'ith*
recess v.i. pihhun; n. pihhuna
recline v.i. wohthch*
recognition n. amichuthadag
recognize v.t. amichuth
recreation area n. chichwikud
red adj. hetmagi*; wegi*
reduce v.t. chum*; chumthajith,
chemthajith; shoniwin*
reed n. wahpk
refreshment stand n. kan-tihna
refugee n. ahhimedtham
refuse n. wosuna
register one's NAME
regurgitate v.t. wihot
regurgitation n. wihos
rein n. lihntha
reject v.t. ohhoth*; n. ohhotha
relation n. hajuni; hajuni*; form a
~ship with __t; ~ship n. ³juni*
relative n. abkam; hajuni; hajuni*
relax v.i. ohshan; ~ation n.
ulinihogig‡
release v.t. thagito
relieve (pain) v.t. hewajith, hewbajith
religious adj. pahl; ~ LEADer
remain v.i. wi'i; wi'is*
remind v.t. chegito*
remnant n. wi'ikam
remote adj. hujed*

remove v.t. huhpan*; wuahawua; DIG
up and ~; ~ far away mehkoth; ~
from v.t. __pig
renew v.t. hekiagith
repair v.t. ap*; apchuth; kegchuth;
n. apchutha
repay v.t. namkith; ~ment n.
namkith*
repeat v.t. che'isith
reportedly adv. ¹__sh
repress v.t. thaish
repudiate v.t. pi mahch ch e ahg
repulse v.t. uhwaith*; uhwaithchuth
reputation n. chehgig
request n. tahnig
rescue v.t. tho'ibia; ~r n.
tho'ibiakam
resent v.t. ko'okoth*
reservoir n. wachki
reside v.i. kih*; thaha*; establish
~nce chihwia; ~nce n. kih
resign v.i. ha'asa chikpan, ha'asa
chipkan; wuhshani
resilient adj. juhagi*
resin n. chuhwuathag*; ushabi;
ushabi*
respect v.t. ab has elith; elith*; n.
wehog elithadag
responsibility n. chu'ichig; mohtoi;
nuhkutha; take ~ for mawshap
rest v.i. hewbagith†; hewbagith*;
ulinihogith‡; n. hewbagig†;
ulinihogig‡; cause to ~
ulinihogith‡; ~fully adv.
hewbagim*
restrain v.t. shohbith; shohbith*; ~t
n. shohbithadag
retardate n. pi wehsigkam
retire v.i. pihhun; ~ment n. pihhuna
return v.t. heki himchuth; nodagith*;
v.i. nod; nod*; in ~ aigo
reveal v.t. chehgith*; maskogith*;
masko wua; tasho*; tashogith
revelation n. chehgithadag; by ~
tonolithch
revenge n. get ~ nodagith
reverse v.,n. ~ a process __ho*; in
~ kuhgam
reward n. namkithadag; wuikam
rhatany n. edho
rib n. ho'onma; CACTUS ~ cage;
saguaro CACTUS ~
rice n. a-lohs, shohs
rich n.,adj. kais*; ~es n.
kaischutha; ~ly adv. kaisim*
ride v.t. cheshaj; cheshaj*; thaichug*;
n. cheshajig; ~ along on
cheshajchug; ~ bareback kaishch g
kawiyu

ridge pole *n.* wawnadag
ridicule *v.t.* hahsig; nahnko*; nahnko ahg
rifle *n.* gawos; ~ **shell** *n.* u'u; wahl
right *n.* ap'ekam*; shel; wuikam; *adj.* ap*; apko*; *adv.* ap*; **human** ~s *n.* o'othham ap'ethag; ~ NOW; ~s *n.* ap'ethag; ~ THEN
rim *n.* WHEEL ~
ring *v.t.* gew; *n.* anilo; **boxing or wrestling** ~ *n.* cheggiakud
rip *v.t.* wantshp
ripe *adj.* baha*; bahi*; bai__*; baikam; ~n *v.t.* bahijith
ripple of sand *n.* wi'ushanig
rise *v.i.* koshodk*; kowkath*; si'ad*; uhgka; uhgkahim*; wamig*; ~ **above** *v.t.* thahm i cheshaj
rival *n.* hehg; hehgt*; sahyo; ~ry *n.* hehgamthadag
river *n.* akimel
rivulet *n.* wi'ishani
road *n.* wohg; ~runner *n.* tadai
roar *v.i.* kuhk; kuhk*; todk
roast *v.t.* ga'a; hahk*; [2]kuhag*; kuhagith*; sitdoi*; *n.* chuamai; [1]kuhag; ~ **in ashes** *v.t.* chuama; PIT ~
rock *v.t.* ugijith, ujugith; *n.* hothai; a ~ *n.* waw; ~ (**a baby**) *v.t.* ulugith
roll *v.* ~ **over** *v.i.* wo'ihim; ~ **up** *v.t.* chul__*; holiwk*; holiwkath; olat; olatahim*; witkwua; *v.i.* holiw; holiwk*
roof *n.* ma'ishpadag; ASPHALT ~ing
room *n.* kih; **make** ~ **for** jegelith
rooster *n.* [1]keli*
root *v.t.* tatkchuth; *v.i.* tatkt; *n.* tatk; tatk*
rope *v.t.* wuhd*; wuhlith*; wulshch*; wulshp; *n.* wijina; wijinat*; wudakud; wulkud*; **make** ~ talwin
rosary *n.* losalo; losalo*
rot *v.t.* jewajith; *v.i.* jew*; jewa; ~ten *adj.* jew*
rough *adj.* chedk*; chel__*; cheodagi*; chepwinag*; hiwk*; ~en *v.t.* i chedkath; ~ly *adv.* chedkam*
round *adj.* sikod; sikol; sikol*; ~ **up** *v.t.* hu'uith; ~up *n.* hu'uitha; shawant*
route *n.* hims*
row *n.* wawnim
rub *v.t.* chelwin; chelwina*; chelshan; hiw; hiw*; __shan*; ~ **off** *v.t.* chemhon

rubber *n.* uhli
rug *n.* wahkus, wahks
ruin *v.t.* wia*
ruler *n.* kuintakud; lai; uhs kuintakud
rumble *v.i.* kodog; kodog*; thoahim*; *n.* bebethk*
rummage through *v.t.* sihowin, sihon
run *v.i.* med; [1]mel*; [2]mel*; [1]mel__*; [2]mel__*; ~ **around** *v.t.* ne'ibim, ne'ibijim; ~ **away** *v.i.* simnolt; ~away *n.* ahhimedtham; ~ **down** *v.t.* melchkwua; ~ **into** *v.t.* melchk; ~ner *n.* medtham; [2]mel*; melchuththam; ~ **over** *v.t.* melchkwua
rush *v.t.,v.i.* hoht__*; ~ **out** *v.i.* tha'iwuni; ~ **past** *v.i.* tha'iwuni
rust *v.i.* wuhsh; *n.* wuhshthag; ~-brown *adj.* lichintog*; ~-colored *adj.* wakumagi*; ~y *adj.* wakumagi*
rustle *v.t.* ~ (**livestock**) *v.t.* kiot

S

sack *n.* tahlk
sacrifice *v.t.* iag__*; *n.* iagchulitha
sad *adj.* ai*
saddle *v.t.* hogi*; hogidath; lomaidag*; *n.* puhst†; sihl; **back of** a ~ *n.* sihl at; ~ **blanket** *n.* shuwijel; ~ **girth** *n.* sihnju; GRASS ~; ~ **horn** *n.* sihl mo'o
Sadducee *n.* Sajusi*
sadness *n.* oh'ith*
sagebrush *n.* ongoi
saguaro CACTUS (**button, fruit, fruit jam, wine**)
saguaro seed GRAVY
saliva *n.* siswuadag; ~te *v.i.* siswua
salmon *n.* watopi hithod
saloon *n.* kan-tihna
salt *v.t.* onmath; *n.* on; on*; ~bush *n.* onk ihwagi; tatshagi; ~ **grass** *n.* onk washai; ~iness *n.* on*; onkthag*; ~y *adj.* on*; onk*
salvation *n.* tho'ibiathag
same *adj.* masmo*; wepo; **do the** ~ **as** i wepot
sand *n.* o'od, o'ohia; ~ **dune** *n.* hia; ~ LIZARD; ~paper *n.* o'od tapial; ~piper *n.* chiwi-chuhch; RIPPLE **of** ~; ~-root *n.* hia tatk
sandal *n.* kaigia shuhshk
sap *n.* ushagi; ushagi*
sarcastic *adj.* ko'okoth*

sardine *n.* watopi hithod
Satan *n.* Niawul
Saturday *n.* Shahwai
save *v.t.* tho'ibia; ~ **up bit by bit** wi'ahim
savior *n.* tho'ibiakam
say *v.t.* ahg; ahg*; ahga*; che'is*; kaij*; kaijelith*; **a** ~**ing** *n.* ahga; **it is said (that)** ¹__sh
scab *n.* komipig*
scale *n.* pisaltakud
scalp *n.* mo'otk
scandal *n.* eda__*; edathag; ~**ize** *v.t.* edawua*; ~**ous** *adj.* eda__*
scar *v.t.* balwuani*; balwuanigith
scare *v.t.* ebkioth
scatter *v.t.* gantan; gantan*
schlep *v.i.* wuichuthahim
school *n.* mashchamakud
scissors *n.* chihil
scold *v.t.* keh'ith*
scoop *n.* ihtakud; uskonakud; ~ **(up)** *v.t.* iht*; ihta*
scorch *v.t.* kuh__*
scorpion *n.* nakshel
scout *v.t.* githahim*; githahimed*; *n.* githaihimdam; ~**ing** *adj.* githaihimdam; ~**ing** EXPEDITION
scrape *v.t.* chemhon*; hiwkon; hiwkona*; oshkon; ~ **(corn)** *v.t.* kaipig*; ~ **off** *v.t.* chemhon; ~**r** *n.* chemhonakud; hiwkonakud; shajkonakud; ~ **smooth** hiwshan; hiwshana*
scratch *v.t.* huk__*; hukshan, hukshom; __shan*; *n.* hukshanakud; BACK ~**er**; ~ **off** *v.t.* chelkon; ~ **out (a hole)** *v.t.* golshan
screech *v.i.* kuhi*; kuhu*
screen *n.* s-jehjeg wainomi
screw *v.t.* sihshp; *n.* sihshpakud; FASTEN **with a** ~
screwbean *n.* kuwithchuls
screwpod mesquite = SCREWBEAN
scum *n.* mamadhod; ~**my** *adj.* mamadhodag*
scythe *n.* ohso
sea *n.* ge'e shuhthagi; kahchk; ~**shell** *n.* kokodki
seal *v.t.* bithshch*; kuhp; kuhp*; *n.* kuhpadag
seam *n.* shohma; ~**stress** *n.* shohshomiththam
sear *v.t.* kuhthshp*
search *v.* ~ **for** *v.t.* hoan; hoanith*; ~**through** *v.t.* hoan
season *n.* **at this** ~ ithani

seat *n.* thaikud; ~ **of government/ office/official** *n.* kownal-thaikud
seclude *v.t.* **in a** ~**d place** chu'iko ~; oneself hejelko
second *n.* gohk; *adj.* gohk; gohkkam
secret *adj.* a'agi; ~**ly** *adv.* a'ag__*; a'agim
section *n.* sha'adk*
security *n.* plihntha
see *v.t.* neith; neith*; *v.i.* nea; nehnthag*
seed *n.* kai; kai*
seek *v.t.* ~ **(an enemy)** *v.t.* githaihun
seem *v.i.* ap'ema*; ap'etama*; __ma; sha heg wepo; ~ **alike** mahs*; ~**ingly** *adv.* hab hi; ~ **like** mahs*; ~ **to know** hab hi machma
self *n.* hejel*; *combining form* e*; e-*; ~**control** *n.* thotholim*; thotholimthag*; ~**discipline** *n.* thotholimthag*
selfish *adj.* tha'a*; ~**ly** *adv.* tha'a*
sell *v.t.* gagda
semen *n.* kai; kedwuathag; **ejaculate** ~ kedwua
send *v.t.* ah'ath; ah'ath*; hotsh†; ~**er** *n.* ah'aththam
senita CACTUS
senna *n.* ko'owi-tahtami
sense *n.* **come to one's** ~**s** tahtk
separate *v.t.* gawulkath; *adj.* gawul; gawul*; ~**ly** *adv.* gawul
September *n.* Washai Gak Mashath
series *n.* wawnim
Seri Indian *n.* Shehl
serrate *v.t.* hikwon; sisidchelig*
servant *n.* nehol
serve *v.t.* bihth*
set *v.t.* chekith*; *v.i.* huduni*; ~ **aside** *v.t.* chehkith*; to'ith*; ~ **out** *v.t.* to'ith*; ~ **up** *v.t.* thashwua
settle *v.i.* chihwia; chihwiapa*
seven *n.,adj.* wewa'ak, wewkam, wewa'am; ~**th** *n.,adj.* wewa'ak, wewkam
sew *v.t.* shohm; shohm*; ~**ing** MACHINE
sex *n.* **have** ~**ual intercourse** thohm
shackle *v.t.* mako
shade *n.* ehhegwua; ehk*; ehkajith; ehkegwua; *n.* ehk*; ehkeg, ehheg; ehkeg*; ehkthag; **a** ~ *n.* ehkakud
shadow *n.* ehkthag; **cast a** ~ ehkeg*
shady *adj.* ehkeg*
shaft *n.* ARROW ~
shake *v.t.* ihgith*; shahmug; shahmuth; ugijith, ujugith; ~ **oneself** hongith; wokjith; ~ **one's HIPS**; ~ **one's LEG**

shallow *adj.* komal; komal*; ~ **in
concavity** chepelk; chepelk*; ~ly
adv. chepelim*; komalim
shame *v.t.* edawua*; *n.* eda__*;
edathag; ~**ful** *adj.* eda__*; ~**fully**
adv. eda__*; sai eda†
share with *v.t.* ho'ith
sharp *adj.* mu'uk*; ~**-edged** *adj.*
mu'uhug*; ~**en** *v.t.* lihmhun;
mu'ukath; ~**ly** *adv.* mu'ukam*;
~**ness** *n.* mu'ukthag
shave *v.t.* hiwkon; hiwkona*; ~ **(the
skin)** *v.t.* hiwium†
shawl *n.* tahpalo
she *pron.* ihtha, ihtha'a
sheep *n.* kahwul, kahwal; **a bighorn**
~ *n.* cheshoni
shelf *n.* **hanging** ~ *n.* kuhkta
shell *n.* komi*; komi__*; RIFLE ~;
SEA ~; SNAIL ~; STRING of ~s
shelter *n.* watto
sheriff *n.* chi-lihhi
shield *n.* WAR ~
shine *v.i.* tonod; tonolith*
shining *adj.* tondam
shiny *adj.* wathathk*
ship *n.* ge'e kanaho; ge'e wahiko
-ship *suffix that forms nouns* __dag*
shirt *n.* ipud; kamish; kotoni
shiver *v.i.* gigiwuk; gigiwuk*
shoat *n.* kohji mad
shoe *v.t.* shuhshkdag*; shuhshkdath;
n. shuhshk; shuhshkdath*; ~ **polish**
n. shuhshk chuchkathakud
shoo *intj.* habba; ~ **(away)** *v.t.*
habbagith; shahmuth
shoot *v.t.* gatwua*; gatwuith; shel*;
v.i. shelwuithag*; ~ **at** *v.t.*
mummu; mummu*; ~**er** *n.*
gatwuatham
shop *v.i.* pasam*; *n.* gagdakud;
nolawttham; **go** GROCERY ~**ping;**
~**per** *n.* nolawttham; ~**ping** *n.*
nolawta
short *adj.* kawud*; shopol; shopol*;
~**en** *v.t.* shopolkath; shopolkthas*;
~**-legged person** *n.* chahbo*
shoulder *v.t.* kushwi'ot;
kushwi'otch*; *n.* gegkio; kotwa*
shovel *n.* kuppiad; pahla
show *v.t.* chehgith*; **a** ~**ing** *n.*
chehgithadag; ~ **off** *v.i.* gimaihun;
woikchuth; ~**-off** *n.*
woikshanimkam
shuck *v.t.* ~ **(corn)** *v.t.* keliw
shut in *v.t.* kuhp
shy *adj.* edtham; elith*
sick *adj.* mumki__*; ~**ness** *n.*
mumkithag

sickle *n.* ohso
side *n.* aigo*; hab*; hiwchu*; huda;
hugithag; thathpk-washai; ~**burn**
n. kampo; ~ **by side** shakal; **on
each** ~ **of** gahi; **on the other** ~ **of**
gahi; ~**ways** *adv.* gahnai*;
~**winder** *n.* a'agam ko'owi
sift *v.t.* sihskith; sihskith*; ~**er** *n.*
sihskithakud
sigh *v.i.* si i ihbheiwua
sight *n.* nea*; nehnthag; nena*;
nenchuth*; **gain** ~ nehnt; **in plain**
~ mahsko
sign *v.t.* ~ **(one's name)** *v.t.* wohth
silent *adj.* bahbagi*
silk *n.* maskal
silver *n.* plahtha; ~**ware** *n.* kusal
similar *adj.* ~**ly** *adv.* masma; ~ **to**
masma
simmer *v.i.* siwk*; totpk; totpsith*
Simon *n.* Si-mohn
sin *n.* pi ap chu'ichig
since *conj.* hekaj; ~...**then**
correlative conj. eda...hekaj
sinew *n.* ohtk*; tatai
sing *v.t.* ne'e; *v.i.* jupij ne'e*; ne'i*;
~**er** *n.* ne'etham; ~**er in a harvest
ceremony** *n.* wihnim; ~ **for** *v.t.*
ne'ichuth
singe *v.t.* wohiw
sink *v.i.* huduni*; juhpin; wachum; ~
in *v.i.* wahk
siren *n.* **sound a** ~ **for** kuhijith
sissy *n.* uwikwuad; uwikwuadag*
sister *n.* nawoj; nawoj*; uwiga;
wehnag; ~**-in-law** *n.*
chuhchud-je'e*; hakima-je'e*
sit *v.i.* habadk*; thaha*; thahi__*;
thahiwua; thai__*; ~ **on** *v.t.*
thai__*
situated *adj.* thaha*
six *n.,adj.* chuhthp; ~**th** *n.,adj.*
chuhthp; ~ **times** *adv.* chuhthpo
size *n.* ha'aschu*; ha'asig*; kuintadag
skill *n.* mahch*; ~**ed** *adj.* amichuth;
thahithag*
skin *v.t.* el__*; elkon; *n.* elithag; **a**
~ *n.* elkona; ~**ny** *adj.* gaki*;
oh'o*
skip (along) *v.i.* halibwua
skirt *n.* ~ **of ancient style** *n.*
ihnagi, nahgi
skull *n.* koshwa
skunk *n.* uhpio
slant *v.i.* hudunikodag*; *n.*
agshpadag
slash *v.t.* hukitsh
slaughter *v.t.* me'akud*; ~**house** *n.*
me'akud kih, mu'akud kih

slave *n.* nehol
sleep *v.i.* kohsh; *n.* kohsi__*;
kohsig; ~**iness** *n.* kohsimthag;
~**ing** BAG; ~**ing** PILL; ~**y-headed**
adj. kohsk*
sleeve *n.* nowikud
slender *adj.* aj; aj*; chu'alk*
slice *v.t.* hihitsh
slide *v.i.* hehlwua; hehlwuahim*;
hehlwuisk*; thapithwua; *n.*
hehlwuisk; = PLAYGROUND ~
sling *n.* wudakud*; ~**shot** *n.*
wewkud
slip *v.i.* lepithwua*; thapithwua
slippery *adj.* thahpk*
slow *adj.* bahbagi*; *adv.* bahbagi*;
bahbagim*; bahbgihm*; ~**ly** *adv.*
bahbagi*; bahbagim*; bahbgihm*; ~
up/down *v.i.* bahbgih
small *adj.* chum, chem; chum*
smell *v.t.* hewagith; *n.* hewagith*;
hewgig*; uhw*; ~ **around for** *v.t.*
hewgia; hewgia*; ~**y** *adj.* uhw*
smile *v.i.* he'edkath; he'edkath*
smoke *v.t.* jehjena*; kummun; *v.i.*
jehni*; jehnimk; *n.* kuhb__*;
kuhbs; **blow** ~ **on** kummun; **puff**
out ~ kubswua; ~**r** *n.* jehniktham;
~ TOBACCO
smoky *adj.* kudshani*; kuhbsig*
smooth *v.t.* hiwkon; hiwkona*;
thahpiun; thahpiun*; *adj.* thahpk*;
wa'athk*; ~**ly** *adv.* thahpkam*
snail shell *n.* hohlwiki
snake *n.* nehbig*; wamad*; **black**
racer ~ *n.* chuk wamad; wegi
wamad; **bull** ~ *n.* sho'owa; **king** ~
n. jewekag; **water** ~ *n.*
wahhigam*
snapshot = PHOTOGRAPH
sneak *v.i.* jupij him*; ~ **up on** *v.t.*
wi'ahim
sneeze *v.i.* bischk; bischk*
sniff *v.i.* hohowo; ~ **for** *v.t.* hewshan
sniffle *v.i.* henihopt
snore *v.i.* todk
snow *n.* gew; ~ **on** *v.t.* gewshp
soak *v.t.* wahg; *v.i.* wakch*; ~ **in**
v.i. juhpin; ~ **underground**
hiowichuth
soap *v.t.* shawonimath; *n.* shawoni;
~ **plant** *n.* utko*; utko-jehj; ~**tree**
or ~**weed** YUCCA
sob *v.i.* kuishani
sock *n.* kal-sihtho
soda pop = **soft** DRINK
soft *adj.* moik*; ~**en** *v.t.* moihun;
moihun*; moikajith; ~**ly** *adv.*
moikam*; moima*

soil *v.t.* uam*; uamhun; *n.* jewed;
~**ed** *adj.* uam*
sojourn *v.i.* chewed; ~**er** *n.*
chihpiatham
soldier *n.* shonthal; wual
solely *adv.* wa'i
solid *adj.* kawk*
solve *v.t.* a'amichuth; matog
some *pron.,adj.* ha*; ha'i; ha'ichu*;
do ~**thing to** thohththa; **from**
~**where** hebaijed, heba'ijed; ~**how**
adv. has i masma; ~**one** *pron.* ha;
ha'ichu*; __m; ~**one's** *pron.* ha__;
~**thing** *pron.* hab*; ~**time** *adv.*
hekith; ~**what** *adv.* sha; ~**where**
adv. am hu hebai, am hu heba'i;
hasko; hasko*
song *n.* ne'i; **begin a** ~ atchuth
son-in-law *n.* ba'amad-ohg*;
ba'amad-o'ogam*; mohs-ohg*
Sonora *n.* So-nohla
soon *adv.* hemu, hemuch; oi
soot *n.* ihmki
sore *n.* hihw__*; hihwthag; wuddag
sorghum *n.* kahnia*
sorrel *adj.* alshani
sotol *n.* umug
soul *n.* thoakag, thoakthag
sound *n.* che'ithag; kai__*; kaithag;
make a ~ shahmuni
soup *n.* sohba
sour *adj.* he'ek*; he'ekchu
source *n.* shon
south *n.* wakoliw, wakolim; *adv.*
wakoliw thahgio, wakolim thahgio;
wakoliw wui, wakolim wui; **in the** ~
wakoliw thahgio, wakolim thahgio;
the ~ *n.* tohono; ~**ward** *adv.*
wakoliw wui, wakolim wui
sow thistle *n.* ho'ithkam-ihwagi;
wai-hehewo
Spain *n.* I-spahnia
Spanish *n.* **speak** ~ juhkam-neok
spank *v.t.* gewittan
sparing *adj.* **be** ~ **of** tha'a*
sparkle *v.i.* nanawuk
sparrow *n.* o'odopiwa; o'odopiwis;
tamtol; **black-throated desert** ~ *n.*
ba'i-chukulim; ~ HAWK
speak *v.* **electronic** ~**er** *n.*
neoktham; ~**er** *n.* jehnigiththam;
neoktham; ~ **on behalf of** neokith;
~ **to** *v.t.* jehnigith
spear *n.* is-pahyo; lahnis
speech *n.* ne'oki; neoksith*
spend *v.t.* heki gehsh; hugiog;
hugiogahim*
sphere *n.* olas; ~ **(of influence)** *n.*
ap'ethag

spherical *adj.* olas; olas*; ~**ly** *adv.*
olasim*
spider *n.* muhla wanimedtham*;
tokithhud; **black-widow** ~ *n.*
hiwchu-wegi; ~ **web** *n.* tokithhud
chuaggia
spill *v.t.* iawu; iawu*
spin *v.i.* mualig*
spinach *n.* chuhugia
spine *n.* eda wa'ug*
spirit *n.* ~ **level** *n.* wuhlu-ihbthag,
wuhlo-ihbthag; ~ **of the dead** *n.*
kok'oi
spit *v.i.* siswua; *n.* siswuadag; ~ **on**
v.t. siswuamath
splash *v.i.* shabani*
split *v.t.* tahpan; tahpan*; *n.*
tahpani; **an implement for** ~**ting**
n. hahtshakud
spoil *v.t.* jewajith; padchuth;
padchuthas*; *v.i.* jew*; jewa; padt;
~**age** *n.* padchutha; ~**ed** *adj.*
pad; pad*; ~**s** *n.* gehgewi,
gehgthag
spool *n.* bihakud; tanglo
spoon *n.* kusal
spot *v.t.* pihnto*; ~**ted** *adj.*
jejewk*; kaimagi*; pihnto
spouse *n.* wehm kihkam; wehm
kihkam*
sprawl *v.i.* napad*; napadwua
spray *v.t.* hip__*
spread *v.t.* tadan*; ~ **apart** *v.i.*
shakal*; *v.t.* shakalkath; ~ **(a**
rumor) *v.t.* kaithag; ~ **out** *v.i.*
chewelhim*; komad*; ~ **the** LEGS;
~ **to dry** helig; helig*
spring *n.* shonkam
sprinkle *v.t.* hathsith; *v.i.* sihbani;
~ **with liquid** wa'akpan
sprout *v.i.* i'iwegith*; mo'okat;
PLANT ~
spur *n.* ispul*
sputter *v.i.* siwk*
square *n.* chuhchpul; *adj.*
chuhchpul; chuhchpulk*; *adv.*
chuhchpulim*; CARPENTER'**s** ~;
TOWN ~
squash *n.* hahl; hihwai*; shapijk*
squat *v.i.* chu'al thaha; sipud*; sipud
thahiwua; thaha*
squaw *n.* **do a** ~ **dance** chuhth
squeeze *v.t.* wak'e
squirrel *n.* chehkul, chehkol; **ground**
~ *n.* chuawi
stagger *v.i.* shakalwua
staghorn CACTUS
stalk *v.t.* wia; wipi'a; *n.* wa'ug
stallion *n.* kalioni

stamp *n.* mo'o; ~**ing ground** *n.*
oimmelig; ~ **out (an illness)** *v.t.*
kehijuni
stand *v.t.* kehkud*; keshwua; *v.i.*
chu'awogi*; [1]kehk; [2]kehk; kekiwua;
n. kehshakud; ~ **against** *v.t.* ab
wui kehk; ~ **facing** ab wui kekiwua;
~ **firm** gegokath*; ~ **for cooking**
n. chetto; ~ **on tiptoe** chu'alkalith,
chu'adkalith; ~ **up** *v.t.* kehsh
star *n.* hu'u; **falling** ~ *n.* siawogi
starch *v.t.* gewkajith; *n.*
gewkthakud
stare *v.i.* neith*; ~**r** *n.* neith*
start to go i hih
startle *v.t.* ha'athka*; tothsith
starve *v.i.* bihugim*
stay *v.i.* wi'i; ~ **overnight** wohp
steadfast *adj.* gegokath*
steal *v.t.* ehs__*
steam *n.* s-wadagi kuhbs
steer *n.* nowiyu
stem *n.* wa'ug
step *v.,n.* ~ **on** *v.t.* keishp; **take a**
~ kehkhim
sternum *n.* bahsho oh'o
stick *v.t.* sha'i*; *v.i.* kuh__*; *n.*
[2]kuhag*; kuhagith*; uhs; **burning** ~
n. kuhchki; ~**er** *n.* ho'i; ~**y** *adj.*
hadam; hadam*; **walking** ~ *n.*
gakimchul
stiff *adj.* gewk*; kushathk*; ~**en**
v.t. gewkajith
still *adj.* pi shahmunim; shahmuni*;
adv. wabsh kia, hash kia
sting *n.* ke'i; ~**er** *n.* uhsh
stingy *adj.* tha'a*
stir *v.t.* iolagith; nonoig; sihowin,
sihon; widwua; *v.i.* hoin
stirrup *n.* istliw
stocking *n.* kal-sihtho
stomach *n.* wohk; ~ **ache** *n.* wohk
ko'okthag
stone *n.* hothai; wihthakud*
stoop *v.i.* sipud*; ~**ed** *adj.* kehk*
stop *v.t.* ha'asa; ha'asa*; keshwua;
v.i. chehmo'o*; i ha'asa; kekiwua;
n. keki__*; ~ **burning** *v.i.*
chuhk; ~ **crying** *v.i.* ehb;
ehb*
storage *n.* CONTAINer **for** ~; ~
place *n.* chekkud; **woven** ~ **case**
n. washa
store *v.t.* ba'iham; ba'iham*; chehk;
chehk*; chehkith; chek__*; *n.*
nolawtakud; tianna, chiantho; ~
away *v.t.* ba'iham
storm *n.* jegos
story *n.* ahga; ha'ichu ahgithadag;

begin a ~ atchuth; **end of a** ~ at hoabdag*
stove *n.* is-tuhhua; ol-nihyo*
stow (away) *v.t.* ba'iham; ba'iham*
straight *adj.* shelini*; *adv.* shelinim*; ~**en** *v.t.* shelin; shelinakud*; ~ **up** *adv.* chu'al*
strain *v.t.* o'osith; ~**er** *n.* o'osithakud
strand *n.* **pull** ~**s from** wanimun
strange *adj.* ge
strangleweed *n.* wamad-gihko
strap *n.* giwud; giwud*; wudakud*
straw *n.* mohg; wa'ug; ~ **mat** *n.* main
street *n.* kahya
strength *n.* gewkthag; gewkthagkam*; ~**en** *v.t.* gewkajith; gewkath
stretch *v.t.* wani'on; *v.i.* ohshan
strict *adj.* kawk*
strike *v.t.* gew; gewi__*; gewichk; __hin*; jehka'ich*; shoni*; shonikon; ~ **(a match)** *v.t.* giummud†; guishani‡; ~ **together loudly** kapanith
string *v.t.* baiukt*; *n.* gi'a*; tokih*; ~ **(beads, shells, etc.)** *v.t.* koawgith; ~ **of beads, shells, etc.** koawgi'a
striped *adj.* jejewk*; o'oi*
strive *v.i.* gewkathch*
strong *adj.* gewk*; gewkthagkam; ~**ly** *adv.* gewkam*
struggle *v.i.* thathgechuth, thathgichuth
strut *v.i.* chu'adkim
stub one's TOE
student *n.* mashchamtham
studies *n.* mahchimig
study *v.t.* mashcham
stumble *v.i.* gehsim*; huchin; keikon; pialhain
stump *n.* shon
stupefy *v.t.* hothaichuth
stupid *adj.* koshwa*
sty *n.* wuichwig
submerge *v.t.* hiashp; *v.i.* wachum
subsequently *adv.* am i thahm; amjed; hahawa*
suck *v.t.,v.i.* si'i; ~ **in** *v.t.* howichkwua*
sue *v.t.* lothait
suffer *v.t.* __kam*; *v.i.* sho'igchuth; sho'igchuth*; ~**ing** *n.* sho'igchuthadag; sho'igthag; ~ **the** CONSEQUENCES
suffice *v.i.* nakog
sufficient *adj.* ahim; ~**ly** *adv.* ahim

sugar *n.* asugal, a-suhga; **powdered** ~ *n.* chu'i asugal, chu'i a-suhga; **unrefined** ~ *n.* pa-nohji
suicide *n.* **commit** ~ hejel e me'a
suit *n.* **bring legal** ~ **against** wahkith chehanig-ch-ed; ~**case** *n.* washa; ~ **of clothes** *n.* e-wehngam eniga
summer *n.* toniabkam
summon *v.t.* waith; waitha*; ~**er** *n.* waiththam; ~**s** *n.* waithadag
sun *v.t.* tashogith; *n.* juh*; tash; ~**dial** *n.* tash; ~**down** *n.* hudunith*; ~**flower** *n.* hihwai; ~**set** *n.* huduni, hudunig
Sunday *n.* Thomig
superintendent *n.* maliom; malioni
supper *n.* gegosig
supply *n.* ba'ihama
support *v.t.* thagio'ith
suppose *v.* ²chum*; ~**dly** *adv.* hab hi; pehegia
sure *adv.* pegih
surpass *v.t.* ba'iwichkhim
surround *v.t.* bih__*; bihad; bihag; bihag*; bijimith; iajith
survivor *n.* wi'ikam
suspect *v.t.* elith*
suspend *v.t.* naggia; naggia*; ~**ers** *n.* ti-lahnthi
suspicion *n.* elith*
swallow *v.t.* ba'a; ba'i__*; *n.* githwal
swamp *n.* wahmul
swarm over *v.t.* iajith
sway *v.i.* winogim*
sweat *v.i.* wahud; wahulchuth*; *n.* wahulthag; ~**y** *adj.* wahulthag*
sweater *n.* sahgo; wuakithalig†
sweep *v.t.* wosun; wosuna*
sweet *adj.* i'owi*; ~**en** *v.t.* i'owijith*; ~**ly** *adv.* i'owim*; ~ POTATO; ~**s** *n.* pi-lohn
swell *v.i.* kopoth*; toskoni; toskoni*
swift *adj.* hottk*
swim *v.i.* wachchui; wachchuimk*
swing *v.t.* widut; *n.* holwuikud
swollen *adj.* kopoth; kopoth*
sword *n.* cheggiakud; is-pahyo
sympathetically *adv.* hemajim*
sympathy *n.* hemajimatalig
syrup *n.* sit'ol; ~**y** *adj.* kushul*

T

table *n.* mihsa, mihsh
tack *n.* sihshpakud
tadpole *n.* mo'okwad

tail *n.* bahi*; baik___*; ~ **end** *n.*
bahi*; ~ **feathers** *n.* bahbhaij
tailor *n.* shohsomiththam
take *v.t.* behe; he'eni*; ~**a** NAP; ~
away from *v.t.* wohppo'ith; ~
(into) *v.t.* wahkith; ~ **off** *v.t.*
wuahawua; *v.i.* tha'a; ~ **over** *v.t.*
behe*; ~ **somewhere** beka'i; ~ **to**
COURT; ~ **up** *v.t.* ___chug*;
mashcham
tale *n.* ahga
talent *n.* ulinithag
talk *v.i.* neok; neokimk*; ~ **about**
v.t. ahg; ~ **about oneself** ahg; ~**er**
n. neoktham
tall *adj.* chew; chew*; chu'alk*
tamale *n.* tamal
tamarack *n.* onk kui
tamarix *n.* wegi uhs
tame *v.t.* mahsho*
tamp *v.t.* chu'amun; chu'amuna*
tan *v.t.* moikajith; ~**ner** *n.*
momoikantham
tangerine *n.* tanja-lohn
tangle *v.t.* hahwulith*
tank *n.* tahngih
tansy mustard *n.* shuh'uwad
tap *v.t.,v.i.* chepwin; chepwin*
tape *n.* **measuring** ~ *n.* kuintakud
tarantula *n.* hiani
target *n.* wuliwga*
tarpaper *n.* tapial
tassle *n.* muda___*; mudathag
taste *v.t.* jehk; *n.* kahk*; ~**less**
adj. kahk*; **sense of** ~ jehkig; **to**
like the ~ **of** nahk
tasty *adj.* i'owi*
tatoo *v.t.* e'eshshelig*
tea *n.* tih; ~ **grounds** *n.* mohg
teach *v.t.* mashcham*; **a** ~**ing** *n.*
mashchamthag; ~**er** *n.*
mashchamtham
team *n.* wehm*
tear *v.t.* wantp; wantshp; *n.* oh'og;
~ **down** *v.t.* wuahawua
tease *v.t.* nahnko*; nahnkogith; *n.*
nahnkogiththam
telephone *v.t.* aj-wainommath; *n.*
aj-wainomi; ~ **wire** *n.* aj-wainomi
television *n.* jiawul wuhi; ~ **set** *n.*
hemako wuhikam; jiawul wuhi
tell *v.t.* ahg*; ahgith*
temper *n.* **an even** ~ *n.*
bamuistkthag; EVEN-~**ed**
temple *n.* ge'e cheopi
temporal *adj.* huhugetham
temporary *adj.* huhugetham
ten *n.,adj.* west-mahm; ~**th** *n.,adj.*
west-mahm

tend *v.t.* nuhkuth
tender *adj.* moik*
tendon *n.* tatai; ~ **in the neck** *n.*
kusta
tent *n.* ikus kih
tepary BEAN
termite *n.* hiopch
test *v.t.* a'appem; *n.* a'appem*;
a'appema; apkoma
testicle *n.* wihpedho
testify *v.t.* wohohkamchuth,
wehohkamchuth
testimony *n.* wohohkamchutha
than *conj.* ba'ich i*
thank *v.t.* ab ho'ige'ith; ab
ho'ige'elith; ~**fully** *adv.*
ho'ige'ith*; ~**fulness** *n.*
ho'ige'ithadag; ho'ige'elithadag
that *pron.* hegai; hega'i; hegai*;
conj. hab*; ~ **is** *connective phrase*
koi; ~ KIND **of;** ~ MUCH
thaw *v.t.* hahgith; *v.i.* hahg
the *article* g, heg
theft *n.* ehsig
their *pron.* ha-
them *pron.* ha; hegam*; itham*; **by**
~**selves** hejelko; ~**selves** *pron.*
e*; e-*
then *adv.* amjed; eda; hahawa, haha;
oi wa; wenog; **right** ~ *adv.* am i;
SINCE . . . ~
there *adv.* abai*; ga'aba'i*; ga'ajed*;
gahnai*; gahsh*; gamai*; ganai*;
wahshan*; ALL ~ **is; far over** ~
gahmai, gahma'i; ~ **facing away**
amai, ama'i; **from over** ~ hujed;
over ~ gamai, gama'i; wahshaj; **up**
~ wahshan
these *pron.* ihtham
they *pron.* hegam*; itham*; ___m
thick *adj.* kowk*; shawad; ~**ly** *adv.*
shawadkam
thief *n.* ehs___*
thievery *n.* ehsig
thieving *adj.* ehs___*
thievish *adj.* behi___*
thigh *n.* um
thimble *n.* nu'ichkwuikud
thin *adj.* aj; aj*; komal; komal*; ~
and long muhwij*; ~**ly** *adv.*
komalim
think *v.t.* ahg*; chegito; chegito*;
elith*; pen*; ~ **about** *v.t.* i
oithahim; oithachug; oithahim;
~**er** *n.* chegitokam; ~**ing** *adj.*
chegitokam; ~ **of** *v.t.* elith*; ~
over *v.t.* oithachug
third *n.,adj.* waik
thirst *n.* kuhst___*; tonom*;

tonomthag; **quench the** ~ wawini; wawinig*; ~**y** *adj.* tonom*; tonomkam
this *pron.* ihtha, ihtha'a; ~ KIND of; ~ **one** ihtha, ihtha'a
thorn *n.* ho'i; ho'i*; **Anderson** ~**bush** *n.* koawul; ~**y** *adj.* ho'i*
thoroughly *adv.* ap*
those *pron.* hegam
though *conj.* chum as, chem as; wa chum
thought *n.* chegitoi; elithadag*
thousand *n.,adj.* mihl
thrasher *n.* **curve-billed** ~ *n.* keli-huch; kul-wichigam
thread *v.t.* hihlodath; *n.* hihlo
threat *n.* ebkiotha
three *n.,adj.* waik
thresh *v.t.* mohon; mohon*; ~**er** *n.* mohonakud*; ~ **(grain)** *v.t.* kehiwin; ~**ing** FLOOR
thrifty *adj.* huwith*; tha'a*
throat *n.* ba'itk; **clear the** ~ ioshan
throne *n.* kownal thaikud
through *prep.* gahi wuhshanim; ~**out** *adv.* shuhthgim
throw *v.t.* tha'ichuth; ~ **away** *v.t.* wua; ~**away** *n.* ohhotha
thump *v.i.* podoni; podoni*; *n.* podonitham; ~ **on** *v.t.* chedeni
thunder *n.* bebethki; kopki*; tataniki; ~ **sharply** kopk; kopk*; **with a** ~**ing sound** tatanikim
Thursday *n.* Gi'ik-tash; Huiwis
tick *n.* mahmsh
tickle *v.t.* kedkolith
tiger *n.* ohshad
tight *adj.* wihnk*; ~**en** *v.t.* wihnkath; ~**ly** *adv.* wihnk*; ~**rope** **walk** *n.* ma-lohma
tie *v.t.* koaw; wuhd; wul*; wulshp; *n.* = NECK**tie**; ~ **pin** *n.* sihshpakud; ~ **together** koaw; ~ **up** *v.t.* alast k wuhd
tilt *v.t.* gahi i ulin
timber *n.* forest ~ *n.* uhs
time *v.t.* kuint g tash; *n.* chekith*; heki*; juh*; tash; tiampo; **any** ~ *adv.* wabsh chum hekith, hash chum hekith; **at that** ~ am i; eda; **at this** ~ ia i; **at this very** ~ edapk; **count the** ~ kuint g tash; **for a long** ~ ge'eho; tash; ~ **of day** tash; **on** ~ oi; ~**piece** *n.* tash; **waste** ~ pihchuth
timid *adj.* thoajk*
tip *n.* kug; kug*; STAND **on** ~**toe**
tire *v.i.* gewkog; gewkog*; *n.* shuhshk; mahgina shuhshk; yahntha. *See also* TIRED

tired *adj.* gehsith*; ~hog*; **be** ~ **of** seeing neith*; ~**ly** *adv.* ta gewkogim
to *prep.* tahgio*; wui, wuij; ~ **and** fro aigo; WALK ~ **and fro**
toad *n.* babath; mo'ochwig; **horned** ~ *n.* chemamagi; ~**stool** *n.* okstakud
toast *n.* oamajitha; sitdoi pahn
tobacco *n.* ta-wahgo, tawago; **coyote** ~ **plant** *n.* ban-wiwga; **desert** ~ *n.* wiw; **smoke** ~ jehni; **wild** ~ *n.* wiw
today *adv.* hemu tash
toe *n.* tadpod; **stub one's** ~ huchin; huchwuag
together *adv.* e wehm
toilet *n.* bihtkud
tolerate *v.t.* nakog
tomahawk *n.* shonchki
tomato *n.* to-mahti
tongs *n.* wah'o; **saguaro rib** ~ *n.* wah'o
tongue *n.* nehni; wihni*; ~ **on a** **wagon** *n.* chi-mohn
tonight *adv.* hudunk
tool *n.* chikpanakud, chipkanakud; **iron** ~ **for splitting wood** *n.* yuhngih
tooth *n.* ki'i__*; tahtami; tam__*; tamsh*; ~**ache** *n.* tahtami ko'okthag
top *n.* **on** ~ **of** thahm; **play spin the** ~ binashwua; **spinning** ~ *n.* tanglo
topple *v.t.* nu'ichkwua
torch *n.* kuhthagi; kuhthch*
torment *v.t.* che'owith
tornado *n.* siwulogi, siwuliki
tornillo = SCREWBEAN
tortilla *n.* chemait; chemait*; ~ **griddle** *n.* chemaitakud
totem *n.* wehmkal
touch *v.t.* tahtam; tahtchulith*; thagshp; thagshpa*
tough *adj.* ha'ahama*; wihnk*
toward *prep.* ga'aba'i*; gahsh*; wui, wuij
towel *n.* toaya; towash
town *n.* puiwlo; **see the** ~ pasam; pasam*; ~ **square** *n.* kuaya
toy *n.* chichwikud
track *v.t.* jekiamed*; *n.* gohki; jehkch*; memelkud; **make** ~**s** mahst; mahstahim*
tractor *n.* judumi
trade *v.t.* kammialt, kambialt; *n.* kammialta, kambialta
tradition *n.* ha'ichu ahgithadag; ~**al** *adj.* kehi__*; ~**s** *n.* himthag

tragedy *n.* neijig*
trail *n.* wohg
train *v.t.* mahsho*; mahshochuth; *n.* wainomi-kalit
tramp *n.* tlahmba
translate *v.t.* gagda
trap *v.t.* kuhp; la'a__*; la'ashp; wulshch*; wulshp; *n.* la'ashpakud; wulshpakud; ~ **door** *n.* kuhpadag
trash *n.* sha'i; tahnhadagi
traucoma *n.* kuiji
travel *v.i.* oimmed; *n.* chihpiathag; oimmelig; ~**er** *n.* chihpiatham; oimmedtham; ~**ing** *adj.* chihpiatham
traverse *v.t.* gahi cheshaj
treat *n.* pi-lohn; ~ **like a human** hemajkamchuth; o'othhamchuth; ~ **variously or deviously** nahnko wua; ~ **with heat** kuhthshp*; kuhtpa
treatise *n.* o'ohana
tree *n.* uhs
tremble *v.i.* __gew; gigiwuk; gigiwuk*
trial *n.* a'appema; COURT ~
triangular *adj.* muhwij*
tribesman *n.* o'othham; HOPI ~; lower PIMA ~; PLAINS ~; YAQUI ~
trick *v.t.* banmath; heki himchuth
trifle *v.i.* chichwi; chichwi*; *n.* chichwithag; ~ **with** *v.t.* chichwi
trifling *adj.* pehegi*
trim *v.t.* hik__*; hikshan
trip *v.i.* keikon; pialhain; *n.* oimmelig
tripe *n.* hihijga; **cooked** ~ *n.* mi-nuhtho*
trot *v.i.* jejewuakhim; wo'olakhim, woshthakhim
trouble *v.t.* kudut; kudut*; *n.* pihthag; **cause** ~ **for** pihchuth
trough *n.* ka-nohwa; wahlko
trousers *n.* shaliw
trowel *n.* bithhunakud; kusal
truck *n.* tlohgih; **pickup** ~ *n.* pig-ab
true *adj.* wohoma*
truly *adv.* wohoh, wehoh; wohohm*
trunk *n.* shon; wawli
trust *v.t.* hiwig
truth *n.* wohoh*; wohohkam, wehohkam
try *v.t.* nakog*; ~ **out** *v.t.* a'appem
T-shirt *n.* kamish; wechothag
tub *n.* tihna
tube *n.* tuhwo
tuber *n.* thahithag
tuberculosis *n.* i'ihogig

tuck *v.t.* chul__*
Tuesday *n.* Gohk-tash; Mahltis
tumble *v.i.* huhl matagiwua†
tumor *n.* ola
tunic *n.* tuhngo
turkey *n.* tohwa; ~ **poult** *n.* tohwa mad; ~ VULTURE
turn *v.t.* nahshp; *v.i.* nod; nod*; __nod*; nodagith*; ~ **around** *v.i.* sikol i kekiwua; ~ **in a circle** i sikolkath
tweezers *n.* ki'ishpakud
twice *adv.* gokko
twig *n.* i'iwonig
twin *n.* kuathi
twinkle *v.i.* tonod
twirl *v.t.* sikol widut
twist *v.t.* tohb; wijin; ~**er** *n.* siwulogi, siwuliki
twitch *v.i.* __gew
two *n.,adj.* gohk

U

udder *n.* wipih
uh *intj.* heh
ultimate *adj.* si
umbilical CORD
umbrella *n.* ehkakud
unashamed *adj.* elith*
uncivilized *adj.* mischini
uncle *n.* chuhchudam*; hakit*; je'es*; jisk*; ¹keli*; ²keli*; oks*; oksi*; tatal*; thahth*; wowoit*; GREAT-~
uncover *v.t.* ma'ishpi'ok
under *prep* wecho*; ~**clothes** *n.* wechothag; ~**ling** *n.* jumalkchu; wechokam; ~**pants** *n.* kalshani; ~**pants/shorts** *n.* wechothag; ~**shirt** *n.* kamish
undergo *v.t.* gahi wuhshani
undermine *v.t.* chekopig
understand *v.t.* amichuth; amichuth*; kah; ~**able** *adj.* amichuth*; ~**ably** *adv.* ta amichutham; ~**ing** *n.* amichuth*; amichuthadag; ~**ingly** *adv.* chu amichutham
undesirable *adj.* neith*; ohhoth*
undesirably *adv.* neith*
undulate *v.i.* __gew; mudagew*
unflinching *adj.* bamuistk*
unharness *v.t.* bibithshpi'ok; bibithshpi'okas*
unhook *v.t.* ol__*; olshpi'ok

unicorn plant *n.* ban-ihugga
unique *adj.* ge; hekiakam
unite *v.t.* hemakochuth
unity *n.* hemakothag
unless *conj.* hi wa, hi-a
unlock *v.t.* yahwidpi'ok
unpredictable *adj.* luhya
unravel *v.t.* matog
unruffle *v.t.* edastk*
untie *v.t.* hahwul'ok; wul'ok
until *conj.* hugkam; ~ after *conj.*
  ip, op; not ~ *conj.* ho'ip; ho'ip kia,
  ho'ip kiap
unusual *adj.* ge
unyoke *v.t.* yehwadpi'ok;
  yehwadpi'okas*
up *adv.* ta'i; uhg; ~root *v.t.*
  huhpan; wohni; ~side down kupal
upset *adj.* hudwua*
up-to-date *adj.* hemuchkam*
urinate *v.i.* hi'a; hi'a*
urine *n.* hi'__*; hi'a
us *pron.* ahchim; __ch*; t-
usable *adj.* apkog*
use *v.t.* hekaj; ih'e*; yuhs; *n.*
  hugioga; ~ up *v.t.* hugiog;
  hugiogahim*
uterus *n.* wo'o*
utterance *n.* ahga
uvula *n.* kampani

V

vaccinate *v.t.* chekith
vagina *n.* muhs; shuhth†
vain *n.* chum*
valise *n.* wawli
valley *n.* wo'otk
valuable *adj.* namkig*
valuably *adv.* namkigam*
variance *n.* nahnko*
varied *adj.* nahnko mahs*
various *adj.* nahnko; ~ly *adv.*
  nahnko
veal *n.* wisilo chuhkug
vehicle *n.* mo'o*; any self-propelled
  ~ *n.* hejel memdatham; CARRY
  in a ~
venereal disease *n.* cheomidag;
  contract ~ cheomi; meihim
vengeance *n.* agwuithag
venison *n.* huawi chuhkug, huai
  chuhkug; sihki chuhkug
verbena *n.* chedkotham; sand ~ *n.*
  kaska-lohn

verse *n.* wawnim
vertebra *n.* cervical ~ *n.* kuswo
  oh'o
very *adj.* hegai*; si; *adv.* sha'i,
  sha__wa'i; si; wohoh'i
vest *n.* cha-lihgo
vibratory *adj.* kuhgkim*
victory *n.* gewitoidag
view *n.* nena*
vigil *n.* wilanta*
vigorously *adv.* gewkam*
vile *adj.* uam*
village *n.* kihhim; ~r *n.* kihkam
vine CACTUS
vinegar *n.* wi-nahl
violin *n.* wio-lihn
virgin *n.* si s-ap chehia
visit *v.t.* neal*; wisit; ~ briefly *v.i.*
  ma'ikon; go to ~ chehgimed;
  chehgimelhim; chehgimelimk*
visualize *v.t.* neith
voice *n.* CLEAR-~d; ~lessly *adv.*
  hewelim*
volume *n.* at low ~ bahbagi*
vomit *v.i.* wihoschuth*; wihot; *n.*
  wihos
vote *v.i.* wothalt
vulture *n.* nuwi; black ~ *n.*
  nuwiopa; turkey ~ *n.* nuwi

W

waffle *n.* oamajitha
wage *n.* gehgewa; namkithadag; ~s
  n. namkithadag
wagon *n.* kalit; TONGUE on a ~
wail *v.i.* si shoak
waistline *n.* giwulkthag
wait *v.i.* kia*; ki'agani; wo'isheg; ~
  for *v.t.* neahim; nealkam*; nenida‡;
  tamiam
wake *v.t.* wuhan; *v.i.* nehhim;
  nenashan*; *n.* wilant*; wilanta; ~
  up *v.t.* wuhan; *v.i.* neh; nehhim
walk *v.i.* him; himchuth*; himith*;
  himlu*; himthag*; ialhim*; ~
  around/about *v.i.* oimmed; ~
  beside *v.t.* honwua; ~er *n.*
  himthag*; ~ing STICK
wall *v.t.* kolhaidag*; *n.* kih;
  kolhaidag; uhksha*
wallet *n.* huashomi; lial kih
walnut *n.* English ~ tree *n.* uhpio
wander *v.i.* himhim; oimmed; ~er
  n. oimmedtham

want v.t. __kam*; tachchu, tachchua;
tachchu*; wi'am*; ~ **to** v.t. __imk*
war n. ~ **arrow** n. u'u; ~ **club** n.
shonchki; ~**like** adj. cheggia*;
~**rior** n. chu-cheggiadkam;
~ **shield** n. kawad; ~**ship** n.
cheggiakud wahlko
ward n. nuhkutha
-ward suffix that forms adjectives and
adverbs __tgio
warlock n. hihointham
warm v.t. huhkajith; huhkalith*;
adj. huhk*; ~ **up** v.t. huhkajith
warn v.t. tha'iwuni; ~**ing of danger**
n. siawogi
wart n. upulig
was v. __ahim*; __d*. See also BE
wash v.t. wakon; wakon*; n. aki;
wi'ishani; ~ **against** v.t. wi'ichk;
wi'ichkwua*; ~ **away** v.t. wi'ihin;
~ CLOTHES; ~**er** n. tihha; ~
oneself wakon
wasp n. wihpsh; **wingless** ~ = COW
killer
waste v.t. heki wua; nahnko*;
nahnkogith; n. sha'i; ~ **of time**
pihthag; ~ TIME
watch v.t. neithahim; n. tash;
wilant*
water n. shuhthagi; wa'ig*; ~ BIRD;
canvas ~ **bag** n. lohna wako;
DIVE **into** ~; ~ **gourd** n. wako;
~**melon** n. gepi; ~**shed** n.
wo'oshani; ~ SNAKE; ~ **(stock)** v.t.
i'ichuth
wave v.t. widut; v.i. __gew; n.
tohnk; **cause a** ~ tohnkath; ~ **the**
HAND
wavy LINES
way n. masma*; **any** ~ adv. has; **in**
a certain ~ has masma; **in any** ~
ha*; **in the** ~ **of** tahgio; ~ **of life**
himthag
we pron. ahchim; __ch*
weak adj. gewk*; gishaliwua*; pi
gewk; ~**ly** adv. pi gewkam; ~**ness**
n. pi gewk
wealth n. kaischutha; kaistalig; ~**y**
n.,adj. kais*
weapon n. **lethal** ~ n. me'akud,
mu'akud
wear v.t. juhkch; wua*; ~ **out** v.t.
wia*
weave v.i. winogim*; ~ **(cotton)**
v.t. ikust; MAT ~**r**
web n. chuaggia; SPIDER ~
wedding n. hohnita
wedge v.t. wah'osith

Wednesday n. Mialklos
week n. thomig; thomig*
weigh v.t. pisalt; pisalta*; **lose** ~**t**
gi'iho; ~**t** n. wehchthag
well n. wawhia, wahia; adv. ap*;
~**-being** n. ap'ethag; ~**-formed**
adj. apkog*; ~**-formedness** n.
apkothag; GET ~; ~ **then** adv.
pegih
west n. huduni, hudunig; adv.
huduni tahgio; **in the** ~ huduniko;
kuiwo; ~**ward** adv huduni tahgio
wet v.t. wadagith; wa'uch; adj.
wadag*; wa'u*
what pron. hab*
wheat n. pilkani; thahpk*; **Pima** ~
n. ola pilkan
wheel n. ~**barrow** n. noli kalit;
nu'ihimtham kalit; ~ **rim** n.
shuhshk
when adv. hekith; conj. __k*
where adv. ¹hebai*; ²hebai; **from** ~
hebaijed, heba'ijed
whetstone n. lihma
which pron. hedai*
while n. kia, kiap; **in a** ~ sha i alo
whimper v.i. kuishani
whine v.i. kuishani
whip v.t. gewittan; n. gewikud
whippletree n. chi-mohn
whippoorwill n. kohlo'ogam
whir v.i. kuhgkim*; weweg;
wewegim*
whirl n. ~ **of wind** siwulogi,
siwuliki; ~**wind** n. siwulogi,
siwuliki
whiskers n. chiniwo; chiniwo*
whiskey n. wihnui
whisper v.i. jupij neok*
whistle v.i. gikuj; kuhgkim*; n.
gikujig; kuikud; ~ **at** v.t. gikujith;
blow a ~ hihnk; ~ **for** v.t.
gikujith
white adj. toha*; ~**n** v.t. tohajith;
tohajithakud*; ~ **person** n.
mil-gahn, milgan
who pron. hedai*
whole adj. hekia; ~**some** adj.
tahtk
whom pron. hedai*
whooping cough n. hehnig
whose pron.,adj. hedai*
wide adj. tadan*; tadani; ~**ly** adv.
tadnim*
widow n. hejel wi'ikam; ~**er** n.
hejel wi'ikam
wife n. hehg*; hohni__*
wiggle v.i. hongith

wild *adj.* mischini; thoajk*; ~**cat** *n.* gewho
wilt *v.i.* bahtkhim*
will *modal auxiliary* wo*; *n.* tachchui
will-o'-the-wisp *n.* nahj oimmedtham
willow *n.* uhpio; **Goodding** ~ **tree** *n.* che'ul
win *v.t.* wanichkwua*; *v.i.* gewito*; ~**ner** *n.* gehgewkam; ~**nings** *n.* gehgewa
winch *n.* si-wihnia
wind *n.* hewastk*; hewel; hewelchuth*; ~**ily** *adv.* hewelim*; ~ **instrument** *n.* kuikud; wahpk kuikud; ~**y** *adj.* hewelhog*
window *n.* winthani; ~-**shop** *v.i.* pasam; pasam*; ~-**shopper** *n.* pasamtham; ~-**shopping** *n.* pasama
wine *n.* nawait; ti-kihla; **make** ~ nawait; **saguaro** CACTUS ~
wing *n.* a'an; a'an*; **flap the** ~**s** anagith; ~ **feather** *n.* hehekaj; machwithag
wink *v.i.* chuishp; kupsh
wino *n.* i'imkam*
winter *n.* hehpch'ed*; hehpch'edkam*
wipe *v.t.* thagion; thagkon, thagkuan; thagkonith*; ~ **off** *v.t.* oan
wire *n.* METAL ~
wisdom *n.* amichuthadag
wish *v.t.* elith*; tachchu, tachchua
witch *n.* hihointham; ho'ok; ~**craft** *n.* hihoina
with *prep.* hekaj; wehm, wehmaj; wehnathch
wobble *v.i.* shakalwua
wolf *n.* sheh'e; ~**berry** *n.* koawul
woman *n.* oks; uwi; uwi*; **an immoral** ~ *n.* chehpa'awi
wood *n.* shontsith*; uhs; **a** ~/~**s** *n.* uhs; ~**cutter** *n.* shoniakam; ~**en** *adj.* uhs; **Gila** ~**pecker** *n.* hikiwigi; komalk mo'okam; ~**pecker** *n.* chehegam
wool *n.* kahwal wopo
word *n.* kailig*; ne'oki
work *v.t.,v.i.* chikpan, chikpan; *n.* chikpan, chikpan; ~**er** *n.* chikpantham, chikpantham; pion; **finish** ~ pihhun; ~**ing** *adj.* chikpantham, chikpantham; ~ **on** *v.t.* chikpan, chikpan; chikpan*; **put to** ~ chikpanachuth, chikpanachuth
world *n.* jewed
worm *n.* watopi; watopad*
worry *v.t.* gihug*; kudut; *v.i.* kudut

worship *v.t.* elith*; *v.i.* mihshmath; **lead in** ~ **or mass** mihshmath
worth *n.* **human** ~ *n.* o'othhamthag
would *modal auxiliary* wo*; ~ **rather** ba'ich i s-hohho'ith
wound *v.t.* mummadag*; mu'u; *n.* muhthag; mummudag; wuddag; PUNCTURE ~
wrap *v.t.* bih__*; bihag*; bihinod; bihinod*; bihshp; chekosh*; hobinod; hobinodag*; hobinol*; ~ **around** *v.t.* bihag; bihiwig; bihiwin; bihiwin*
wreck *v.t.* padchuth; padchuthas; ~**age** *n.* padchutha
wren *n.* **cactus** ~ *n.* hokkad
wrench *v.,n.* ~ **apart** wantp; ~ **away** wanichkwua; PIPE ~ **with chain**
wrestle *v.t.* cheggia; cheggia*; thathge, thathgi__; ~**r** *n.* cheggiatham
wrestling MATCH, RING
wring *v.t.* tohb
wrinkle *v.t.* wijini*
wrist *n.* mashwua; ~**band** *n.* shohshoba
writ *n.* tapial
write *v.t.* o'ohadag*; o'ohan, o'ohon; o'ohan*; o'ohana*; ~ **down** *v.t.* wohth; ~**r** *n.* o'ohantham, o'ohontham
wrong *adj.* GO ~

Y

yam *n.* ihkowi; ka-mohthi
Yaqui tribesman *n.* hiakim
yard *n.* keishpa; ~**stick** *n.* uhs kuintakud
yawn *v.i.* chinniak
year *n.* ahith__*; ahithag; ha'akith*; **fiscal** ~ *n.* kownal ahithag; ~**ling** *n.* ahithkam; **New Y**~ *n.* Wechij Ahithag
yeast *n.* jewajithakud
yell *v.i.* hihnk; ~ **at** *v.t.* hihnko'ith; ~ **to** *v.t.* hihnath
yelp *v.i.* hihnk
yes *adv.* heu'u, hau'u; ho-e-juh, ho-ni-juh, ni-juh
yesterday *adv.* tako; **day before** ~ d hema tako
yet *conj.* eda; oi wa; **not** ~ kia, kia koi; koi
yield *v.t.* thagito

yoke *v.t.* yehwadag*; yehwadath; *n.*
yehwa
you *pron.* m-*; ⁴__m*; ²__p*; (*sing.*)
ahpih, ahpi'i; (*pl*) ahpim, ahham
young *adj.* wechij; wechij*
your *adj.* (*sing.*) m-; **by** ~**self/selves**
hejelko; ~**self/selves** *pron.* e*; e-*
yucca *n.* ; utko*; **banana** ~ *n.*
howij-je'e; **fruit of banana** ~ *n.*

howij; ~ **shoot** *n.* wupaj; **soaptree**
or soapweed ~ *n.* takui

Z

zig-zag *adj.* jujul*; ~**ed** *adj.* jujul*;
~**edly** *adv.* jujulim*
zoo *n.* mischini ha'ichu thoakam
chehgitha

APPENDIX ONE
Phonology

Consonants*

Manner	Position					
	Bilabial	Dental	Alveolar	Palatal	Velar	Glottal
Tense stop	p	t		tʃ¹	k	
Lax stop	b	d²	d	dʒ³	g	ʔ⁴
Fricative			s	ʃ		h
Nasal	m	n				
Lateral				l⁵		
Glide	w					

¹ č is used in this description.
² ḏ is used in this description.
³ j is used in this description
⁴ a (') is used in this description.
⁵ a palatal lateral flap.

Vowels*

	Position		
	Front	Central	Back
High	i	ɨ	u
Low		a	o

*International Phonetic Alphabet

Distribution and Allophones
Allophonic variation depends on distribution of phonemes in syllables, words, and sentences.

The syllable is the unit of stress placement. There are three degrees of stress: primary, secondary, and unstressed. Stress is predictable, but for descriptive purposes, primary stress is indicated by (´), and secondary stress by (`) over the stressed vowel. Syllables have a nucleus of one or two vowels. All vowel sequences occur except ao, uo, ou, aɨ, uɨ, and oɨ. Vowel sequences in syllable nucleus may be interrupted by the glottal stop ('), or the glottal spirant (h) under primary stress, and by the glottal stop under secondary stress, as shown with (/) for syllable division as in: hó'i/gɨ'iḏáa 'blessing'. The glottal stop and glottal spirant do not occur in the posterior margin of syllables. The vowel i forms the anterior margin of syllables that are not word

113

initial, as in 'oiopo 'to walk around (pl.)' and ḏadhaiwuia 'to sit down (pl. imperative)'. Primary stress occurs on the first syllable of major class words and parts of compounds, on any non-back vowel immediately following hu, ku, or wu, and on the first vowel otherwise, as in: Huán 'John', Huíwis 'Thursday', kuí 'mesquite', wuá 'to put (something) down', kóa 'forehead', wáid 'to invite', páal-wákon 'to baptize', etc. Secondary stress occurs on certain syllables with no primary stress. On vowel sequences, secondary stress occurs on the first of identical-vowel, or high-low vowel, or interrupted sequences, and on the last vowel otherwise, as in: 'íidà'a/'íidàa 'this', tóhàa 'to become white', wígìi 'to become red', ho'ige'iḏàa 'blessing', 'ámài 'there', ɨ́gòi 'greasewood bush', hɨ́kià 'of one substance', ḏáapiùn 'to smooth', táccuì 'a need', etc.

On single vowels, secondary stress occurs on the last vowel in a word that precedes a voiced consonant without a following stressed vowel, as in: 'ɨ̀dàgi, 'ídagìda 'to own'; 'ídagidàa 'ownership'; híwìgi, híwigìda 'to permit'; híwigidàa 'permission'; etc. All sequences of vowel-plus-consonant occur. All sequences of consonant-plus-vowel occur except: ʃ or d plus i; t, ḏ, d, s, or l plus ɨ; and b or g plus u. Consonants are unaspirated, but have a neutral release under conditions described later. No consonants have lip rounding, except before u or o. N is palatalized (ñ) before i, ɨ, or u. W is fricative before i or a, and before certain other vowels in some dialects.

Certain allophones of voiced phonemes are formed by devoicing and vowel offglide phenomena. The voiced phonemes are b, ḏ, d, j, g, m, n, l, w, i, ɨ, u, a, and o. Devoiced allophones are indicated here by capital letters, B, G, I, A, etc. In primary-stressed syllables, unstressed vowels devoice sentence finally, as in: maI 'to learn'; miA 'near'; maA 'to give', etc. In primary-stressed syllables, unstressed vowels after glottals devoice if not before a voiced consonant or ('), as in: s-tohA 'white', mo'O 'head', etc. When not primary stressed, both double and single vowels are reduced in length, giving the impression of single and extra-short vowels, respectively. In secondary-stressed syllables, unstressed vowels devoice utterance finally and before h, as in: ʃɨ́gòI 'greasewood'; 'ámàI 'there'; etc. Single unstressed vowels devoice utterance finally, before h, and between a stop and a voiceless consonant, as in: komI 'the lower back'; čúuwI 'a jackrabbit'; wáak UsI 'a rug'; hɨ́kI húU 'already', ḏágItoO 'to drop something'; etc. Consonants are devoiced if not before a voiced sound, as in: kóMI, čúuWI, dáGItòO; etc. Vowels that are not devoiced have a glottal offglide before devoiced stops, and an aspirated offglide otherwise when not before a voiced phoneme or ('), as in: tóo'BI 'a cottontail rabbit', 'á'JI 'narrow', dá'GItòO 'to drop something', cúuʰWI 'a jackrabbit', kóʰMI 'the lower back', hɨ́ʰKI húʰU 'already', etc. In Totoguani, ḏ is treated as a stop, and as a nonstop in other dialects, accounting for a difference in offglide phenomena, as in: mɨ́'DA or mɨ́ʰDA 'to run'. Unstressed word-final i metathesizes with any following glottal, as in: s-tóni 'oO → s-tón'iòO 'It's hot'; s-tóni hóḏai → s-tóNhióḏaI 'hot stone'; etc. Other unstressed final vowels are deleted before any glottal. Unstressed vowels are also deleted between: identical consonants; any stop and homorganic tense stop; s or ʃ and tense stop; m and p or b; n and dental, alveolar, or palatal stop, as in: ʃúuḍagi + kaji → ʃúuḍagkaji 'with water'.

In the formation of consonant sequences, n assimilates to the point of articulation of any following stop. Nasal consonants are lengthened to compensate for the deletion of a following vowel. Under conditions where unstressed single vowels are not deleted, they may be reduced to schwa, a neutral release. The schwa retains the voiced or devoiced condition of the vowel it is reduced from. The following unstressed single vowels reduce to schwa: all a and o; word-final u after k; and i when between w and a voiced consonant that does not precede a stressed vowel, or when not following a bilabial or velar consonant, as in: wóoga →wóo'Gə 'a road'; tónolìda → tonəli'də 'to enlighten'; s-čúku → s-čúʰkə 'black'; híwigìda → hiwəgì'Də 'to permit'; wáakusi → wáaʰkUsə 'a rug'; etc.

The sounds of h and w are deleted in certain words as they are in certain English words—as in: I saw (h)im; I'll go; etc. The following words delete initial h or w following a consonant or i: ha (negative adjunct), háhawaa 'afterward', ha-hékaj 'immediately', wa 'as previously mentioned', haʃ/wabʃ 'just', haʃaba/wabʃaba 'but', wa'i 'in particular', wo 'will', wud (existential marker).

The main part of each clause and each phrase has a tone contour. The tone level in a contour is high from the first through the last primary stress in the main part of the construction, and low elsewhere, as in:

napə|pìi mä|acə masə|híbai hì|i hígai čí|ojə
'Don't you know where that man may have gone?'

Traditional chanting style introduced ŋ by a rule changing voiced stops to nasals at the same point of articulation, and y by a rule changing (') to y in word-initial position, and to h noninitially, as in: ʃúudagi →ʃúunaŋi 'water', 'á'ai → yáahai 'back and forth', etc. Spanish loanwords incorporated n and y as phonemes in normal speech, as in: 'áŋhil 'angel', and yáawi 'key'.

Unstressed short and long vowels contrast after h, n, and g, as in: s-toha 'white' and tohah 'to become white'; s-toni 'hot' and tonih 'to become hot'; s-wegi 'red' and wegih 'to become red'; etc. When a vowel is required where none is specified following a consonant, the vowel is i after ch, j, l, or s, otherwise the vowel is a, as in: huhch + j = huhchij 'hoof of'; wehs + g = wehsig 'complete'; etc.

Since ŋ occurs in only a few Spanish loan words, it is written ng, as in anghil; or not differentiated, as in chahngo 'monkey' and wahngo 'bank'.

In certain Spanish loan words, n does not palatalize before i or u. In these words in the dictionary, n is italicized, as in: mi-*n*uhto 'minute'; mi-*n*uhlo 'tripe'; *n*i 'neither, nor'; *n*uhmilo 'number'.

Dialect Differences

The dictionary lists major dialect variances but lists only a standard form when words of other dialects can be formed by rule.

The greatest dialect differences occur between the groups of dialects called Papago and Pima, where there are different words for the same item, such as:

Papago	Pima	English meaning
ah'ath	hotsh	to send
nenida	tamiam	to wait for
s-hehogi	s-heubagi	to be cool
sisish	ho'iumi	to fasten
pih ha'ichug	piach	to be absent
ulinihogig	heubagig	relaxation

Another dialect difference results from reduction of sequences of tense stop plus h. Southern dialects delete the tense stop and assimilate the vowel following h to the preceding vowel. Northern dialects delete the h.

Early	Southern	Northern	English meaning
ahphim	ahham	ahpim	you
chuhkhug	chuhhug	chuhkug	flesh
ehkheg	ehheg	ehkeg	to be shaded
uhpham	uhhum	uhpam	back to a previous place or condition

The Chukud Kuk dialect deletes voiced bilabials medially in certain words:

Other Dialects	Chukud Kuk	English meaning
jiwia, jiwa	jiia	to arrive
u'uwhig	u'uhig	a bird
wabsh	hash	just, only
wabshaba, shaba	hashaba	but

In sequences of vowels that are together or separated by a ('), Totogwuani changes e to i before a or o, and o to u before a:

Standard	Totogwuani	English meaning
cheadagi	chiadagi	the Gila monster
chehani	chihani	to command
heosig	hiosig	a blossom
ne'oki	ni'oki	a word
tho'ag	thu'ag	a mountain
s-toha	s-tuha	white

Totogwuani plural forms in which the vowels do not form a sequence have the same vowels as the standard forms, as in: chechadagi 'Gila monsters', thohtha'ag 'mountains', s-tohta 'white (pl.)', etc.

The following are the dialects of Papago and Pima:

Papago	Pima
Chukud Kuk	Eastern Gila
Gigimai	Kohathk
Huhhu'ula	Salt River
Huhuwosh	Western Gila
Totogwuani	

Correlation of Alphabets

The practical alphabet, because it was formed by testing native speakers with English reading experience, differs in some respects from the IPA and phonemic alphabets. The symbols that differ are:

IPA	Phonemic	Practical
tʃ	č	ch
d	ḍ	th
dʒ	j	j
ʃ	ṣ	sh
ɨ	ɨ	e
ʔ	ʔ	'

Although word-initial (') is not written, it must be used in the formation of reduplicated syllables, as in esh ('chin')→e'esh ('chins').

Geminate vowel sequences are treated as long vowels in the practical alphabet, and represented as vowel plus h, as in ah, eh, ih, oh, and uh. Any h which occurs between vowels is the consonant h. In certain repetitive action verb forms, a medial h reduplicates, as in hihhim 'to go repeatedly', and hehhem 'to laugh repeatedly'.

Vowels that reduce to schwa are not written except in verbs in which they are required for the perfective truncated form. Thus in verbs like the following, the middle vowel reduces to schwa in the basic form, but not in the truncated form: edagith→edagi 'to own'; jegelith→jegel 'to make room for'; hiwigith→hiwigi 'to permit'; tonolith→tonol 'to enlighten'; etc.

In word positions where a single unstressed vowel is reduced to schwa and not written, contrast is clear when double vowels are written as single vowels, like the contrast between: hiwigith 'to permit' and hiwigitha 'permission', etc.

The alphabet introduced by Albert Alvarez employs the same symbols for most of the sounds, making transfer from one alphabet to the other relatively easy. Primary stress is indicated by (´) over the vowel in the Alvarez alphabet. The symbols that differ are:

Practical		Alvarez		English meaning
ch	chuchul	c	cúcul	a chicken
d	tadai	ḍ	táḍaĭ	a roadrunner
n	huniga	ñ	húñĭga	a bunion
sh	shopol	ṣ	ṣópol	short
th	thag	d	dág	caliche

Word-initial (') is indicated in the Alvarez alphabet:

Practical	Alvarez	English meaning
esh	'éṣ	chin
a'ag	'a'ag	a horn

Stressed long vowels in Alvarez are indicated by a colon rather than h:

mahk	má:k	to give
oh'o	'ó:'o	a bone

Unstressed short vowels in Alvarez are indicated by (ˇ) over the vowel:

s-wegi	s-wĕgi	red
i'ito	'i'ĭto	to drink up
edagith	'edăgid	to own

In Alvarez the phoneme ŋ is differentiated from n, as in: 'aŋhil 'angel' and cá:ŋgo 'monkey'. Also, words that delete initial h or w after consonants or i are written without it in Alvarez whether it is sounded or not, as in: 'am 'ant aha o hi 'I'm going to go there afterward'.

APPENDIX TWO
Time and Calendar

Time

Time is measured traditionally by the movements of the sun and the moon. *Tash*, which means 'sun', also means 'time', 'a day', and 'a period of daylight'. Since the sun is a timepiece, *tash* is extended in meaning to designate any timepiece. As a period of daylight, *tash* is bounded by *si'alig* 'morning' (from *si'ad* '[of the sun] to rise') and *hudunik* 'evening' (from *huduni* 'to descend'). Night is *s-chuhugam* 'darkness, night'.

A year is a cycle of the sun, *ahithag* (from *aha, ahi__* 'to complete a cycle'). A month is a cycle of the moon, both being called *mashath*. Any present unit of time is indicated by *hemu* 'now, present' before the unit name, as in *hemu tash* 'today', *hemu mashath* 'this month', *hemu ahithag* 'this year'.

Some immediate past and future time periods have specific names, such as *tako* 'yesterday', *si'alim* 'tomorrow', *chuhug* 'last night', *ha'akith* 'last year'. 'Tomorrow night' is *si'alim hudunik*. Otherwise, the immediate future period is indicated by *ba'ich* 'beyond, next' before the unit name, as in *ba'ich mashath* 'next month', *ba'ich ahithag* 'next year'. Two periods of time away is indicated by *d hema*, and three periods of time away by *d hu hema* before the specific unit name. Examples are *d hema tako* 'two days ago', *d hu hema tako* 'three days ago', *d hema si'alim* 'two days from now', *d hu hema si'alim* 'three days from now', *d hema ha'akith* 'two years ago', etc. Other past periods are indicated by *wehgaj* 'behind' after the period designation, as in *gi'ik tash wehgaj* 'four days ago', etc. Other future periods are indicated by *ba'ich* 'beyond' after the period designation, as in *gi'ik tash ba'ich* 'four days from now', etc.

Time of day is indicated by the verb *juh, jujju* '(of the sun) to reach a specified position'. A modifier before the verb indicates the part of the day by the direction of the sun's movement, as in *ga hu* 'approaching', *thahm* 'above', *gam hu* 'retreating'. The position may be specified by gesture. Examples are: *Ga at hu i juh g tash* 'A certain time of morning arrived (lit. The sun rose so far)', *Gam at hu i juh g tash* 'A certain time of the afternoon arrived (lit. The sun went down so far)', *Thahm at juh g tash* 'Noon arrived (lit. The sun arrived overhead)'. The form *jujju* indicates repetitiveness, as in *thahm jujju* 'every noon', and *ga hu i jujju* 'every morning at a (specified) time'.

The non-continuative (perfective) connector *k* forms adverbial phrases, as in *Am ant hih gam hu i juhk* 'I went there in the afternoon (lit. I went there when the sun had descended to a certain position)'.

Since the introduction of the clock and of the Spanish loan words *ohla* 'hour' (from Spanish *hora*) and *mi-nuhto* 'minute' (from Spanish *minuto*), time may also be expressed by hour and minute.

Papago/Pima		*English*						
hemako	**ohla-ch-ed**	at one o'clock						
one	hour -in							

west-mahm	**gamai**	**hetasp**	**mi-nuhto**	**mat -o**	**e**	**ai**	**g**	**waik**	**ohla**
ten	plus	five	minutes	INT+it	FUT	RE	reach	ART	three	hour

English: fifteen minutes (or a quarter) to three

gokko	**west-mahm**	**gamai**	**hetasp**	**mi-nuhto**	**waik**	**ohla**	**ba'ich**
twice	ten	plus	five	minutes	three	hour	beyond

English: twenty-five (minutes) after/past three

The week as a measure of time, and days of the week, were introduced from Spanish, as *Thomig* 'Sunday', (from Spanish *domingo*), etc. In some dialects Tuesday, Wednesday, and Thursday are designated as the second, third, and fourth days respectively, with Monday considered the first day. Here, Tuesday is *Gohk Tash* (lit. second day), Wednesday is *Waik Tash* (lit. third day), and Thursday is *Gi'ik Tash* (lit. fourth day).

Calendar

Traditionally the year began with the saguaro cactus harvest at the summer solstice, and the names of months, which differ in different areas, reflect seasonal features and activities (such as hunting and gathering for Papagos versus farming for Pimas) and different environments (the lower elevation of Pimas causes an earlier spring, and irrigation results in different vegetation). Common names of the months are given below, with Pima names, where they are different, in parentheses.

Hahshani Bahithag Mashath is June, 'The Saguaro Cactus Fruit Month', when the Desert People go to the camps or areas where they harvest the fruit of the giant saguaro cactus.

Jukiabig Mashath is July, 'The Rainy Month', when most crops are planted. Before the digging of wells made year-round living at the field sites possible, people would move there in time to irrigate and prepare for planting.

Shopol Eshabig Mashath is August, 'The Short Crop Month', when the late summer rains end and short crops are planted.

Washai Gakithag Mashath is September, 'The Dry Grass Month', (*Vashai Gakithag Mashath*), when the harvest is finished. Before there were wells, people would move in September to their mountain homes where there would be a winter water supply.

Wi'ihanig Mashath is October, 'The Gleaning Month' (*Vi'ihanig Mashath*), the time to gather left-over fruits, acorns, and tubers for the winter food supply.

Kehg S-hehpijig Mashath is November, 'The Fair Cold Month'. This is the deer rutting season, so the month is also called *Uhwalig Mashath* (*Uhvalig Mashath*), 'The Rutting Odor Month'.

Ge'e S-hehpijig Mashath is December, 'The Extreme Cold Month'. Since it is the month of the winter solstice (which divides the year), December is also called *Eda Wa'ugath Mashath* 'The Backbone Month'.

Gi'ihothag Mashath is January, 'The Weight Loss Month' *(Kohmagi Mashath*—see February following), when game animals lose their reserve of flesh.

Kohmagi Mashath is February, 'The Gray Month' *(Chehthagi Mashath*—see March following), when vegetation is scant and trees are bare.

Chehthagi Mashath is March, 'The Green Month' *(Oam Mashath*—see April following). The greening begins with the leafing out of mesquite trees.

Oam Mashath is April, 'The Yellow Month' *(S-gevk Mashath* 'The Strong Month'), when the trees begin to bloom, beginning with mesquite.

Ko'ok Mashath is May, 'The Painful Month' for the Papago because of hunger *(Pilkani Bahithag Mashath* 'The Wheat Harvest Month', so called since the introduction of winter wheat).

There are also other names for the months. Among the Desert People, June is *Kaij Chukalig* 'Blackened Saguaro Seed', October is *Hehogiabk* 'Cooling' and *Al Jujukiabig* 'Little Rains', February is *Uhwalig* 'Mating Odor' (for whitetail deer), March is *Kui I'iwagithag* 'Mesquite budding', April is *Kui Heosig* 'Mesquite Blooming', May is *U'us Wihogtalig* 'Tree Bean'. Among the River People, January is *Auppa Heosig* 'Cottonwood Blooming', February is *Auppa I'iwagithag* 'Cottonwood Leafing'.

The specific calendar of an area may be determined by consulting dependable resource people of the area.

APPENDIX THREE
Cultural Terms
Ceremonial Groups and Totems
Since ancient times, the Papago and Pima people have belonged to two main moieties, which took part in ceremonies and games. One group has the buzzard, and the other the coyote, as its totem or helper (*wehmkal*). The buzzard moiety has two clans, *Mahmgam* and *Wahwgam*, and the coyote moiety has two clans, *Apapagam* and *Apkihgam*. Representatives of these four clans took part at the four directions in ceremonies. There is also a clan called *Ogolgam* which has the bear as its totem. Each clan derives its name from its father term *mahm, wahw, apapa, apkih,* and *ogol,* since clan membership comes from one's father. There was great rivalry and competition in games and races between the groups, and, although moiety and clan functions have disappeared, those who remember their group still tease each other about characteristics they are assumed to have derived from their totem.

Completeness of Ceremonies
A ceremony or ritual is completed (*am hugith*) by four repetitions or by four days of activity. The importance of completion is seen by a striking contrast in versions of the Ogress (*Ho'ok*) story.

The Ogress is driven out of the village of Green Well (*Chehthagi Wawhia*), but returns, feigning love for children, and takes them off, one by one, to fill out her menu. The people call on *I'itoi*, the cultural hero, to resolve the problem. He tells them to invite the Ogress to the village for four days and nights of dancing. When she is exhausted, they will drug her cigarettes, then carry her unconscious to her cave where they will burn her up. In the version from this side of the Mexican border, the people complete the ritual number of days, and all goes well at the burning. She jumps and cracks the roof as the fire reaches her, but I'itoi steps on the crack and prevents the smoke from escaping. (*Legends* 243–61). But in the version from the other side of the border, the Ogress gives out after three days and they carry her to the cave and burn her. Her spirit escapes through the crack in the form of smoke and rises to become a great blue hawk, which turns out to be more devastating than the Ogress (*Legends* 281–95).

Manhood
There were four degrees in attaining manhood. Each degree progressed in danger, but gave further power to those who attained it.

Killing a small animal was the first degree. It would be said of any novitiate *Koi at mea g ban* 'He hasn't yet killed a coyote (or other small animal)', meaning that he had not yet attained the first degree of manhood.

Another degree was attained when the candidate went on his first journey with the men to get salt (*onamed*). The danger faced was meeting the ocean (Gulf of California), a source of power as well as salt.

Another degree was attained by meeting an animal or bird with power in a dream or vision (*Legends* 181–82, 193–96). The candidate who attained this degree might be called by the name of the animal or bird he saw, such as

Wisag Namkam 'Hawk Meeter' (*Legends* 199), to indicate that he had acquired its powers.

The final degree of manhood was attained by killing an enemy tribesman. Accomplishing this feat was attended not just with physical danger but with the greatest spiritual danger. The enemy slayer acquired spiritual power from the slain but must guard himself and his relatives from the ill-effects of having this power by retreating from society for a fast, especially from salt, to be purified (*e lihmhun*). Whereas the normal period for completing a ritual was four days, the solemnity of the final degree and its accompanying power required four times that period, or sixteen days.

Improper conduct in seeking a degree of manhood might result in spiritual illness, which is described in the next section.

Spirit Power

In traditional ideology, certain people and things have inherent spirit power that may be appropriated by proper treatment but that may bring ill-fortune when treated improperly.

Rain (*Juhki*) abandoned the people because they drove away his guide Wind (*Hewel*). Now they must be invited back each year by singing to them (*Legends* 321–36). Crops must be sung to for good production (*Legends* 37–39). Proper precautions must be taken to avoid calamity, such as grasping the back of the neck at the sight of a tarantula (*kusho thagshpa*). Certain things are taboo, such as the badger (*Legends* 341–46) and quail (*Legends* 121–24).

Danger of illness results from contact with, or improper conduct toward, certain animals, certain moving or lifelike things such as lightning and smoke, and humans in certain conditions. The animals concerned have spirit power *ha'ichu thoakam gewkthag,* also called by the specific animal, such as *ban gewkthag* 'coyote spirit power'. The illness is called after the specific causative agent, such as *ban mumkithag* 'coyote illness'. Such an illness is non-contagious, called *kahchim mumkithag* 'immobile illness' in contrast to any contagious disease, called *oimmedtham mumkithag* 'mobile illness' (Bahr et al. 19). Such an illness is said to overtake a person (*aha, ai*). It might result from improper conduct in killing an enemy tribesman, or contact with a prostitute. If a menstruating woman contacted a man *huhulmad* '(of a menstruating woman) to contact a male', he would lose his strength. Thus a menstrual house was provided to isolate her from any contact.

An illness caused by spirit power might occur long after the causative incident. Thus it would be necessary to call on a shaman (*mahkai*) to determine the cause. A diagnostic chant (*kuadk*) might be used for this purpose. When the cause had been determined, a practitioner who had the cure for the specific disease was called on. The cure may include drawing a line around the patient *kihchuth* 'to house or contain (the spirit power)'; singing the song or songs for the specific illness (*ne'ichuth*); blowing smoke on the patient (*kummun*); treating with a fetish, a part, product, or replica of the causative agent by waving over, or pressing on, the patient; blowing breath on the patient (*wusot*); reciting ritual orations (*hambdho*) (Bahr et al. 297); rubbing a notched stick for percussion (*hiwchulith*); using a healing stick (*omina*); etc.

APPENDIX FOUR
Kinship

Papago-Pima kinship is an equilateral system, with primary and reciprocal terms for four ascending generations of blood relatives, plus marriage-related relatives, and those related by legal or religious means. Any blood relative may be referred to as *hajuni* 'a relative, relatives', as in *Do ni-hajuni* 'He (or she) is my relative', or 'They are my relatives'. Any specific but unspecified relative may be referred to as *hab juni* 'that relation', or *has juni* 'what relation', as in *K has d m-juni?* 'What relation is he to you?', *No d m-hakit?* 'Is he your uncle (here, specifically, your father's younger brother)?', and *Heu'u, heg o hab d ni-juni* 'Yes, he's that relation to me'.

Terms that specify a relationship are used when referring to anyone's relatives and when addressing one's own relatives. Relatives are addressed by relationship rather than by name or relationship plus name. Addressing a relative by relationship is expressed by the verb *ihm* 'to address by kin relationship', or by the noun *ihmigi* 'the terms, or the custom, of addressing by kin relationship'. Relatives are addressed by relationship to greet them, to get their attention, or to encourage them in an endeavor.

Terms for older generation blood relatives and younger generation relatives by marriage are primary, and the response terms are reciprocal. Both primary and reciprocal terms carry information about the person named in the primary term. The information carried is: relative generation, relative rank of same-generation relatives to oneself or one's parent, and sex and side of family in one's parent- and grandparent-generation and in one's son- and daughter-in-law generation. Examples are *ni-hakit* 'my uncle of lower rank than my father' and *ni-hakimad* 'my nephew or niece, of whose father I am of lower rank'.

In the nuclear or immediate family, parent-child terms do not express rank. Examples are *ni-je'e* 'my mother', *ni-mad* 'my child (spoken by the mother)' and *ni-mahmad* 'my children (spoken by the mother)'.

The noun suffix __kam or __m refers to one who possesses the item named. With relationship terms, the suffix refers to one who has the relative named. Examples are *je'ekam* (or *je'em*) 'one who has a mother', *madkam* (or *madam*) 'a woman who has a child', and *mahmadkam* (or *mahmadam*) 'a woman who has children'.

The reflexive person indicator *e-* combines with the plural reciprocal relationship term to refer to those who have the mutual relationship that includes the person named, as in *e-mahmadkam* (or *e-mahmadam*) 'those who are related to each other as mother and child or children'. Those who are related to each other in any way are *e-hajunim*.

In my own generation, any brother, sister, or cousin is *ni-wehnag*. I call my older brother or sister *ni-sihs, ni-si'ihe*, or *ni-si'ihegi*, expressing higher rank and responsibility. They call me *ni-shehpij* or *ni-sikul,* expressing lower rank. Rank is passed to descendents, so the rank of cousins depends on the age of their ancestors who are brothers and sisters. I call my higher rank cousins *ni-sihs,* and they call me *ni-shehpij,* regardless of our age. The relationship group of brothers, sisters, and cousins is called *e-wepnagam* or *e-sheshepijim.*

The same terms are used between those who are four generations apart as between those of the same generation, but rank is inverted. My great-great-grandparents and their brothers, sisters, and cousins call me by the higher rank term *ni-sihs,* and I call any of them *ni-shehpij* or *ni-sikul.* The inversion of rank indicates the responsibility of the younger generation for the aged. Old timers say *Am o sikol bijim g ihmigi* 'There's where kinship turns around'. The inversion of terms also marks the vertical limits of the kinship system.

I call my great grandparents and their brother, sister, and cousin *ni-wihkol,* and they call me *ni-wihshad.* Some dialects reverse these terms. Our relationship group is called *e-wipishadam* or *e-wipikolim.*

I call my paternal grandfather, his brother, and his male cousin *ni-wosk* or *ni-woji* (informal). I may also call his brother and his male cousin *ni-wosk-keli,* and call his sister and female cousin *ni-wosk-oks.* They all call me *ni-wosmad.* Our relationship group is called *e-wopsmadam.*

I call my paternal grandmother, her sister and her female cousin *ni-kahk* or *ni-gagih* (informal). I may also call her sister and her female cousin *ni-kahk-oks,* and I call her brother and her male cousin *ni-kahk-keli.* They all call me *ni-ka'amad.* Our relationship group is called *e-kahkmadam.*

I call my maternal grandfather and his brother and his male cousin *ni-bahb* or *ni-babih* (informal). I may also call his brother and his male cousin *ni-bahb-keli.* I call his sister and his female cousin *ni-bahb-oks.* They all call me *ni-ba'amad.* Our relationship group is called *e-bahbmadam.*

I call my maternal grandmother, her sister, and her female cousin *ni-hu'ul* or *ni-hu'uli* (informal). I may also call her sister and her female cousin *ni-hu'ul-oks.* I call her brother and her male cousin *ni-hu'ul-keli.* They all call me *ni-mohs* or *ni-mohsi* (informal). Our relationship group is called *e-mohmsim.*

The immediate or nuclear family is indicated in the terms for parents. My parents are *ni-jehj.* I call my father *ni-ohg,* and he calls me *ni-alithag.* Our relationship group is called *e-a'alithkam.* I call my mother *ni-je'e,* and she calls me *ni-mad.* Our relationship group is called *e-mahmadam.* A number of nuclear families in the extended family may live in a group of dwellings, usually around the dwelling of the patriarch of the family. Clan names for father are given in Appendix 3.

My parents' cousins as well as their brothers and sisters are my uncles and aunts. My relationship names for them indicate their sex and their rank in relation to my father or my mother.

I call a person of higher rank than my father *ni-keli* if male, and *ni-oksi* if female, and they call me *ni-chuhchud.* Our relationship group is called *e-chuhchudam.* I call a person of lower rank than my father *ni-hakit* if male,

Blood Relationships

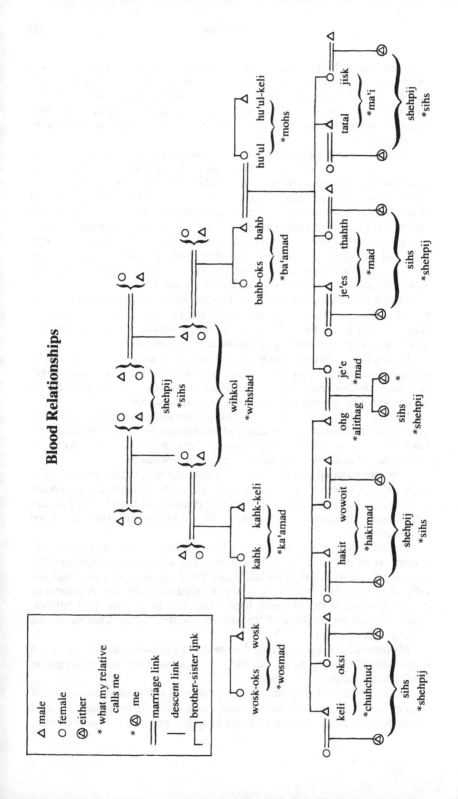

Legend:
- △ male
- ○ female
- ⊕ either
- * what my relative calls me
- *Ⓐ me
- ═══ marriage link
- │ descent link
- ⌐⌐ brother-sister link

shehpij / *sihs
wihkol / *wihshad

hu'ul   hu'ul-keli
*mohs

bahb   bahb
bahb-oks
*ba'amad

kahk   kahk-keli
*ka'amad

wosk-oks   wosk
*wosmad

tatal   jisk
*ma'i
shehpij / *sihs

je'es   thahth
*mad
sihs / *shehpij

je'e   *mad
ohg   *alithag
sihs / *shehpij   *

hakit   wowoit
*hakimad
shehpij / *sihs

keli   oksi
*chuhchud
sihs / *shehpij

and *ni-wowoit* if female, and they call me *ni-hakimad*. Our relationship group is called *e-hahakimadam*.

I call a person of higher rank than my mother *ni-je'es* if male, and *ni-thahth* if female, and they call me *ni-mad*. Our relationship group is called *e-mahmadam*. I call a person of lower rank than my mother *ni-tatal* if male, and *ni-jisk* if female, and they call me *ni-ma'i*. Our relationship group is called *e-mama'ikam*.

The relationships given previously are by blood, established by birth. Other relationships are created by marriage, legal means, and religious tradition.

A man calls his wife *ni-hohnig* or *ni-oksga*. A woman calls her husband *ni-kun* or *ni-keliga*. A man and wife are called *e-hohonigam*. When a man had more than one wife, each called the other *ni-hehg*, and the pair or group was called *e-hehegam*.

The relationship names of my in-laws are formed by adding the term for mother or father to my relationship name for a child or children in the union. Thus, when a child is born, the in-law acquires a name, and when another child is born the name changes, like *ni-hakima-je'e* and *ni-hahakimad-ha-je'e*.

If my relative is higher rank than myself, I call his wife *ni-hakima-je'e*, or her husband *ni-ma'i-ohg*. If my relative is lower, I call his wife *ni-chuhchud-je'e*, or her husband *ni-mad-ohg*. They call me *ni-kiheh*. Our relationship groups are *e-hakima-jehjim*, *e-ma'i-o'ogam*, *e-chuhchud-jehjim*, and *e-mad-o'ogam*.

A man calls his son's or nephew's wife *ni-wosma-je'e*, and his daughter's or niece's husband *ni-ba'amad-ohg*. A woman calls her son's or nephew's wife *ni-ka'ama-je'e*, and her daughter's or niece's husband *ni-mohs-ohg* or *ni-moi-ohg*. The reciprocal terms are identical to the primary terms. The relationship groups are *e-wosma-jehjim*, *e-ba'amad-o'ogam*, *e-ka'ama-jehjim*, and *e-mohs-o'ogam*.

I call the spouses in my grandchild generation *ni-wihshad-ohg* and *ni-wihshad-je'e*, and they call me the same. Our relationship groups are *e-wihshad-o'ogam* and *e-wihshad-jehjim*.

I call the spouses in my great-grandchild generation *ni-sihs-ohg* and *ni-sihs-je'e*, and they call me the same. Our relationship groups are *e-sihs-o'ogam* and *e-sihs-jehjim*.

I call my stepfather *ni-hakit* or *ni-keishpa-ohg*, and he responds *ni-hakimad*. I call my stepmother *ni-jisk* or *ni-keishpa-je'e*, and she responds *ni-ma'i*. Our relationship groups are *e-hahakimadam* and *e-mama'ikam*.

I call my godfather *ni-paw-lihna*, and my godmother *ni-thahth*, and they call me *ni-wakona* or *ni-mad*.

The godfather of my child and I call each other *ni-kompal*, and our relationship group is *e-kokompalim*. The godmother of my child and I call each other *ni-komal*, and our relationship group is *e-kokomalim*.

Maps and Place Names

The Language Family
The language of the Pima and Papago belongs to the Utoaztecan language family, which is now found throughout the central and western United States and northern Mexico. Linguistic evidence indicates that the Utoaztecan family all spoke one language long ago. However, as the centuries passed, general mobility resulted in scattered groups which progressively brought about division in language groups as shown (from left to right) on the chart below.

The Utoaztecan Language Family

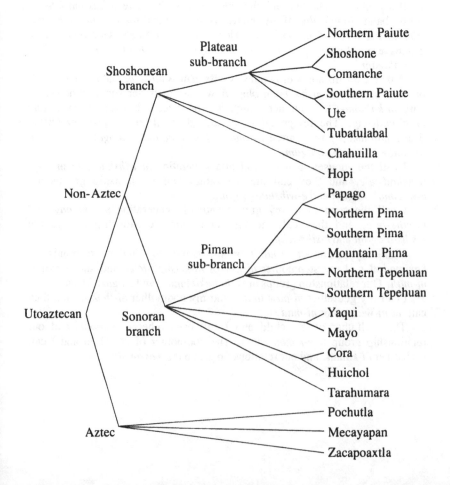

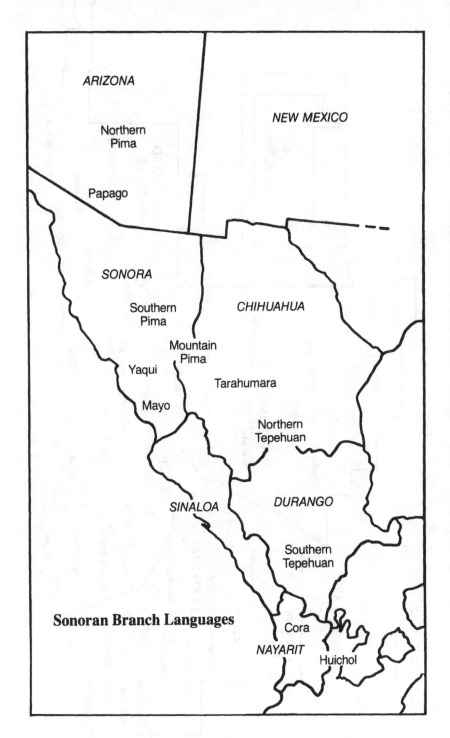

Sonoran Branch Languages

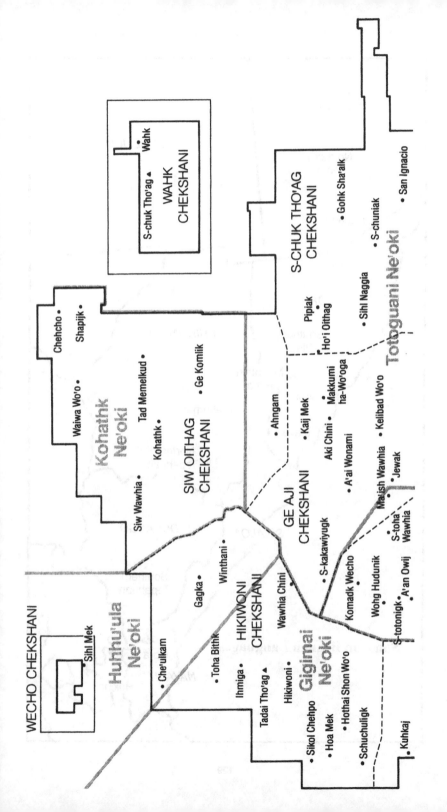

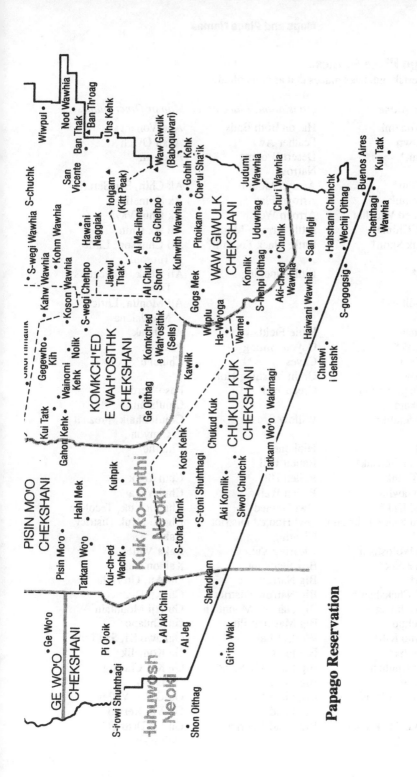

Papago Reservation

Papago Place Names
An asterisk indicates places that are inhabited.

Papago Name	Translation: Place of...	Map or Other Names
A'ai Wonami	Hat on Both Ends	Aha Vonam
A'an Owij	Feather Awl	Ahan Ovich
Ahngam*	Desert Brooms	Anegam
Aji	Narrow	
Aki Chini*	Arroyo Mouth	Ak Chin, San Serafin
Aki Komlik	Arroyo Flat	Ak Komelik
Aki-ch-ed Wawhia	Arroyo Well	Ak Chut Vaya
Al Aki Chini*	Little Arroyo Mouth	Ali Ak Chin
Al Chuk Shon*	Little Black Foothill	Ali Chukson, Little Tucson
Al Jeg*	Little Opening	Ali Chuk, Meneger's Dam
Al Ma-lihna*		Ali Monila, Little Magdalena
Al Oithag	Little Field	Ali Oidak
Ban Thak*	Coyote Sitting	Pan Tak
Chehcho*	Caves	Chuichu
Chehpog	Grain Mashing Hole	
Chehthagi Wawhia*	Green Well	Poso Verde
Che'ulkam		Chiulikam
Che'ul Sha'ik*	Willow Brush	Chiuli Shaik, Freznal Canyon
Chuhlk*	Hipbone	Choulic
Chuhwi i Gehshk*	Rabbit Fell	
Chu'i Tohnk	Pollen Hill	Chui Tonk
Chu'i Wawhia	Pollen Well	Chui Vaya
Chukud Kuk*	Owl Hooted	Chukut Kuk, Tecolote
Chukud Kuk Chekshani*	Owl Hooted District	Chukud Kuk District
Gagka*	Clearing	Kaka
Gagka Wo'oshani	Clearing Valley	Kaka Valley
Gahon Kehk*	Box Standing	Kaihon Kug
Ge Aji*	Big Narrow	Gu Aji, Gu Achi
Ge Aji Chekshani*	Big Narrow District	Gu Aji District
Ge Aji Tho'ag	Big Narrow Mountain	Gu Aji Mountain
Ge Chehpo	Big Mashing Pit	Gu Chuapo
Gegewho Kih*	Wildcat Lair	Gukawo Ki, San Luis
Ge Komlik*	Big Flats	Gu Komelik
Ge Kui Chuhchk	Big Mesquite Stand	Gu Kui Chuchg
Ge Oithag*	Big Field	Gu Oidak
Ge Oithag Wo'oshani	Big Field Valley	Gu Oidak Valley
Ge Wo'o*	Big Pond	Gu Vo, Kerwo
Ge Wo'o Chekshani*	Big Pond District	Gu Vo District
Gi'ito Wak*		Quitovak

Papago Name	Translation: Place of...	Map or Other Names
Giwho Tho'ag		
Gogs Mek*	Burnt Dog	Topawa
Gohih Kehk	Mulberry Standing	Kohi Kug
Gohk Sha'alk*	Two Clefts	Quinn's Well, Aguirre Vaya
Hahl Mek	Burnt Squash	Hali Murk
Hahshani Chuhchk	Saguaro Standing	Hashan Chuchg
Haiwani Wawhia	Cattle Well	Haivan Vaya
Hawani Naggiak*	Crow Hanging	Havana Nakya, Crow Hang
Hikiwoni*	Jagged Cut	Hickwan
Hikiwoni Aki	Jagged Cut Arroyo	Hickwan Wash
Hikiwoni Chekshani*	Jagged Cut District	Hickwan District
Hila Wihn Chekshani*	see Wecho Chekshani	Gila Bend District
Hoa Mek	Burnt Basket	Hoa Murk
Ho'i Oithag	Thorn Field	Hoi Oidak
Ihmiga*	Kinship Names	Emika
Iolgam	Mansanita	Kitt Peak
Jewak*	Rotten	Covered Well
Jewed Mek	Burnt Earth	Dirt Burn
Jiawul Thak*	Barrel Cactus Sitting	Chiawuli Tak, Freznal Village
Judumi Wawhia	Bear Well	Chutum Vaya
Kahw Wawhia*	Badger Well	Ko Vaya, Cobabi
Kaij Mek*	Burnt Seed	Santa Rosa
Kawlik*	The Hill	Cowlic
Kelibad Wo'o	Dead Man's Pond	Gurli Put Vo
Kohathk*	Hollow	Kohatk, Quohate
Kohm Wawhia*	Hackberry Well	Comobabi
Kohm Wawhia Thohtha'ag	Hackberry Well Mountains	Comobabi Mountains
Kohm Wo'o*	Hackberry Pond	Kom Vo, Santa Cruz
Kohm Wo'o Wo'oshani	Hackberry Valley	Kom Vo Valley
Komadk Wecho	Below the Flats	Komak Wuacho
Komlik*	Low Flat Place	Komelik
Koson Wawhia	Woodrat Well	Koson Vaya
Kots Kehk*	Cross Standing	Kots Kug
Komkch'ed e Wah'osithk*	Turtle Got Wedged	Indian Oasis, Sells
Komkch'ed e Wah'osithk Chekshani	Turtle Got Wedged District	Sells District
Kuhpik	The Dike	Kupk
Kuhpik Ka'akwulik	Dike Hills	Kupk Hills
Kuhkaj	End of the Mountain	Kuakatch
Kuhwith Wawhia	Pronghorn Antelope Well	Kuit Va'ya

Papago Name	Translation: Place of...	Map or Other Names
Kui Tatk	Mesquite Root	Kuk Tatk
Kui-ch-ed Wachk	Pond in the Mesquite	Kui Chut Vachk
Ma'ish Wawhia*	Covered Well	Maish Vaya, Upper Village
Makkumi Ha-Wo'oga	Caterpillars' Pond	Makgum Havoka
Moi Wawhia	? Well	Moi Vaya
Naggia	Hanging	Nakya
Nod Wawhia	Pampas Grass Well	Nawt Vaya
Nolik*	The Bend	Nolia, Nolic
Nowipakam		Noipa Kam
Pi O'oik*	Not Striped	Pi Oik
Pisin Mo'o*	Buffalo Head	Pisinimo
Pisin Mo'o Chekshani*	Buffalo Head District	Pisinimo District
San Migil		San Miguel
S-chuchk*	Black (Hills)	S-chuchk
S-chuchuligk*	Many Chickens	Schuchulik, Gunsight
S-chuk Tho'ag	Black Mountain	Shuk Toak
S-chuk Tho'ag Chekshani*	Black Mountain District	Schuk Toak District
S-gogogsig*	Many Dogs	
Shahdkam	Wild Sweet Potato	Shaotkam
Shapijk		
S-hehpi Oithag*	Cold Field	Supi Oidak
Shon Oithag*	Spring Field	Sonoita
Sihl Mek*	Burnt Saddle	San Lucy
Sihl Naggia*	Hanging Saddle	Sil Nakya
Sihl Naggia Ka'akwulk	Hanging Saddle Hills	Sil Nakya Hills
Sihl Naggia Wo'oshani	Hanging Saddle Valley	Sil Nakya Valley
Sikol Chehpo	Round Mashing Pit	Sikort Chuapo
Sikol Himathk*	Whirling (Water)	Sikul Himatk
Siw Oithag Chekshani*	Bitter Field District	Sif Oidag District
Siwol Chuhchk	Onions Standing	Siwili Chuchg
Siw Wawhia	Bitter Well	Sif Vaya
S-kakawiyugk	Many Horses	Shakaveyok
S-kokawagk	Many Staghorn Cactus	Skokaonak
S-nenepodagk	Many Nighthawks	
S-toha Tahnk	White Bank	Stoa Tonk
S-toha Wawhia	White Well	Stoa Vaya
S-toni Shuhthagi	Hot Water	Stan Shuatuk
S-totonigk*	Many Ants	(suburb of Santa Rosa)
S-wegi Chehpo	Red Mashing Pit	Suwuki Chuapo
Tadai Tho'ag		
Tad Memelkud*	Foot Running Place	Tat Momoli
Tad Memel Wo'oshani	Foot Running Valley	Tat Momoli Valley
Tatkam Wo'o	Root Pond	Tatk Kam Vo
Tiko-lohthi		Tecolote

Papago Name	Translation: Place of...	Map and Other Names
Toha Bithk*		
Uduwhag	Cattails	Utevak
Uhs Kehk	Stick Standing	Uhs Kug
Wahk*	Standing Water	San Xavier del Bac
Wahk Chekshani*	Standing Water District	San Xavier District
Wahpk	Reeds	
Wainomi Kehk*	Iron Standing	Vainom Kug
Waiwa Wo'o*	Cocklebur Pond	Vaiva Vo
Wakimagi	Worn	Vakamok
Wamel*	Swamp	Vamori
Waw Giwulk	Constricted Rock	Baboquivari
Waw Giwulk Chekshani*	Constricted Rock District	Baboquivari District
Wawhia Chini*	Well Mouth	Vaya Chin
Wechij Oithag*	New Field	
Wecho Chekshani*	Lower District	Gila Bend District
Winthani*	Window	Ventana
Wiwpul*	Wild Tobacco	Viopul, San Pedro
Wohg Hudunik*	Road Dip	Wahak Hotronik, San Simon
Wuplu Ha-Wo'oga	Burros' Pond	Vopolo Havoka

Pima Place Names
An asterisk indicates places that are inhabited.

Pima Name	Translation: Place of...	Map and Other Names
Chichino*	Chinese	Co-op
Chukma Shuhthagi*	Blackwater	Uhs Kehk
Ge'e Kih*	Big House	Sacaton
Hahshani Kehk*	Saguaro Standing	Sacaton Flats
Hia-t-ab	On the Dune	Santa Cruz
Kohko'i ha-Kih	Rattlesnake House	Snaketown
Kuiwa/Kuiva*	West Village	Gila Crossing
Komadk*		Komatke
Lihai*		Lehi
Onk Akimel*	Salt River	
Pihpchul*		
Santan*		Santa Ana
S-i'owi/S-i 'ovi Shuhthagi*	Sweet Water	
S-totonigk*	Many Ants	
Uhs Kehk*	Tree Standing	Chukma Shuhthagi
Wa'akih/Va'akih*	Ancient House	Vahki
Walin/Valin Thak*	Barrel Sitting	Goodyear

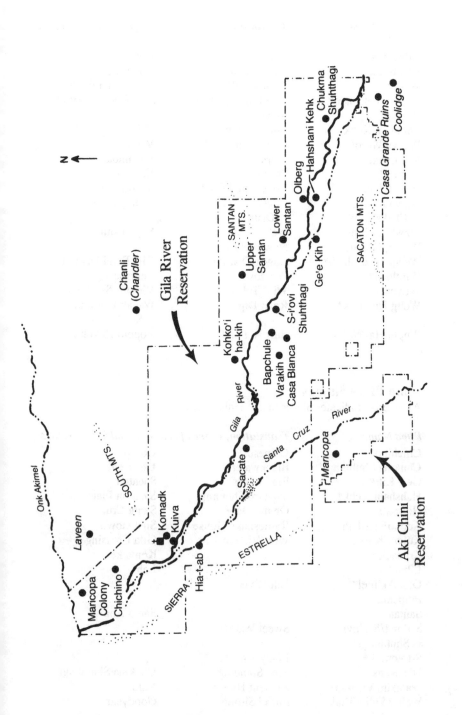

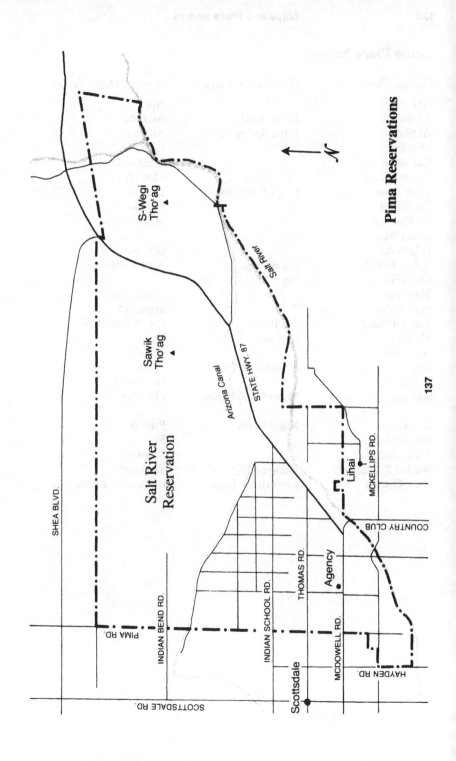

Pima Reservations

Other Place Names

Papago-Pima	*Translation: Place of . . .*	*Map and Other Names*
Aho		Ajo
Al Wahpk	Little Reeds	Arivaca
Al Shon	Little Spring	Arizona
Chanli		Chandler
Chi-wuawua		Chihuahua
Cheho Wawhia	Cave Well	Chui Vaya
Chuk Shon	Black Foothills	Tucson
Do Bawui		Topawa
Ge Pihchkin		Mexico City
Gi'ito Wak		
Hila Wihn		Gila Bend
Kohki Pi Bak	Pig not cooked	Avra Valley
Kohji Wo'o	Pig Pond	
Ma-lihna		Magdalena
Mali-kohba		Maricopa
Mihstol Komi	Cat Back	Cat Mountain
Mohmli	Mormon	Mesa
No-wahl		Nogales
Oithbad	Abandoned Field	Tempe
Pihchkin		Hermosillo
S-auppag	Many Cottonwood Trees	Florence
S-hukag	Many Pines	Prescott
So-nohla		Sonora
Tiko-lohthi		Tecolote
Washai S-washoni	Decayed Hay	Scottsdale
Waw Giwulk	Constricted Rock	Baboquivari Peak

APPENDIX SIX
Numbers

Numbers form a decimal system in Papago-Pima as in English. The simple numbers are:

1. hemako
2. gohk (gok— before —ko)
3. waik
4. gi'ik
5. hetasp
6. chuhthp
7. wewa'ak, wewkam
8. gigi'ik
9. humukt

Higher numbers are complex words or loanwords. Ten is derived from *wehs t-mahm* 'all our fingers.' Multiples of ten consist of the simple number plus suffix —*ho* (—*ko* after k, —*o* after other stops), modifying ten.

10. west-mahm
20. gokko west-mahm
30. waikko west-mahm
40. gi'ikko west-mahm
50. hetaspo west-mahm
60. chuhthpo west-mahm
70. wewa'akko west-mahm
80. gigi'ikko west-mahm
90. humukto west-mahm

Teens and numbers within multiples of ten are formed by adding *gamai* 'plus' and the number. The word *west-mahm* can be omitted before the word *gamai*.

11. west-mahm gamai hemako (*or* gamai hemako)
21. gokko west-mahm gamai hemako (*or* gokko gamai hemako)
54. hetaspo west-mahm gamai gi'ik (*or* hetaspo gamai gi'ik)

Words borrowed from Spanish have generally replaced Papago-Pima for higher decimal numbers hundred, thousand, and million.

100. siant (*or* west-mahmho west-mahm)
1000. mihl (*or* west-mahmho west-mahmho west-mahm)
1,000,000. mi-yohn

The number of a higher decimal precedes the decimal number.

200. gohk siant
3000. waik mihl
10,000. west-mahm mihl
100,000. siant mihl
200,000. gohk siant mihl
4,000,000. gi'ik mi-yohn

Numbers within a higher decimal follow the decimal.

101. siant hemako
211. gohk siant west-mahm gamai hemako
5326. hetasp mihl waik siant gokko west-mahm gamai chuhthp
1,000,001. mi-yohn hemako

Except for *wehpeg* 'first', the ordinal numbers are the same as the cardinal numbers, as in *gohk kuintadag* 'the second chapter', *waik ohla-ch-ed* 'in the third hour' or 'at three o'clock'.

Any number may occur with the following suffixes and meanings.

1. __ *chuth* 'cause to be (the specified number)', as in *waikchuth* 'cause there to be three', *gi'ikchuth* 'cause there to be four'.
2. __ *ho* (__*ko* after k, __*o* after other stops) '(the specified number of) times', as in *hemho* 'once', *gokko* 'twice', *hetaspo* 'five times'.
3. __ *jj* '(the specified number) of a group', as in *gohkajj* 'two of them', *hetaspajj hegam haiwani* 'five of those cattle'.
4. __ *kaj* 'by means of (the specified number)', as in *gi'ikkaj* 'by means of four', *chuhthpkaj* 'by means of six'.
5. __ *pa* (__*iap* after hem__) '(the specified number of) places', as in *hemiap* 'in one place', *gohkpa* 'in two places'.

Bibliography

Alvarez, Albert, and Kenneth Hale
1970   "Toward a manual of Papago grammar: some phonological terms."
        International Journal of American Linguistics, vol. 36, no. 2, pp. 83–97.
Bahr, Donald M., Juan Gregorio, David I. Lopez, Albert Alvarez
1974   *Piman Shamanism and Staying Sickness (Ká:cim Múmkidag).* Tucson:
        The University of Arizona Press.
Barnes, Will C.
1960   *Arizona Place Names.* Revised and enlarged by Byrd H. Granger.
        Tucson: The University of Arizona Press.
Congdon, Russell T.
1954   *Our Beautiful Western Birds.* Exposition Press.
Curtin, Leonora S. M.
1949   *Pima Plants.* Monograph.
Densmore, Frances
1929   "Papago music." *Bulletin of the Bureau of American Ethnology,* no. 90,
        Washington, D.C.: Government Printing Office.
Dillon, George L.
1977   *Introduction to Contemporary Linguistic Semantics.* New Jersey:
        Prentice-Hall, Inc.
Dodge, Natt N.
1951   *Flowers of the Southwest Deserts.* Globe, Arizona: McGrew Printing
        and Lithographing Co., The National Park Service, Popular Series
        no. 4.
Dolores, Juan
1913   "Papago verb stems." *University of California Publications in American
        Archaeology and Ethnology,* vol. 10, no. 5, pp. 241–263.
1923   "Papago nominal stems." *University of California Publications in
        American Archaeology and Ethnology,* vol. 20, no. 1, pp. 19–31.
Fodor, Janet Dean
1977   *Semantics: Theories of Meaning in Generative Grammar.* New York:
        Thomas Y. Crowell Company.
Fontana, Bernard L.
1973   "The cultural dimensions of pottery: ceramics as social documents."
        In *Ceramics in America,* edited by Ian M. G. Quimby, pp. 1–13.
        Charlottesville: University Press of Virginia.
Hale, Kenneth
1962   "Some preliminary observations on Papago morphophonemics." *International Journal of American Linguistics,* vol. 3, no. 4.
1965   "A Papago grammar." Indiana doctoral dissertation in *International
        Journal of American Linguistics,* vol. 31, no. 4, pp. 295–305.
_____, C. F. Voeglin, and F. M. Voeglin
1962   "Typological and comparative grammar of Uto-Aztecan: I (phonology)." *International Journal of American Linguistics,* vol. 28, no. 1.

Hale, Kenneth (*cont.*)
————, and Joseph B. Casagrande
Undated   Semantic Relationships in Papago Folk-definitions. University of Illinois (dittoed).
Jaeger, Edward
1940   *Desert Wild Flowers*. Stanford: Stanford University Press.
Joseph, Alice, Rosamund B. Spicer, and Jane Chesky
1949   *The Desert People: A Study of the Papago Indians*. Chicago: The University of Chicago Press.
Lehrer, Adrienne
1977   *Semantic Fields and Lexical Structure*. Amsterdam: North-Holland.
Lumholtz, Carl
1971   *New Trails in Mexico*. Glorrietta, New Mexico: The Rio Grande Press (reissue of the 1912 publication).
Mason, J. Alden
1950   *The Language of the Papago of Arizona*. Philadelphia: The University of Pennsylvania, Museum Monographs.
Mathiot, Madeleine
1962   "Noun classes and folk taxonomy," *American Anthropologist*, vol. 64, no. 2, pp. 340–350.
1973   *A Dictionary of Papago Usage*. 2 vols. Bloomington: Indiana University Press.
Olin, George
1950   *Mammals of the Southwest Deserts*. Santa Fe, New Mexico: National Park Service, Popular Series no. 8.
Parker, Kittie F.
1958   *Arizona Ranch, Farm, and Garden Weeds*. Tucson, University of Arizona Press, Circular 265.
Pilcher, William
1967   "Some comments on the folk taxonomy of the Papago." *American Anthropologist* 69, no. 2, pp. 204–208.
Russell, Frank
1908   *The Pima Indians*. Washington, D.C.: Bureau of American Ethnology, Annual Report 26. Reedition 1974. Tucson: University of Arizona Press.
Saxton, Dean
1963   "Papago phonemes," *International Journal of American Linguistics* 29, no. 1, pp. 29–35.
1982   "Papago" *Studies in Uto-Aztecan Grammar* 3, pp. 92–266. Edited by Ronald Langacker.
————, and Lucille Saxton
1969   *Papago and Pima to English, English to Papago and Pima Dictionary*. Tucson: University of Arizona Press.
1973   *Legends and Lore of the Papago and Pima Indians*. Tucson: University of Arizona Press.
Scott, S. H.
1958   *The Observer's Book of Cacti and Other Succulents*. London, England: Frederick Warne and Co. Ltd.
Shaw, Anne Moore
1968   *Pima Indian Legends*. Tucson: The University of Arizona Press.
1974   *A Pima Past*. Tucson: The University of Arizona Press.

Smith, Gusse Thomas
  1941   *Birds of the Southwest Desert.* Scottsdale, Arizona: Doubleshoe Publishers.
Underhill, Ruth
  1939   *The Social Organization of the Papago Indians.* New York: Columbia University Press.
  1951   *People of the Crimson Evening.* United States Indian Service. *The Papago Indians of Arizona and their Relatives the Pima.* Bureau of Indian Affairs: Haskell Press, Sherman Pamphlet no. 3.
  1946   "Papago Indian Religion" *Columbia University Contributions to Anthropology,* vol. 33. New York: Columbia University.
Zepeda, Ofelia
  1983   *A Papago Grammar.* Tucson: The University of Arizona Press.

Papago and Pima translators
  1975   *Jiosh Wechij O'ohana: The New Testament in O'othham (Papago-Pima).* South Holland, Illinois: The World Home Bible League.
Joint authors
  1980   *Indian Greens.* Tucson, Arizona: Meals for Millions Foundation, Love the Children joint publishers.

Pronunciation Guide

LETTER		ENGLISH		PAPAGO/PIMA
a	*as in*	Father	*as in*	Pahl
b		ball		bohl
ch		chicken		chuchul
d		roadrunner		tadai
e		open		jeg
g		gun		gawos
h		hooves		huhch
i		police		chi-lihhi
j		jostling		ugijith
k		kicking		keihin
l		lariat		liat
m		moon		mashath
n		noisy		s-nakosig
ni		bunion		huniga
o		short		shopol
p		pickax		pihgo
s		saddle		sihl
sh		shoes		shuhshk
t		teeth		tahtami
th		smooth		s-thahpk
u		ruler		kuintokud
w		window		winthani
y		yoke		yehwo
' (glottal stop)		(unwritten)		ho'i ('thorn')

NOTES:

1. The stressed or loudest part of a word is the vowel following initial *ku* or *wu*, the first vowel otherwise.
2. Any vowel followed by an *h* with no vowel after it is held longer, as in *pahl* and *wehs*.
3. The glottal stop, ('), as in *ho'i*, is made by stopping the breath in the throat. It is the sound between the parts of *Oh oh*, an expression of surprise in English. A glottal stop is also pronounced automatically in Papago-Pima before any vowel which begins a word, as in *ohg*.
4. *e* is pronounced like the *u* in put, but with unrounded lips.
5. The lips are not rounded for any consonant, except before *u* or *o*.

6. Voiced consonants, *b*, *d*, *g*, *j*, *l*, *m*, *n*, *ng*, *th*, and *w*, are unvoiced or whispered at the end of speech or before *h*.

7. *n* before *e*, *i*, or *u*, has the sound of English *n* before the same letters in words like *sinew*, *senior*, and *genuine*, or of Spanish *ñ* as in *señor*.

8. *t*, *th*, and *n* (when not before *e*, *i*, or *u*), are made with the tongue against the teeth as for English *th* or Spanish *t*.

9. The consonants *ch*, *k*, *p*, and *t*, are unaspirated (without a puff of air after them), like the similar Spanish consonants rather than the English consonants.

10. The vowels *a*, *e*, *i*, *o*, and *u*, are aspirated (with a puff of air after them) when they do not precede a voiced sound or a glottal stop.

11. An unwritten transition sound (schwa) is inserted automatically between consonants made at different positions in the mouth (as in *ton lig*), but not before *h* or (') nor between a stop (*b*, *d*, *ch*, *j*, *g*, *k*, *p*, *t*, *th*) and a sibilant (*s* or *sh*).

12. Vowels are unvoiced in certain positions. These and other phonetic details are given in Appendix 1.

About the Authors...

DEAN and LUCILLE SAXTON have been working with Papago and Pima authors and translators since 1953, helping in the task of putting the Papago and Pima language into writing and producing its literature. The Saxtons were prepared for their part in this task by studies in language, linguistics, and translation, and by work under the direction of the Summer Institute of Linguistics.

SUZANNE IGNACIO ENOS was a native Papago speaker and an early writer of her language. She studied English at the Tucson Indian Training School, and later at the University of Arizona where, under Dr. William Kurath, she transcribed Papago legends. She studied linguistics and translation theory at the Summer Institute of Linguistics (Mexico), worked in translation for the Papago Tribal Council, did interpreting for the Indian Health Services, and taught conversational Papago at Pima Community College. She was co-translator of the *Papago-Pima New Testament*.